Learn Objective-C
on the Mac

For iOS and OS X

Scott Knaster
Waqar Malik
Mark Dalrymple

Apress·

Learn Objective-C for iOS and OS X

ISBN-13 (pbk): 978-1-4302-4188-1

ISBN-13 (electronic): 978-1-4302-4189-8

President and Publisher: Paul Manning
Lead Editor: Steve Anglin
Development Editors: Gwenan Spearing, Matthew Moodie
Technical Reviewer: Nick Waynik
Editorial Board: Steve Anglin, Ewan Buckingham, Gary Cornell, Louise Corrigan, Morgan Ertel, Jonathan Gennick, Jonathan Hassell, Robert Hutchinson, Michelle Lowman, James Markham, Matthew Moodie, Jeff Olson, Jeffrey Pepper, Douglas Pundick, Ben Renow-Clarke, Dominic Shakeshaft, Gwenan Spearing, Matt Wade, Tom Welsh
Coordinating Editor: Brent Dubi
Copy Editor: Heather Lang
Compositor: SPi Global
Indexer: SPi Global
Artist: SPi Global
Cover Designer: Anna Ishchenko

Distributed to the book trade worldwide by Springer Science+Business Media New York, 233 Spring Street, 6th Floor, New York, NY 10013. Phone 1-800-SPRINGER, fax (201) 348-4505, e-mail orders-ny@springer-sbm.com, or visit www.springeronline.com.

For information on translations, please e-mail rights@apress.com, or visit www.apress.com.

Apress and friends of ED books may be purchased in bulk for academic, corporate, or promotional use. eBook versions and licenses are also available for most titles. For more information, reference our Special Bulk Sales–eBook Licensing web page at www.apress.com/bulk-sales.

Any source code or other supplementary materials referenced by the author in this text is available to readers at www.apress.com. For detailed information about how to locate your book's source code, go to www.apress.com/source-code/.

This is for my family—of course!

–Scott

For my parents, M. Saleem and Kalsoom A. Malik,
who have always provided unconditional encouragement, support and help
in all of my endeavors.

–Waqar

Contents at a Glance

v

Contents

Foreword

Whenever software developers adopt a new platform, they are faced with the daunting task of familiarizing themselves with the programming language, development tools, design patterns, and standard software libraries available in the new environment.

Typically, this must be done simultaneously with writing code under pressure to deliver it as quickly as possible, and developers are tempted to fall back on approaches they know from previous systems. This often results in code that doesn't really fit the platform, that may duplicate functionality that already existed, and can cause maintenance headaches down the road.

In an ideal world, new developers would have the benefit of colleagues who are already familiar with the platform, who can offer their guidance to get them started and moving in the right direction. Unfortunately, the very success of the iOS platform has made for many cases where this just isn't possible.

If you don't have a mentor handy, what's the next best thing?

The authors of this book are veterans of Apple's Developer Technical Services organization, and they have each answered countless questions from software engineers who are new to Apple's technology. They have been responsible for instilling good habits in those they've helped. That experience results in a book that anticipates the most common misunderstandings and takes care to explain not only the how, but also the why of Apple's development platform.

For example, the conceptual basis provided in Chapter 3, "Introduction to Object-Oriented Programming," gives you the means to place the material that follows it into a coherent picture, instead of just tossing you into the midst of a flurry of unfamiliar classes, methods, and techniques and hoping that you'll somehow sort it all out with practice.

Learn Objective-C on the Mac is a fine guide to the language at the heart of Apple's iOS and OS X development platform.

John C. Randolph

About the Authors

 **Scott Knaster** was at Apple when Apple wasn't cool. Scott worked at Apple helping developers write Mac software in the earliest days of the platform, when Cocoa was just a great idea waiting to be born. Scott now works on Google's Developer Relations team and runs the Google Mac Blog. He lives in Silicon Valley among his nerdy peers.

 **Waqar Malik** is a UNIX nerd and has been for long time. He worked at Apple during the early days of Mac OS X, helping developers with Cocoa and UNIX. He now works for MeLLmo, Inc. in San Diego, writing great iOS Software.

 **Mark Dalrymple** is a longtime Mac and Unix programmer who has worked on cross-platform toolkits, Internet publishing tools, high-performance web servers, and end-user desktop applications. He's also the principal author of *Advanced Mac OS X Programming* (Big Nerd Ranch 2005). In his spare time, he plays trombone and bassoon and makes balloon animals.

About the Technical Reviewer

Nick Waynik has been working in the IT field for over 13 years and has done everything from network administration to web development. He started writing iOS apps at the beginning of 2008 when the SDK was released. Since then, he has gone on to start his own business focusing on iOS development. In his spare time, he loves to spend time with his wife and family and play golf. He blogs at nickwaynik.com and can be found on Twitter as @n_dubbs.

Acknowledgments

This book didn't write itself, you know. And we, the authors, didn't do all the work either—not even close. Sure, we typed a bunch of words and code, but without our amazing book team, what would we have? A really long blog post, maybe.

Enormous thanks go to Brent Dubi, who held everything together with relentlessly cheerful e-mails and focused phone calls, both vital tools in coordinating a virtual team of people from around the world. Thanks to Nick Waynik for keeping us technically honest, which is not an easy task given the power and complexity that Apple packs into Xcode and Cocoa nowadays. We thank Gwenan Spearing, who scoured every word we wrote, even the bad puns, to help us make sure we were as clear and concise as possible. And second-edition thanks to our excellent first-edition copy editor, Heather Lang, who returned and once again allowed us to push the limits of proper grammar and style just so we could make yet another nerdy *Star Wars* joke. Each of these folks improved this book immeasurably and so have made us look our best.

Waqar would also like to thank his wonderful children, Adam and Mishal, and his beautiful wife, Irrum, for giving him enough time to work on this book.

Working with This Book

To download source code or report an error, please see this book's page on the Apress site: www.apress.com/9781430241881.

For best results when using this book, have your computer close by while you read. Having your favorite beverage at hand is also nice, but keep it away from the computer, because liquid damage repair prices will ruin your whole day.

Most of all, have fun while you learn this stuff!

Chapter 1

Hello

Welcome to *Learn Objective-C on the Mac*! This book is designed to teach you the basics of the Objective-C language. Objective-C is a superset of C and is the language used by many (if not most) applications that have a true OS X or iOS look and feel.

In addition to presenting Objective-C, this book introduces you to its companion, Apple's Cocoa (for OS X) and Cocoa Touch (for iOS) toolkits. Cocoa and Cocoa Touch are written in Objective-C and contain all the elements of the OS X and iOS user interfaces, plus a whole lot more. Once you learn Objective-C, you'll be ready to dive into Cocoa with a full-blown project or another book such as *Learn Cocoa on the Mac* (Apress 2010) or *Beginning iOS 5 Development* (Apress 2011).

In this chapter, we'll let you know the basic information you need before you get started with Objective-C itself. We'll also serve up a bit of history about Objective-C and give you a thumbnail sketch of what's to come in future chapters.

Before You Start

Before you read this book, you should have some experience with a C-like programming language such as C++, Java, or venerable C itself. Whatever the language, you should feel comfortable with its basic principles. You should know what variables, methods, and functions are and understand how to control your program's flow using conditionals and loops. Our focus is the features Objective-C adds to its base language, C, along with some goodies chosen from Apple's Cocoa toolkits.

Are you coming to Objective-C from a non-C language? You'll still be able to follow along, but you might want to take a look at this book's Appendix or check out *Learn C on the Mac* (Apress 2009).

Where the Future Was Made Yesterday

Cocoa and Objective-C are at the heart of Apple's OS X and iOS operating systems. Although OS X and especially iOS are relatively new, Objective-C and Cocoa are much older. Brad Cox invented Objective-C in the early 1980s to meld the popular and portable C language with the elegant Smalltalk language. In 1985, Steve Jobs founded NeXT, Inc., to create powerful, affordable workstations. NeXT chose Unix as its operating system and created NextSTEP, a powerful user interface toolkit developed in Objective-C. Despite its features and a small, loyal following, NextSTEP achieved little commercial success.

When Apple acquired NeXT in 1996 (or was it the other way around?), NextSTEP was renamed Cocoa and brought to the wider audience of Macintosh programmers. Apple gives away its development tools—including Cocoa—for free, so any programmer can take advantage of them. All you need is a bit of programming experience, basic knowledge of Objective-C, and the desire to dig in and learn stuff.

You might wonder, "If Objective-C and Cocoa were invented in the '80s—in the days of *Alf* and *The A-Team*, not to mention stuffy old Unix—aren't they old and moldy by now?" Absolutely not! Objective-C and Cocoa are the result of years of effort by a team of excellent programmers, and they have been continually updated and enhanced. Over time, Objective-C and Cocoa have evolved into an incredibly elegant and powerful set of tools. Over the past few years, iOS has become the hottest development platform in computing, and Objective-C is the key to writing great iOS applications. So now, twenty-some years after NeXT adopted Objective-C, all the cool kids are using it.

What's Coming Up

Objective-C is a superset of C: it begins with C and then adds a couple of small but significant additions to the language. If you've ever looked at C++ or Java, you may be surprised at how small Objective-C really is. We'll cover Objective-C's additions to C in detail in this book's chapters:

- Chapter 2, "Extensions to C," focuses on the basic features that Objective-C introduces.

- In Chapter 3, "An Introduction to Object-Oriented Programming," we kick off the learning by showing you the basics of object-oriented programming.

- Chapter 4, "Inheritance," describes how to create classes that gain the features of their parent classes.

- Chapter 5, "Composition," discusses techniques for combining objects so they can work together.

- Chapter 6, "Source File Organization and Using Xcode 4," presents real-world strategies for creating your program's sources.

- Chapter 7, "More about Xcode," shows you some shortcuts and power-user features to help you get the most out of your programming day.

- We take a brief respite from Objective-C in Chapter 8, "A Quick Tour of the Foundation Kit," to impress you with some of Cocoa's cool features using one of its primary frameworks.

- You'll spend a lot of time in your Cocoa applications dealing with Chapter 9's topic, "Memory Management and ARC".

- Chapter 10, "Object Initialization," is all about what happens at that magical time when objects are born.

- Chapter 11, "Properties," gives you the lowdown on Objective-C's dot notation and an easier way to make object accessors.

- Chapter 12, "Categories," describes the super cool Objective-C feature that lets you add your own methods to existing classes—even those you didn't write.

- Chapter 13, "Protocols," tells about a form of inheritance in Objective-C that allows classes to implement packaged sets of features.

- Chapter 14, "Blocks and Concurrency" shows you how to use a new Objective-C feature that enhances functions into blocks that can include data as well as code.

- Chapter 15, "Introduction to UIKit" gives you a taste of the gorgeous applications you can develop for iOS using its primary framework.

- Chapter 16, "Introduction to AppKit," is similar to Chapter 15 except that it introduces the basic framework for OS X applications.

- Chapter 17, "File Loading and Saving," shows you how to save and retrieve your data.

- Chapter 18, "Key-Value Coding," gives you ways to deal with your data indirectly.

- Chapter 19, "Using the Static Analyzer" shows you how to use a powerful Xcode tool to find common mistakes programmers make.

- And finally, in Chapter 20, "NSPredicate," we show you how to slice and dice your data.

If you're coming from another language like Java or C++, or from another platform like Windows or Linux, you may want to check out this book's Appendix, "Coming to Objective-C from Other Languages," which points out some of the mental hurdles you'll need to jump to embrace Objective-C.

Getting Ready

Xcode is the development environment provided by Apple for creating iOS and OS X applications. Macs don't come with Xcode preinstalled, but downloading and installing it is easy and free. All you need is a Mac running OS X 10.7 Lion or later.

The first step on the long and awesome road to programming for OS X or iOS is acquiring a copy of Xcode. If you don't have it already, you can download it from the Mac App Store. To get there, click the App Store icon in the dock (see Figure 1-1), or find the App Store in the *Applications* folder.

In the Mac App Store, click in the search box in the upper right, and search for Xcode (see Figure 1-2).

Figure 1-1. App Store icon in the dock

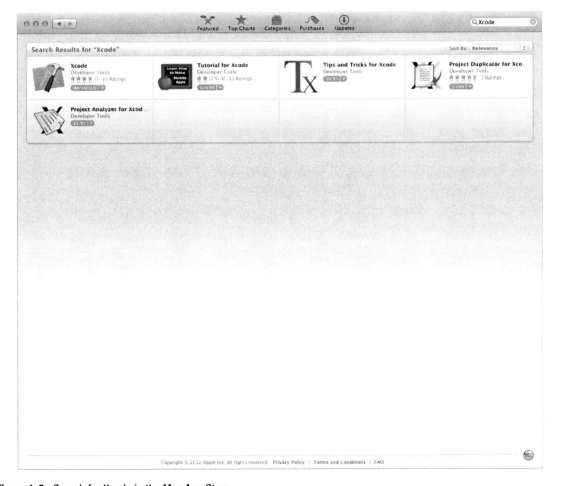

Figure 1-2. Search for Xcode in the Mac App Store

Or, click *Categories* and then *Developer Tools*, and you'll see Xcode on the top left (see Figure 1-3) or somewhere nearby. Click *Xcode* to see its download page (see Figure 1-4).

Figure 1-3. Developer Tools Apps

Figure 1-4. Xcode download page in Mac App Store

Click *Free* and then *Install App*. The App Store installs Xcode in your Applications folder.

Now, you're ready to start your journey. Good luck! We'll be there with you for at least the first part of your trip.

Summary

OS X and iOS programs are written in Objective-C, using technology from way back in the 1980s that has matured into a powerful set of tools. In this book, we'll start by assuming you know something about C programming or another general-purpose programming language and go from there.

We hope you enjoy your adventure!

Chapter 2

Extensions to C

Objective-C is nothing more than the C language with some extra features drizzled on top—it's delicious! In this chapter, we'll cover some of those key extras as we take you through building your first Objective-C program—and your second one too.

The Simplest Objective-C Program

You've probably seen the C version of the classic Hello World program, which prints out the text "Hello, world!" or a similar pithy remark. Hello World is usually the first program that neophyte C programmers learn. We don't want to buck tradition, so we're going to write a similar program here called Hello Objective-C.

Building Hello Objective-C

As you work through this book, we're assuming you have Apple's Xcode tools installed. If you don't already have Xcode, or if you've never used it before, an excellent section in Chapter 2 of Dave Mark's *Learn C on the Mac* (Apress 2008) walks you through the steps of acquiring, installing, and creating programs with Xcode.

In this section, we'll step through the process of using Xcode to create your first Objective-C project. If you are already familiar with Xcode, feel free to skip ahead; you won't hurt our feelings. Before you go, be sure to expand the Learn ObjC Projects archive from this book's archive (which you can download from the Source Code/Download page of the Apress web site). This project is located in the 02.01 - Hello Objective-C folder.

To create the project, start by launching Xcode. You can find the Xcode application in /Developer/Applications. We put the Xcode icon in the Dock for easy access. You might want to do that too.

Once Xcode finishes launching, you'll see the Welcome screen, as shown in Figure 2-1. On the left side, you can select the next thing you want to do. Or, you can choose to open a recent project from the list on the right. (If you're brand new with Xcode, you won't see any recent

Figure 2-1. *Xcode Welcome screen*

projects.) If you don't see the Welcome screen, you can always show it by selecting "Welcome to Xcode" on the Window menu or by typing ⌘⇧1.

On the Welcome screen, click "Create a new Xcode project" (see Figure 2-1), or just choose **File ➤ New ➤ New Project**. Xcode shows you a list of the various kinds of projects it can create. Use your focus to ignore most of the intriguing project types there, and choose Application on the left-hand side of the window and Command Line Tool on the right-hand side, as shown in Figure 2-2. Click Next.

On the next screen (Figure 2-3), you'll select options for your new project. For Product Name, enter the timeless classic "Hello Objective-C". For Company Identifier, you'll typically enter a reverse DNS version of your company or website name, such as com.mywebsite; for now, you can just enter com.thinkofsomethingclever.

This screen saves the best for last, as the most important option is the type of command line tool you want to create: be sure to choose Foundation. Once you're done, your screen should look a lot like Figure 2-3. After you've done this, click Next.

Xcode drops a sheet and asks you where to save your project (see Figure 2-4). We're putting it into one of our Projects directories here to keep things organized, but you can put it anywhere you want.

After you click Save, Xcode shows you its main window, called the project window (see Figure 2-5). This window displays the pieces that compose your project along with an editing pane. main.m is the source file that contains the code for Hello Objective-C.

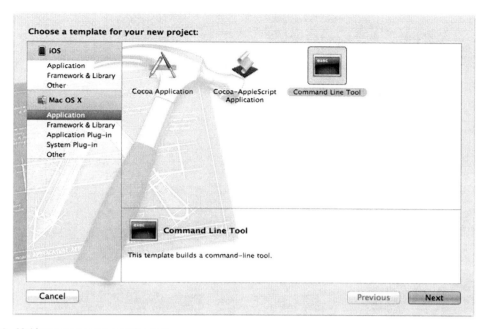

Figure 2-2. *Making a new command line tool*

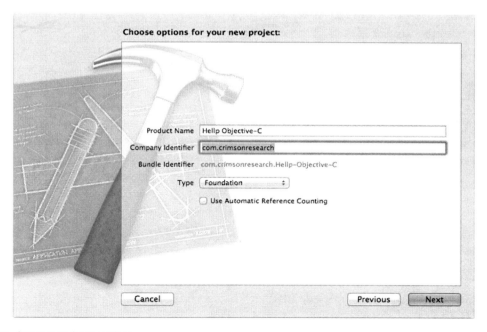

Figure 2-3. *Set your project's options*

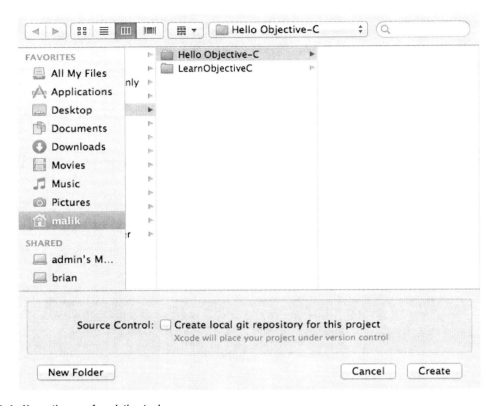

Figure 2-4. *Name the new foundation tool*

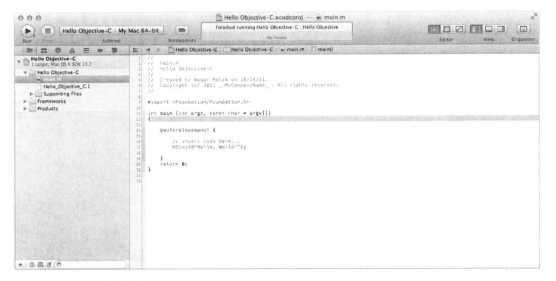

Figure 2-5. *XCode's main window*

main.m contains boilerplate code, kindly provided by Xcode for each new project. We can make our Hello Objective-C application a little simpler than the sample Xcode supplies. Delete everything in main.m and replace it with this code:

```
#import <Foundation/Foundation.h>
int main (int argc, const char *argv[])
{
 NSLog (@"Hello, Objective-C!");

 return (0);
} // main
```

If you don't understand all the code right now, don't worry about it. We'll go through this program in excruciating, line-by-line detail soon.

Source code is no fun if you can't turn it into a running program. Build and run the program by clicking the Run button or pressing ⌘R. If there aren't any nasty syntax errors, Xcode compiles and links your program and then runs it. Open the Xcode console window (by selecting **View ➤ Debug Area ➤ Activate Console** or pressing ⌘⇧C), which displays your program's output, as shown in Figure 2-6.

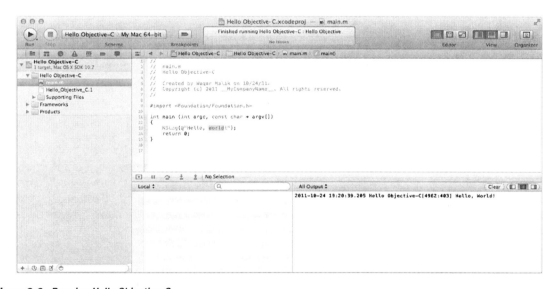

Figure 2-6. Running Hello Objective-C

And there you have it: your first working Objective-C program. Congratulations! Let's pull it apart and see how it works.

Deconstructing Hello Objective-C

Here, again, are the contents of `main.m`:

```
#import <Foundation/Foundation.h>
int main (int argc, const char *argv[])
{
  NSLog (@"Hello, Objective-C!");
  return (0);
} // main
```

Xcode uses the `.m` extension to indicate a file that holds Objective-C code and will be processed by the Objective-C compiler. File names ending in `.c` are handled by the C compiler, and `.cpp` files are the province of the C++ compiler. (In Xcode, all this compiling is handled by the LLVM compiler by default), a single compiler that understands all three variations of the language.)

The `main` file contains two lines of code that should be familiar to you already if you know plain C: the declaration of `main()` and the `return (0)` statement at the end. Remember that Objective-C really is C at heart, and the syntax for declaring `main()` and returning a value is the same as in C. The rest of the code looks slightly different from regular C. For example, what is that wacky #import thing? To find out, read on!

> **Note**   The `.m` extension originally stood for "messages" when Objective-C was first introduced, referring to a central feature of Objective-C that we'll talk about in future chapters. Nowadays, we just call them "dot-m files."

That Wacky #import Thing

Just like C, Objective-C uses **header files** to hold the declarations of elements such as structs, symbolic constants, and function prototypes. In C, you use the #include statement to inform the compiler that it should consult a header file for some definitions. You can use #include in Objective-C programs for the same purpose, but you probably never will. Instead, you'll use #import, like this:

```
#import <Foundation/Foundation.h>
```

#import is a feature provided by the compiler that Xcode uses, which is what Xcode uses when you're compiling Objective-C, C, and C++ programs. #import guarantees that a header file will be included only once, no matter how many times the #import directive is actually seen for that file.

> **Note**   In C, programmers typically use a scheme based on the #ifdef directive to avoid the situation where one file includes a second file, which then, recursively, includes the first.
>
> In Objective-C, programmers use #import to accomplish the same thing.

The #import <Foundation/Foundation.h> statement tells the compiler to look at the *Foundation.h* header file in the Foundation framework.

Introducing Frameworks

What's a framework? We're glad you asked. A **framework** is a collection of parts—header files, libraries, images, sounds, and more—collected together into a single unit. Apple ships technologies such as Cocoa, Carbon, QuickTime, and OpenGL as sets of frameworks. Cocoa consists of a pair of frameworks, Foundation and Application Kit (also known as AppKit), along with a suite of supporting frameworks, including Core Animation and Core Image, which add all sorts of cool stuff to Cocoa.

The Foundation framework handles features found in the layers beneath the user interface, such as data structures and communication mechanisms. All the programs in this book are based on the Foundation framework.

> **Note**   Once you finish this book, your next step along the road to becoming a Cocoa guru is to master Cocoa's Application Kit, which contains Cocoa's high-level features: user interface elements, printing, color and sound management, AppleScript support, and so on. To find out more, check out *Learn Cocoa on the Mac* by Jack Nutting, David Mark, and Jeff LaMarche (Apress 2010).

Each framework is a significant collection of technology, often containing dozens or even hundreds of header files. Each framework has a master header file that includes all the framework's individual header files. By using #import on the master header file, you have access to all the framework's features.

The header files for the Foundation framework take up nearly a megabyte of disk storage and contain more than 14,000 lines of code, spread across over a hundred files. When you include the master header file with #import <Foundation/Foundation.h>, you get that whole vast collection. You might think wading through all that text for every file would take the compiler a lot of time, but Xcode is smart: it speeds up the task by using precompiled headers, a compressed and digested form of the header that's loaded quickly when you #import it.

If you're curious about which headers are included with the Foundation framework, you can peek inside its *Headers* directory (*/System/Library/Frameworks/Foundation.framework/Headers/*). You won't break anything if you browse the files in there; just don't remove or change anything.

NSLog() and @"strings"

Now that we have used #import on the master header file for the Foundation framework, you're ready to write code that takes advantage of some Cocoa features. The first (and only) real line of code in Hello Objective-C uses the NSLog() function, like so:

```
NSLog (@"Hello, Objective-C!");
```

This prints "Hello, Objective-C!" to the console. If you've used C at all, you have undoubtedly encountered `printf()` in your travels. `NSLog()` is a Cocoa function that works very much like `printf()`.

Just like `printf()`, `NSLog()` takes a string as its first argument. This string can contain format specifiers (such as %d), and the function takes additional parameters that match the format specifiers. `printf()` plugs these extra parameters into the string before it gets printed.

As we've said before, Objective-C is just C with a little bit of special sauce, so you're welcome to use `printf()` instead of `NSLog()` if you want. We recommend `NSLog()`, however, because it adds features such as time and date stamps, as well as automatically appending the newline ('\n') character for you.

The NS Prefix: A Prescription Against Name Collisions

You might be thinking that `NSLog()` is kind of a strange name for a function. What is that "NS" doing there? It turns out that Cocoa prefixes all its function, constant, and type names with "NS". This prefix tells you the function comes from Cocoa instead of some other toolkit.

The prefix helps prevent **name collisions**, big problems that result when the same identifier is used for two different things. If Cocoa had named this function `Log()`, there's a good chance the name would clash with a `Log()` function created by some innocent programmer somewhere. When a program containing `Log()` is built with Cocoa included, Xcode complains that `Log()` is defined multiple times, and sadness results.

Now that you have an idea why a prefix is a good idea, you might wonder about the specific choice: why "NS" instead of "Cocoa," for example? Well, the "NS" prefix dates back from the time when the toolkit was called NextSTEP and was the product of NeXT Software (formerly NeXT, Inc.), which was acquired by Apple in 1996. Rather than break compatibility with code already written for NextSTEP, Apple just continued to use the "NS" prefix. It's a historical curiosity now, like your appendix.

Cocoa has staked its claim on the "NS" prefix, so obviously, you should not prefix any of your own variables or function names with "NS". If you do, you will confuse the readers of your code, making them think your stuff actually belongs to Cocoa. Also, your code might break in the future if Apple happens to add a function to Cocoa with the same name as yours. There is no centralized prefix registry, so you can pick your own prefix. Many people prefix names with their initials or company names. To make our examples a little simpler, we won't use a prefix for the code in this book.

NSString: Where it's @

Let's take another look at that `NSLog()` statement: `NSLog (@"Hello, Objective-C!");`

Did you notice the at sign before the string? It's not a typo that made it past our vigilant editors. The at sign is one of the features that Objective-C adds to standard C. A string in double quotes preceded by an at sign means that the quoted string should be treated as a Cocoa NSString element.

So what's an `NSString` element? Peel the "NS" prefix off the name and you see a familiar term: "String." You already know that a string is a sequence of characters, usually human-readable, so you can probably guess (correctly) that an `NSString` is a sequence of characters in Cocoa.

NSString elements have a huge number of features packed into them and are used by Cocoa any time a string is needed. Here are just a few of the things an NSString can do:

- Tell you its length

- Compare itself to another string

- Convert itself to an integer or floating-point value

That's a whole lot more than you can do with C-style strings. We'll be using and exploring NSString elements much more in Chapter 8.

WATCH THOSE STRINGS

One mistake that's easy to make is to pass a C-style string to NSLog() instead of one of the fancy NSString @"strings" elements. If you do this, the compiler will give you a warning:

```
main.m:46: warning: passing arg 1 of 'NSLog' from incompatible pointer type
```

If you run this program, it might crash. To catch problems like this, you can tell Xcode to always treat warnings as errors. To do that, select the Project file in the Project Navigator, Hello Objective-C under targets, then the Build Settings tab, type *error* into the search field, and check the Treat Warnings as Errors checkbox, as shown in the following image. Also make sure that the Configuration pop-up menu at the top says All.

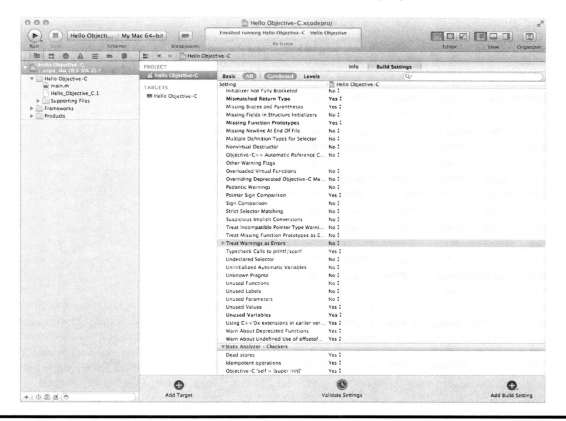

Here's another cool fact about NSString: the name itself highlights one of the nice features of Cocoa. Most Cocoa elements are named in a very straightforward manner, striving to describe the features they implement. For instance, NSArray provides arrays; NSDateFormatter helps you format dates in different ways; NSThread gives you tools for multithreaded programming; and NSSpeechSynthesizer lets you hear speech.

Now, we'll get back to stepping through our little program. The last line of the program is the return statement that ends the execution of main() and finishes the program:

```
return (0);
```

The zero value returned says that our program completed successfully. This is just the way return statements work in C.

Congratulations, again! You've just written, compiled, run, and dissected your first Objective-C program.

Are You the Boolean Type?

Many languages have a Boolean type, which is, of course, a fancy term for variables that store true and false values. Objective-C is no exception.

C has a Boolean data type, bool, which can take on the values true and false. Objective-C provides a similar type, BOOL, which can have the values YES and NO. Objective-C's BOOL type, incidentally, predates C's bool type by over a decade. The two different Boolean types can coexist in the same program, but when you're writing Cocoa code, you'll be using BOOL.

> **Note**   BOOL in Objective-C is actually just a type definition (typedef) for the signed character type (signed char), which uses 8 bits of storage. YES is defined as 1 and NO as 0 (using #define).
>
> Objective-C doesn't treat BOOL as a true Boolean type that can hold only YES or NO values. The compiler considers BOOL to be an 8-bit number, and the values of YES and NO are just a convention. This causes a subtle gotcha: if you inadvertently assign an integer value that's more than 1 byte long, such as a short or an int value, to a BOOL variable, only the lowest byte is used for the value of the BOOL. If that byte happens to be zero (as with 8960, which in hexadecimal is 0x2300), the BOOL value will be zero, the NO value.

Mighty BOOL in Action

To show mighty BOOL in action, we move on to our next project, *02.02 - BOOL Party*, which compares pairs of integers to see if they're different. Aside from main(), the program defines two functions. The first, areIntsDifferent(), takes two integer values and returns a BOOL: YES if the integers are different and NO if they are the same. A second function, boolString(), takes a BOOL parameter and returns the string @"YES" if the parameter is YES and @"NO" if the parameter is NO. This function is handy to have around when you want to print out a human-readable representation of BOOL values. main() uses these two functions to compare integers and print out the results.

Creating the project for BOOL Party is exactly the same process as making the project for Hello Objective-C:

1. Launch Xcode, if it's not already running.

2. Select **File ➤ New ➤ New Project**.

3. Choose *Application* on the left and *Command Line Tool* on the right.

4. Click *Next*.

5. Type BOOL Party as the Project Name, and click Next.

6. Click *Create*.

Edit *main.m* to make it look like this:

```
#import <Foundation/Foundation.h>
// returns NO if the two integers have the same
// value, YES otherwise

BOOL areIntsDifferent (int thing1, int thing2)
{
  if (thing1 == thing2) {
   return (NO);
  } else {
   return (YES);
  }

} // areIntsDifferent
// given a NO value, return the human-readable
// string "NO". Otherwise return "YES"

NSString *boolString (BOOL yesNo)
{
  if (yesNo == NO) {
   return (@"NO");
  } else {
   return (@"YES");
  }

} // boolString
int main (int argc, const char *argv[])
{
  BOOL areTheyDifferent;
  areTheyDifferent = areIntsDifferent (5, 5);
  NSLog (@"are %d and %d different? %@",
   5, 5, boolString(areTheyDifferent));

  areTheyDifferent = areIntsDifferent (23, 42);
  NSLog (@"are %d and %d different? %@",
   23, 42, boolString(areTheyDifferent));

  return (0);
} // main
```

Build and run your program. You'll need to bring up the console to see the output, by choosing **View ➤ Debug Area ➤ Activate Console**, or by using the keyboard shortcut ⌘⇧R. You should see output like the following:

```
2012-01-20 16:47:09.528 02 BOOL Party[16991:10b] are 5 and 5 different? NO
2012-01-20 16:47:09.542 02 BOOL Party[16991:10b] are 23 and 42 different? YES
The Debugger has exited with status 0.
```

Once again, let's pull this program apart, function by function, and see what's going on.

The First Function

The first function in our tour is areIntsDifferent().

```
BOOL areIntsDifferent (int thing1, int thing2)
{
  if (thing1 == thing2) {
   return (NO);
  } else {
   return (YES);
  }
} // areIntsDifferent
```

The areIntsDifferent() function that takes two integer parameters and returns a BOOL value. The syntax should be familiar to you from your C experience. Here, you can see thing1 being compared to thing2. If they're the same, NO is returned (since they're not different). If they're different, YES is returned. That's pretty straightforward, isn't it?

WON'T GET BOOLED AGAIN

Experienced C programmers might be tempted to write the areIntsDifferent() function as a single statement:

```
BOOL areIntsDifferent_faulty (int thing1, int thing2)
{
  return (thing1 - thing2);
} // areIntsDifferent_faulty
```

They'd do so operating under the assumption that a nonzero value is the same as YES. But that's not the case. Yes, this function returns a value, as far as C is concerned, that is true or false, but callers of functions returning BOOL will expect either YES or NO to be returned. If a programmer tries to use this function as follows, it will fail, since 23 minus 5 is 18:

```
if (areIntsDifferent_faulty(23, 5) == YES) {
 // …. }
```

While the preceding function may be a true value in C, it is not equal to YES (a value of 1) in Objective-C.

It's a good idea never to compare a BOOL value directly to YES, because too-clever programmers sometimes pull stunts similar to areIntsDifferent_faulty(). Instead, write the preceding if statement like this:

```
if (areIntsDifferent_faulty(5, 23)) {
  // …. }
```

Comparing directly to NO is always safe, since falsehood in C has a single value: zero.

The Second Function

The second function, boolString(), maps a numeric BOOL value to a string that's readable by mere humans:

```
NSString *boolString (BOOL yesNo)
{
  if (yesNo == NO) {
   return (@"NO");
  } else {
   return (@"YES");
}
}
} // boolString
```

The if statement in the middle of the function should come as no surprise. It just compares yesNo to the constant NO, and returns @"NO" if they match. Otherwise, yesNo must be a true value, so it returns @"YES".

Notice that the return type of boolString() is a pointer to an NSString. This means the function returns one of the fancy Cocoa strings that you saw earlier when you first met NSLog(). If you look at the return statements, you'll see the at sign in front of the returned values, a dead giveaway that they're NSString values.

main() is the final function. After the preliminaries of declaring the return type and arguments for main(), there is a local BOOL variable:

```
int main (int argc, const char *argv[])
{
  BOOL areTheyDifferent;
```

The areTheyDifferent variable holds onto the YES or NO value returned by areIntsDifferent(). We could simply use the function's BOOL return value directly in an if statement, but there's no harm in adding an extra variable like this to make the code easier to read. Deeply nested constructs are often confusing and hard to understand, and they're a good place for bugs to hide.

The Comparison Itself

The next two lines of code compare a couple of integers with areIntsDifferent() and store the return value into the areTheyDifferent variable. NSLog() prints out the numeric values and the human-readable string returned by boolString():

```
areTheyDifferent = areIntsDifferent (5, 5);
NSLog (@"are %d and %d different? %@",
  5, 5, boolString(areTheyDifferent));
```

As you saw earlier, NSLog() is basically a Cocoa-flavored printf() function that takes a format string and uses the additional parameters for values to plug in the format specifiers. You can see that the two fives will replace the two %d format placeholders in our call to NSLog().

At the end of the string we're giving to NSLog(), you see another at sign. This time, it's %@. What's that all about? boolString() returns an NSString pointer. printf() has no idea how to work with an NSString, so there is no a format specifier we can use. The makers of NSLog() added the %@ format specifier to instruct NSLog() to take the appropriate argument, treat it as an NSString, use the characters from that string, and send it out to the console.

> **Note**   We haven't officially introduced you to objects yet, but here's a sneak preview: when you print the values of arbitrary objects with NSLog(), you'll use the %@ format specification. When you use this specifier, the object supplies its own NSLog() format via a method named description. The description method for NSString simply prints the string's characters.

The next two lines are very similar to those you just saw:

```
areTheyDifferent = areIntsDifferent (23, 42);
NSLog (@"are %d and %d different? %@",
 23, 42, boolString(areTheyDifferent));
```

The function compares the values 23 and 42. This time, because they're different, areIntsDifferent() returns YES, and the user sees text stating the monumental fact that 23 and 42 are different values.

Here's the final return statement, which wraps up our BOOL Party:

```
  return (0);
} // main
```

In this program, you saw Objective-C's BOOL type, and the constants YES and NO for indicating true and false values. You can use BOOL in the same way you use types such as int and float: as variables, parameters to functions, and return values from functions.

Summary

In this chapter, you wrote your first two Objective-C programs, and it was fun! You also met some of Objective-C's extensions to the language, such as #import, which tells the compiler to bring in header files and to do so only once. You learned about NSString literals, those strings preceded by an at sign, such as @"hello". You used the important and versatile NSLog(), a function Cocoa provides for writing text to the console, and the NSLog() special format specifier, %@, that lets you plug NSString values into NSLog() output. You also gained the secret knowledge that when you see an at sign in code, you know you're looking at an Objective-C extension to the C language. Finally, you learned about Objective-C's BOOL type.

Stay tuned for our next chapter, in which we'll enter the mysterious world of object-oriented programming.

Chapter 3

Introduction to Object-Oriented Programming

If you've been using and programming computers for any length of time, you've probably heard the term "object-oriented programming" more than once. **Object-oriented programming**, frequently shortened to its initials, OOP, is a programming technique originally developed for writing simulation programs. OOP soon caught on with developers of other kinds of software, such as those involving graphical user interfaces. Before long, "OOP" became a major industry buzzword. It promised to be the magical silver bullet that would make programming simple and joyous.

Of course, nothing can live up to that kind of hype. Like most pursuits, OOP requires study and practice to gain proficiency, but it truly does make some kinds of programming tasks easier and, in some cases, even fun. In this book, we'll be talking about OOP a lot, mainly because Cocoa is based on OOP concepts, and Objective-C is a language that is designed to be object oriented.

So what is OOP? OOP is a way of constructing software composed of objects. Objects are like little machines living inside your computer and talking to each other to get work done. In this chapter, we'll look at some basic OOP concepts. After that, we'll examine the style of programming that leads to OOP, describing the motivation behind some OOP features. We'll wrap up with a thorough description of the mechanics of OOP.

> **Note** Like many "new" technologies, the roots of OOP stretch way back into the mists of time. OOP evolved from Simula in the 1960s, Smalltalk in the 1970s, Clascal in the 1980s, and other related languages. Modern languages such as C++, Java, Python, and of course, Objective-C draw inspiration from these older languages.

As we dive into OOP, stick a Babel fish in your ear, and be prepared to encounter some strange terminology along the way. OOP comes with a lot of fancy-sounding lingo that makes it seem more mysterious and difficult than it actually is. You might even think that computer scientists create long, impressive-sounding words to show everyone how smart they are, but of course, they don't all do that. Well, don't worry. We'll explain each term as we encounter it.

Before we get into OOP itself, let's take a look at a key concept of OOP: indirection.

It's All Indirection

An old saying in programming goes something like this, "There is no problem in computer science that can't be solved by adding another level of indirection." **Indirection** is a fancy word with a simple meaning—instead of using a value directly in your code, use a pointer to the value. Here's a real-world example: you might not know the phone number of your favorite pizza place, but you know that you can look in the phone book to find it. Using the phone book like this is a form of indirection.

Indirection can also mean that you ask another person to do something rather than doing it yourself. Let's say you have a box of books to return to your friend Andrew who lives across town. You know that your next-door neighbor is going to visit Andrew tonight. Rather than driving across town, dropping off the books, and driving back, you ask your friendly neighbor to deliver the box. This is another kind of indirection: you have someone else do the work instead of doing it yourself.

In programming, you can take indirection to multiple levels, writing code that consults other code, which accesses yet another level of code. You've probably had the experience of calling a technical support line. You explain your problem to the support person, who then directs you to the specific department that can handle your problem. The person there then directs you to the second-level technician with the skills to help you out. And if you're like us, at this point, you find out you called the wrong number, and you have to be transferred to some other department for help. This runaround is a form of indirection. Luckily, computers have infinite patience and can handle being sent from place to place to place looking for an answer.

Variables and Indirection

You might be surprised to find out that you have already used indirection in your programs. The humble variable is a real-world use of indirection. Consider this small program that prints the numbers from one to five. You can find this program in the *Learn ObjC Projects* folder, in *03.01 Count-1*:

```
#import <Foundation/Foundation.h>

int main (int argc, const char *argv[])
{
 NSLog (@"The numbers from 1 to 5:");

 for (int i = 1; i <= 5; i++) {
  NSLog (@"%d\n", i);
 }
```

```
 return (0);

} // main
```

Count-1 has a for loop that runs five times, using NSLog() to display the value of i each time around. When you run this program, you see output like this:

```
2012-01-21 11:52:01.940 03.01 Count-1[26429:903] The numbers from 1 to 5:
2012-01-21 11:52:01.943 03.01 Count-1[26429:903] 1
2012-01-21 11:52:01.944 03.01 Count-1[26429:903] 2
2012-01-21 11:52:01.944 03.01 Count-1[26429:903] 3
2012-01-21 11:52:01.945 03.01 Count-1[26429:903] 4
2012-01-21 11:52:01.947 03.01 Count-1[26429:903] 5
```

Now, suppose you want to upgrade your program to print the numbers from one to ten. You have to edit your code in two places, which are highlighted in bold in the following listing, and then rebuild the program (this version is in the folder *03.02 Count-2*):

```
#import <Foundation/Foundation.h>

int main (int argc, const char * argv[])
{
 NSLog (@"The numbers from 1 to 10:");

 for (int i = 1; i <= 10; i++) {
  NSLog (@"%d\n", i);
 }

 return (0);

} // main
```

Count-2 produces this output:

```
2012-01-21 12:03:13.433 03.02 Count-2[26507:903] The numbers from 1 to 10:
2012-01-21 12:03:13.435 03.02 Count-2[26507:903] 1
2012-01-21 12:03:13.436 03.02 Count-2[26507:903] 2
2012-01-21 12:03:13.436 03.02 Count-2[26507:903] 3
2012-01-21 12:03:13.437 03.02 Count-2[26507:903] 4
2012-01-21 12:03:13.437 03.02 Count-2[26507:903] 5
2012-01-21 12:03:13.438 03.02 Count-2[26507:903] 6
2012-01-21 12:03:13.438 03.02 Count-2[26507:903] 7
2012-01-21 12:03:13.438 03.02 Count-2[26507:903] 8
2012-01-21 12:03:13.439 03.02 Count-2[26507:903] 9
2012-01-21 12:03:13.439 03.02 Count-2[26507:903] 10
```

Modifying the program in this way is obviously not a very tricky change to make: you can do it with a simple search-and-replace action, and only two places need to be changed. However, doing a similar search and replace in a larger program, consisting of, say, tens of thousands of lines of code would be a lot trickier. We would have to be careful about simply replacing 5 with 10: no doubt, there would be some instances of the number five that aren't related to this and so shouldn't be changed to ten.

Solving this problem is what variables are for. Rather than sticking the upper loop value (five or ten) directly in the code, we can solve this problem by putting the number in a variable, thus adding a layer of indirection. When you add the variable, instead of telling the program to "go through the loop five times," you're telling it to "go look in this variable named count, which will say how many times to run the loop." Now, the program is called Count-3 and looks like this:

```
#import <Foundation/Foundation.h>

int main (int argc, const char * argv[])
{
 int count = 5;

 NSLog (@"The numbers from 1 to %d:", count);

 for (int i = 1; i <= count; i++) {
  NSLog (@"%d\n", i);
 }

 return (0);

} // main
```

The program's output should be unsurprising:

```
2012-01-21 12:16:51.442 03.03 Count-3[26596:903] The numbers from 1 to 5:
2012-01-21 12:16:51.446 03.03 Count-3[26596:903] 1
2012-01-21 12:16:51.447 03.03 Count-3[26596:903] 2
2012-01-21 12:16:51.448 03.03 Count-3[26596:903] 3
2012-01-21 12:16:51.449 03.03 Count-3[26596:903] 4
2012-01-21 12:16:51.449 03.03 Count-3[26596:903] 5
```

> **Note**   The NSLog() time stamp and other information take up a lot of space, so for clarity, we'll leave that information out of future listings.

If you want to print the numbers from 1 to 100, you just have to touch the code in one obvious place:

```
#import <Foundation/Foundation.h>

int main (int argc, const char * argv[])
{
 int count = 100;

 NSLog (@"The numbers from 1 to %d:", count);

 for (int i = 1; i <= count; i++) {
  NSLog (@"%d\n", i);
 }

 return (0);

} // main
```

By adding a variable, our code is now much cleaner and easier to extend, especially when other programmers need to change the code. To change the loop values, they won't have to scrutinize every use of the number five to see if they need to modify it. Instead, they can just change the count variable to get the result they want.

Indirection Through Filenames

Files provide another example of indirection. Consider Word-Length-1, a program that prints a list of words along with their lengths; it is in the *03.04 Word-Length-1* folder. This vital program is the key technology for your new Web 2.0 start-up, Length-o-words.com. Here's the listing:

```
#import <Foundation/Foundation.h>

int main (int argc, const char * argv[])
{
 const char *words[4] = { "aardvark", "abacus",
        "allude", "zygote" };
 int wordCount = 4;

 for (int i = 0; i < wordCount; i++) {
  NSLog (@"%s is %lu characters long", words[i], strlen(words[i]));
 }

 return (0);

} // main
```

The for loop determines which word in the words array is being processed at any time. The NSLog() function inside the loop prints out the word using the %s format specifier. We use %s, because words is an array of C strings rather than of @"NSString" objects. The %lu format specifier takes the integer value of the strlen() function, which calculates the length of the string, and prints it out along with the word itself.

When you run Word-Length-1, you see informative output like this:

```
aardvark is 8 characters long
abacus is 6 characters long
allude is 6 characters long
zygote is 6 characters long
```

> **Note** Once again, we're leaving out the time stamp and process ID that NSLog() adds to the output of Word-Length-1.

Now, suppose the venture capitalists investing in Length-o-words.com want you to use a different set of words. They've scrutinized your business plan and have concluded that you can sell to a broader market if you use the names of country music stars.

Because we stored the words directly in the program, we have to edit the source, replacing the original word list with the new names. When we edit, we have to be careful with the punctuation, such as the quotes in Joe Bob's name and the commas between entries. Here is the updated program, which can be found in the *03.05 Word-Length-2* folder:

```
#import <Foundation/Foundation.h>

int main (int argc, const char * argv[])
{
  const char *words[4] = { "Joe-Bob \"Handyman\" Brown",
   "Jacksonville \"Sly\" Murphy",
   "Shinara Bain",
   "George \"Guitar\" Books" };
  int wordCount = 4;

  for (int i = 0; i < wordCount; i++) {
  NSLog (@"%s is %lu characters long", words[i], strlen(words[i]));
  }

  return (0);

} // main
```

Because we were careful with the surgery, the program still works as we expect (note that spaces and punctuation count as characters):

```
Joe-Bob "Handyman" Brown is 24 characters long
Jacksonville "Sly" Murphy is 25 characters long
Shinara Bain is 12 characters long
George "Guitar" Books is 21 characters long
```

Making this change required entirely too much work: we had to edit *Word-Length-2.m*, fix any typos, and then rebuild the program. If the program runs on a web site, we then have to retest and redeploy the program to upgrade to Word-Length-2.

Another way to construct this program is to move the names completely out of the code and put them all into a text file, one name on each line. Let's all say it together: this is indirection. Rather than putting the names directly in the source code, the program looks for the names elsewhere. The program reads a list of names from a text file and proceeds to print them out, along with their lengths. The project files for this new program live in the *03.06 Word-Length-3* folder, and the code looks like this:

```
#import <Foundation/Foundation.h>

int main (int argc, const char * argv[])
{
  FILE *wordFile = fopen ("/tmp/words.txt", "r");
  char word[100];

  while (fgets(word, 100, wordFile))
   {
   // strip off the trailing \n
   word[strlen(word) - 1] = '\0';
```

```
    NSLog (@"%s is %lu characters long", word, strlen(word));
    }
    fclose (wordFile);

    return (0);

} // main
```

Let's stroll through Word-Length-3 and see what it's doing. First, fopen() opens the *words.txt* file for reading. Next, fgets() reads a line of text from the file and places it into word. The fgets() call preserves the newline character that separates each line, but we really don't want it: if we leave it, it will be counted as a character in the word. To fix this, we replace the newline character with a zero, which indicates the end of the string. Finally, we use our old friend NSLog() to print out the word and its length.

> **Note**   Take a look at the path name we used with fopen(). It's */tmp/words.txt*. This means that *words.txt* is a file that lives in the */tmp* directory, the Unix temporary directory, which gets emptied when the computer reboots. You can use */tmp* to store scratch files that you want to mess around with but really don't care about keeping. For a real, live program, you'd put your file in a more permanent location, such as the home directory.

Before you run the program, use your text editor to create the file *words.txt* in the */tmp* directory. Type the following names into the file:

```
Joe-Bob "Handyman" Brown
Jacksonville "Sly" Murphy
Shinara Bain
George "Guitar" Books
```

To save a file to the */tmp* directory from a text editor, type the file's text, choose Save, press the slash key (/), type **tmp**, and press Enter.

If you prefer, instead of typing the names, you can copy *words.txt* from the *03.06 Word-Length-3* directory into */tmp*. To see */tmp* in the Finder, choose **Go ➤ Go to Folder**.

> **Tip**   If you're using our prebuilt Word-Length-3 project, we've done a little Xcode magic to copy the *words. txt* file to */tmp* for you. See if you can discover what we did. Here's a hint: look in the Targets area in the Groups & Files pane.

When you run Word-Length-3, the program's output looks just as it did before:

```
Joe-Bob "Handyman" Brown is 24 characters long
Jacksonville "Sly" Murphy is 25 characters long
Shinara Bain is 12 characters long
George "Guitar" Books is 21 characters long
```

Word-Length-3 is a shining example of indirection. Rather than coding the words directly into your program, you're instead saying, "Go look in */tmp/words.txt* to get the words." With this scheme, we can change the set of words anytime we want, just by editing this text file, without having to change the program. Go ahead and try it out: add a couple of words to your *words.txt* file and rerun the program. We'll wait for you here.

This approach is better, because text files are easier to edit and far less fragile than source code. You can get your nonprogrammer friends to use TextEdit to do the editing. Your marketing staff can keep the list of words up to date, which frees you to work on more interesting tasks.

As you know, people always come along with new ideas for upgrading or enhancing a program. Maybe your investors have decided that counting the length of cooking terms is the new path to profit. Now that your program looks at a file for its data, you can change the set of words all you want without ever having to touch the code.

Despite great advances in indirection, Word-Length-3 is still rather fragile, because it insists on using a full path name to the words file. And that file itself is in a precarious position: if the computer reboots, */tmp/words.txt* vanishes. Also, if others are using the program on your machine with their own */tmp/words.txt* files, they could accidentally stomp on your copy. You could edit the program each time to use a different path, but we already know that that's no fun, so let's add another indirection trick to make our lives easier.

Instead of looking in */tmp/words.txt* to get the words, we'll change the program and tell it to "go look at the first launch parameter of the program to figure out the location of the words file." Here is the Word-Length-4 program (which can be found in the *03.07 Word-Length-4* folder). It uses a command-line parameter to specify the file name. The changes we made to Word-Length-3 are highlighted:

```
#import <Foundation/Foundation.h>

int main (int argc, const char * argv[])
{
  if (argc == 1) {
   NSLog (@"you need to provide a file name");
   return (1);
  }

  FILE *wordFile = fopen (argv[1], "r");
  char word[100];
  while (fgets(word, 100, wordFile))
   {
   // strip off the trailing \n
   word[strlen(word) - 1] = '\0';

   NSLog (@"%s is %lu characters long", word, strlen(word));
   }

  fclose (wordFile);

  return (0);

} // main
```

The loop that processes the file is the same as in Word-Length-3, but the code that sets it up is new and improved. The if statement verifies that the user supplied a path name as a launch parameter. The code consults the argc parameter to main(), which holds the number of launch parameters. Because the program name is always passed as a launch parameter, `argc` is always 1 or greater. If the user doesn't pass a file path, the value of `argc` is 1, and we have no file to read, so we print an error message and stop the program.

If the user was thoughtful and provided a file path, `argc` is greater than 1. We then look in the `argv` array to see what that file path is. `argv[1]` contains the filename the user has given us. (In case you're curious, the `argv[0]` parameter holds the name of the program.)

If you're running the program in Terminal, it's easy to specify the name of the file on the command line, like so:

```
$ ./Word-Length-4 /tmp/words.txt
Joe-Bob "Handyman" Brown is 24 characters long
Jacksonville "Sly" Murphy is 25 characters long
Shinara Bain is 12 characters long
George "Guitar" Books is 21 characters long
```

SUPPLYING A FILE PATH IN XCODE

If you're editing the program along with us in Xcode, supplying a file path as you run it is a little more complicated. **Launch arguments**, also called **command-line parameters**, are a little trickier to control from Xcode than from Terminal. Here's what you need to do to change the launch arguments:

First, in Xcode, choose Product ➤ Edit Scheme and then click the Arguments tab.

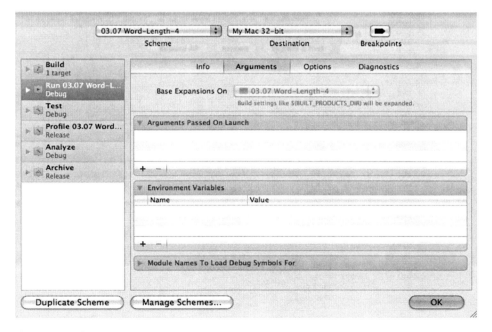

Figure 3-1. Arguments tab

Next, as shown in the following screen shot, click the plus sign in the Arguments Passed On Launch section, and type the launch argument—in this case, the path to the *words.txt* file:

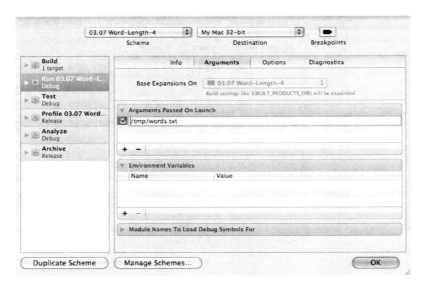

Figure 3-2. Arguments Passed On Launch

Now, when you run the program, Xcode passes your launch argument into Word-Length-4's `argv` array. Here's what you'll see when you run the program:

```
All Output ↕                                    Clear  ⬛ ⬛ ⬛
GNU gdb 6.3.50-20050815 (Apple version gdb-1708) (Mon Aug 15
16:03:10 UTC 2011)
Copyright 2004 Free Software Foundation, Inc.
GDB is free software, covered by the GNU General Public
License, and you are
welcome to change it and/or distribute copies of it under
certain conditions.
Type "show copying" to see the conditions.
There is absolutely no warranty for GDB.   Type "show
warranty" for details.
This GDB was configured as "x86_64-apple-darwin".tty /dev/
ttys000
[Switching to process 77578 thread 0x0]
2012-01-23 18:32:05.312 03.07 Word-Length-4[77578:903] Joe-
Bob "Handyman" Brown
 is 25 characters long
2012-01-23 18:32:05.315 03.07 Word-Length-4[77578:903]
Jacksonville "Sly" Murphy
 is 26 characters long
2012-01-23 18:32:05.316 03.07 Word-Length-4[77578:903]
Shinara Bain
 is 13 characters long
2012-01-23 18:32:05.316 03.07 Word-Length-4[77578:903] George
"Guitar" Books
 is 22 characters long
Program ended with exit code: 0
```

Figure 3-3. argv array output

Just for fun, run your program with *usr/share/dict/words*, which has over 230,000 words in it. Your program can handle huge amounts of data! When you get tired of watching words whiz by in the Xcode console window, click the Stop button to make the program stop.

Because you're supplying arguments at runtime, everybody can use your program to get the length of *any* set of words they want to, even absurdly large sets of words. Users can change the data without changing the code, just as nature intended. This is the essence of indirection: it's telling us where to get the data we need.

Using Indirection in Object-Oriented Programming

Object-oriented programming is all about indirection. OOP uses indirection for accessing data, just as we did in the previous examples by employing variables, files, and arguments. The real revolution of OOP is that it uses indirection for calling *code*. Rather than calling a function directly, you end up calling it indirectly.

Now that you know that, you're an expert in OOP. Everything else is a side effect of this indirection.

Procedural Programming

To complete your appreciation of the flexibility of OOP, we'll take a quick look at procedural programming, so you can get an idea of the kinds of problems that OOP was created to solve. Procedural programming has been around a long, long time, since just after the invention of dirt. Procedural programming is the kind typically taught in introductory programming books and classes. Most programming in languages like BASIC, C, Tcl, and Perl is procedural.

In procedural programs, data is typically kept in simple structures, such as C `struct` elements. There are also more complex data structures, such as linked lists and trees. When you call a function, you pass the data to the function, and it manipulates the data. Functions are the center of the procedural programming experience: you decide which functions you want to use, and then you call those functions, passing in the data they need.

The Shape of Things to Draw

Consider a program that draws a bunch of geometric shapes on the screen. Thanks to the magic of computers, you can do more than consider it—you'll find the source code to this program in the *03.08 Shapes-Procedural* folder. For simplicity's sake, the Shapes-Procedural program doesn't actually draw shapes on the screen, it just quaintly prints out some shape-related text. We left out the code that actually draws shapes because that would add complexity and remove our desired focus, which is to write a program that processes several kinds of elements in similar ways.

Shapes-Procedural uses plain C and the procedural programming style. The code starts out by defining some constants and a structure.

After the obligatory inclusion of the foundation headers is an enumeration that specifies the different kinds of shapes that can be drawn: circle, rectangle, and an egg-shaped solid:

```
#import <Foundation/Foundation.h>
```

```
typedef enum {
 kCircle,
 kRectangle,
 kEgg } ShapeType;
```

Next is an enum that defines the colors that can be used to draw the shape:

```
typedef enum {
 kRedColor,
 kGreenColor,
 kBlueColor } ShapeColor;
```

After that, we have a structure that describes a rectangle, which specifies the area on the screen where the shape will be drawn. For this chapter's examples, we're not worrying about exactly how this rectangle will be used to place each shape, just that it will happen somehow.

```
typedef struct {
 int x, y, width, height;
} ShapeRect;
```

Finally, we have a structure that pulls all these things together to describe a shape:

```
typedef struct {
 ShapeType type;
 ShapeColor fillColor;
 ShapeRect bounds;
} Shape;
```

The Part That Does the Work

Next up in our example, `main()` declares an array of shapes we're going to draw. After declaring the array, each shape structure in the array is initialized by assigning its fields. The following code gives us a red circle, a green rectangle, and a blue egg, at various random locations:

```
int main (int argc, const char * argv[])
{
 Shape shapes[3];

 ShapeRect rect0 = { 0, 0, 10, 30 };
 shapes[0].type = kCircle;
 shapes[0].fillColor = kRedColor;
 shapes[0].bounds = rect0;

 ShapeRect rect1 = { 30, 40, 50, 60 };
 shapes[1].type = kRectangle;
 shapes[1].fillColor = kGreenColor;
 shapes[1].bounds = rect1;

 ShapeRect rect2 = { 15, 18, 37, 29 };
 shapes[2].type = kEgg;
 shapes[2].fillColor = kBlueColor;
 shapes[2].bounds = rect2;
```

```
drawShapes (shapes, 3);

return (0);

} // main
```

```
┌──────────────────────────────────────────────────────────────┐
│                      A HANDY C SHORTCUT                        │
└──────────────────────────────────────────────────────────────┘
```

The rectangles in the Shapes-Procedural program's `main()` method are declared using a handy little C trick: when you declare a variable that's a structure, you can initialize all the elements of that structure at once.

```
ShapeRect rect0 = { 0, 0, 10, 30 };
```

The structure elements get values in the order they're declared. Recall that ShapeRect is declared like this:

```
typedef struct {
int x, y, width, height; } ShapeRect;
```

The preceding assignment to `rect0` means that `rect0.x` and `rect0.y` will both have the value 0; `rect0.width` will be 10; and `rect0.height` will be 30.

This technique lets you reduce the amount of typing in your program without sacrificing readability.

After initializing the shapes array, `main()` calls the `drawShapes()` function to draw the shapes.

`drawShapes()` has a loop that inspects each Shape structure in the array. A `switch` statement looks at the `type` field of the structure and chooses a function that draws the shape. The program calls the appropriate drawing function, passing parameters for the screen area and color to use for drawing. Check it out:

```
void drawShapes (Shape shapes[], int count)
{
  for (int i = 0; i < count; i++) {

    switch (shapes[i].type) {

      case kCircle:
       drawCircle (shapes[i].bounds,
           shapes[i].fillColor);
       break;

      case kRectangle:
       drawRectangle (shapes[i].bounds,
            shapes[i].fillColor);
       break;

      case kEgg:
       drawEgg (shapes[i].bounds,
           shapes[i].fillColor);
       break;

    }
  }
} // drawShapes
```

Here is the code for drawCircle(), which just prints out the bounding rectangle and the color passed to it:

```
void drawCircle (ShapeRect bounds, ShapeColor fillColor)
{
  NSLog (@"drawing a circle at (%d %d %d %d) in %@",
      bounds.x, bounds.y,
      bounds.width, bounds.height,
      colorName(fillColor));

} // drawCircle
```

The colorName() function called inside NSLog() simply does a switch on the passed-in color value and returns a literal NSString such as @"red" or @"blue":

```
NSString *colorName (ShapeColor colorName)
{
  switch (colorName) {
   case kRedColor:
    return @"red";
    break;
   case kGreenColor:
    return @"green";
    break;
   case kBlueColor:
    return @"blue";
    break;
  }

  return @"no clue";

} // colorName
```

The other draw functions are almost identical to drawCircle, except that they draw a rectangle and an egg.

Here is the output of Shapes-Procedural (minus the time stamp and other information added by NSLog()):

```
drawing a circle at (0 0 10 30) in red
drawing a rectangle at (30 40 50 60) in green
drawing an egg at (15 18 37 29) in blue
```

This all seems pretty simple and straightforward, right? When you use procedural programming, you spend your time connecting data with the functions designed to deal with that type of data. You have to be careful to use the right function for each data type: for example, you must call drawRectangle() for a shape of type kRectangle. It's disappointingly easy to pass a rectangle to a function meant to work with circles.

Another problem with coding like this is that it can make extending and maintaining the program difficult. To illustrate, let's enhance Shapes-Procedural to add a new kind of shape: a triangle. You can find the modified program in the *03.09 Shapes-Procedural-2* project. We have to modify the program in at least four different places to accomplish this task.

First, we'll add a kTriangle constant to the ShapeType enum:

```
typedef enum {
 kCircle,
 kRectangle,
 kEgg,
 kTriangle
} ShapeType;
```

Then, we'll implement a drawTriangle() function that looks just like its siblings:

```
void drawTriangle (ShapeRect bounds,
      ShapeColor fillColor)
{
 NSLog (@"drawing triangle at (%d %d %d %d) in %@",
    bounds.x, bounds.y,
    bounds.width, bounds.height,
    colorName(fillColor));

} // drawTriangle
```

Next, we'll add a new case to the switch statement in drawShapes(). This will test for kTriangle and will call drawTriangle() if appropriate:

```
void drawShapes (Shape shapes[], int count)
{
 for (int i = 0; i < count; i++) {

  switch (shapes[i].type) {

   case kCircle:
    drawCircle (shapes[i].bounds, shapes[i].fillColor);
    break;

   case kRectangle:
    drawRectangle (shapes[i].bounds, shapes[i].fillColor);
    break;

   case kEgg:
    drawEgg (shapes[i].bounds, shapes[i].fillColor);
    break;

   case kTriangle:
    drawTriangle (shapes[i].bounds, shapes[i].fillColor);
    break;
  }
 }

} // drawShapes
```

Finally, we'll add a triangle to the shapes array. Don't forget to increase the number of shapes in the shapes array:

```
int main (int argc, const char * argv[])
{
 Shape shapes[4];

 ShapeRect rect0 = { 0, 0, 10, 30 };
 shapes[0].type = kCircle;
```

```
shapes[0].fillColor = kRedColor;
shapes[0].bounds = rect0;

ShapeRect rect1 = { 30, 40, 50, 60 };
shapes[1].type = kRectangle;
shapes[1].fillColor = kGreenColor;
shapes[1].bounds = rect1;

ShapeRect rect2 = { 15, 18, 37, 29 };
shapes[2].type = kEgg;
shapes[2].fillColor = kBlueColor;
shapes[2].bounds = rect2;

ShapeRect rect3 = { 47, 32, 80, 50 };
shapes[3].type = kTriangle;
shapes[3].fillColor = kRedColor;
shapes[3].bounds = rect3;

drawShapes (shapes, 4);

return (0);

} // main
```

OK, let's take a look at Shapes-Procedural-2 in action:

```
drawing a circle at (0 0 10 30) in red
drawing a rectangle at (30 40 50 60) in green
drawing an egg at (15 18 37 29) in blue
drawing a triangle at (47 32 80 50) in red
```

Adding support for triangles wasn't too bad, but our little program only does one kind of action—drawing shapes (or at least, printing out text about drawing shapes). The more complex the program, the trickier it is to extend. For example, let's say the program does more messing around with shapes; suppose it computes their areas and determines if the mouse pointer lies within them. In that case, you'll have to modify every function that performs an action on shapes, touching code that has been working perfectly and possibly introducing errors.

Here's another scenario that's fraught with peril: adding a new shape that needs more information to describe it. For example, a rounded rectangle needs information none of our other shapes has needed: the radius of its rounded corners. To support rounded rectangles, you could add a radius field to the Shape structure, which is a waste of space, because the field won't be used by other shapes, or you could use a C union to overlay different data layouts in the same structure, which complicates things by making all shapes dig into the union to get to their interesting data.

OOP addresses these problems elegantly. As we teach our program to use OOP, we'll see how OOP handles the first problem, modifying already-working code to add new kinds of shapes.

Implementing Object Orientation

Procedural programs are based on functions. The data orbits around the functions. Object orientation reverses this point of view, placing a program's data at the center, with the functions orbiting around the data. Instead of focusing on functions in your programs, you concentrate on the data.

That sounds interesting, but how does it work? In OOP, data contains references to the code that operates on it, using indirection. Rather than telling the `drawRectangle()` function to "go draw a rectangle using this shape structure," you instead ask a rectangle to "go draw yourself" (gosh, that sounds rude, but it's really not). Through the magic of indirection, the rectangle's data knows how to find the function that will perform the drawing.

So what exactly is an object? It's nothing more than a fancy C `struct` that has the ability to find code it's associated with, usually via a function pointer. Figure 3-4 shows four Shape objects: two rectangles, a circle, and an egg. Each object is able to find a function to do its drawing.

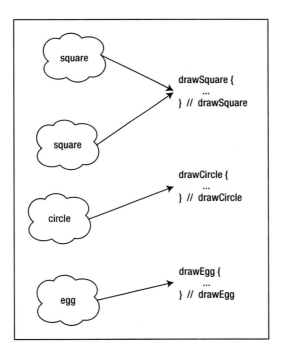

Figure 3-4. Basic Shape objects

Each object has its own `draw()` function that knows how to "draw" its specific shape. For example, a `Circle` object's `draw()` knows to draw a circle. A `Rectangle`'s `draw()` knows to draw a rectangle.

The Shapes-Object program (available at *03.10 -Shapes-Object*) does the same stuff as Shapes-Procedural but uses Objective-C's object-oriented features to do it. Here's `drawShapes()` from Shapes-Object:

```
void drawShapes (id shapes[], int count)
{
  for (int i = 0; i < count; i++) {
```

```
   id shape = shapes[i];
   [shape draw];
 }

} // drawShapes
```

This function contains a loop that looks at each shape in the array. In the loop, the program tells the shape to draw itself.

Notice the differences between this version of drawShapes() and the original. For one thing, this one is a lot shorter! The code doesn't have to ask each individual shape what kind it is.

Another change is shapes[], the first argument to the function: it's now an array of id objects. What is an id? Is it a psychological term referring to the part of the mind in which innate instinctive impulses and primary processes are manifest? Not in this case: it stands for **identifier**, and it's pronounced "eye dee." An id is a generic type that's used to refer to any kind of object. Recall that an object is just a C struct with some code attached, so an id is actually a pointer to one of these structures; in this case, the structures make various kinds of shapes.

The third change to drawShapes() is the body of the loop:

```
id shape = shapes[i];
[shape draw];
```

The first line looks like ordinary C. The code gets the id—that is, a pointer to an object— from the shapes array and sticks it into the variable named shape, which has the type id. This is just a pointer assignment: it doesn't actually copy the entire contents of the shape. Take a look at Figure 3-5 to see the various shapes available in Shapes-Object. shapes[0] is a pointer to the red circle; shapes[1] is a pointer to a green rectangle; and shapes[2] is a pointer to a blue egg.

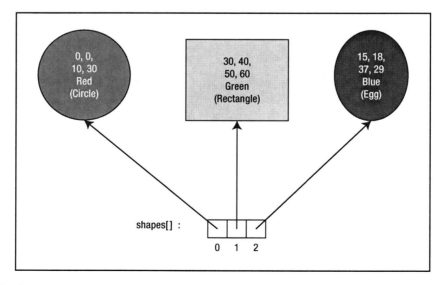

Figure 3-5. *The shapes array*

Now we've come to the last line of code in the function:

```
[shape draw];
```

This is seriously weird. What's going on? We know that C uses square brackets to refer to array elements, but we don't seem to be doing anything with arrays here. In Objective-C, square brackets have an additional meaning: they're used to tell an object what to do. Inside the square brackets, the first item is an object, and the rest is an action that you want the object to perform. In this case, we're telling an object named shape to perform the action draw. If shape is a circle, a circle is "drawn." If shape is a rectangle, we'll get a rectangle.

In Objective-C, telling an object to do an action is called **sending a message** (although some folks also say "calling a method"). The code [shape draw] sends the message draw to the object shape. One way to pronounce [shape draw] is "send draw to shape." How the shape actually does the drawing is up to the shape's implementation.

When you send a message to an object, how does the necessary code get called? This happens with the assistance of behind-the-scenes helpers called **classes**.

Take a look at Figure 3-6 please. The left side of the figure shows that this is the circle object at index zero of the shapes array, last seen in Figure 3-2. The object has a pointer to its class. The class is a structure that tells how to be an object of its kind. In Figure 3-3, the Circle class has a pointer to code for drawing circles, for calculating the area of circles, and other stuff required in order to be a good Circle citizen.

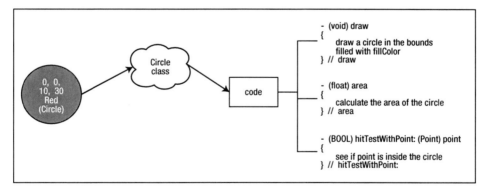

Figure 3-6. *A circle and its class*

What's the point of having class objects? Wouldn't it be simpler just to have each object point directly to its code? Indeed, it would be simpler, and some OOP systems do just that. But having class objects is a great advantage: if you change the class at runtime, all objects of that class automatically pick up the changes (we'll discuss this more in later chapters).

Figure 3-7 shows how the draw message ends up calling the right function for the circle object.

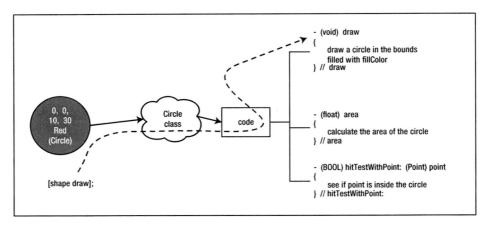

Figure 3-7. A circle finds its draw code.

Here are the steps illustrated in Figure 3-4:

1. The object that is the target of the message (the red circle in this case) is consulted to see what its class is.

2. The class looks through its code and finds out where the draw function is.

3. Once it's found, the function that draws circles is executed.

Figure 3-8 shows what happens when you call [shape draw] on the second shape in the array, which is the green rectangle.

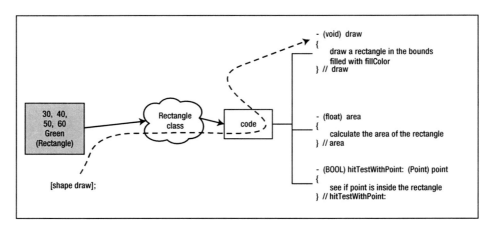

Figure 3-8. A rectangle finds its draw code.

The steps used in Figure 3-5 are nearly identical those in the previous image:

1. The target object of the message (the green rectangle) is consulted to see what its class is.

2. The rectangle class checks its pile of code and gets the address of the `draw` function.

3. Objective-C runs the code that draws a rectangle.

This program shows some very cool indirection in action! In the procedural version of the program, we had to write code that determined which function to call. Now, that decision is made behind the scenes by Objective-C, as it asks the objects which class they belong to. This reduces the chance of calling the wrong function and makes our code easier to maintain.

Time Out for Terminology

Before we dig into the rest of the Shapes-Object program, let's take a moment to go over some object-oriented terminology. We've already talked about some of these terms; others are brand new.

▪   **class** is a structure that represents an object's type. An object refers to its class to get various information about itself, particularly what code to run to handle each action. Simple programs might have a handful of classes; moderately complex ones will have a couple of dozen. Objective-C style encourages developers to capitalize class names.

▪   An **object** is structure containing values and a hidden pointer to its class. Running programs typically have hundreds or thousands of objects. Objective-C variables that refer to objects are typically not capitalized.

▪   **Instance** is another word for "object." For example, a `circle` object can also be called an instance of class `Circle`.

▪   **message** is an action that an object can perform. This is what you send to an object to tell it to do something. In the `[shape draw]` code, the `draw` message is sent to the `shape` object to tell it to draw itself. When an object receives a message, its class is consulted to find the proper code to run.

▪   **method** is code that runs in response to a message. A message, such as `draw`, can invoke different methods depending on the class of the object.

▪   The **method dispatcher** is the mechanism used by Objective-C to divine which method will be executed in response to a particular message. We'll get out our shovels and dig a lot more into the Objective-C method dispatch mechanism in the next chapter.

Those are the key OOP terms you'll need for the rest of this book. In addition, there are a couple of generic programming terms that will soon become very important:

■ The **interface** is the description of the features provided by a class of objects. For example, the interface for class `Circle` declares that circles can accept the draw message.

> **Note**   The concept of interfaces is not limited to OOP. For example, header files in C provide interfaces for libraries such as the standard I/O library (which you get when you `#include <stdio.h>`), and the math library (`#include <math.h>`). Interfaces do not provide implementation details, and the general idea is that you shouldn't care about them.

■ The **implementation** is the code that makes the interface work. In our examples, the implementation for the circle object holds the code for drawing a circle on the screen. When you send the draw message to a circle object, you don't know or care how the function works, just that it draws a circle on the screen.

OOP in Objective-C

If your brain is starting to hurt now, that's OK. We've been filling it up with a lot of new stuff, and assimilating all the terms and technology will take awhile. While your subconscious is chewing on the previous couple of sections, let's take a look at the rest of the code for Shapes-Object, including some new syntax for declaring classes.

The @interface Section

Before you can create objects of a particular class, the Objective-C compiler needs some information about that class. Specifically, it has to know about the data members of the object (that is, what the C `struct` for the object looks like) and which features it provides. You use the @ `interface` directive to give this information to the compiler.

> **Note**   In Shapes-Object, we put everything into its *Shapes-Object.m* file. In larger programs, you'll use multiple files, giving each class its own set of files. We'll explore ways of organizing classes and files in Chapter 6.

Here is the interface for the `Circle` class:

```
@interface Circle : NSObject
{
@private
 ShapeColor fillColor;
 ShapeRect  bounds;
}
```

```
- (void) setFillColor: (ShapeColor) fillColor;

- (void) setBounds: (ShapeRect) bounds;

- (void) draw;

@end // Circle
```

This code includes some syntax we haven't talked about yet, so let's do that. A lot of information is packed into these few lines. Let's pull them apart.

The first line looks like this:

```
@interface Circle : NSObject
```

As we said in Chapter 2, whenever you see an at sign in Objective-C, you're looking at an extension to the C language. `@interface Circle` says to the compiler, "Here comes the interface for a new class named `Circle`."

> **Note**   NSObject in the `@interface` line tells the compiler that the `Circle` class is based on the NSObject class. This statement says that every `Circle` is also an NSObject, and every `Circle` will inherit all the behaviors that are defined by class NSObject. We'll explore inheritance in much greater detail in the next chapter.

What follows are some lines that look kind of like C function prototypes:

```
- (void) draw;
- (void) setFillColor: (ShapeColor) fillColor;
- (void) setBounds: (ShapeRect) bounds;
```

In Objective-C, these are called **method declarations**. They're a lot like good old-fashioned C function prototypes, which are a way of saying, "Here are the features I support." The method declarations give the name of each method, the method's return type, and any arguments.

Let's start out with the simplest one, `draw`:

```
- (void) draw;
```

The leading dash signals that this is the declaration for an Objective-C method. That's one way you can distinguish a method declaration from a function prototype, which has no leading dash. Following the dash is the return type for the method, enclosed in parentheses. In our case, `draw` just draws and won't be returning anything. Objective-C uses `void` to indicate that there's no return value.

Objective-C methods can return the same types as C functions: standard types (`int`, `float`, and `char`), pointers, object references, and structures.

The next method declarations are more interesting:

```
- (void) setFillColor: (ShapeColor) fillColor;
- (void) setBounds: (ShapeRect) bounds;
```

Each of these methods takes a single argument. setFillColor: takes a color for its argument. Circles use this color when they draw themselves. setBounds: takes a rectangle. Circles use this rectangle to define their bounds.

GET YOUR INFIX HERE

Objective-C uses a syntax technique called **infix notation**. The name of the method and its arguments are all intertwined. For instance, you call a single-argument method like this:

```
[circle setFillColor: kRedColor];
```

A method that takes two arguments is called like this:

```
[textThing setStringValue: @"hello there" color: kBlueColor];
```

The setStringValue: and color: thingies are the names of the arguments (and are actually part of the method name—more on that later), and @"hello there" and kBlueColor are the arguments being passed.

This syntax differs from C, in which you call a function with its name followed by all its arguments, like so:

```
setTextThingValueColor (textThing, @"hello there", kBlueColor);
```

We really like the infix syntax, although it does look a little weird at first. It makes the code very readable, and matching arguments with what they do is easy. With C and C++ code, you'll sometimes have four or five arguments to a function, and knowing exactly which argument does what without consulting the documentation can be difficult.

The setFillColor: declaration starts out with the usual leading dash and the return type in parentheses:

```
- (void)
```

As with the draw method, the leading dash says, "This is the declaration for a new method." The (void) says that this method will not return anything. Let's continue with the code:

```
setFillColor:
```

The name of the method is setFillColor:. The trailing colon is part of the name. It's a clue to compilers and humans that a parameter is coming next.

```
(ShapeColor) fillColor;
```

The type of the argument is specified in parentheses, and in this case, it's one of our ShapeColor values (kRedColor, kBlueColor, and so on). The name that follows, fillColor, is the parameter name. You use this name to refer to the parameter in the body of the method. You can make your code easier to read by choosing meaningful parameter names, rather than naming them after your pets or favorite superheroes.

CALLIN' ALL COLONS

It's important to remember that the colon is a very significant part of the method's name. The method

```
- (void) scratchTheCat;
```

is distinct from

```
- (void) scratchTheCat: (CatType) critter;
```

A common mistake made by many freshly minted Objective-C programmers is to indiscriminately add a colon to the end of a method name that has no arguments. In the face of a compiler error, you might be tempted to toss in an extra colon and hope it fixes things. The rule to follow is this: If a method takes an argument, it has a colon. If it takes no arguments, it has no colons.

The declaration of `setBounds:` is exactly the same as the one for `setFillColor:`, except that the type of the argument is `ShapeRect` rather than `ShapeColor`.

The last line tells the compiler we're finished with the declaration of the `Circle` class:

```
@end // Circle
```

Even though it's not required, we advocate putting comments on all @end statements noting the class name. This makes it easy to know what you're looking at if you've scrolled to the end of a file or you're on the last page of a long printout.

That's the complete interface for the `Circle` class. Now, anyone reading the code knows that this class has a couple of instance variables and three methods. One method sets the bounds; one sets the color; and the third draws the shape.

Now that we have the interface done, it's time to write the code that makes this class actually do stuff. You didn't think we were done, did you?

The @implementation Section

The @interface section, which we just discussed, defines a class's public interface. The interface is often called the API, which is a TLA for "application programming interface" (and TLA is a TLA for "three-letter acronym"). The actual code to make objects work is found in the @ implementation section.

Here is the implementation for class `Circle` in its entirety:

```
@implementation Circle

- (void) setFillColor: (ShapeColor) c
{
 fillColor = c;
} // setFillColor

- (void) setBounds: (ShapeRect) b
{
 bounds = b;
} // setBounds
```

Now, we'll examine the code in detail, in our customary fashion. The implementation for `Circle` starts out with this line:

```
@implementation Circle
```

`@implementation` is a compiler directive that says you're about to present the code for the guts of a class. The name of the class appears after `@implementation`. There is no trailing semicolon on this line, because you don't need semicolons after Objective-C compiler directives.

After starting to declare a new class, we tell the compiler about the various pieces of data that circle objects need:

```
{
  ShapeColor fillColor;
  ShapeRect bounds;
}
```

The stuff between the curly braces is a template used to churn out new `Circle` objects. It says that when a new `Circle` object is created, it will be made up of two elements. The first, `fillColor`, of type `ShapeColor`, is the color used to draw the circle. The second, `bounds`, is the circle's bounding rectangle. Its type is `ShapeRect`. This rectangle tells where the circle will be drawn on the screen. Again, the vital concept is that the rectangle is part of the shape's data; *how* that data is used is not important here.

You specify `fillColor` and bounds in the class declaration. Then, every time a `Circle` object is created, it includes these two elements. So, every object of class `Circle` has its own `fillColor` and its own bounds. The `fillColor` and bounds values are called **instance variables** for objects of class `Circle`.

The closing brace tells the compiler we're finished specifying the instance variables for `Circle`.

The definitions of the individual methods are next. They don't have to appear in the same order as they do in the `@interface` directive. You can even define methods in an `@implementation` that don't have a corresponding declaration in the `@interface`. You can think of these as private methods, used just in the implementation of the class.

> **Note**   You might think that defining a method solely in the `@implementation` directive makes it inaccessible from outside the implementation, but that's not the case. Objective-C doesn't really have private methods. There is no way to mark a method as being private and preventing other code from calling it. This is a side effect of Objective-C's dynamic nature.

`setFillColor:` is the first method defined:

```
- (void) setFillColor: (ShapeColor) c
{
  fillColor = c;
} // setFillColor
```

The first line of the definition of setFillColor: looks a lot like the declaration in the @interface section. The main difference is that this one doesn't have a semicolon at the end. You may notice that we renamed the parameter to simply c. It's OK for the parameter names to differ between the @interface and the @implementation. In this case, if we had left the parameter name as fillColor, it would have hidden the fillColor instance variable and generated a warning from the compiler.

> **Note**   Why exactly do we have to rename fillColor? We already have an instance variable named
> fillColor defined by the class. We can refer to that variable in this method—it's in scope. So, if we
> define another variable with the same name, the compiler will cut off our access from the instance
> variable. Using the same variable name hides the original variable. We avoid this problem by using a new
> name for the parameter. We could have named the instance variable something else, like myFillColor,
> and then we could have kept fillColor as the parameter name. As you'll see later in Chapter 16, Cocoa
> can do some magic if we name our instance variable similarly to how we name our methods.

In the @interface section, we used the name fillColor in the method declaration because it tells the reader exactly what the argument is for. In the implementation, we have to distinguish between the parameter name and the instance variable name, and it's easiest to simply rename the parameter.

The body of the method is one line:

```
fillColor = c;
```

If you're extra curious, you might wonder where the instance variables are stored. When you call a method in Objective-C, a secret hidden parameter called self is passed to the receiving object that refers to the receiving object. For example, in the code [circle setFillColor: kRedColor], the method passes circle as its self parameter. Because self is passed secretly and automatically, you don't have to do it yourself. Code inside a method that refers to instance variables works like this:

```
self->fillColor = c;
```

By the way, passing hidden arguments is yet another example of indirection in action (bet you thought we were all finished talking about indirection, huh?). Because the Objective-C runtime can pass different objects as the hidden self parameter, it can change which objects get their instance variables changed.

> **Note**   The Objective-C runtime is the chunk of code that supports applications, including ours, when
> users are running them. The runtime performs important tasks like sending messages to objects and
> passing parameters. You'll learn more about the runtime in future chapters, starting with Chapter 9.

The second method, `setBounds:`, is just like our `setFillColor:` method:

```
- (void) setBounds: (ShapeRect) b
{
 bounds = b;
} // setBounds
```

This code sets a circle object's bounding rectangle to be the rectangle that's passed in.

The last method is our `draw` method. Note that there's not a colon at the end of the method's name, which tells us that it doesn't take any arguments:

```
- (void) draw
{
 NSLog (@"drawing a circle at (%d %d %d %d) in %@",
    bounds.x, bounds.y,
    bounds.width, bounds.height,
    colorName(fillColor));
} // draw
```

The `draw` method uses the hidden `self` parameter to find the values of its instance variables, just as `setFillColor:` and `setBounds:` did. This method then uses `NSLog()` to print out the text for all the world to see.

The `@interface` and `@implementation` for the other classes (`Rectangle` and `Egg`) are nearly identical to those for `Circle`.

Instantiating Objects

Now, we're ready for the final, meaty part of Shapes-Object, in which we create lovely shape objects, such as red circles and green rectangles. The big-money word for this process is **instantiation**. When you instantiate an object, memory is allocated, and then that memory is initialized to some useful default values—that is, something other than the random values you get with freshly allocated memory. When the allocation and initialization steps are done, we say that a new **instance** has been created.

> **Note**   Because an object's local variables are specific to that instance of the object, we call them instance variables, often shortened to "ivars."

To create a new object, we send the `new` message to the class we're interested in. Once the class receives and handles the `new` message, we'll have a new object instance to play with.

One of the nifty features of Objective-C is that you can treat a class just like an object and send it messages. This is handy for behavior that isn't tied to one particular object but is global to the class. The best example of this kind of message is allocating a new object. When you want a new circle, it's appropriate to ask the `Circle` class for that new object, rather than asking an existing circle.

Here is Shapes-Object's `main()` function, which creates the circle, rectangle, and egg:

```
int main (int argc, const char * argv[])
{
 id shapes[3];

 ShapeRect rect0 = { 0, 0, 10, 30 };
 shapes[0] = [Circle new];
 [shapes[0] setBounds: rect0];
 [shapes[0] setFillColor: kRedColor];

 ShapeRect rect1 = { 30, 40, 50, 60 };
 shapes[1] = [Rectangle new];
 [shapes[1] setBounds: rect1];
 [shapes[1] setFillColor: kGreenColor];

 ShapeRect rect2 = { 15, 19, 37, 29 };
 shapes[2] = [Egg new];
 [shapes[2] setBounds: rect2];
 [shapes[2] setFillColor: kBlueColor];

 drawShapes (shapes, 3);

 return (0);

} // main
```

You can see that Shapes-Object's main() is very similar to Shapes-Procedural's. There are a couple of differences, though. Instead of an array of shapes, Shapes-Object has an array of id elements (which you probably remember are pointers to any kind of object). You create individual objects by sending the new message to the class of object you want to create:

```
shapes[0] = [Circle new];
...
shapes[1] = [Rectangle new];
...
shapes[2] = [Egg new];
```

Another difference is that Shapes-Procedural initializes objects by assigning struct members directly. Shapes-Object, on the other hand, doesn't muck with the object directly. Instead, Shapes-Object uses messages to ask each object to set its bounding rectangle and fill color:

```
[shapes[0] setBounds: rect0]; [shapes[0] setFillColor: kRedColor];

[shapes[1] setBounds: rect1]; [shapes[1] setFillColor: kGreenColor];

[shapes[2] setBounds: rect2]; [shapes[2] setFillColor: kBlueColor];
```

After this initialization frenzy, the shapes are drawn using the drawShapes() function we looked at earlier, like so:

```
drawShapes (shapes, 3);
```

Extending Shapes-Object

Remember when we added triangles to the Shapes-Procedural program? Let's do the same for Shapes-Object. The task should be a lot neater this time. You can find the project for this in the *03.11 Shapes-Object-2* folder of *Learn ObjC Projects*.

We had to do a lot of stuff to teach Shapes-Procedural-2 about triangles: edit the ShapeType enum, add a drawTriangle() function, add a triangle to the list of shapes, and modify the drawShapes() function. Some of the work was pretty invasive, especially the surgery done to drawShapes(), in which we had to edit the loop that controls the drawing of all shapes, potentially introducing errors.

With Shapes-Object-2, we only have to do two things: create a new Triangle class, and then add a Triangle object to the list of objects to draw.

Here is the Triangle class, which happens to be exactly the same as the Circle class with all occurrences of "Circle" changed to "Triangle". (Of course, we're just printing text instead of doing real drawing. If we were actually drawing, the code would be more distinctive.)

```
@interface Triangle : NSObject
{
 ShapeColor fillColor;
 ShapeRect bounds;
}

- (void) setFillColor: (ShapeColor) fillColor;

- (void) setBounds: (ShapeRect) bounds;

- (void) draw;

@end // Triangle

@implementation Triangle

- (void) setFillColor: (ShapeColor) c
{
 fillColor = c;
} // setFillColor

- (void) setBounds: (ShapeRect) b
{
 bounds = b;
} // setBounds

- (void) draw
{
 NSLog (@"drawing a triangle at (%d %d %d %d) in %@",
    bounds.x, bounds.y,
    bounds.width, bounds.height,
    colorName(fillColor));
} // draw

@end // Triangle
```

> **Note**   One drawback to cut and paste programming, like our Triangle class, is that it tends to create a lot of duplicated code, like the setBounds: and setFillColor: methods. We'll introduce you to inheritance in the next chapter, which is a fine way to avoid redundant code like this.

Next, we need to edit `main()` so it will create the new triangle. First, change the size of the shapes array from 3 to 4 so it will have enough room to store the new object:

```
id shapes[4];
```

After that, add a block of code that creates a new `Triangle`, just like we create a new `Rectangle` or `Circle`:

```
ShapeRect rect3 = { 47, 32, 80, 50 };
shapes[3] = [Triangle new];
[shapes[3] setBounds: rect3];
[shapes[3] setFillColor: kRedColor];
```

And finally, update the call to `drawShapes()`with the new length of the shapes array:

```
drawShapes (shapes, 4);
```

And that's it. Our program now understands triangles:

```
drawing a circle at (0 0 10 30) in red
drawing a rectangle at (30 40 50 60) in green
drawing an egg at (15 19 37 29) in blue
drawing a triangle at (47 32 80 50) in red
```

Note that we were able to add this new functionality without touching the `drawShapes()` function or any other functions that deal with shapes. That's the power of object-oriented programming at work.

> **Note**   The code in Shapes-Object-2 provides an example of object-oriented programming guru Bertrand Meyer's Open/Closed Principle, which says that software entities should be open for extension but closed for modification. The `drawShapes()` function is open to extension: just add a new kind of shape object to the array to draw. `drawShapes()` is also closed to modification: we can extend it without modifying it. Software that adheres to the Open/Closed Principle tends to be more robust in the face of change, because you don't have to edit code that's already working correctly.

Summary

This is a big, head-space chapter—one with lots of concepts and ideas—and it's a long chapter, too. We talked about the powerful concept of indirection and showed that you've already been using indirection in your programs, such as when you deal with variables and files. Then, we discussed procedural programming and showed you some of the limitations caused by its "functions first, data second" view of the world.

We introduced object-oriented programming, which uses indirection to tightly associate data with code that operates on it. This permits a "data first, functions second" style of programming. We talked about messages, which are sent to objects. The objects handle these messages by executing methods, the chunks of code that make the object sing and dance. You also learned that every method call includes a hidden parameter named self, which is the object itself. By using this self parameter, methods find and manipulate the object's data. The implementation for the methods and a template for the object's data are defined by the object's class. You create a new object by sending the new message to the class.

Coming up in our next chapter is inheritance, a feature that lets you leverage the behavior of existing objects so you can write less code to do your work. Hey, that sounds great! We'll see you there!

Chapter 4

Inheritance

When you write an object-oriented program—and we hope you're going to write *a lot* of them—the classes and objects you create have relationships with each other. They work together to make your program do its thing.

Two aspects of OOP are most important when dealing with relationships between classes and objects. The first is **inheritance**, the subject of this chapter. When you create a new class, it's often useful to define the new class in terms of its differences from another, already existing class. Using inheritance, you can define a class that has all the capabilities of a parent class: it *inherits* those capabilities.

The other OOP technique used with related classes is **composition**, in which objects contain references to other objects. For example, a car object in a racing simulator might have four tire objects that it uses during game play. When your object keeps references to others, you can take advantage of features offered by the others: that's composition. We'll cover composition in the next chapter.

Why Use Inheritance?

Remember our old friend the Shapes-Object program from the previous chapter? It contained several classes that had very similar interfaces and implementations. And, of course, they're similar because we created them by cutting and pasting.

We'll jog your memory by presenting the interfaces for the Circle and Rectangle classes:

```
@interface Circle : NSObject
{
@private
 ShapeColor   fillColor;
 ShapeRect    bounds;
}
- (void) setFillColor:(ShapeColor)fillColor;
- (void) setBounds:(ShapeRect)bounds;
- (void) draw;
@end // Circle
```

```
@interface Rectangle : NSObject
{
@private
  ShapeColor fillColor;
  ShapeRect bounds;
}
- (void) setFillColor:(ShapeColor)fillColor;
- (void) setBounds:(ShapeRect)bounds;
- (void) draw;
@end // Rectangle
```

The interfaces for these classes are much alike—very, *very* much alike. In fact, except for the class names, they're identical twins.

The implementations of Circle and Rectangle are also very similar. Recall from the previous chapter that setFillColor: and setBounds: are identical in the two classes:

```
@implementation Circle
- (void)setFillColor:(ShapeColor)c
{
  fillColor = c;
} // setFillColor
- (void)setBounds:(ShapeRect)b
{
  bounds = b;
} // setBounds
// …
@end // Circle
@implementation Rectangle
- (void) setFillColor: (ShapeColor) c
{
fillColor = c; } // setFillColor
- (void)setBounds:(ShapeRect)b
{
  bounds = b;
} // setBounds
// …
@end // Rectangle
```

These methods do exactly the same job; they set the fillColor and bounds instance variables. However, the implementations of Circle and Rectangle are not identical. For example, the draw method's signature, that is, the method's name and parameters, is the same in both classes, but the implementations differ:

```
@implementation Circle // …
- (void) draw
{
   NSLog (@"drawing a circle at (%d %d %d %d) in %@",
   bounds.x, bounds.y,
   bounds.width, bounds.height,
   colorName(fillColor));
} // draw @end // Circle
@implementation Rectangle
```

```
// …
- (void) draw
{
    NSLog (@"drawing rect at (%d %d %d %d) in %@",
    bounds.x, bounds.y,
    bounds.width, bounds.height,
    colorName(fillColor));
} // draw @end // Rectangle
```

Shapes-Object clearly duplicates a lot of code and behavior between the Circle and Rectangle classes. Figure 4-1 is a diagram of the classes.

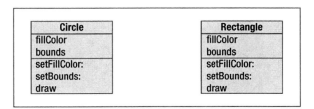

Figure 4-1. *Shapes-Object architecture without inheritance*

Note   In Figure 4-1, the name of the class is at the top of each box. The middle section gives the instance variables, and the bottom shows the methods provided by the class. This kind of diagram is defined by the Unified Modeling Language (UML), which is a common way to diagram classes, their contents, and their relationships.

There's a lot of duplication in Figure 4-1, and that just smells like inefficiency. When you're programming, duplication like this suggests bad architecture. You have twice as much code to maintain, and you have to make changes in two (or more) places when you modify code, which greatly increases your chances of introducing errors. If you forget to make a change in one of these places, weird bugs can occur.

Wouldn't it be nice if all this duplicated stuff could be consolidated in one place? And it would be nicer still if we could maintain the ability to have custom methods where we need them, such as when we have to draw circles and rectangles. We need a system that allows us to tell the compiler, "The Circle class is just like this other thing, with a couple of tweaks here and there." Well, you probably already figured out that the powerful OOP feature for exactly this is inheritance.

Figure 4-2 shows how our architecture looks after we sprinkle in some inheritance. We have created Shape, a brand new class, to hold the common instance variables and declare the methods. Class Shape holds the implementation of setFillColor: and setBounds:.

Take a look (in Figure 4-2) at our spiffy new Circle and Rectangle classes. They're a lot smaller than they were before. All the common elements got pulled up into Shape. The only things left in Circle and Rectangle are elements that make them unique, the draw method in particular. We now say that Circle and Rectangle *inherit* from Shape.

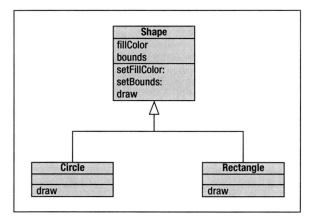

Figure 4-2. *Improved Shapes-Object architecture using inheritance*

> **Note**   A line with an arrow on the end, as shown in Figure 4-2, is the UML way to indicate inheritance. This line shows the inheritance relationship between `Circle` and `Shape` and between `Rectangle` and `Shape`.

Just as you might have inherited features like your hair color, shape of your nose, or your desire to use a Mac from your biological parents, inheritance in OOP means that a class acquires features from another class, its parent or **superclass**. `Circle` and `Rectangle`, because they inherit from `Shape`, pick up `Shape`'s two instance variables.

> **Note**   Directly changing the value of inherited instance variables is considered bad form. Be sure to use methods or properties to change them.

In addition to instance variables, inheritance also brings methods along for the ride. Every `Circle` and every `Rectangle` knows how to respond to `setFillColor:` and `setBounds:`. They inherit that ability from class `Shape`.

Inheritance Syntax

Let's take a look at the syntax we've been using to declare a new class: `@interface Circle :` `NSObject`.

The identifier following the colon is the class you're inheriting from. You can inherit from no class in Objective-C, but if you're using Cocoa, you'll want to inherit from `NSObject`, because it provides a lot of useful features (you also get those features when you inherit from a class that inherits from `NSObject`). We'll cover more of `NSObject`'s features when we talk about memory management in Chapter 9.

INHERIT THE ONE

Some languages, such as C++, include a feature called *multiple inheritance*, in which a class can inherit directly from two or more classes. Objective-C does not support multiple inheritance. If you tried to use multiple inheritance in Objective-C, which might look something like the following statement, you would make the compiler very unhappy:

```
@interface Circle : NSObject, PrintableObject
```

You can get many of the benefits of multiple inheritance by using other features of Objective-C, such as categories (see Chapter 12) and protocols (see Chapter 13).

Now that you've discovered inheritance and we're fixing up our architecture so that our classes inherit from Shape, the interfaces for Circle and Rectangle change to look like the following listing (you can find the code for this program in *04.01 Shapes-Inheritance*):

```
@interface Circle : Shape
@end // Circle

@interface Rectangle : Shape
@end // Rectangle
```

You can't get much simpler than that. When code is simple, bugs have no place to hide.

Notice that we don't declare the instance variables anymore: we get them from Shape as part of our inheritance. You'll notice we didn't include the curly braces for the missing instance variables: if you don't have any ivars, you can omit the braces. We also don't declare the methods we get from Shape (setBounds: and setFillColor:).

Now, let's look at the code that makes Shape do its thing. Here's the declaration of Shape:

```
@interface Shape : NSObject {
  ShapeColor fillColor;
  ShapeRect bounds;
}
- (void) setFillColor:(ShapeColor)fillColor;
- (void) setBounds:(ShapeRect)bounds;
- (void) draw;
@end // Shape
```

You can see that Shape ties up in one neat package all the stuff that was duplicated in different classes before.

The implementation of Shape is lovely and unsurprising:

```
@implementation Shape
- (void)setFillColor:(ShapeColor)c
{
 fillColor = c;
} // setFillColor
- (void)setBounds:(ShapeRect)b
{
  bounds = b;
} // setBounds
```

```
- (void) draw
{
} // draw
@end // Shape
```

Although the draw method doesn't do anything, we define it anyway so that all of Shape's subclasses can implement their versions. It's OK to have an empty body, or one that returns a dummy value, for a method definition.

Now, let's examine the implementation of Circle. As you probably figured out, it's a lot simpler now:

```
@implementation Circle
- (void) draw
{
    NSLog(@"drawing a circle at (%d %d %d %d) in %@", bounds.x, bounds.y, bounds.width,↩
    bounds.height, colorName(fillColor));
} // draw
@end // Circle
```

Here's the new, simplified Rectangle implementation:

```
@implementation Rectangle
- (void)draw
{
 NSLog(@"drawing rect at (%d %d %d %d) in %@",
      bounds.x, bounds.y,
      bounds.width, bounds.height,
      colorName(fillColor));
} // draw
@end // Rectangle
```

The Triangle and Egg classes are similarly skinnier. Take a look at the *04.01 Shapes-Inheritance* folder for details.

You can now run Shapes-Inheritance and see that it works exactly as it did before. Notice this fascinating fact: we didn't have to touch any of the code in main() that sets up and uses the objects. That's because we didn't change which methods the objects respond to, and we didn't modify their behavior.

Note   Moving and simplifying code this way is called **refactoring**, a subject that is quite trendy in the OOP community. When you refactor, you move code around to improve the architecture, as we did here to eliminate duplicate code, without changing the code's behavior or results. A typical development cycle involves adding some features to your code and then refactoring to take out any duplication.

You might be surprised to learn that object-oriented programs often become simpler after new features are *added*, which is exactly what happened when we added the Shapes class.

Time Out for Terminology

What would new technology be without new terms to learn? Here are the words you'll need to be fully inheritance literate:

- The **superclass** is the class you're inheriting from. The superclass of Circle is Shape. The superclass of Shape is NSObject.

- **Parent class** is another word for "superclass." For example, Shape is the parent class of Rectangle.

- The **subclass** is the class doing the inheriting. Circle is a subclass of Shape, and Shape is a subclass of NSObject.

- **Child class** is another word for "subclass." Circle is a child class of Shape. It's your choice whether to use subclass/superclass or parent class/child class. You'll come across both pairs in the real world. In this book, we use superclass and subclass, possibly because we're more nerdy than parental.

- You **override** an inherited method when you want to change its implementation. Circle has its own draw method, so we say it overrides draw. Objective-C makes sure that the appropriate class's implementation of an overridden method is called when the code runs.

How Inheritance Works

We did major surgery to Shapes-Object, taking all that code out of Circle and Rectangle and moving it into Shape. It's very cool that the rest of the program still works, without modification. Creating and initializing all the different shapes in main() didn't change, and the drawShapes() function is the same, yet the program still works:

```
drawing a circle at (0 0 10 30) in red
drawing a rect at (30 40 50 60) in green
drawing an egg at (15 19 37 29) in blue
drawing a triangle at (47 32 80 50) in red
```

Here, you can see another aspect of the power of OOP: you can make radical changes to a program, and if you're careful, things will still work when you're done. Of course, you can do that with procedural programming, but your chances of success are usually higher with OOP.

Method Dispatching

How do objects know which methods to run when they receive messages? For example, setFillColor:'s code has been moved out of the Circle and Rectangle classes, so how does the Shape code know what to do when you send setFillColor: to a Circle object? Here's the secret: When code sends a message, the Objective-C method dispatcher searches for the method in the current class. If the dispatcher doesn't find the method in the class of the object receiving the message, it looks at the object's superclasses.

Figure 4-3 shows how method dispatching works for code sending the setFillColor: message to a Circle object, using the old, pre-Shape version of our program. To handle code like [shape setFillColor:kRedColor], the Objective-C method dispatcher looks at the object receiving the message; in this case, it's an object of class Circle. The object has a pointer to its class, and the class has a pointer to its code. The dispatcher uses these pointers to find the right code to run.

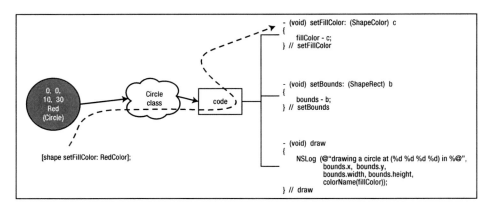

Figure 4-3. *Method dispatch without inheritance*

Check out Figure 4-4, which shows our snazzy new inheritance-enhanced structure. In this code, class Circle has a reference to its superclass, Shape. The Objective-C method dispatcher uses this information to find the right implementation of a method when a message comes in.

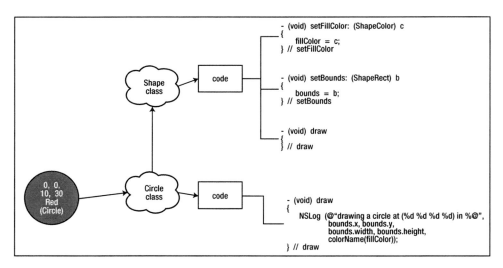

Figure 4-4. *Inheritance and class code*

Figure 4-5 shows the method dispatch process when inheritance is involved. When you send the setFillColor: message to the Circle object, the dispatcher first consults the Circle class to see if it can respond to setFillColor: with its own code. In this case, the answer is no: the dispatcher discovers that Circle has no definition for setFillColor:, so it's time to look in the superclass, Shape. The dispatcher then roots around in Shape and finds the definition of setFillColor:, and it runs that code.

This action of saying, "I can't find it here, so I'll go look in the superclass," is repeated for every class in the inheritance chain, as necessary. If a method can't be found in either the Circle or Shape class, the dispatcher checks class NSObject, because it's the next superclass in the chain. If the method doesn't exist in NSObject, the most super of the superclasses, you'll get a runtime error (and you would also have gotten a compile-time warning).

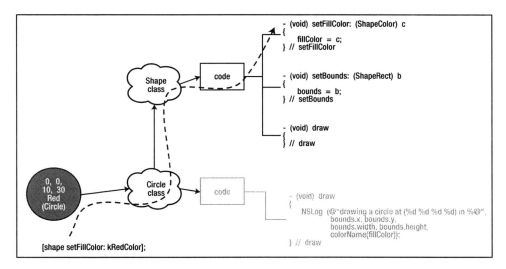

Figure 4-5. Method dispatch with inheritance

Instance Variables

We've spent time discussing how methods are called in response to messages. Now, let's look at how Objective-C accesses instance variables. How does Circle's draw method find the bounds and fillColor instance variables declared in Shape?

When you create a new class, its objects inherit the instance variables from its superclasses and then (optionally) add their own instance variables. To see how instance variable inheritance works, let's invent a new shape that adds a new instance variable. This new class, RoundedRectangle, needs a variable to hold the radius to use when drawing the corners of the rectangle. The class definition goes a little something like this:

```
@interface RoundedRectangle : Shape
{
@private
 int radius;
}
@end // RoundedRectangle
```

Figure 4-6 shows the memory layout of a rounded rectangle object. NSObject declares one instance variable, called isa, which holds the pointer to the object's class. Next come two instance variables declared by Shape: fillColor and bounds. Finally, there's radius, the instance variable that RoundedRectangle declares.

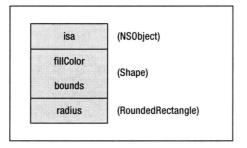

Figure 4-6. *Object instance variable layout*

> **Note**   The NSObject instance variable is called isa because inheritance sets up an "is a" relationship between the subclass and the superclass; that is, a Rectangle *is a* Shape, and a Circle *is a* Shape. Code that uses a Shape can also use a Rectangle or Circle instead.
>
> The ability to use a more specific kind of object (a Rectangle or Circle) instead of a general type (Shape) is called **polymorphism**, a Greek word meaning "many shapes," appropriately enough.

Remember that every method call gets a hidden parameter, called self, which is a pointer to the object that receives the message. Methods use the self parameter to find the instance variables they use.

Figure 4-7 shows self pointing to a rounded rectangle object. self points to the first instance variable of the first class in the chain of inheritance. For RoundedRectangle, the inheritance chain starts with NSObject, then continues with Shape, and finally ends with RoundedRectangle, so self points to isa, the first instance variable. The Objective-C compiler knows the layout of the instance variables in an object because it has seen the @interface declarations for each of these classes. With this important knowledge, the compiler can generate code to find any instance variable.

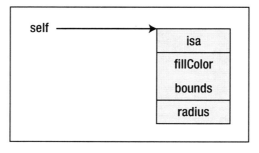

Figure 4-7. *The self parameter pointing to a circle object*

> **CAUTION FRAGILE!**
>
> The compiler works its magic by using a "base plus offset" mechanism. Given the base address of an object—that is, the memory location of the first byte of the first instance variable—the compiler can find all other instance variables by adding an offset to that address.
>
> For example, if the base address of the rounded rectangle object is 0x1000, the isa instance variable is at 0x1000 + 0, which is 0x1000. isa is a 4-byte value, so the next instance variable, fillColor, starts at an offset of four, at 0x1000 + 4, or 0x1004. Every instance variable has an offset from the object's base.
>
> When you access the fillColor instance variable in a method, the compiler generates code to take the value that self holds and add the value of the offset (4, in this case) to point to the location where the variable's value is stored.
>
> This does lead to problems over time. These offsets are now hard-coded into the program generated by the compiler. Even if Apple's engineers wanted to add another instance variable to NSObject, they couldn't, because that would change all of the instance variable offsets. This is called the **fragile base class problem**. Apple has fixed this problem with the new 64-bit Objective-C runtime introduced with Leopard, which uses indirection for determining ivar locations.

Overriding Methods

When you're making your own fresh subclasses, you often add your own methods. Sometimes, you'll add a new method that introduces a unique feature to your class. Other times, you'll replace or enhance an existing method defined by one of your new class's superclasses.

For instance, you could start with the Cocoa NSTableView class, which shows a scrolling list of stuff for users to click, and add a new behavior, such as announcing the contents of the list with a speech synthesizer. You might add a new method called speakRows that feeds the contents of the table to the speech synthesizer.

Or, instead of adding an entirely new feature, you might create a subclass that tweaks an existing behavior inherited from one of its superclasses. In Shapes-Inheritance, Shape already does most of what we want a shape to do by setting the fill color and bounds of the shape, but Shape doesn't know how to draw anything. And it can't know how to draw: Shape is a generic, abstract class, and every shape is drawn differently. So when we want to make a Circle class, we subclass Shape and write a draw method that knows how to draw a circle.

When we created Shape, we knew that all its subclasses would have to draw, even though we didn't know exactly what they would do to implement their drawing. So we gave Shape a draw method but made it empty so that every subclass could do its own thing. When classes such as Circle and Rectangle implement their own draw methods, we say that they have **overridden** the draw method.

When a draw message is sent to a circle object, the method dispatcher runs the overridden method—Circle's implementation of draw. Any implementation of draw defined by a superclass, such as Shape, is completely ignored. That's fine in this case—Shape has no code in its implementation of draw. But other times, you might *not* want to ignore the superclass's version of a method. For more on this, read on.

I Feel Super!

Objective-C provides a way to override a method and still call the superclass's implementation—useful when you want to let the superclass do its thing and perform some additional work before or after. To call the inherited method implementation, you use super as the target for a method call.

For example, let's suppose we just learned that some cultures are offended by red circles, and we want to sell our Shapes-Inheritance software in those countries. Instead of drawing red circles, as we've been doing all along, we want all the circles to be drawn in green. Because this limitation affects only circles, one way to do this is to modify Circle so that all circles are drawn green. Other shapes drawn in red aren't a problem, so we don't need to eliminate them. Why not just bash Circle's fill color methods directly? Here, we could. You don't always have this luxury, though; for example, you don't have the code for the class you want to modify.

Remember that setFillColor: is defined in class Shape. We can therefore fix the problem for circles only by overriding setFillColor: in the Circle class. We'll look at the color parameter, and if it's red, we'll change it to green. We'll then use super to tell the superclass (Shape) to store this changed color into the fillColor instance variable (the complete code listing for this program is in *04.02 Shapes-Green-Circles*).

The @interface section of Circle doesn't change, because we're not adding any new methods or instance variables. We only need to add code to the @implementation section:

```
@implementation Circle
- (void)setFillColor:(ShapeColor)c
{
 if (c == kRedColor)
 {
  c = kGreenColor;
 }
 [super setFillColor: c];
} // setFillColor
// and the rest of the Circle @implementation // is unchanged
@end // Circle
```

In this new implementation of setFillColor:, we examine the ShapeColor parameter to see if it's red. If so, we change it to green. Next, we ask the superclass to do the work of putting the color in the instance variable with the code [super setFillColor: c].

Where does super come from? It's not a parameter or an instance variable, but instead a bit of magic provided by the Objective-C compiler. When you send a message to super, you're asking Objective-C to send the message to the class's superclass. If it's not defined there, Objective-C continues looking up the inheritance chain in the usual fashion.

Figure 4-8 shows the flow of execution for Circle's setFillColor: method. The circle object is sent the setFillColor: message. The method dispatcher finds the custom version of setFillColor: that's implemented by class Circle.

After Circle's version of setFillColor: does its check for kRedColor and changes the color if needed, the superclass's method is invoked by calling [super setFillColor: c]. The super call runs Shape's version of the setFillColor: method.

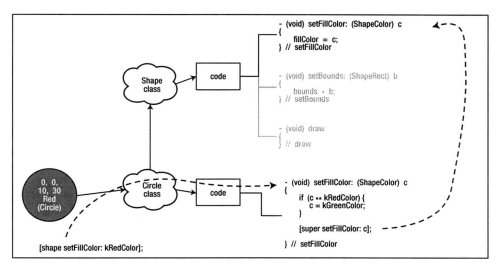

Figure 4-8. *Calling the superclass method*

Note   When you override a method, invoking the superclass method is almost always a good idea, in case it's doing more work than you're aware of. In this case, we have access to the source for Shape, so we know that all Shape does in its setFillColor: method is stick the new color into an instance variable. But if we weren't so well versed in Shape, we wouldn't know if Shape was doing something else. And even though we know what Shape does now, we might not if the class is changed or enhanced later. By calling the inherited method, we make sure we get all the features it implements.

Summary

Inheritance is a vital concept in object-oriented programming, because many advanced techniques of OOP involve it. In this chapter, you met inheritance and saw how it was used to beautify and simplify the Shapes-Object code. We discussed how new classes can be made from existing classes, and you saw how instance variables of a superclass appear in subclasses.

We went over the Objective-C method dispatch machinery and noted how it crawls up the inheritance chain looking for the method to run in response to a particular message. Finally, we introduced the super keyword and showed how you can use it to take advantage of a superclass's code in an overridden method.

You'll get to know composition in the next chapter, which is another way of having different objects collaborate to get work done. It might not be quite as geeky-cool as inheritance, but it's very important, so we'll see you there.

Chapter 5

Composition

In the previous chapter, you got hip to inheritance, a way to set up a relationship between two classes that removes the need for a lot of duplicated code. And we (briefly) mentioned that you can also set up relationships using composition, which is the subject of this chapter. You can use composition to combine objects so they can work together. In a typical program, you'll use both inheritance and composition when creating your own classes, so it's important to have a good handle on both concepts.

What Is Composition?

Composition in programming is like composition in music: you're bringing individual components together and making them work to build something bigger. In music, you might bring together a bassoon part and an oboe part in creating a symphony. In software, you might bring together a pedal object and a tire object as part of a virtual unicycle.

In Objective-C, you compose by including pointers to objects as instance variables. So, our virtual unicycle would have a pointer to a Pedal object and a pointer to a Tire object and would look something like this:

```
@interface Unicycle : NSObject
{
 Pedal *pedal;
 Tire *tire;
}
@end // Unicycle
```

Through composition, a Unicycle consists of a Pedal and a Tire.

> **Note** You've already seen a form of composition in the Shapes-Object program: the Shape class makes use of rectangles (a struct) and colors (an enum). Strictly speaking, only objects are said to be composed. More primitive types like int, float, enum, and struct are considered to just be part of the object.

Car Talk

Let's put the Shapes program aside for awhile (are those sighs of relief we hear?) and take a look at modeling an automobile. A car, in our simplified model, has an engine and four tires. Rather than wading through the physics modeling of actual tires and engines, we'll use a couple of classes that have only a method to print out which part they represent: tire objects will say that they're tires, and the engine object will say that it's an engine. In a real program, the tires would have attributes like air pressure and handling ability, and the engine would have variables like horsepower and gas mileage. The code for this program can be found in *05.01 CarParts*.

Like the Shapes program, CarParts has everything in its *mainCarParts.m*. CarParts starts out by importing the Foundation framework header:

```
#import <Foundation/Foundation.h>
```

The Tire class follows; there's not much to it except a description method:

```
@interface Tire : NSObject
@end // Tire

@implementation Tire
- (NSString *) description {
  return (@"I am a tire. I last a while.");
} // description
@end // Tire
```

> **Note**   You can leave out the curly braces in your class definitions if you don't have any instance variables.

The only method in Tire is description, and it wasn't declared in the interface. Where did it come from? How can anybody know to use description with a Tire if it's not included in the interface? It happens with the help of a little Cocoa magic.

Customizing for NSLog()

Remember that NSLog() lets you use the %@ format specifier to print objects. When NSLog() processes the %@ specifier, it asks the corresponding object in the parameter list for its description. Speaking technically, NSLog() sends the description message to the object, and the object's description method builds an NSString and returns it. NSLog() then includes that string in its output. By supplying a description method in your class, you can customize how your objects are printed by NSLog().

In your description methods, you can return a literal NSString, such as @"I am a cheese Danish object", or you can construct a string that describes all sorts of information about the object, such as the fat content and calories for the cheese Danish. The description method for Cocoa's NSArray class, which manages a collection of objects, provides information about the array itself, such as the number of objects it contains and descriptions of each object it contains. These descriptions, naturally, are acquired by sending the description message to each of the objects the array contains.

Getting back to CarParts, let's have a look at the Engine class. Like Tire, it has just a description method. In a real program, your engine would have methods such as start and accelerate and instance variables like RPMs. But we're here to see a simple example of composition at work, so we've given Engine just a description:

```
@interface Engine : NSObject
@end // Engine
@implementation Engine
- (NSString *) description
{
   return (@"I am an engine. Vrooom!");
} // description
@end // Engine
```

The last part is the car itself, which has an engine and a C array of four tires. The car uses composition to assemble itself. Car also has a method called print that uses NSLog() to print out the tires and engine:

```
@interface Car : NSObject
{
   Engine *engine;
   Tire *tires[4];
}
- (void) print;
@end // Car
```

The engine and tires instance variables are the composition, because tires and engine are instance variables of Car. You can say that Car is *composed* of four tires and an engine. Of course, people don't usually talk like that, so you can also say that Car has four tires and an engine.

Each car object allocates memory for *pointers* to the engine and tires. An entire engine and four tires aren't embedded into the car, just references to other objects floating around in memory. When a new Car is allocated, these pointers are initialized to nil (a zero value) indicating that the car does not have an engine or any tires. You can picture it just sitting up on blocks.

Let's take a look at the implementation of the Car class. First is an init method, which initializes the instance variables. The init method creates an engine and four tires to outfit the car. When you create a new object with new, two steps actually happen under the hood. First, the object is allocated, meaning that a chunk of memory is obtained that will hold your instance variables. The init method is then called automatically to get the object into a workable state.

```
@implementation Car
- (id) init
{
   if (self = [super init]) {
      engine = [Engine new];
      tires[0] = [Tire new];
      tires[1] = [Tire new];
      tires[2] = [Tire new];
      tires[3] = [Tire new];
   }
   return (self);
} // init
```

The init method for Car creates four new tires and assigns them to the tires array. init then makes a new engine and assigns it to the engine instance variable.

Next comes Car's print method:

```
- (void) print
{
  NSLog (@"%@", engine);
  NSLog (@"%@", tires[0]);
  NSLog (@"%@", tires[1]);
  NSLog (@"%@", tires[2]);
  NSLog (@"%@", tires[3]);
} // print
@end // Car
```

About That If Statement...   This line of code in the init method looks a little odd:

```
if (self = [super init]) {
```

We'll explain what's happening here. You need to call [super init] so that the superclass (NSObject, in this case) can do any one-time initialization that it needs to do. The init method returns a value (of type id, a generic object pointer) representing the object that was initialized.

Assigning the result of [super init] back to self is a standard Objective-C convention. We do this in case the superclass, as part of its initialization work, returns a different object than the one originally created. We'll explore this in depth in a later chapter when we cover init methods in more detail, so for now, please just nod and smile over this line of code, and we'll move on.

The print method uses NSLog() to print out the instance variables. Remember that %@ simply calls the description method of each object, and the results are displayed. In a real program, you would use the tires and the engine to figure out how well the car was holding the road.

The last part of *CarParts.m* is the main() function, the *driver* of this program. (Sorry about that.) main() creates a new car, tells it to do its thing by asking the car to print itself, and then exits.

```
int main (int argc, const char * argv[])
{
  Car *car;
  car = [Car new];
  [car print];
  return (0);
} // main
```

Build and run CarParts, and you should see output similar to this:

```
I am an engine. Vrooom!
I am a tire. I last a while.
I am a tire. I last a while.
I am a tire. I last a while.
I am a tire. I last a while.
```

It won't win any car awards, but it works!

Accessor Methods

Programmers are rarely satisfied with the programs they write, because software is never finished. There's always one more bug to fix, one more feature to add, or one more way to make the program bigger, stronger, or faster. So it's no surprise that CarParts isn't perfect yet. We can improve it and make its code more flexible by using accessor methods. The code for this new version can be found in the *05.02 CarParts-Accessors* folder.

An experienced programmer looking at Car's init method might say, "Why is the car creating its own tires and engine?" The program would be much better if you could customize the car to use different kinds of tires (such as snow tires for the winter months) or various types of engines (fuel injected rather than carbureted).

It would be nice if we could instruct the car to use a particular tire or engine. We could then let users mix and match car parts to create custom vehicles.

We can make this happen by adding accessor methods. An **accessor** method is one that reads or changes a specific attribute for an object. For instance, setFillColor: in Shapes-Object is an accessor method. If we added a new method to change the engine in a Car object, it would be an accessor method. This particular kind of accessor method is called a **setter** method, because it sets a value on an object. You might hear the term **mutator** used for a method that changes an object state.

You've probably already guessed that another kind of accessor method is a **getter**. A getter method provides a way for code that uses an object to access its attributes. In a racing game, the physics logic would want to access attributes of the car's tires to figure out if the car will skid on wet pavement at its current speed.

> **Note**   You should always use any provided accessor methods when manipulating another object's attributes—never reach into an object and change values directly. For example, main() should not directly access the Car's engine instance variable (using car->engine) to change its engine. Instead, your code should use a setter method to make the change.
>
> Accessor methods are yet another example of indirection at work. By accessing the car's engine indirectly via an accessor method, you're allowing for flexibility in the car's implementation.

Let's add some setter and getter methods to Car so the code that uses it has control over the kinds of tires and engine used. Here is the new interface for Car, with the new items in bold:

```
@interface Car : NSObject
{
  Engine *engine;
  Tire *tires[4];
}
- (Engine *) engine;
- (void) setEngine: (Engine *) newEngine;
- (Tire *) tireAtIndex: (int) index;
```

```
- (void) setTire: (Tire *) tire atIndex: (int) index;
- (void) print;
@end // Car
```

The set of instance variables hasn't changed, but there are two new pairs of methods: engine and setEngine: deal with the engine attributes, and tireAtIndex: and setTire:atIndex: work with the tires. Accessor methods almost always come in pairs, one to set the value and one to get it. Occasionally, having only a getter (for a read-only attribute, like the size of a file on disk) or only a setter (like setting a secret password) might make sense, but most often, you'll be writing both setters and getters.

Cocoa has conventions for naming accessor methods. When you're writing accessor methods for your own classes, you should follow these conventions so that you and other people reading your code won't get confused.

Setter methods are named after the attribute they change, preceded by the word "set." Here are examples of names of setter methods: setEngine:, setStringValue:, setFont:, setFillColor:, and setTextLineHeight:.

Getter methods are simply named after the attribute they return. The getters corresponding to the preceding setters would be named engine, stringValue, font, fillColor, and textLineHeight. Don't use the word "get" in the name of the method. For example, methods named getStringValue and getFont would violate the convention. Some languages, such as Java, have different conventions that use "get" in the name of accessor methods, but if you're writing Cocoa code, don't use it.

> **Note**   The word "get" has a special meaning in Cocoa: in a Cocoa method name, it means the method returns a value via a pointer that you pass in as a parameter. For example, NSData (a Cocoa class for objects that store an arbitrary sequence of bytes) has a method called getBytes:, which takes a parameter that is the address of a memory buffer for holding the bytes. NSBezierPath (used for drawing) has a method called getLineDash:count:phase:, which takes a pointer to a float array for the line dash pattern, a pointer to an integer for the number of elements in the dash pattern, and a pointer to a float for the place in the pattern to start drawing.
>
> If you use "get" in your accessor method names, experienced Cocoa programmers using your code will expect to provide pointers as arguments to your method and will then be confused when they discover that it's just a simple accessor. It's best not to confuse the programmers.

Setting the Engine

The first pair of accessor methods affect the engine:

```
- (Engine *) engine;
- (void) setEngine: (Engine *) newEngine;
```

Code that uses `Car` objects calls `engine` to access the engine and `setEngine:` to change it. Here is what the implementation of these methods look like:

```
- (Engine *) engine
{
  return (engine);
} // engine
- (void) setEngine: (Engine *) newEngine
{
  engine = newEngine;
} // setEngine
```

The getter method `engine` returns the current value of the `engine` instance variable. Remember that all object interaction in Objective-C happens via pointers, so the `engine` method returns a pointer to the engine object that the `Car` contains.

Similarly, the setter method `setEngine:` sets the value of the engine instance variable to the value that's pointed in. The actual engine itself is not copied, just the value of the pointer that points to the engine. Here's another way to say this: after you call `setEngine:` on a car object, only one engine exists in the world, not two engines.

> **Note**   In the interests of full disclosure, we'll state that there are a couple of problems with the `Engine` getter and setter in the areas of memory management and object ownership. Throwing memory and object life cycle management at you right now would be both confusing and frustrating, so we'll defer the discussion of the absolutely correct way to write accessor methods until Chapter 8.

To actually use these accessors, you write code like this:

```
Engine *engine = [Engine new];
[car setEngine: engine];
NSLog (@"the car's engine is %@", [car engine]);
```

Setting the Tires

The accessor methods for the tires are a little more sophisticated:

```
- (void) setTire: (Tire *) tire atIndex: (int) index;
- (Tire *) tireAtIndex: (int) index;
```

Because a car has multiple spots for tires (one on each of the four corners of the vehicle), `Car` objects contain an array of tires. Rather than exposing the `tires` array to the world, an indexed accessor is used. When setting a tire for a car, you tell the car not only which tire to use but also which position on the car to use for each tire. Likewise, when accessing a tire for a car, you ask for the tire in a particular location.

Here is the implementation of tire accessors:

```
- (void) setTire: (Tire *) tire atIndex: (int) index
  {
  if (index < 0 || index > 3) {
   NSLog (@"bad index (%d) in setTire:atIndex:",index);
   exit (1);
  }
  tires[index] = tire;
} // setTire:atIndex:
- (Tire *) tireAtIndex: (int) index
{
  if (index < 0 || index > 3) {
   NSLog (@"bad index (%d) in "tireAtIndex:", index);
   exit (1);
  }
  return (tires[index]);
} // tireAtIndex:
```

The tire accessors have some common code that checks to make sure the array index for the `tires` instance variable is a valid value. If it's outside of the range of 0 through 3, the program prints a complaint and exits. This code is what's known as **defensive programming**, and it's a good idea. Defensive programming catches errors, such as using a bad index for a tire location, early in the development cycle.

We have to check the validity of the array index because `tires` is a C-style array, and the compiler doesn't do any error checking on the index used when accessing the array. We could write `tires[-5]` or `tires[23]` without a compiler complaint. Of course, the array has only four elements, so using –5 or 23 for the index will access random memory and lead to bugs and program crashes.

After the index check, the `tires` array is manipulated to put the new tire in its proper place. Code that uses these accessors looks like this:

```
Tire *tire = [Tire new];
[car setTire: tire atIndex: 2];
NSLog (@"tire number two is %@", [car tireAtIndex: 2]);
```

Tracking Changes to Car

There are a couple of details left to clean up before we can declare CarParts-Accessors to be done.

The first detail is Car's init method. Because Car now has accessors for its engine and tires, its init method doesn't need to create any. The code that creates the car is responsible for outfitting the engine and tires. In fact, we can remove the init method entirely, since there's no need to do that work in Car any more. People who get a new car will get one without tires or an engine, but these can easily be made (sometimes, life in software is so much easier than it is out here in the real world).

Because Car no longer creates its own moving parts, main() must be updated to create them. Change your main() function to look like this:

```
int main (int argc, const char * argv[]) {
  Car *car = [Car new];
  Engine *engine = [Engine new];
  [car setEngine: engine];
  for (int i = 0; i < 4; i++) {
   Tire *tire = [Tire new];
   [car setTire: tire atIndex: i];
  }
  [car print];
  return (0);
} // main
```

main() creates a new car, as it did in its previous incarnation. Then, a new Engine is made and placed in the car. Then a for loop spins around four times. Each time through the loop, a new tire is created, and the car is told to use the new tire. Finally, the car is printed and the program exits.

From the user's point of view, the program hasn't changed at all:

```
I am an engine. Vrooom!
I am a tire. I last a while.
I am a tire. I last a while.
I am a tire. I last a while.
I am a tire. I last a while.
```

As with Shapes-Object, we've refactored the program, improving the internal structure but leaving the external behavior the same.

Extending CarParts

Now that Car has accessors, let's take advantage of them. Instead of the stock engine and tires, we'll implement variations on these parts. We'll use inheritance to make the new kinds of engines and tires and then use Car's accessors (that's composition) to give the car its new moving pieces. The code for this program can be found in the *05.03 CarParts-2* folder.

First is a new kind of engine, a Slant6 (if you prefer a V8 or a ThreeFiftyOneWindsor, go for it).

```
@interface Slant6 : Engine
@end // Slant6
@implementation Slant6
- (NSString *) description
{
   return (@"I am a slant- 6. VROOOM!");
} // description
@end // Slant6
```

A Slant6 is a kind of engine, so it makes sense for us to subclass Engine. Remember that inheritance sets up a relationship that allows us to pass subclasses (Slant6) where the superclass (Engine) is expected. Because Car takes an argument of type Engine for the setEngine: method, we can safely pass in a Slant6.

Slant6 overrides description to make it print a new message. Because Slant6 does not invoke the superclass's description method (that is, it doesn't include [super description]), it completely replaces its inherited description.

The steps for implementing a new class of tires, called AllWeatherRadial, are a lot like the ones we used for Slant6. We subclass an existing class (Tire) and provide a new description method:

```
@interface AllWeatherRadial : Tire
@end // AllWeatherRadial
@implementation AllWeatherRadial
- (NSString *) description
{
    return (@"I am a tire for rain or shine.");
} // description
@end // AllWeatherRadial
```

And finally, we tweak main() to use the new engine and tire types (the changed code is in bold):

```
int main (int argc, const char * argv[]) {
    Car *car = [Car new];
    for (int i = 0; i < 4; i++) {
     Tire *tire = [AllWeatherRadial new];
     [car setTire: tire atIndex: i];
    }
    Engine *engine = [Slant6 new];
    [car setEngine: engine];
    [car print];
    return (0);
} // main
```

We added two new classes and slightly changed two lines of code. We didn't touch Car at all. Our Car happily uses whatever kind of engine and tires you devise without having to change Car itself. The behavior of the program is now radically different:

```
I am a slant- 6. VROOOM!
I am a tire for rain or shine.
I am a tire for rain or shine.
I am a tire for rain or shine.
I am a tire for rain or shine.
```

Composition or Inheritance?

CarParts-2 uses both inheritance and composition, the two new tools in your utility belt introduced here and in the previous chapter. A good question—no, a great question—to ask is, "When do I use inheritance, and when do I use composition?"

Inheritance sets up an "is a" relationship. A triangle *is a* shape. Slant6 *is an* engine. AllWeatherRadial *is a* tire. When you can say, "X is a Y," you can use inheritance.

Composition, on the other hand, sets up a "has a" relationship. A shape *has a* fill color. A car *has an* engine, and it *has a* tire. In contrast, a car is not an engine, and a car is not a tire. When you can say, "X has a Y," you should use composition.

Programmers new to object-oriented programming often make the mistake of trying to use inheritance for everything, such as having Car inherit from Engine. Inheritance is a fun new toy, but it's not appropriate for every situation. You can create a working program with such a structure, because you can access stuff that makes an engine work from inside the Car code. But it doesn't make sense to people reading the code. A car is an engine? Huh? So, use inheritance only when it's appropriate.

Here's an example of how your thinking might go when designing your data structures: when creating new objects, take some thinking time to out when inheritance should be used and when composition should be used. For instance, in designing car stuff, you might think, "A car has tires, and an engine, and a transmission." So you'd use composition and make instance variables in your Car class for all of those.

In other circumstances, you would use inheritance. For instance, you might need the idea of a licensed vehicle, that is, one requires some kind of license before it is legal to use. An automobile, motorcycle, and tractor-trailer rig would all be licensed vehicles. An automobile *is a* licensed vehicle, and a motorcycle *is a* licensed vehicle—sounds like a good job for inheritance. So you'd probably have a LicensedVehicle class that holds things like the municipality and license number (using composition!), and Automobile, MotorCycle, and so on would inherit from LicensedVehicle.

Summary

Composition, the technique of creating objects that have references to other objects, is a fundamental concept of OOP. For instance, a car object has references to the engine object and four tire objects. During this chapter's discussion of composition, we introduced accessor methods, which provide a way for outside objects to change attributes while keeping the instance variables shielded.

Accessor methods and composition go hand in hand, because you usually write accessor methods for each object that's being composed. You also learned about two types of accessor methods: setter methods tell an object what to change an attribute to, and getter methods ask an object for the value of an attribute.

In this chapter, you also heard about Cocoa rules for naming accessor methods. In particular, we cautioned you to not use "get" in the name of accessor methods that return an attribute value.

In the next chapter, we'll take a breather from all this fabulous OOP theory so we can look at how to split classes among multiple source files, rather than keeping everything in one big file.

Chapter 6

Source File Organization

So far, every project we've talked about has had all its source code crammed into its *main.m* file. The `main()` function and all the `@interface` and `@implementation` sections for our classes are piled into the same file. That structure's fine for small programs and quick hacks, but it doesn't scale to larger projects. As your program gets bigger, you'll have a ponderous file to scroll through, making finding stuff harder.

Back in your school days (assuming you're finished with them), you didn't put every term paper into the same word processing document (assuming you had word processors). You kept each paper in its own document, with a descriptive name. Likewise, it's a good idea to split your program's source code into multiple files, and you can give each one a helpful name.

Compartmentalizing your program into smaller files gives you a chance to find important bits of code more quickly, and it helps others get a quick overview when they look at your project. Putting your code in multiple files also makes sending the source for an interesting class to a friend easier: you just pack up a couple of files rather than your entire project. In this chapter, we'll discuss strategies and ideas for keeping various bits of your program in separate files.

Split Interface and Implementation

As you've seen, the source code for Objective-C classes is divided into two parts. One part is the interface, which provides the public view of the class. The interface contains all the information necessary for someone to use the class. By showing the compiler the `@interface` section, you'll be able to use objects of that class, call class methods, compose objects into another class, and make subclasses.

The other part of a class's source is the implementation. The `@implementation` section tells the Objective-C compiler how to make the class actually work. This section contains the code that implements the methods declared in the interface.

Because of the natural split in the definition of a class into interface and implementation, a class's code is often split into two files along the same lines. One part holds the interface components: the `@interface` directive for the class, any public `struct` definitions, `enum` constants, `#defines`, `extern` global variables, and so on. Because of Objective-C's C heritage, this stuff typically goes into a header file, which has the same name as the class with a .h at the end. For example, class Engine's header file would be called *Engine.h*, and Circle's header file would be *Circle.h*.

All the implementation details, such as the @implementation directive for the class, definitions of global variables, private structs, and so on, go into a file with the same name as the class and a .m at the end (sometimes called a **dot-m file**). *Engine.m* and *Circle.m* would be the implementation files for those classes.

> **Note**   If you use *.mm* for the file extension, you're telling the compiler you've written your code in Objective-C++, which lets you use C++ and Objective-C together.

Making New Files in Xcode

When you build a new class, Xcode makes your life easier by automatically creating the .h and .m files for you. When you choose **File ➤ New ➤ New File** in Xcode, you get a window like the one shown in Figure 6-1, which presents you with a list of the kinds of files that Xcode knows how to create.

Select "Objective-C class", and click Next. You'll get another window asking you to fill in the name of the class, as shown in Figure 6-2.

You also get to choose the parent class of your new class. By default, this is NSObject. Every class must have a parent class (except NSObject itself, which is the parent to every class). You can specify the parent for your new class by selecting from the pop-up menu or just typing the name of the class if you don't see it listed in the pop-up.

When you click Next, Xcode asks where you want to save the file (see Figure 6-3). Choose the directory where you keep other files for this project.

You can see a few other interesting things in that window. For example, you can choose which group should contain the new files. We won't discuss the Targets section right now, except to say that complex projects can have multiple targets, each with its own configuration of source files and build rules.

Once you create the new class, Xcode adds the appropriate files to the project and displays the results in the project window, as shown in Figure 6-4.

Xcode creates a new group with the project name and then puts the files into folders within that group. (You can see the project's structure in the Project Navigator pane.) These folders (called *groups* by Xcode) provide a way to organize the source files in your project. For example, you can make one group for your user interface classes and another for your data-manipulation classes to make your project easier to navigate. When you set up groups, Xcode doesn't actually move any files or create any directories on your hard drive. The group relationship is just a lovely fantasy maintained by Xcode. If you want, you can set up a group so that it points to a particular place in the file system. Xcode will then put newly created files into that directory for you.

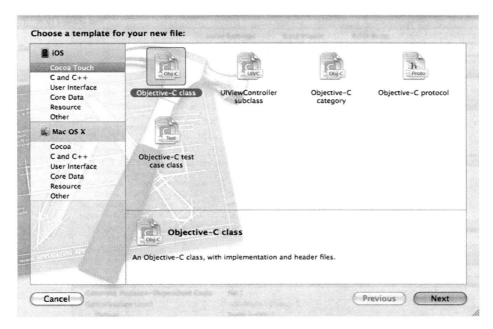

Figure 6-1. *Creating a new file in Xcode*

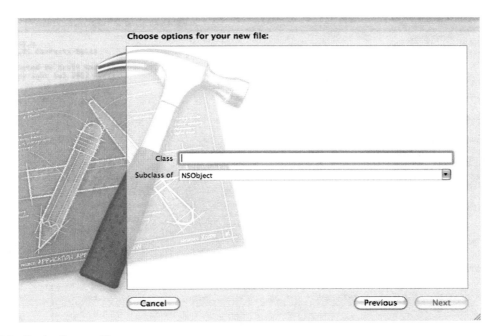

Figure 6-2. *Naming the new files*

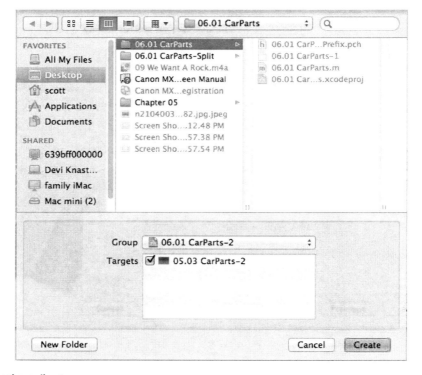

Figure 6-3. *Choosing a directory*

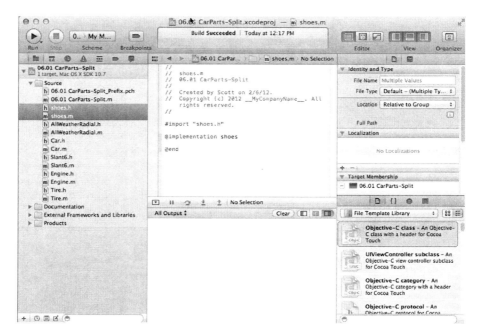

Figure 6-4. *The new files displayed in the Xcode project window*

Once you've created the files, you can click them in the list to edit them. Xcode helpfully includes some of the standard boilerplate code, stuff you'll always need to have in these files, such as #import <Cocoa/Cocoa.h>, as well as empty @interface and @implementation sections for you to fill in.

Note   So far in this book, we've had #import <Foundation/Foundation.h> in our programs because we're using only that part of Cocoa. But it's OK to use #import <Cocoa/Cocoa.h> instead. That statement brings in the Foundation framework headers for us, along with some other stuff.

Breaking Apart the Car

CarParts-Split, found in the *06.01 CarParts-Split* project folder, takes all the classes out of the *CarParts-Split.m* file and moves them into their own files. Each class lives in its own header (*.h*) and implementation (*.m*) files. Let's see what it takes to create this project ourselves. We'll start with two classes that inherit from NSObject: Tire and Engine. Choose New File, and then pick Objective-C Class, and enter the name *Tire*. Do the same with *Engine*. Figure 6-5 shows the four new files in the project list.

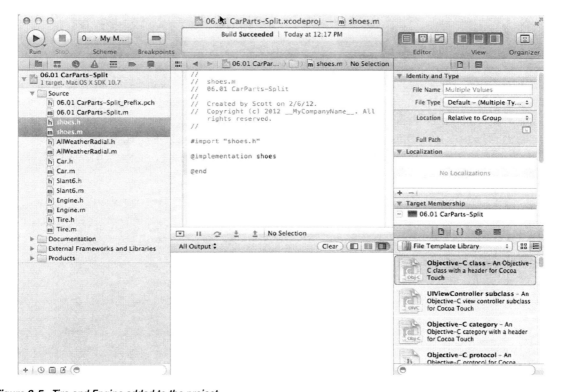

Figure 6-5. Tire and Engine added to the project

Now, cut `Tire`'s `@interface` from *CarParts-Split.m*, and paste it into *Tire.h*. The file should look like this:

```
#import <Cocoa/Cocoa.h>

@interface Tire : NSObject
@end // Tire
```

Next, we'll cut the `Tire` `@implementation` from *CarParts-Split.m* and paste it into *Tire.m*. You'll also need to add an `#import "Tire.h"` at the top. This is what *Tire.m* should look like:

```
#import "Tire.h"

@implementation Tire

- (NSString *) description
{
   return (@"I am a tire. I last a while");
} // description

@end // Tire
```

The first `#import` of the file is interesting. It's not importing the *Cocoa.h* or *Foundation.h* header files, as we've done before. Instead, it imports the header file for the class. This is standard procedure, and you'll end up doing this in virtually every project you create. The compiler needs the layout of instance variables in the class so it can generate the proper code, but it doesn't automatically know there is a header file to go along with this source file. So, we need to inform the compiler by adding the `#import "Tire.h"` statement. When compiling, if you encounter an error message like "Cannot find interface declaration for Tire," that usually means you forgot to `#import` the class's header file.

> **Import Center**   Notice that there are two different ways of doing imports: with quotation marks and with angle brackets. For example, there's `#import <Cocoa/Cocoa.h>` and `#import "Tire.h"`. The version with angle brackets is used for importing system header files. The quoted version indicates a header file that's local to the project. If you see a header file name in angle brackets, it's read only for your project, because it's owned by the system. When a header file name is in quotes, you know that you (or someone else on the project) can make changes to it.

Now do the same procedure for class `Engine`. Cut the `Engine` `@interface` out of *CarParts-Split.m*, and paste it into *Engine.h*. *Engine.h* now looks like this:

```
#import <Cocoa/Cocoa.h>

@interface Engine : NSObject

@end // Engine
```

Next, cut the `@implementation` from `Engine`, and paste it into *Engine.m*, which should now look like the following:

```
#import "Engine.h"

@implementation Engine
```

```
- (NSString *) description
{
  return (@"I am an engine. Vrooom!");
} // description

@end // Engine
```

If you try to compile the program now, *CarParts-Split.m* will report errors because of the missing declarations of Tire and Engine. Those are pretty easy to fix. Just add the following two lines to the top of *CarParts-Split*.m, just after the #import <Foundation/Foundation.h> statement:

```
#import "Tire.h" #import "Engine.h"
```

> **Note**   Remember that #import is like #include, a command that's handled by the C preprocessor. In this case, the C preprocessor is essentially just doing cut and paste, sticking the contents of *Tire.h* and *Engine.h* into *CarParts-Split.m* before continuing.

You can build and run CarParts-Split now, and you'll find its behavior unchanged from the original version, which is the one that uses AllWeatherRadials and Slant6:

```
I am a slant-6. VROOOM!
I am a tire for rain or shine
I am a tire for rain or shine
I am a tire for rain or shine
I am a tire for rain or shine
```

Using Cross-File Dependencies

A **dependency** is a relationship between two entities. Issues with dependencies pop up frequently during program design and development. Dependencies can exist between two classes: for example, Slant6 depends on Engine because of their inheritance relationship. If Engine changes, such as by adding a new instance variable, Slant6 will need to be recompiled to adapt to the change.

Dependencies can exist between two or more files. *CarParts-Split.m* is dependent on *Tire.h* and *Engine.h*. If either of those files change, *CarParts-Split.m* will need to be recompiled to pick up the changes. For instance, *Tire.h* might have a constant called kDefaultTirePressure with a value of 30 psi. The programmer who wrote *Tire.h* might decide that the default tire pressure should be changed to 40 psi in the header file. *CarParts-Split.m* now needs to be recompiled to use the new value of 40 rather than the old value of 30.

Importing a header file sets up a strong dependency relationship between the header file and the source file that does the importing. If the header file changes, all the files dependent on that header file must be recompiled. This can lead to a cascade of changes in the files that need to be recompiled. Imagine you have a hundred *.m* files, all of which include the same header file— let's call it *UserInterfaceConstants.h*. If you make a change to *UserInterfaceConstants.h*, all 100 of the *.m* files will be rebuilt, which can take a significant amount of time, even with a cluster of souped-up, zillion-core Mac Pros at your disposal.

The recompilation issue can get even worse, because dependencies are transitive: header files can be dependent on each other. For example, if *Thing1.h* imports *Thing2.h*, which in turn imports *Thing3.h*, any change to *Thing3.h* will cause files that import *Thing1.h* to be recompiled. Although compilation can take a long time, at least Xcode keeps track of all dependencies for you.

Recompiling on a Need-to-Know Basis

But there's good news: Objective-C provides a way to limit the effects of dependency-caused recompilations. Dependency issues exist because the Objective-C compiler needs certain pieces of information to be able to do its work. Sometimes, the compiler needs to know everything about a class, such as its instance variable layout and which classes it ultimately inherits from. But sometimes, the compiler needs to know only the name of the class, rather than its entire definition.

For example, when objects are composed (as you saw in the preceding chapter), the composition uses pointers to objects. This works because all Objective-C objects use dynamically allocated memory. The compiler needs to know only that a particular item is a class. It then knows that the instance variable is the size of a pointer, which is always the same for the whole program.

Objective-C introduces the @class keyword as a way to tell the compiler, "This thing is a class, and therefore I'm only going to refer to it via a pointer." This calms the compiler down: it doesn't need to know more about the class, just that it's something referred to by a pointer.

We'll use @class while moving class Car into its own file. Go ahead and make the *Car.h* and *Car.m* files with Xcode, just as you did with Tire and Engine. Copy and paste the @interface for Car into *Car.h*, which now looks like this:

```
#import <Cocoa/Cocoa.h>

@interface Car : NSObject
- (void) setEngine: (Engine *) newEngine;
- (Engine *) engine;

- (void) setTire: (Tire *) tire
      atIndex: (int) index;

- (Tire *) tireAtIndex: (int) index;

- (void) print;

@end // Car
```

If we now try using this header file, we'll get errors from the compiler stating that it doesn't understand what Tire or Engine is. The message will most likely be error: expected a type "Tire", which is compiler-speak for "I don't understand this."

We have two choices for how to fix this error. The first is to just #import *Tire.h* and *Engine.h*, which will give the compiler oodles of information about these two classes.

But there's a better way. If you look carefully at the interface for Car, you'll see that it only refers to Tire and Engine by pointer. This is a job for @class. Here is what *Car.h* looks like with the @class lines added:

```
#import <Cocoa/Cocoa.h>

@class Tire;
@class Engine;

@interface Car : NSObject

- (void) setEngine: (Engine *) newEngine;

- (Engine *) engine;

- (void) setTire: (Tire *) tire
      atIndex: (int) index;

- (Tire *) tireAtIndex: (int) index;

- (void) print;

@end // Car
```

That's enough information to tell the compiler everything it needs to know to handle the @interface for Car.

> **Note**   @class sets up a forward reference. This is a way to tell the compiler, "Trust me; you'll learn eventually what this class is, but for now, this is all you need to know."
>
> @class is also useful if you have a circular dependency. That is, class A uses class B, and class B uses class A. If you try having each class #import the other, you'll end up with compilation errors. But if you use @class B in *A.h* and @class A in *B.h*, the two classes can refer to each other happily.

Making the Car Go

That takes care of Car's header file. But *Car.m* needs more information about Tires and Engines. The compiler has to see which classes Tire and Engine inherit from, so it can do some checking to make sure the objects can respond to messages sent to them. To do this, we'll import *Tire.h* and *Engine.h* in *Car.m*. We also need to cut the @implementation for Car out of *CarParts-Split.m*. *Car.m* now looks like this:

```
#import "Car.h"
#import "Tire.h"
#import "Engine.h"

@implementation Car {
Tire *tires[4];
Engine *engine;
}

- (void) setEngine: (Engine *) newEngine
{
   engine = newEngine;
} // setEngine
```

```
- (Engine *) engine
{
    return (engine);
} // engine

- (void) setTire: (Tire *) tire
      atIndex: (int) index
{
 if (index < 0 || index > 3) {
    NSLog (@"bad index (%d) in setTire:atIndex:",
       index);
    exit (1);
}

tires[index] = tire;

} // setTire:atIndex:

- (Tire *) tireAtIndex: (int) index
{
 if (index < 0 || index > 3) {
    NSLog (@"bad index (%d) in setTire:atIndex:",
       index);
    exit (1);
}

return (tires[index]);

} // tireAtIndex:

- (void) print
{
    NSLog (@"%@", tires[0]);
    NSLog (@"%@", tires[1]);
    NSLog (@"%@", tires[2]);
    NSLog (@"%@", tires[3]);

    NSLog (@"%@", engine);
} // print

@end // Car
```

You can build and run the program again and get the same output as before. Yep, we're refactoring again (shh, don't tell anybody). We've been improving the internal structure of our program while keeping its behavior the same.

Importation and Inheritance

We need to liberate two more classes from *CarParts-Split*.m: Slant6 and AllWeatherRadial. These are a little trickier to handle because they inherit from classes we've created: Slant6 inherits from Engine, and AllWeatherRadial inherits from Tire. Because we're inheriting from these classes rather than just using pointers to the classes, we can't use the @class trick in their header files. We'll have to use #import "Engine.h" in *Slant6.h* and #import "Tire.h" in *AllWeatherRadial.h*.

So why, exactly, can't we just use @class here? Because the compiler needs to know all about a superclass before it can successfully compile the @interface for its subclass. The compiler needs the layout (types, sizes, and ordering) of the instance variables of the superclass. Recall that when you add instance variables in a subclass, they get tacked onto the end of the superclass's instance variables. The compiler then uses that information to figure out where in memory to find instance variables, starting with the hidden self pointer that comes with each method call. The compiler needs to see the entire contents of the class to correctly calculate the location of the instance variables.

Next on the operating table is Slant6. Create the *Slant6.m* and *Slant6.h* files in Xcode, and then cut Slant6's @interface out of *CarParts-Split.m*. If you've done your carving and gluing properly, *Slant6.h* should look like this now:

```
#import "Engine.h"

@interface Slant6 : Engine

@end // Slant6
```

The file only imports *Engine.h* and not <Cocoa/Cocoa.h>. Why? We know that *Engine.h* already imports <Cocoa/Cocoa.h>, so we don't have to do it ourselves here. However, it's OK if you want to put #import <Cocoa/Cocoa.h> in this file, because #import is smart enough not to include any file more than once.

Slant6.m is just a cut-and-paste version of the @implementation section from *CarParts-Split.m*, with the customary #import of the *Slant6.h* header file:

```
#import "Slant6.h"

@implementation Slant6

- (NSString *) description
{
    return (@"I am a slant-6. VROOOM!");
} // description

@end // Slant6
```

Do the same steps to move AllWeatherRadial to its own pair of files. No doubt you've got the hang of this by now. Here's a look at *AllWeatherRadial.h*:

```
#import "Tire.h"

@interface AllWeatherRadial : Tire

@end // AllWeatherRadial
```

And here's *AllWeatherRadial.m*:

```
#import "AllWeatherRadial.h"

@implementation AllWeatherRadial

- (NSString *) description
{
    return (@"I am a tire for rain or shine");
} // description

@end // AllWeatherRadial
```

Poor *CarParts-Split.m* is just a shell of its former self. It's now a bunch of #imports and one lonely function, like so:

```
#import <Foundation/Foundation.h>
#import "Tire.h"
#import "Engine.h"
#import "Car.h"
#import "Slant6.h"
#import "AllWeatherRadial.h"

int main (int argc, const char * argv[])
{
   Car *car = [Car new];

   int i;
   for (i = 0; i < 4; i++) {
    Tire *tire = [AllWeatherRadial new];

    [car setTire: tire
        atIndex: i];
}
Engine *engine = [Slant6 new];
[car setEngine: engine];

[car print];

return (0);

} // main
```

If we build and run the project now, we'll get exactly the same output as before we started spreading stuff around into various files.

Summary

In this chapter, you learned the essential skill of using multiple files to organize your source code. Typically, each class gets two files: a header file that contains the @interface for the class and a dot-m file that holds the @implementation. Users of the class then import (using #import) the header file to gain access to the class's features.

Along the way we encountered cross-file dependencies, in which a header file or source file needs information from another header file. A tangled web of imports can increase your compile times and can cause unnecessary recompilations. Judicious use of the @class directive, in which you tell the compiler "trust that you'll see a class by this name eventually," can reduce compile time by cutting down on the number of header files you have to import.

Next up is a tour of some interesting Xcode features. See you there.

Chapter 7

More About Xcode

Mac and iOS programmers spend most of their time writing code inside Xcode. Xcode is an excellent tool with a lot of wonderful features, not all of which are obvious. When you're going to be living inside a powerful tool for a long time, you'll want to learn as much about it as you can. In this chapter, we'll introduce you to some Xcode tips and tricks that are useful when you're writing and navigating your code and locating information you need. We'll also touch on some ways Xcode can help you debug your code.

Xcode is a huge application, and it is extremely customizable, sometimes ridiculously so. (Did we mention that it's huge?) Entire books can be (and have been) written about just Xcode, so we'll stick to the highlights to get you productive quickly. We recommend using the Xcode defaults when you're starting out. When something bugs you, though, you'll find there's probably a setting that can be tweaked to your liking.

When faced with a big tool like Xcode, a good strategy is to skim through the documentation until just about the point when your eyes glaze over. Use Xcode for a while, and then skim the documents again. Each time you read, more will make sense. Lather, rinse, repeat, and you'll have terrific hair.

We'll be talking about Xcode 4.3.2, the current version at the time of this writing. Apple loves adding new things and moving old things around between Xcode versions, so if you're using Xcode 42.0, the screen shots are probably out of date. Now, on to the tips!

One Window to Rule Them All

As an Xcode programmer, you live in the main Xcode window. Let's discuss the various parts of this window, just to make sure we know what we're talking about.

- *Toolbar*: This is the topmost part of the window, where most of the controls live.

- *Navigator pane*: This is the left pane. This pane usually contains lists of files in your project, but you can see other views there as well: Symbol, Search,

Issue, Debug, Breakpoints, and Logs. You can switch between views by pressing command (⌘) plus a number key (1 through 7) or clicking the icons at the top of the pane.

■ *Editor pane*: This pane, right smack in the middle, is where you'll spend most of your time as you write your amazing source code that will change the world and earn you a fortune.

■ *Inspector pane*: At the right, this area displays context-sensitive information and controls you can use to modify the attributes of selected items.

■ *Debugger pane*: This is the bottom-center pane. When the debugger is running, the stack and debugger console appear here.

■ *Library pane*: Stashed away in the lower right corner of the window, this pane is where you'll find the project assets, the objects, code snippets, and other goodies you'll use in your projects.

Now you have the basic layout. Let's jump right in and start our tour.

Figure 7-1. *The window you stare at all day if you're an OS X or iOS developer*

Changing the Company Name

One thing you might have noticed when you create a new Objective-C source file is the comment block that Xcode generates for you:

```
//
// Calculator
// CKStoreManager.m
//
// Created by Waqar Malik on 4/15/12.
// Copyright 2012 __MyCompanyName__. All rights reserved.
//
```

Xcode includes the file name and the project name, as well as the creation user and time, because this information lets you know at a glance which file you're looking at and who was responsible for its creation, as well as giving you a clue as to its general vintage. The default company name, though, is unfortunate. Last time we checked, __MyCompanyName__ wasn't hiring Mac programmers, only TPS report creators.

Figure 7-2. Changing the company name

Changing the company name is a simple process. Select the project in the navigator pane and in the editor pane. Look at the inspector pane on the right. Under Project Document, you'll see the Organization field. Type your company name there. From now on, the project will use your company name instead of __MyCompanyName__.

Using Editor Tips and Tricks

Xcode provides you with a couple of basic ways of organizing the project and source code editors. So far, we've shown the default interface, which is mostly an all-in-one window for your minute-by-minute project and coding tasks. A single editing pane is used for all source files, and the contents of the editor change based on which source file is selected in the navigator pane at the left side of the window.

Here's a little more detail about what you see in the navigator pane. The files list shows you all the moving parts of your project: your source files, the frameworks you link to, and the *Products* folder that describe how to actually build your individual programs. You'll also find some utilities, for example, to access to source code control repositories (handy if you're collaborating with other programmers); all your project symbols; and some smart folders.

When you select a file, you'll see a file path at the top of the window under the toolbar showing where the file is located in your project. You can use the search box at the bottom of the navigator pane to narrow down the list of files shown. Figure 7-3 shows a search for the word "car" in file names. You can use this filter box with any navigator view.

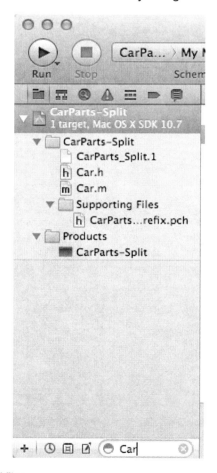

Figure 7-3. Narrowing down the list of files

The browser shows each of the matching source files with "car" in its name. You can click files in the browser to put them into the editor. Because larger projects may have over a hundred source files, the browser is a handy way to navigate around if you have lots of files. We'll talk a bit more about navigating through your source files later in this chapter.

When you're working on code, you'll want to hide the browser to maximize the use of your screen real estate. One of the toolbar icons on the far right side of the window is labeled *View*. It has three buttons; you can hover over them to see what they do (but we'll tell you here anyway). The left one hides or shows the navigator pane, or you can use ⌘0 as a shortcut. The middle button toggles the debugger area, and the right button is for the inspector.

Having each source file in its own window can be useful, especially if you're comparing two different files. Double-clicking a source file in the navigator pane opens the file in a new window. You can have the same file open in two windows, but be warned that sometimes the two windows can get out of sync (you can click each of them to sync).

You might prefer to use tabs (just like in Safari) instead of multiple windows—Xcode has you covered. It's almost as if the Xcode people know the Safari people or something. To make tabs appear, choose **View ➤ Show Tab Bar** (see Figure 7-4). To add more tabs, click the + on the right side of the tab bar.

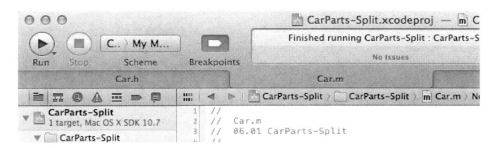

Figure 7-4. Running a tab at the bar

Writing Your Code with a Little Help from Xcode

Many programmers write code all day. Many programmers write code all night, too. For all of those programmers, Xcode has some features that make writing code easier and more fun.

Indentation (Pretty Printing)

You've probably noticed that all the code in this book is nicely indented, with bodies of `if` statements and `for` loops shifted over so they're indented farther than surrounding code. Objective-C does not require you to indent your code, but doing so is a good idea because it makes seeing the structure of your code easier at a glance. Xcode automatically indents your code as you type it.

Sometimes, heavy editing can leave the code in a messy state. Xcode can help here, too. With text selected, control-click (or right-click) to see the editor's contextual menu, and then choose **Structure ➤ Re-Indent**. Xcode will go through the selection, tidying everything up. You can use the shortcut control-I for the same feature.

Use the Structure menu, or press ⌘[and ⌘], to shift the selected code left or right. This bit of reformatting is handy if you just put an `if` statement around some code.

Let's say you have this in the editor:

```
Engine *engine = [Slant6 new];
[car setEngine: engine];
```

Later, you decide you want to create a new engine only if the user set a preference:

```
if (userWantsANewEngine) {
 Engine *engine = [Slant6 new];
 [car setEngine: engine];
}
```

You can select the two middle lines of code and press ⌘] to shift them over.

You can infinitely tweak Xcode's indentation engine. You might prefer spaces to tabs. You might like each of your opening braces to be put on a new line instead of up on the same lines with the `if` statement. Whatever you want to do, chances are you can tailor Xcode to abide by your One True Code formatting style: much of the magic is found in **Xcode ➤ Preferences ➤ Text Editing ➤ Indentation**. Here's a handy tip: if you want to quickly and easily start a heated Internet discussion among programmers, begin talking about code formatting preferences.

You Complete Me

You might have noticed that Xcode sometimes offers suggestions while you're typing code. This is Xcode's Code Sense feature, often just called **code completion**. As you're writing your program, Xcode builds an index of a whole lot of stuff, including names of variables and methods in your projects and the frameworks you include. It knows about local variable names and their types. It probably even knows if you've been naughty or nice. As you're typing, Xcode is constantly comparing what you're typing with its index of symbols. If there's a match, Xcode will offer a suggestion, as shown in Figure 7-5.

```
16
17   int main(int argc, const char * argv[])
18   {
19       Car *car = [Car new];
20       for (int i = 0; i < 4; i++)
21       {
22           Tire *tire = [AllWeatherRadial
23
24           [car setTire: tire atIndex: i];
25       }
26
```

Figure 7-5. Xcode code completion

Here, we've started typing *[All*, and Xcode thinks we might be wanting to send a message to the AllWeatherRadial class (see the gray text following *[AllW* in Figure 7-5). Xcode happened to guess correctly, so we can press tab to accept *AllWeatherRadial* as the completion.

"Aww," you say, "that's too easy! We only have one class that starts with 'All'!" That's true, but Xcode offers a completion menu (Figure 7-6) even if there are many possibilities. If you want the menu to go away, just press escape, or press escape again to bring it back.

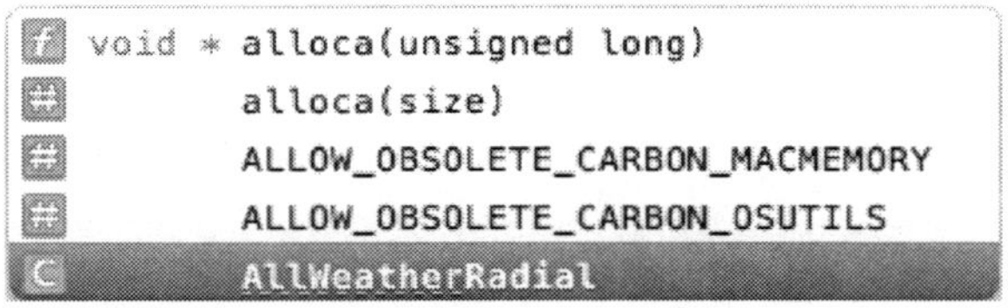

```
f   void * alloca(unsigned long)
#           alloca(size)
#           ALLOW_OBSOLETE_CARBON_MACMEMORY
#           ALLOW_OBSOLETE_CARBON_OSUTILS
C           AllWeatherRadial
```

Figure 7-6. Possible completions for "all"

You can see there are quite a few possibilities that start with "all." Xcode realizes that the current project contains one symbol that starts with "all" and assumes that's the logical first choice. The colored boxes next to the name indicate what the symbol is: E for an enumerated symbol, f for a function, # for a #define, m for a method, C for a class, and so on.

You can type control+.(period) to page through the options or shift+control+. to page backward. And don't worry if you don't catch all these keyboard shortcuts as we go along. There's a handy cheat sheet at the end of this chapter.

You can use the completion menu as a quick API reference for a class. Consider NSDictionary, which has a method that lets you specify a list of arguments representing the keys and objects used to build a dictionary. Is it +dictionaryWithKeysAndObjects, or is it +dictionaryWithObjectsAndKeys? Who can remember? One easy way to find out is to start a method call to [NSDictionary, type a space to indicate you've finished typing the class name, and press escape. Xcode will realize that you're going to be putting the name of a method there and will display all the methods that NSDictionary responds to. Sure enough, there's dictionaryWithObjectsAndKeys, shown near the bottom of the menu in Figure 7-7.

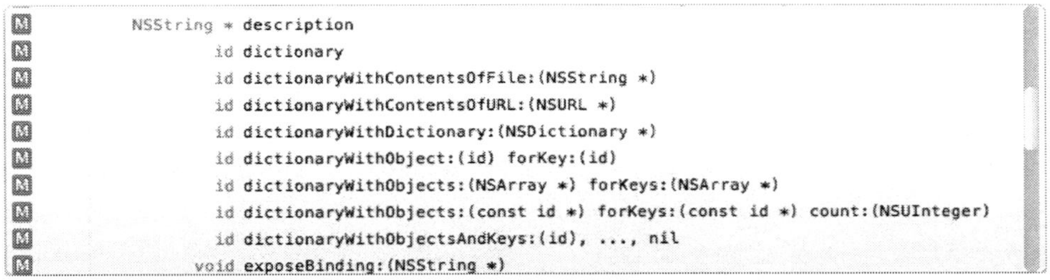

```
M       NSString * description
M              id dictionary
M              id dictionaryWithContentsOfFile:(NSString *)
M              id dictionaryWithContentsOfURL:(NSURL *)
M              id dictionaryWithDictionary:(NSDictionary *)
M              id dictionaryWithObject:(id) forKey:(id)
M              id dictionaryWithObjects:(NSArray *) forKeys:(NSArray *)
M              id dictionaryWithObjects:(const id *) forKeys:(const id *) count:(NSUInteger)
M              id dictionaryWithObjectsAndKeys:(id), ..., nil
M           void exposeBinding:(NSString *)
```

Figure 7-7. Exploring a class with Code Sense

It gets even better. If you hover over a method name, you'll see that each one has a little question mark on the right side of the window. Click any method's question mark, and you'll get a small help window for the method (see Figure 7-8).

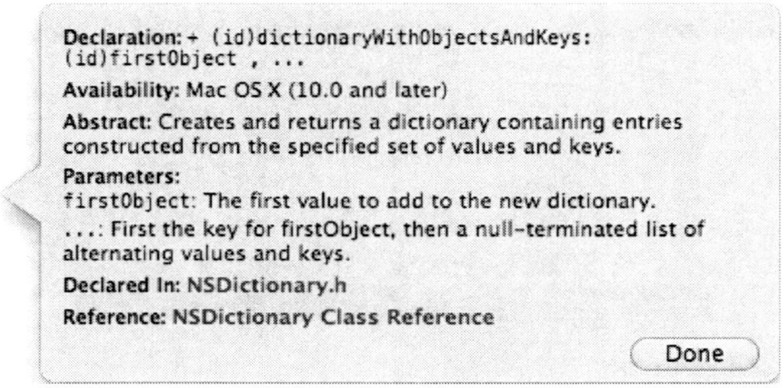

Declaration: + (id)dictionaryWithObjectsAndKeys:
(id)firstObject , ...

Availability: Mac OS X (10.0 and later)

Abstract: Creates and returns a dictionary containing entries constructed from the specified set of values and keys.

Parameters:
firstObject: The first value to add to the new dictionary.
...: First the key for firstObject, then a null-terminated list of alternating values and keys.

Declared In: NSDictionary.h

Reference: NSDictionary Class Reference

Done

Figure 7-8. In the Help window for a method, the file names are links; click one to open it in a new window

Sometimes, when you use code completion, you'll get strange little boxes in among your completion, as illustrated in Figure 7-9. What's going on there?

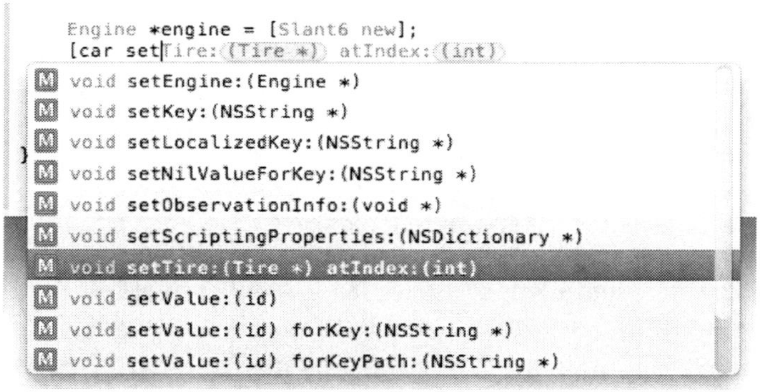

```
Engine *engine = [Slant6 new];
[car setTire:(Tire *) atIndex:(int)
 M  void setEngine:(Engine *)
 M  void setKey:(NSString *)
 M  void setLocalizedKey:(NSString *)
 M  void setNilValueForKey:(NSString *)
 M  void setObservationInfo:(void *)
 M  void setScriptingProperties:(NSDictionary *)
 M  void setTire:(Tire *) atIndex:(int)
 M  void setValue:(id)
 M  void setValue:(id) forKey:(NSString *)
 M  void setValue:(id) forKeyPath:(NSString *)
```

Figure 7-9. Code completion placeholders

Notice that Xcode is suggesting -setTire:atIndex:, which takes two parameters. Xcode's Code Sense goes further than just filling out names. The two parameters shown there are actually placeholders. If you press tab again, the method completes to setTire, as shown in Figure 7-10.

```
Engine *engine = [Slant6 new];
[car setTire:(Tire *) atIndex:(int)
```

Figure 7-10. Selecting a placeholder

The first placeholder is highlighted. Type anything to replace it with a real argument. You can click the second placeholder and replace it too. You don't even have to take your hands off the keyboard. You can move to the next placeholder by pressing tab again.

Kissing Parentheses

As you type your code, you might sometimes notice the screen flash a little when you type certain characters, such as),], or }. When this happens, Xcode is showing you the opening symbol that matches the closing symbol you just typed. In Figure 7-11, we're just now typing the right parenthesis at the end of the second line. As we do, the matching left parenthesis earlier in that line flashes briefly with a colored background.

```
Car *car = [Car new];
    for (int i = 0; i < 4; i++)|
```

Figure 7-11. Kissing the parentheses

This feature is sometimes called "kissing the parentheses" and can be really handy when you're closing up a complex set of delimiters. Make sure that every closing character you type matches with the opening character you expect. If you cross the streams, like trying to type] when should really type), Xcode will beep at you and won't show the kissy-kissy stuff.

You can also double-click one of those delimiters, and Xcode will select all the code between it and its mate.

Mass Edits

Sometimes, you have a code change that you want to make in a couple of places, but you don't want to edit every instance individually. Making a lot of similar edits manually is fraught with peril, since humans aren't typically very good at boring repetitive work. Luckily for us, computers thrive on boring and repetitive work.

The first Xcode feature to help us here doesn't actually manipulate code but installs a safety net. Choose **File ➤ Create Snapshot** . . . (or its handy shortcut, ⌘+control+S), and Xcode will remember the state of your project. You're now free to edit source files and fold, spindle, and mutilate your stuff all you want. If you later realize you've made a terrible mistake, you can use the snapshots window, which you can access from **File ➤ Restore Snapshot** . . ., to recover from a previous snapshot. It's a good idea to take a snapshot before doing anything too adventurous.

> **Note**　The snapshots are stored in *~/Library/Developer/Xcode/Snapshots/* .

Of course, Xcode has search-and-replace functionality. The **Edit ➤ Find** submenu contains several handy choices. Select **Find in Workspace** (command+shift+F), or select the search option in the navigator pane. This feature lets you search and replace across the files in your project. Figure 7-12 shows the projectwide search and replace window.

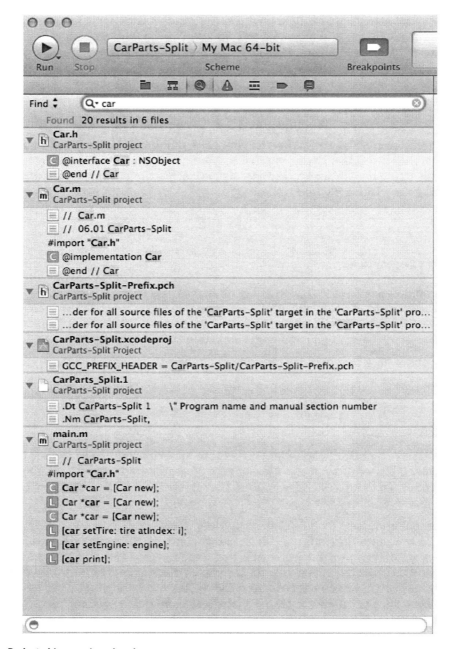

Figure 7-12. Projectwide search and replace

Let's say we're thinking of changing "car" to "automobile." After filling in the blanks and clicking *Find*, you can see that there are references to the Car class and car local variable. You can click *Replace All* to make the change globally.

Search and replace functionality is a blunt instrument for doing this kind of surgery, however. It does too much if you're just trying to rename a variable in a function (because it might clobber stuff in the whole file), and it doesn't do enough if you're trying to rename a class. Specifically, it doesn't rename the source file.

Xcode has two features to fill those gaps. The first has the svelte moniker of "Edit all in Scope." You can choose a symbol, like a local variable or a parameter, and click it to make a drop-down menu arrow appear next to it. Click the arrow to see the menu, and select "Edit all in Scope." Then, as you type, all the occurrences of that symbol are instantly updated. Not only is this a fast way to make a lot of changes, it looks really cool while you're doing it.

Figure 7-13 shows "car" being edited in scope. Notice that each car local variable has box around it. Once you start typing *automobile*, all the boxes change, like in Figure 7-14.

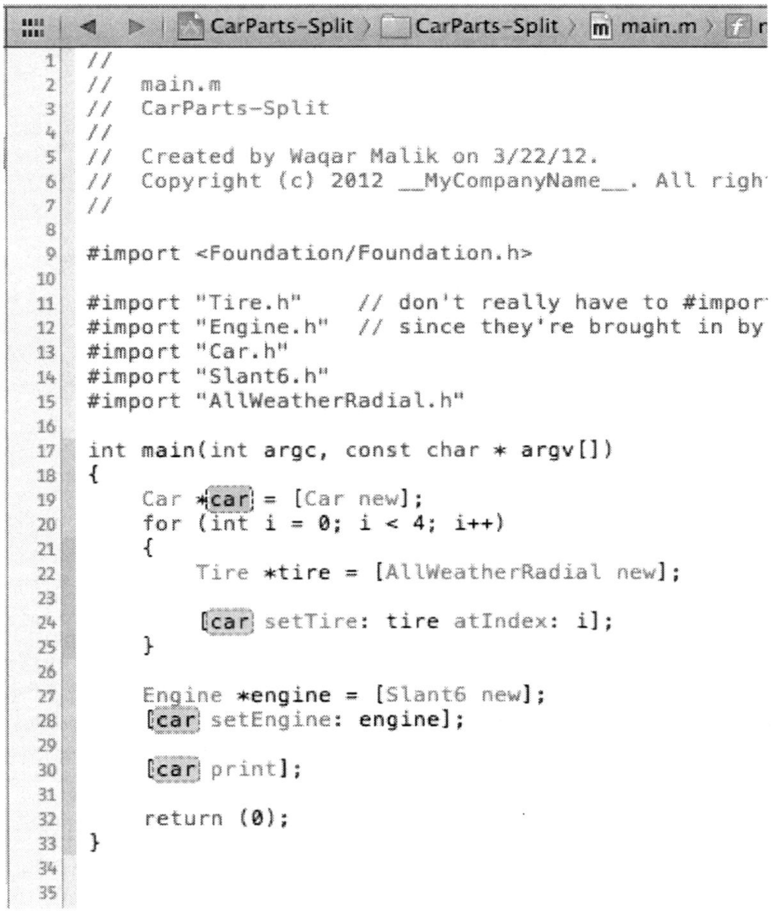

Figure 7-13. Starting to edit all in scope by changing the car to an automobile

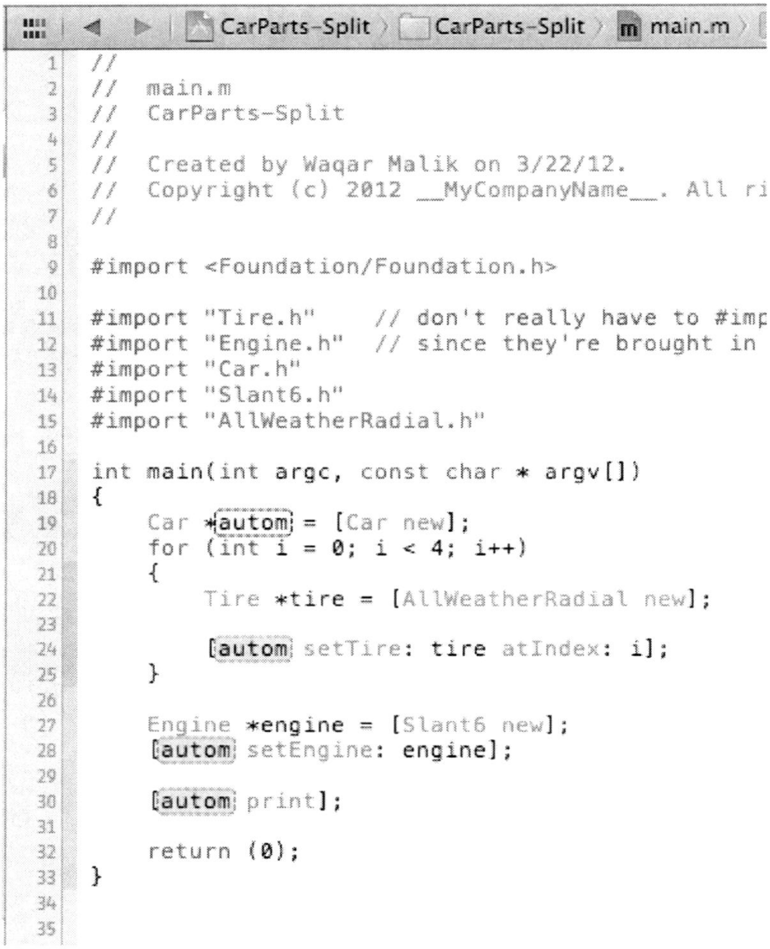

```
        CarParts-Split  >   CarParts-Split  >  m  main.m  >

 1   //
 2   //   main.m
 3   //   CarParts-Split
 4   //
 5   //   Created by Waqar Malik on 3/22/12.
 6   //   Copyright (c) 2012 __MyCompanyName__. All ri
 7   //
 8
 9   #import <Foundation/Foundation.h>
10
11   #import "Tire.h"      // don't really have to #imp
12   #import "Engine.h"    // since they're brought in
13   #import "Car.h"
14   #import "Slant6.h"
15   #import "AllWeatherRadial.h"
16
17   int main(int argc, const char * argv[])
18   {
19       Car *autom = [Car new];
20       for (int i = 0; i < 4; i++)
21       {
22           Tire *tire = [AllWeatherRadial new];
23
24           [autom setTire: tire atIndex: i];
25       }
26
27       Engine *engine = [Slant6 new];
28       [autom setEngine: engine];
29
30       [autom print];
31
32       return (0);
33   }
34
35
```

Figure 7-14. Editing all in scope

When you're finished, just click elsewhere in the source editing window, and you'll get out of "Edit all in Scope" mode.

Sometimes, you'll go to make a change like this and find the "Edit all in Scope" menu item disabled. This feature is tied closely to the syntax coloring in Xcode, so if you have that feature turned off or have fiddled with it a lot, "Edit all in Scope" may refuse to work. To fix it, go back to the preferences and mess around with syntax coloring again until it works–there's a bit of voodoo involved.

Recall our use of the term "refactoring" in previous chapters? We didn't just make up this word to sound really smart. Xcode has some refactoring tools built in. One of the refactoring helpers lets you easily rename a class. Not only does it rename the class but it does fancy things like renaming the source files to match. And if you have a GUI program, it even digs into the nib files and changes things there. (Don't worry if that last sentence is total gibberish to you right now. It's a really cool feature, and we'll explain more about nib files in later chapters.)

Let's try changing all of our Car classes to Automobile ones. Open *Car.h* in the editor, and put your insertion point in the word Car. Choose **Edit ➤ Refactor ➤ Rename . . . .** You'll see a dialog like the one shown in Figure 7-15, where we've entered *Automobile* as the replacement for "Car."

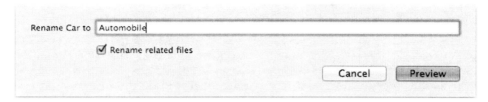

Figure 7-15. *Starting to refactor*

Xcode figures out what it will do after you click Preview and presents it to you as shown in Figure 7-16.

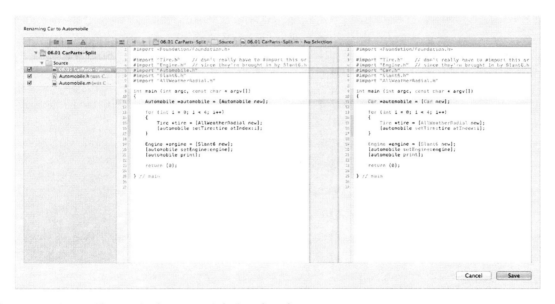

Figure 7-16. *Xcode telling us what it wants to do in the refactoring.*

You can see that Xcode will rename *Car.h* and *Car.m* to the corresponding Automobile-style names. You can click a source file to see what changes Xcode will make in the file merge viewer at the bottom of the window. Looking there, you'll see that Xcode has changed "Car" to "Automobile" in the #import, as well as the class name in the proper places.

After you review the changes, click Save. If this is the first time you have refactored code in this project, Xcode asks if you want to enable automatic snapshots. Saying yes is a good idea, because then if you make a big change and decide it's less than awesome, falling back to your pre-refactoring version is easy.

Sadly, refactoring does not rename things in comments, so end-of-class comments, file header comments generated by Xcode, or any documentation comments you may have written will need to be fixed manually. You can search and replace to make this a bit easier.

Navigating Around in Your Code

Most source files have a familiar life cycle. They're created new and get a lot of code added to them quickly to make them do their magic. Next, they go into a mode where additions and modifications are about fifty-fifty and then into a maintenance mode, in which you have to read a lot of the file before you add new code or make changes. Finally, after a class has matured, you end up browsing its code to figure out how the class works before using it elsewhere in your program. This section explores various ways of navigating around your code as it lives its life.

emacs is Not a Mac

An ancient text editor called emacs, invented in the 1970s, is available on modern Macs. Some throwbacks (including Waqar Malik) use it on a daily basis. We won't talk about emacs much here, except to describe some of its key bindings—and we'll even tell you what that means.

The phrase "emacs key bindings" describes keystrokes that let you move the text cursor without taking your hand off the main part of the keyboard. Just as many folks prefer arrow keys over reaching for the mouse, emacs users prefer to use these cursor movement keys instead of reaching for the arrow keys. And here's the punch line: amazingly enough, these same movement keys work in any Cocoa text field, including not just Xcode but also TextEdit, Safari's URL bar and text fields, Pages and Keynote text areas, and many more. Here they are:

- *control-F*: Move **f**orward, to the right (same as the right arrow).

- *control-B*: Move **b**ackward, to the left (same as the left arrow).

- *control-P*: Move to the **p**revious line (same as the up arrow).

- *control-N*: Move to the **n**ext line (same as the down arrow).

- *control-A*: Move to the beginning of a line (same as the as command-left arrow).

- *control-E*: Move to the **e**nd of a line (same as the as command-right arrow).

- *control-T*: **T**ranspose (swap) the characters on either side of the cursor.

- *control-D*: **D**elete the character to the right of the cursor.

- *control-K*: **K**ill (delete) the rest of the line. This is handy if you want to redo the end of a line of code.

- *control-L*: Center the insertion point in the window. This is great if you've lost your text cursor or want to quickly scroll the window so the insertion point is front and center.

If you get these keystrokes into your head and under your fingers, you can make small cursor movements and editing operations much faster—and not just in Xcode.

Open Sesame Seed!

You're looking at one of your source files, and you see `#import` at the top. Wouldn't it be great if you could open that header file quickly without having to do a lot of mousing around? You can! Just select the file name (you can even leave off the *.h*), and choose **File ➤ Open Quickly**. Xcode opens the header file for you.

If you don't have any text selected, choosing **Open Quickly** opens a dialog box, which is another way of finding a file to look at. You can also perform the **Open Quickly** command by typing the shortcut ⌘⇧O. The Open Quickly dialog is a very simple window containing just a search field and a table, but it is a very quick way to do searches across the contents of your project. Type *tire* in the search box to look for things tire-related, as shown in Figure 7-17. You can also put in other terms, like *NSArray* to see the NSArray header files.

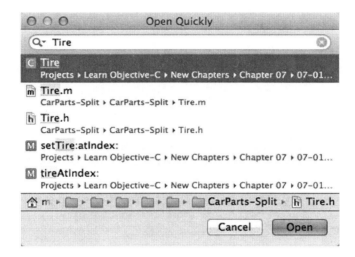

Figure 7-17. The Open Quickly dialog

If you're lucky enough to have a large monitor, you can see windows side by side using the assistant editor (**View ➤ Assistant Editor ➤ Show Assistant Editor**). By default, you'll see the header file in one pane and the implementation in the other, but you can change that if you like. Click *Counterparts* in the toolbar to see your many options.

Focus Your Energy

You may have noticed the columns immediately to the left of your source code. The wider column to the left is known as the **gutter**, and we'll have our minds there later when we discuss debugging. The narrower one is known as the **focus ribbon**, and as its name implies, it allows you to focus your attention on different parts of your code.

Notice the shades of gray in the focus ribbon: the more deeply nested a bit of code is, the darker the gray next to it in the ribbon. This color-coding gives you a hint of the complexity of your code at a glance. You can hover over different gray regions of the focus bar to highlight the corresponding hunk of code, as shown in Figure 7-18.

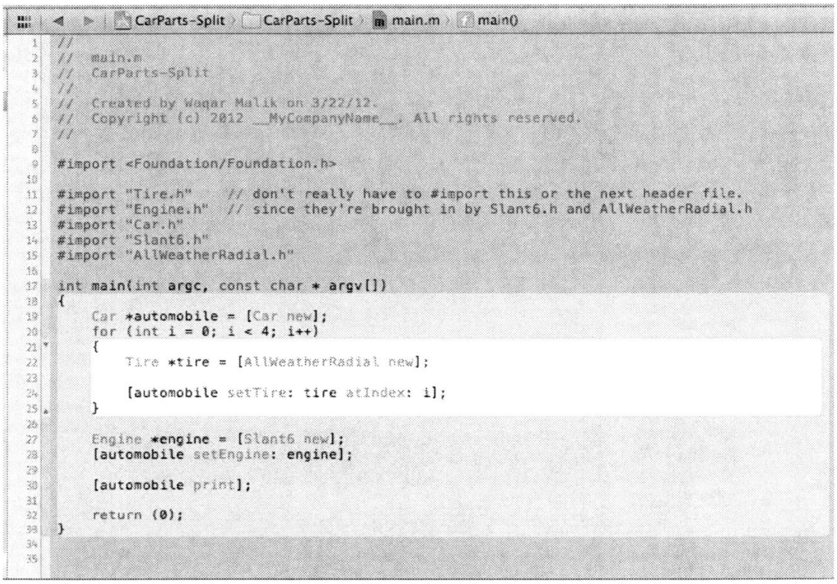

Figure 7-18. Highlighting code with the focus ribbon

You can click in the focus ribbon to collapse chunks of code. Say you're convinced that the if statement and the for loop shown in Figure 7-18 are correct and you don't want to look at them anymore, so you can concentrate (focus your attention, as it were) on the rest of the code in the function. Click to the left of the if statement, and its body will collapse as shown in Figure 7-19.

You can see now that the body of the if statement has been replaced by a box with an ellipsis in it. Double-click the box to expand the code back the way it was, or click the disclosure triangle in the focus ribbon. The code isn't gone; it's just hidden, so your file should compile and work fine even like this. **Code folding** is another name for this kind of feature. Check out the **Editor ➤ Code Folding** menu for a lot of additional options.

The Navigation Bar Is Open

At the top of the code editor is a little ribbon of controls, shown in Figure 7-20, known as the **navigation bar**. Many of its controls are there to let you quickly bounce around your source files in the project.

At the far left, you have a menu button, which provides quick access to recent history for the editor and some other advanced goodies. Next are backward and forward buttons that let you cycle through the history of files you've had open during this editing session. They work like Safari's back and forward arrows. Next to those buttons is a path that shows the current file (*Car.m*) and its position in the project, rather than its directory path. Each entry in the path is a button; click one, and you get a pop-up menu for navigation.

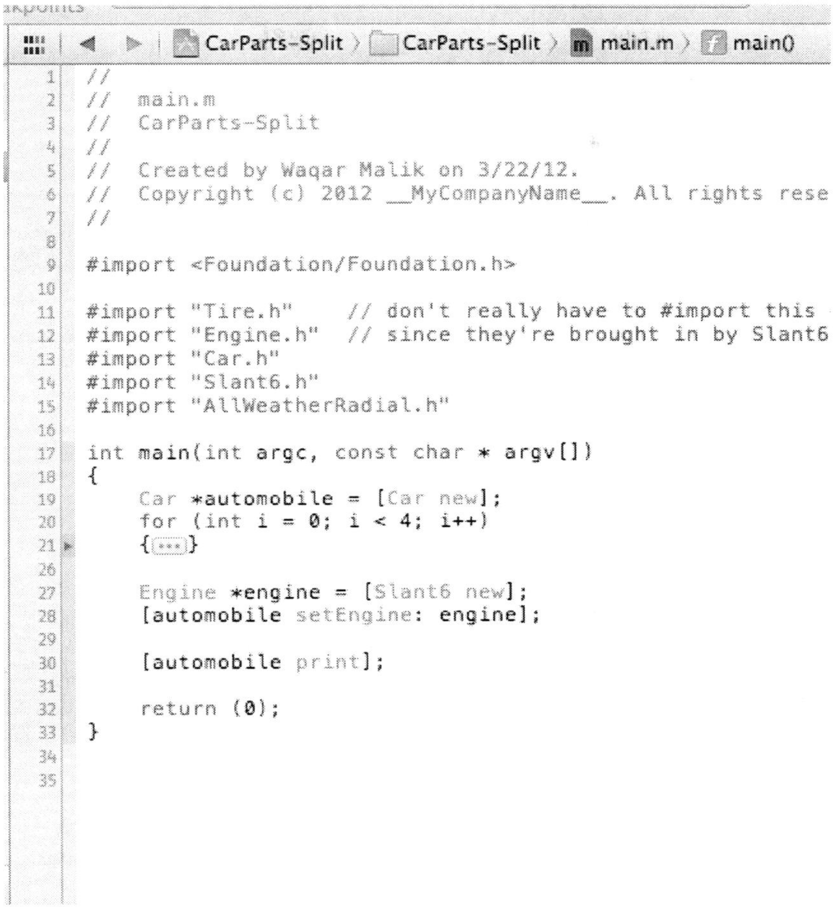

Figure 7-19. *Folding code. You thought we were going to put a Dune reference here, didn't you?*

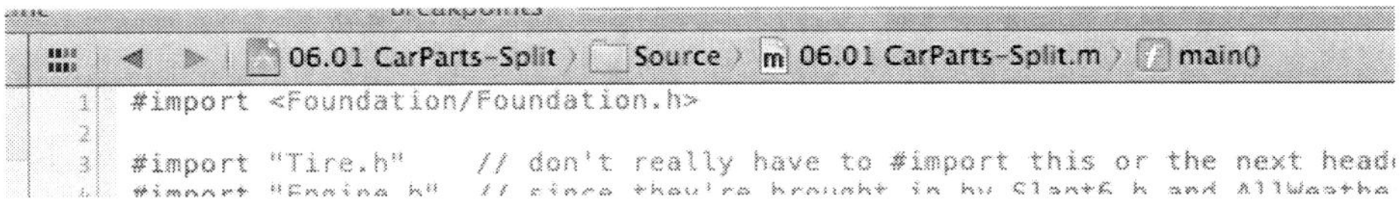

Figure 7-20. *The navigation bar*

The last item in the navigation bar is the function menu. It shows that the insertion point is currently in the method -setTire:atIndex:. Click the menu to see all the interesting symbols, as shown in Figure 7-21.

-setTire:atIndex: is highlighted, because that's where the insertion point is. You can see the other methods above and below it, sorted by their order of appearance in the file. You can ⌘-click the function menu to see it sorted alphabetically.

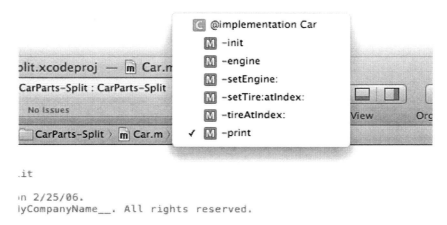

Figure 7-21. Symbols in the file

In addition to method names, you can add your own items to this menu. There are a couple of different ways to add items One way is to use #pragma mark whatever to put the string *whatever* into the menu. This is handy for adding human-readable anchors for you and other biological life forms to see and use. #pragma mark - (minus sign) puts a separator line into the menu. Xcode also looks in comments that begin with the specific strings MARK:, TODO:, FIXME:, !!!:, and ???:. Xcode adds this text to the function menu too. These are all programmer signals for "better come back and look at this before you inflict this program on an unsuspecting public."

> **Note** "Pragma" comes from a Greek word meaning "action." #pragma is a way to pass on information or instructions to compilers and code editors that are outside of the usual lines of Objective-C code. Pragmas are usually ignored, but they may have meaning to tools used in software development. If a tool does not understand a pragma, the tool should nod, smile, and ignore it, without generating a warning or an error.

Getting Information

Bouncing around your code and the Cocoa header files is all fine and dandy, but sometimes, you need to get some information from outside your own code. Luckily, Xcode comes with a treasure trove of documentation and reference material (explaining what a trove is beyond the scope of this book).

A Little Help, Please

The inspector has two icons at the top. So far in our explorations, the first one has been selected, and the inspector has been showing attributes about the current file. The other icon enables Quick Help in the inspector. To use Quick Help, click something in your code and see what appears in the inspector. If you click somewhere else in the source, the quick help panel updates itself.

For instance, say you have your insertion point inside of the word *NSString*. Quick Help will look like Figure 7-22.

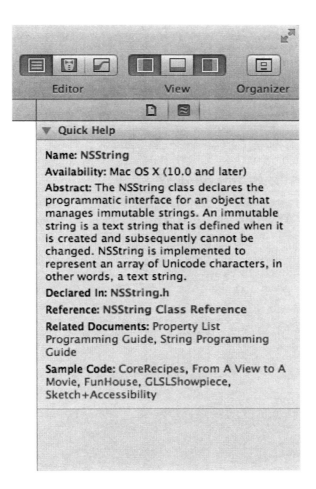

Figure 7-22. Quick Help

There's a huge amount of information available. The first two items bring up the `NSString` class reference documentation in the documentation window. The *NSString.h* item brings up the header file in the editor.

The Abstract section describes the class. If you had your cursor in the middle of a method call, this section would describe the method, along with related calls. There are pointers to higher level documentation and some code samples that use `NSString` a lot. Words in blue are links you can click to get more information. You can also get more from Quick Help by option-clicking the symbol. If you do, you'll see something like Figure 7-23. For still more, click the book icon in the upper-right corner to open the documentation for that symbol.

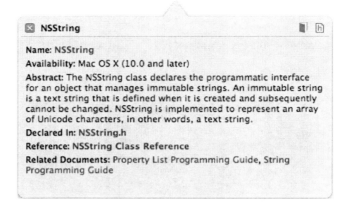

Figure 7-23. We clicked NSString and got more info about it, as promised

Is There a Documentor in the House?

If you want to go directly to Apple's official documentation for an API, a very fast way to do that is to option–double-click a symbol. This is simply a shortcut for doing a documentation search for that symbol.

Say you had a line of code like [someString UTF8String], which converts someString (an NSString) into a C-style string expressed in Unicode. If you option–double-click UTF8String, the documentation browser opens and searches for UTF8String, as shown in Figure 7-24.

Figure 7-24. The Xcode documentation window

That window is mighty busy, and it packs in a lot of information. In the upper-left corner is a search box, which comes prepopulated with UTF8String. The ribbon of buttons underneath the toolbar lets you refine which documentation sets are searched. You can look at all documentation, or just OS X or iOS documentation.

Below the button ribbon is a pane (on the left) that contains documentation sets and a set of bookmarks. You can add bookmarks to specific chunks of documentation by using the pop-up menu. Documentation bookmarks are global to Xcode and are not limited to a specific project.

On the left pane of the window at the top is a browser showing all the search matches. In Figure 7-24, it shows three methods and a constant. The most interesting is the last one, UTF8, which is the call we're actually making here. You will also notice that there are multiple version of the same item listed. This is because you might have multiple sets of documents installed: iOS, OS X, or other. Pick the documents for the platform you're interested in. Keep in mind that some methods may not be available on all platforms.

Below that is a browser that shows the documents. It's kind of a small area for reading documentation, but it's easy to open the documentation into another Xcode window or even into a web browser.

Debugging

Bugs happen. It's a fact of life that errors creep into your programs, especially when you're just starting out with a new language and a new platform. When faced with problems, take a deep breath, take a sip of you favorite beverage, and systematically try to figure out what's gone wrong. This process of figuring out program errors is called **debugging**.

Crush Puny Bugs

The easiest kind of debugging is brute force, sometimes called **caveman debugging**, in which you put in print statements (like NSLog) to show the flow of control of your program, along with some data values. You've probably been doing this all along without knowing its name. You may run into some folks who look down on caveman debugging, but it can be an effective tool, especially if you're just learning a new system. So ignore those naysayers.

Xcode's Debugger

In addition to everything else, Xcode includes a debugger. A **debugger** is a program that sits between your program and the operating system and can interrupt your program, making it stop in its tracks and allowing you to poke around the program's data and even change things. When you finish looking around, you can resume execution to see what happens. You can also single-step through code, slowing the computer down to human speed to see precisely what effect the code is having on your data.

Xcode also has a debugger pane that provides a lot of information at a glance and a debugging console where you can type commands directly to the debugger.

Note   Xcode gives you a choice of two debuggers: GDB and LLDB. GDB, part of the GNU project, is available on a zillion different platforms and has been around for many years. LLDB is the hot new contender, part of the LLVM project that is the source of many other Xcode tools. For now the differences between the debuggers is subtle and mainly internal.

We'll discuss debugging inside the Xcode text editor. You should definitely play around with the other debugging modes if you want to learn more.

Subtle Symbolism

When you're planning on debugging a program, you need to make sure you're using a Debug build configuration. You can check this in the **Edit Scheme** pop-up menu item in the Xcode toolbar. The Build configuration tells the compiler to emit extra debugging symbols, which the debugger uses to figure out what's where in your program.

Let's Debug!

Getting started with the debugger is a bit easier with a GUI program than with the command-line programs we've been using so far. A GUI program is accustomed to sitting around waiting for the user to do something, so using it gives us lots of time to find the debugger buttons, interrupt the program, and start poking around it. Our command-line programs, on the other hand, come and go so fast you can't do much debugging on them. So let's start by setting a breakpoint in main. We'll be using *07.01 CarParts-split*, which is simply a copy of the same project from the previous chapter.

Open *CarParts-Split*.m, and click in the gutter, which, as you saw earlier, is the wide bar to the left of the focus ribbon. You should get a blue arrow thingy (yes, that's a technical term) indicating your new breakpoint, as shown in Figure 7-25. You can delete a breakpoint by dragging it out of the gutter, and you can disable it by clicking it.

Now, select Run to run your program. Your program should stop at the breakpoint, as shown in Figure 7-26. Notice the green arrow pointing at a line of code. This is like the "you are here" sign on the map at the mall.

Once your program has stopped, you'll see you've grown a new control strip above the navigation bar, shown in Figure 7-27.

Yay, more buttons. What do they do? Starting from the left, the first button opens and closes the debug pane.

The next four buttons control what your program does next. The first looks like the play button from a CD player (if you don't know what a CD player is, ask your parents). This is the continue button. After you click it, the program runs until it hits a breakpoint, finishes, or crashes.

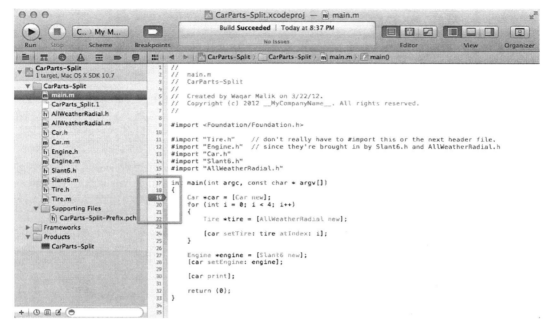

Figure 7-25. Setting a breakpoint

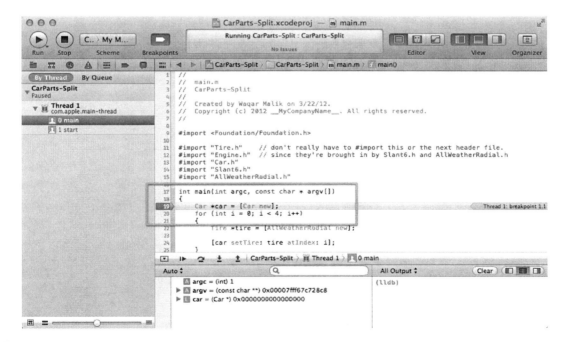

Figure 7-26. You are here

***Figure 7-27.** Debugger controls*

The next control, which looks like a dot with someone jumping over it, is the step over button. This one executes one line of code and then returns control back to you. If you click the step over button three times, the "you are here" arrow will move to the -setTire:atIndex call, as shown in Figure 7-28.

The next button, the arrow pointing down into a dot, is the step into button. If you have the source code for the function or method you're currently sitting on, Xcode will step into that function, bring up its code, and set the "you are here" arrow at the beginning of it, as shown in Figure 7-29.

```
16
17    int main(int argc, const char * argv[])
18    {
19        Car *car = [Car new];
20        for (int i = 0; i < 4; i++)
21        {
22            Tire *tire = [AllWeatherRadial new];
23
24            [car setTire: tire atIndex: i];
25        }
26
27        Engine *engine = [Slant6 new];
28        [car setEngine: engine];
29
30        [car print];
31
32        return (0);
33    }
34
```

***Figure 7-28.** After single stepping three times*

```
40
41    - (void) setEngine: (Engine *) newEngine
42    {
43        engine = newEngine;
44    } // setEngine
45
46
47    - (void) setTire: (Tire *) tire
48              atIndex: (int) index
49    {
50        if (index < 0 || index > 3) {
51            NSLog (@"bad index (%d) in setTire:atIndex:",
52                    index);
53            exit (1);
54        }
55
56        tires[index] = tire;
57
58    } // setTire:atIndex:
59
```

***Figure 7-29.** After stepping into a method (in this case, setTire)*

The last button is step out, which lets the current function finish and then returns control to you on the next line of the calling function. If you're following along, don't use this one just yet. We'll be looking at some data values in this method in a little bit.

The last control is a pop-up that lets you select which thread you want to look at. You won't need to bother with threaded programming for a while, so you can ignore the thread selection for now.

To the right of the buttons, we see the **call stack**, which is the current set of active functions. If A calls B, and B calls C, C is considered to be at the top of the stack, with B and A below it. If you click to open the call stack menu now, it has -[Car setTire:atIndex:], followed by main. That means that main called -setTire:atIndex:. With more complex programs, this call stack, also called a **stack trace**, can have dozens of entries in it. Sometimes, the best question answered during a debugging session is, "How the heck did *this* code get called?" By looking at the call stack, you can see who called whom to get to the current state (of confusion).

Taking a Look-See

Now that you're stopped, what should you do next? Usually, when you set a breakpoint or single-step to a particular part of your program, you're interested in the **program state**—the values of variables.

Xcode has **datatips**, similar to the tooltips that tell you what a button does when you hover over it. In the Xcode editor, you can hover over a variable, or a method argument, and Xcode pops open a little window that shows the value, as shown in Figure 7-30.

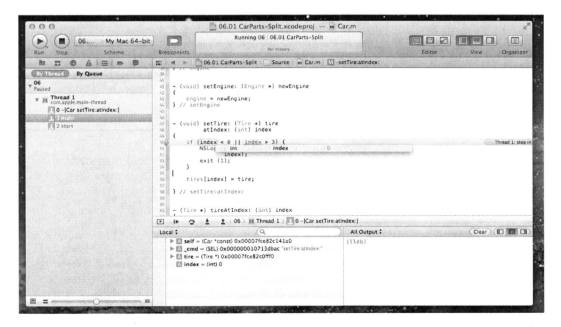

Figure 7-30. Xcode datatip

Figure 7-30 shows us hovering over index. The datatip pops up and shows us the value is zero, as we expect. Now this is really cool: we can change the value by clicking the zero and typing in a new value. For example, you can type *37*, and then use a couple of step over commands to see the program exit from the out-of-bounds index.

While you're still in the loop, hover over tires, and you'll get an array. Scoot the mouse down to hover over the arrow until it expands, showing you all four tires. Next, move down and over the first tire, and Xcode will show the guts of the tire to you. There are no instance variables in our tires, so there's not much to see. But if the class had instance variables, they would be displayed and editable. You can see the result of all this hovering and mousing in Figure 7-31.

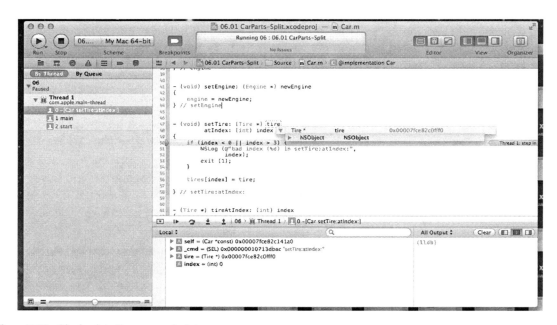

Figure 7-31. *Digging into the program's data*

And that's the whirlwind tour of the Xcode debugger. This information, plus huge amounts of your time, should be enough to let you debug any problems you come across. Happy debugging!

Cheat Sheet

We mentioned a lot of keyboard shortcuts in this chapter. As promised, we've collected them all in one easy place: Table 7-1. We've thrown in a couple we didn't mention, just for your convenience. If you're reading this book on paper, feel free to tear out these pages before you give this book to someone else, unless you think that would be rude.

Table 7-1. Xcode Keyboard Shortcuts

Keystroke	Description
⌘[	Shift the code block to the left
⌘]	Shift the code block to the right.
tab	Accept a completion.
esc	Show or hide the completion menu.
control +. (period)	Cycle through the completions.
control + shift +. (period)	Cycle backward through the completions.
⌘ + control + **S**	Make a snapshot.
control + **F**	Move the cursor forward.
control + **B**	Move the cursor backward.
control + **P**	Move the cursor to the previous line.
control + **N**	Move the cursor to the next line.
control + **A**	Move the cursor to the beginning of the line.
control + **E**	Move the cursor to the end of the line.
control + **T**	Transpose the characters adjacent to the cursor.
control + **D**	Delete the character to the right of the cursor.
control + **K**	Delete the line.
control + **L**	Center the cursor in the text editor.
⌘ + shift + **O**	Show the Open Quickly window.
⌘ + control + ↑	Open the counterpart file.
⌥ + double-click	Search in documentation.
⌘**Y**	Activate / deactivate breakpoints.
⌘**-control-Y**	Continue (in the debugger).
F6	Step over.
F7	Step into.
F8	Step out.

Summary

This chapter was pretty information-dense, and we really didn't talk about Objective-C all that much. What's the deal? Just like woodworkers needs to know more than just wood (for example, they need to know all that stuff about tools), an Objective-C programmer needs to know more than just the language. Being able to quickly write, navigate, and debug your code in Xcode means that you spend less time wrestling with the environment and spend more time doing the fun stuff.

Next up is a meaty introduction to some of the classes in Cocoa. That should be fun!

Chapter 8

A Quick Tour of the Foundation Kit

You've already seen that Objective-C is a pretty nifty language, and we haven't even finished exploring all the features it has to offer. For now, we're going to take a quick side trip and have a look at Cocoa's Foundation framework. Although strictly part of Cocoa and not built in to Objective-C, the Foundation framework is so important that we thought it worth exploring in this book.

As you saw in Chapter 2, Cocoa is actually composed of many different frameworks. Of these, the ones most used for desktop (OS X) applications are Foundation and Application Kit. The Application Kit has all the user interface objects and high-level classes. You'll get a taste of the AppKit (as the cool kids call it) in Chapter 16.

If you are going to be developing applications for iOS, then you will be working with the User Interface Kit (UIKit). We will give a 10,000–foot overview of UIKit in Chapter 15. UIKit is considered parallel to AppKit for iOS. It has all the interface objects for iOS applications.

Solid Foundation

Foundation, as its name implies, is the foundation for both the UI frameworks, and because it has no UI objects, you can use the same objects for iOS and OS X applications.

Foundation framework has a bunch of useful low-level, data-oriented classes and types. We'll be visiting a number of these, such as NSString, NSArray, NSEnumerator, and NSNumber. Foundation has more than a hundred classes, all of which you can explore by looking at the documentation installed with Xcode. You can read the documentation in Xcode's Organizer window by selecting the "Documentation" item in the toolbar.

Foundation framework is built on top of another framework called CoreFoundation. CoreFoundation is written purely in C, and you can use it if you desire, but we will not be discussing it in this book. Don't be confused when talking about two different frameworks that might have similar names. If you come across function names or variable names that start with "CF," they are part of CoreFoundation. Most of them have equivalents in Foundation framework, and some of them can be easily converted from one to the other.

Using the Project Boilerplate Code

Before we continue, here's a note about the projects for this chapter and for the rest of this book. We'll still be making Foundation tool projects, but we'll leave in the boilerplate code, which follows:

```
#import <Foundation/Foundation.h>

int main (int argc, const char * argv[])
{
 @autoreleasepool
 {
  // insert code here…
  NSLog(@"Hello, World!");
 } return 0;
}
```

Take a look through this code. `main()` starts with the keyword `@autoreleasepool`, and all the Cocoa code is written within the brackets that appear between the keyword and the return statement. This is a sneak preview of Cocoa memory management, which we'll discuss in the next chapter. For now, please just nod, smile, and leave the `@autoreleasepool` stuff in there. If you take it out, you won't hurt yourself, but you'll get some very strange messages when you run your programs.

Some Useful Types

Before digging into real live Foundation classes, let's take a look at some `struct`s that Cocoa provides for our benefit.

Home on the Range

The first structure is `NSRange`:

```
typedef struct _NSRange
{
 unsigned int location;
 unsigned int length;
} NSRange;
```

This structure is used to represent a range of things, usually a range of characters in a string or a range of items in an array. The `location` field holds the starting position of the range, and `length` is the number of elements in the range. For the string "Objective-C is a cool language", the word "cool" can be described by the range that starts at `location` 17 and has `length` 4. `location` can have the value `NSNotFound` to indicate that the range doesn't refer to anything, probably because it's uninitialized.

You can make a new NSRange in three different ways. First, you can assign the field values directly:

```
NSRange range;
range.location = 17;
range.length = 4;
```

Second, you can use the C aggregate structure assignment mechanism (doesn't that sound impressive?):

```
NSRange range = { 17, 4 };
```

Finally, Cocoa provides a convenience function called NSMakeRange():

```
NSRange range = NSMakeRange (17, 4);
```

The nice thing about NSMakeRange() is that you can use it anywhere you can use a function, such as in a method call as an argument:

```
[anObject flarbulateWithRange:NSMakeRange (13, 15)];
```

Geometric Types

You'll often see types that deal with geometry and have the prefix "CG," such as CGPoint and CGSize. These types are provided by the Core Graphics framework, used for 2D rendering. Core Graphics is written in C, so we use C types to code with it. CGPoint represents an (x, y) point in the Cartesian plane:

```
struct CGPoint
{
 float x;
 float y;
};
```

CGSize holds a width and a height:

```
struct CGSize
{
 float width;
 float height;
};
```

In the Shapes family of programs, we could have used a CGPoint and a CGSize instead of our custom rectangle struct, but we wanted to keep things as simple as possible at the time. Cocoa provides a rectangle type, which is a composition of a point and a size:

```
struct CGRect
{
 CGPoint origin;
 CGSize size;
};
```

Cocoa gives us convenience functions for making these bad boys too: CGPointMake(), CGSizeMake(), and CGRectMake().

> **Note**   Why are these things C `structs` instead of full-blown objects? It comes down to performance. A program, especially a GUI program, uses a lot of temporary points, sizes, and rectangles to do its work. Remember that all Objective-C objects are dynamically allocated, and dynamic allocation is a relatively expensive operation, consuming a nontrivial amount of time. Making these structures first-class objects would impose a lot of overhead in their use.

Stringing Us Along

The first real live class on our tour is NSString, Cocoa's string handling class. A string is just a sequence of human-readable characters. Since computers tend to interact with humans on a regular basis, having a way to store and manipulate human-readable text is a fine idea. You've met NSStrings before, with the special NSString literal, indicated by an at (@) sign before a double-quoted string, as in @"Hi!". These literal strings are as much NSStrings as the ones you create programmatically.

If you've ever done any string processing in C, such as the stuff covered in *Learn C on the Mac* by Dave Mark (Apress 2009), you know it's pretty painful. C implements strings as simple arrays of characters that mark their end with a trailing zero-byte. Cocoa's NSString has a bunch of built-in methods that make string handling much easier.

Build That String

You've seen functions like printf() and NSLog() that take a format string and some arguments and emit formatted output. NSString's stringWithFormat: method creates a new NSString just like that, with a format and arguments:

```
+ (id) stringWithFormat: (NSString *) format, …;
```

And you make a new string like this:

```
NSString *height;
height = [NSString stringWithFormat:@"Your height is %d feet, %d inches", 5, 11];
```

The resulting string is "Your height is 5 feet, 11 inches".

Class Methods

A couple of interesting things are going on in stringWithFormat:'s declaration. The first is the ellipses (…) at the end, which tells you (and the compiler) that this method will take any number of additional arguments, specified in a comma-separated list, just like printf() and NSLog().

Another wacky and even more important fact about stringWithFormat: is the very special leading character in the declaration: a plus sign. Does this have anything to do with that social network from Google? Well, no. When the Objective-C runtime builds a class, it creates a **class object** that represents the class. The class object contains pointers to the superclass, class name, and the list of the class's methods. The class object also contains a `long` that specifies the size, in bytes, for newly created instance objects of that class.

When you declare a method with the plus sign, you've marked the method as a **class method**. This method belongs to the class object (as opposed to an instance object of the class) and is typically used to create new instances. Class methods used to create new objects are called **factory methods**.

`stringWithFormat:` is a factory method. It creates a new object for you based on the arguments you give it. Using `stringWithFormat:` to make a new string is a whole lot easier than starting off with an empty string and building all the individual components.

Class methods can also be used to access global data. AppKit's `NSColor` for OS X and UIKit's `UIColor` for iOS have some class methods named after various colors, such as `redColor` and `blueColor`. To get hold of a blue color to draw with, you write something like this:

```
NSColor *haveTheBlues = [NSColor blueColor];
```

or

```
UIColor *blueMan = [UIColor blueColor];
```

The vast majority of methods you create will be instance methods and will be declared with a leading minus sign (-). These methods will operate on a specific object instance, such as getting a `Circle`'s color or a `Tire`'s air pressure. If the method performs a more general-purpose function, such as creating an instance object or accessing some global class data, you'll likely declare the method as a class method using the leading plus sign (+).

Size Matters

Another handy `NSString` method (an instance method) is `length`, which returns the number of characters in the string:

```
- (NSUInteger) length;
```

You'd use it like this:

```
NSUInteger length = [height length];
```

or in expressions like so:

```
if ([height length] > 35)
{
   NSLog (@"wow, you're really tall!");
}
```

> **Note**   `NSString`'s `length` method does the right thing when dealing with international strings, such as those containing Russian, Chinese, or Japanese characters, and using the Unicode international character standard under the hood. Dealing with these international strings in straight C is especially painful, because an individual character might take more than 1 byte. This means that functions like `strlen()`, which just counts bytes, can return the wrong value.

Comparative Politics

Comparison is a frequent operation with strings. Sometimes, you want to see if two strings are equal (for example, is username equal to 'wmalik'?). Other times, you want to see how two strings would be ordered against each other, so you can sort a list of names. NSString provides several comparison functions to help you out.

isEqualToString: compares the receiver (the object that the message is being sent to) with a string that's passed in as an argument. isEqualToString: returns a BOOL (YES or NO) indicating if the two strings have the same contents. It's declared like this:

```
- (BOOL) isEqualToString: (NSString *) aString;
```

And this is how you use it:

```
NSString *thing1 = @"hello 5";
NSString *thing2 = [NSString stringWithFormat: @"hello %d", 5];

if ([thing1 isEqualToString: thing2])
{
  NSLog (@"They are the same!");
}
```

To compare strings, use the compare: method, which is declared as follows:

```
- (NSComparisonResult) compare: (NSString *) aString;
```

compare: does a character-by-character comparison of the receiving object against the passed-in string. It returns an NSComparisonResult (which is just an enum) that shows the result of the comparison:

```
enum
{
  NSOrderedAscending = -1,
  NSOrderedSame,
  NSOrderedDescending
};
typedef NSInteger NSComparisonResult;
```

Comparing Strings: Do It Right   When comparing strings for equality, you want to use isEqualToString: rather than just comparing their pointer values, for instance:

```
if ([thing1 isEqualToString: thing2])
{
    NSLog (@"The strings are the same!");
}
```

is different from

```
if (thing1 == thing2)
{
    NSLog (@"They are the same object!");
}
```

That's because the == operator works on only the values of the thing1 and thing2 *pointers*, not what they point to. Because thing1 and thing2 are different strings, the second comparison will think they're different.

Sometimes, you do want to check for identity between two objects: is thing1 exactly the same object as thing2? That's the time to use the == operator. If you want to check for equivalence (that is, do these two strings represent the same thing?), use isEqualToString:.

If you've ever used the C functions qsort() or bsearch(), this might look familiar. If the result from compare: is NSOrderedAscending, the left-hand value is smaller than the right-hand one—that is, the target of compare sorts earlier in the alphabet than the string that's been passed in. For instance, [@"aardvark" compare: @"zygote"] would return NSOrderedAscending.

Similarly, [@"zoinks" compare:@"jinkies"] would return NSOrderedDescending. And, as you'd expect, [@"fnord" compare: @"fnord"] would return NSOrderedSame.

Insensitivity Training

compare: does a case-sensitive comparison. In other words, @"Bork" and @"bork", when compared, won't return NSOrderedSame. There's another method, compare:options:, that gives you more control:

```
- (NSComparisonResult) compare: (NSString *) aString
     options: (NSStringCompareOptions) mask;
```

The options parameter is a bit mask, which is a value that uses each bit to indicate whether an option is on or off. You can use the bitwise OR operator (|) to add option flags together. Some common options follow:

- NSCaseInsensitiveSearch: Uppercase and lowercase characters are considered the same.

- NSLiteralSearch: Perform an exact comparison, including case.

- NSNumericSearch: Numbers in strings are compared as numbers, rather than their character values. Without this, "100" would sort before "99," which strikes most nonprogrammers as rather bizarre, or even wrong.

For example, if you want to perform a comparison ignoring case but ordering numbers correctly, you would do this:

```
if ([thing1 compare: thing2 options: NSCaseInsensitiveSearch | NSNumericSearch]
     == NSOrderedSame)
{
  NSLog (@"They match!");
}
```

Is It Inside?

Sometimes, you want to see if a string has another string inside it. For example, you might want to know if a file name has ".mov" at the end so you can open it in QuickTime Player, or you could check whether it starts with "draft" to see if it's a draft version of a document. Here are two methods that help: the first checks whether a string starts with another string, and the second determines if a string ends with another string:

```
- (BOOL) hasPrefix: (NSString *) aString;
- (BOOL) hasSuffix: (NSString *) aString;
```

And you'd use these methods as follows:

```
NSString *fileName = @"draft-chapter.pages";

if ([fileName hasPrefix: @"draft"])
{
  // this is a draft
}
if ([fileName hasSuffix: @".mov"])
{
  // this is a movie
}
```

So draft-chapters.pages would be recognized as a draft version (because it starts with "draft"), but would not be recognized as a movie (it has ".pages" at the end rather than ".mov").

If you want to see if a string is somewhere inside another string, use rangeOfString:

```
- (NSRange) rangeOfString: (NSString *) aString;
```

When you send rangeOfString: to an NSString object, you pass it the string to look for. It then returns an NSRange struct to show you where the matching part of the string is and how large the match is. So the following example

```
NSRange range = [fileName rangeOfString: @"chapter"];
```

comes back with range.location at 6 and range.length set to 7. If the argument isn't found in the receiver, range.location will be equal to NSNotFound.

Mutability

NSStrings are **immutable**. That doesn't mean you can't keep them quiet; it refers to the fact that once they're created, you can't change them. You can do all sorts of stuff with them, like make new strings with them, find characters in them, and compare them to other strings, but you can't change them by taking off characters or by adding new ones.

Cocoa provides a subclass of NSString called NSMutableString. Use that if you want to slice and dice a string in place.

> **Note** Programmers coming from Java should feel at home with this distinction. NSString behaves like the java String class, and NSMutableString is like Java's StringBuffer class.

You can create a new NSMutableString by using the class method stringWithCapacity:, which is declared like so:

```
+ (id) stringWithCapacity: (NSUInteger) capacity;
```

The capacity is just a suggestion to NSMutableString, like when you tell a teenager what time to be home. The string is not limited to the capacity you supply—it's just an optimization. For example, if you know you're building a string that's 40 megabytes in size, NSMutableString can preallocate a chunk of memory to hold it, making subsequent operations much faster. Create a new mutable string like this:

```
NSMutableString *string = [NSMutableString stringWithCapacity:42];
```

Once you have a mutable string, you can do all sorts of wacky tricks with it. A common operation is to append a new string, using appendString: or appendFormat:, like this:

```
- (void) appendString: (NSString *) aString;
- (void) appendFormat: (NSString *) format, …;
```

appendString: takes its aString parameter and copies it to the end of the receiving object. appendFormat: works like stringWithFormat:, but instead of creating a new string object, it appends the formatted string to the end of the receiving string, for example:

```
NSMutableString *string = [NSMutableString stringWithCapacity:50];
[string appendString: @"Hello there "];
[string appendFormat: @"human %d!", 39];
```

At the end of this code, string will have the friendly value "Hello there human 39!".

You can remove characters from the string with the deleteCharactersInRange: method:

```
- (void) deleteCharactersInRange: (NSRange) aRange;
```

You'll often use deleteCharactersInRange: coupled with rangeOfString:. Remember that NSMutableString is a subclass of NSString. Through the miracle of object-oriented programming, you also can use all the features of NSString with NSMutableStrings, including rangeOfString:, the comparison methods, and everything else. For example, let's say you list all your friends, but then you decide you don't like Jack anymore and you want to remove him from the list:

First, make the list of friends:

```
NSMutableString *friends = [NSMutableString stringWithCapacity:50];
[friends appendString: @"James BethLynn Jack Evan"];
```

Next, find the range of characters where Jack lives:

```
NSRange jackRange = [friends rangeOfString: @"Jack"];
jackRange.length++; // eat the space that follows
```

In this case, the range starts at 15 and has a length of 5. Now, we can remove Jack from our Christmas card list:

```
[friends deleteCharactersInRange: jackRange];
```

This leaves the string as "James BethLynn Evan".

Mutable strings are very handy for implementing description methods. You can use appendString and appendFormat to create a nice description for your object.

We get a couple of behaviors for free because NSMutableString is a subclass of NSString. The first freebie is that anywhere an NSString is used, we can substitute an NSMutableString. Any methods that take an NSString will also take an NSMutableString. The user of the string really doesn't care if it's mutable or not.

The other free behavior comes from the fact that inheritance works just as well with class methods as it does with instance methods. So, the handy stringWithFormat: class method in NSString works for making new NSMutableStrings. You can easily populate a mutable string from a format:

```
NSMutableString *string = [NSMutableString stringWithFormat: @"jo%dy", 2];
```

string starts out with the value "jo2y", but you can perform other operations, such as deleting characters from a given range or inserting characters at a particular position. Check out the documentation for NSString and NSMutableString to learn full details on the dozens of methods available in these classes.

Collection Agency

Individual objects floating around is nifty, but frequently, you'll want to get things organized. Cocoa provides a number of collection classes such as NSArray and NSDictionary whose instances exist just to hold onto other objects.

NSArray

You've used arrays in C. In fact, earlier in this very book, we used an array to hold four tires for a car. You might remember that we ran into some difficulties with that code. For instance, we had to check to make sure the index into the array was valid: it couldn't go below 0 or beyond the end of the array. Another problem: the array length of 4 was hard-coded into the Car class, meaning we couldn't have a car with more than four tires. Sure, that doesn't seem like much of a limitation, but you never know if the Flying Rocket Cars of the Future that we've all been promised will need more than four tires for a smooth landing.

NSArray is a Cocoa class that holds an ordered list of objects. You can put any kind of objects in an NSArray: NSString, Car, Shape, Tire, or whatever else you want, even other arrays and dictionaries.

Once you have an NSArray of objects, you can work with it in various ways, such as by having an object's instance variable point to the array, passing the array as an argument to a method or function, getting a count of the number of objects stored inside it, grabbing an object at a particular index, finding an object in the array, looping over the contents, or a zillion other magic tricks.

NSArray has two limitations. First, it holds only Objective-C objects. You can't have primitive C types, like int, float, enum, struct, or random pointers in an NSArray. Also, you can't store nil (the zero or NULL value for objects) in an NSArray. There are ways of working around these limitations, as you'll see in a little while.

You can create a new NSArray using the class method arrayWithObjects:. You give it a comma-separated list of objects, with nil at the end to signal the end of the list (which, by the way, is one of the reasons you can't store nil in an array):

```
NSArray *array = [NSArray arrayWithObjects:@"one", @"two", @"three", nil];
```

This makes a three-element array composed of literal NSString objects. You can also create an array using the array literal format, which is very similar to the NSString literal format. Instead of quotes, you use square brackets, like so:

```
NSArray *array2 = @[@"one", @"two", @"three"];
```

Even though array and array2 are different objects, their contents are the same, and the second version is obviously much easier to type than the first.

> **Note**   You don't have to include nil at the end when you use the literal syntax.

Once you have an array, you can get a count of the number of objects it contains:

```
- (NSUInteger)count;
```

And you can fetch an object at a particular index:

```
- (id)objectAtIndex:(NSUInteger)index;
```

Accessing objects in the array using the literal syntax is just like accessing an array item in C.

```
id *myObject = array1[1];
```

You can combine counting and fetching to print out the contents of the array:

```
for (NSInteger i = 0; i < [array count]; i++)
{
    NSLog (@"index %d has %@.",i, [array objectAtIndex:i]);
}
```

You can also write the preceding code using the array literal syntax:

```
for (NSInteger i = 0; i < [array count]; i++)
{
  NSLog (@"index %d has %@.",i, array[i]);
}
```

The output looks the same in both cases:

```
index 0 has one.
index 1 has two.
index 2 has three.
```

If you refer to an index that's greater than the number of objects in the array, Cocoa prints a complaint at runtime. For example, run this code:

```
[array objectAtIndex:208000];
array[208000];
```

You'll see this:

```
*** Terminating app due to uncaught exception 'NSRangeException',
reason: '*** -[__NSArray objectAtIndex:]: index 208000 beyond bounds [0 .. 2]'
```

So there.

Because you'll probably see messages like this from time to time in your Cocoa programming career, let's spend a moment taking a closer look. After giving you the smackdown by saying that it terminated your program, the message mentions that it did so because of an "uncaught exception." An **exception** is Cocoa's way of saying "I don't know how to deal with this." There are ways to catch exceptions in code and handle them yourself, but you don't need to do that when you're just starting out. This particular exception is an NSRangeException, which means there's something wrong with a range parameter being passed to a method. The method in particular is NSArray objectAtIndex:.

The last bits of information in the exception message are the most interesting. This part of the message says we're asking for something at index 208000 in an array, but oops, the array only has three items—missed it by *that much*. Using this information, you can trace back to the offending code and find the error.

Tracking down the cause of an exception can be frustrating. All you get is this message in the Console window. With a GUI program, the program keeps running. There's a way to get Xcode to break into the debugger when an exception happens, which is a bit better. To make this happen, choose the breakpoints tab in the navigator panel in the workspace. You'll get a list of breakpoints. Right now, we have one breakpoint set, as shown in Figure 8-1.

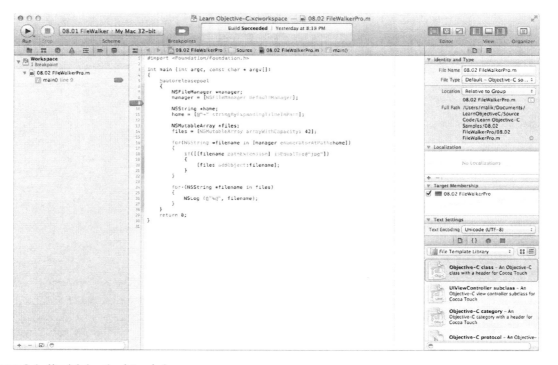

Figure 8-1. Xcode's breakpoints window

To add another breakpoint, just click the + button on the bottom left of the panel, and select the Add Exception Breakpoint… item from the pop-up. You'll see another pop-up, shown in Figure 8-2.

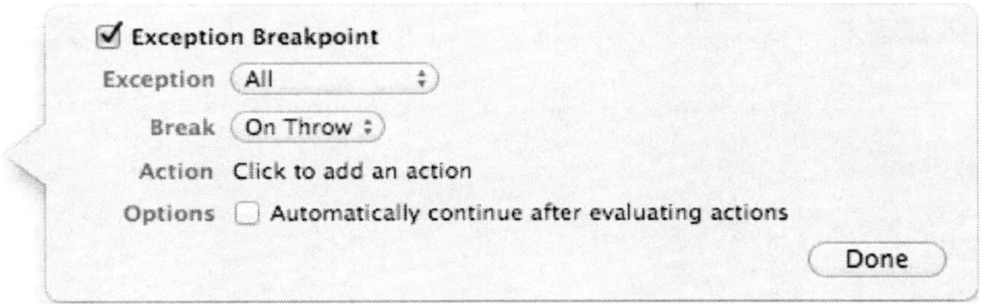

☑ **Exception Breakpoint**

Exception (All   ⬍)

Break (On Throw ⬍)

Action Click to add an action

Options ☐ Automatically continue after evaluating actions

(Done)

Figure 8-2. Adding an exception breakpoint

Before Xcode sets the breakpoint, it allows you to customize the breakpoint's behavior. For instance, you can have it print an error message or stop and execute some commands for you. For now, we're not going to do anything fancy. We'll just let the program stop where the exception is thrown. To finish, we click Done to add the breakpoint. After the breakpoint has been added, the window looks something like Figure 8-3. Now, when you run the program and an exception is thrown, the debugger will stop and point to the line containing the breakpoint, as shown in Figure 8-4.

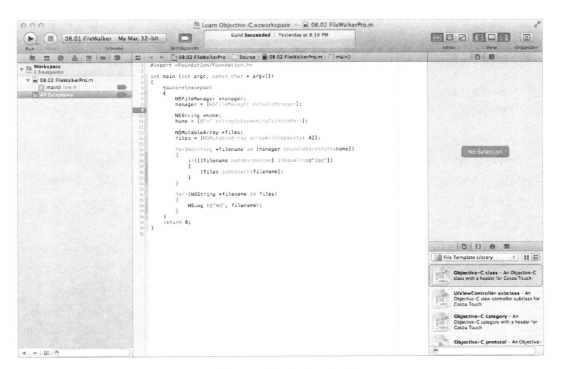

Figure 8-3. The XCode debugger pointing to the line containing the breakpoint

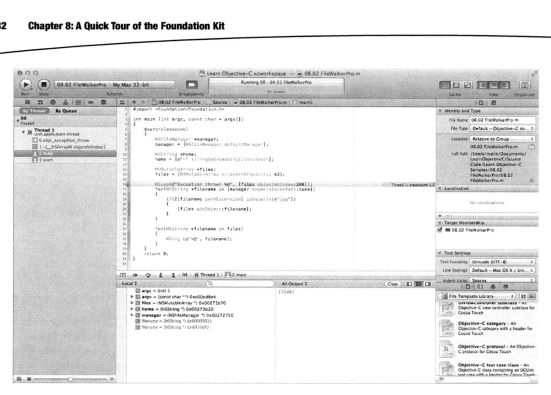

Figure 8-4. *Now, the program stops at the breakpoint*

You might not be happy that Cocoa complains so vehemently if your program merely transgresses the bounds of an array. But trust us: you'll come to realize it's actually a *great thing*, because it allows you to catch errors that otherwise might go undetected.

Like NSString, NSArray has a lot of features. For example, you can tell an array to give you the location of a particular object, make a new array based on a range of elements in the current array, join all the elements into a string with a given separator (that one is handy for making comma-separated lists), or make a new array that's a sorted version of the array you already have.

Doing the Splits   If you've used scripting languages like Perl or Python, you're probably used to splitting a string into an array and joining an array's elements into a single string. You can do that with NSArray too.

To split an NSArray, use -componentsSeparatedByString:, like this:

```
NSString *string = @"oop:ack:bork:greeble:ponies";
NSArray *chunks = [string componentsSeparatedByString: @":"];
```

And to join an NSArray and create a string of its contents, use componentsJoinedByString::

```
string = [chunks componentsJoinedByString: @" :- ) "];
```

The preceding line produces an NSString with the contents "oop :-) ack :-) bork :-) greeble :-) ponies".

Mutable Arrays

NSArray creates immutable objects, just as NSString does. Once you create an array with a certain number of objects, that's it for that array: you can't add or remove any members. The objects contained in the array are free to change, of course (like a Car getting a new set of Tires after it fails a safety inspection), but the array object itself will stay the same forever.

To complement NSArray, NSMutableArray exists so that we can add and remove objects whenever we want. It uses a class method, arrayWithCapacity, to make a new mutable array:

```
+ (id) arrayWithCapacity: (NSUInteger) numItems;
```

Like NSMutableString's stringWithCapacity:, the array's capacity is just a hint about its eventual size. The capacity value exists so that Cocoa can perform some optimizations on the code. Cocoa doesn't prepopulate the array with objects, and it doesn't use the capacity value to limit the array. You create a new mutable array like this:

```
NSMutableArray *array = [NSMutableArray arrayWithCapacity: 17];
```

Add objects to the end of the array by using addObject:.

```
- (void) addObject: (id) anObject;
```

You can add four tires to an array with a loop like this:

```
for (NSInteger i = 0; i < 4; i++)
{
 Tire *tire = [Tire new];
 [array addObject: tire];
}
```

You can remove an object at a particular index. For example, if you don't like the second tire, you can use removeObjectAtIndex: to get rid of it. Here's how the method is defined:

```
- (void) removeObjectAtIndex: (NSUInteger) index;
```

You use it like this:

```
[array removeObjectAtIndex:1];
```

Note that the second tire lives at index 1. NSArray objects are zero-indexed, like C arrays.

There are now three tires left. No hole is created in the array after you remove an object. The objects in the array that follow the removed object all get shifted down to fill the gap.

There are a bunch of cool things you can do with other methods of mutable arrays, like inserting an object at a particular index, replacing an object, sorting the array, plus all the goodies that NSArray provides as an ancestor.

> **Note**   There is no literal syntax for creating NSMutableArray objects.

Enumeration Nation

Performing an operation on each element of the array is a common NSArray operation. For example, you might tell all the shapes in the array to change their color to green, if you really liked green that much. Or you might want every tire in the car to go flat on the driver, for realism in constructing your Pittsburgh-area driving simulator. You can write a loop to index from 0 to [array count] and get the object at the index, or you can use an NSEnumerator, which is Cocoa's way of describing this kind of iteration over a collection. To use NSEnumerator, you ask the array for the enumerator using objectEnumerator:

```
- (NSEnumerator *)objectEnumerator;
```

You use the method like this:

```
NSEnumerator *enumerator = [array objectEnumerator];
```

There's also a reverseObjectEnumerator method if you want to walk the collection from back to front. !looC

After you get an enumerator, you crank up a while loop that asks the enumerator for its nextObject every time through the loop:

```
- (id) nextObject;
```

When nextObject returns nil, the loop is done. This is another reason why you can't store nil values in the array: there's no way to tell whether a nil result was a value stored in the array or the nil that signals the end of the loop.

The whole loop then looks like this:

```
NSEnumerator *enumerator = [array objectEnumerator];
while (id thingie = [enumerator nextObject])
{
 NSLog (@"I found %@", thingie);
}
```

There's one gotcha if you're enumerating over a mutable array: you can't change the container, such as by adding or removing objects. If you do, the enumerator will become confused, and you'll get undefined results. "Undefined results" can mean anything from "Hey, it seems to have worked!" to "Oops, it crashed my program."

Fast Enumeration

Apple introduced a number of small tweaks to Objective-C as it boosted the language version to 2.0. The first of these tweaks we'll examine is called **fast enumeration**, and it uses syntax familiar to users of scripting languages. Here's what it looks like:

```
for (NSString *string in array)
{
 NSLog (@"I found %@", string);
}
```

The body of the loop will spin for each element in the array, with the variable `string` holding each array value. It's much more concise than the enumerator syntax and much faster.

Like all the Objective-C 2.0 features, this is not available on Macs running very old system software (pre-Mac OS X 10.5 Leopard). If you or your users need to run your programs on a system that does not support Objective-C 2.0 or later, you can't use this new syntax. Bummer – but at this point, very unlikely too.

The latest release of the Apple compiler (based on the Clang and LLVM projects) adds a feature called **blocks** to the base C language. We will discuss blocks at length in Chapter 14. To support the blocks feature, Apple has added a method to enumerate objects in NSArray using blocks, and it looks like this.

```
- (void)enumerateObjectsUsingBlock:(void (^)(id obj, NSUInteger idx, BOOL *stop))block
```

Whoa! What the heck is that? You're probably thinking you don't even know how to read it, let alone use it. Well, don't worry. It's much simpler than it looks. Using the previous array, we can rewrite the preceding code as:

```
[array enumerateObjectsUsingBlock:^(NSString *string, NSUInteger index, BOOL *stop) {
    NSLog (@"I found %@", string);
}];
```

Now, the question is, "Why would we use this instead of fast enumeration?" With blocks, one of the options is that the loop can execute in parallel. With fast enumeration, execution proceeds through the items linearly.

OK, so now we have four ways to iterate through an array: by index, with `NSEnumerator`, with fast enumeration, and now with blocks. Which one do you use?

If you don't have to worry about running on ancient, pre-10.5 systems, use fast enumeration or blocks. They are more succinct and much faster. What's more, blocks are only available with the Apple LLVM compiler.

In the unlikely event that you need to support Mac OS X 10.4 Tiger or earlier, go the `NSEnumerator` way. Xcode includes a refactoring to convert code to Objective-C 2.0 and will automatically convert `NSEnumerator` loops into fast enumeration.

Only use `-objectAtIndex` if you really need to access things by index, like if you're skipping around the array (for example, accessing every third object in it) or if you are iterating through multiple arrays at the same time.

NSDictionary

No doubt you've heard of dictionaries. Maybe you even use one occasionally. In programming, a **dictionary** is a collection of keywords and their definitions. Cocoa has a collection class called `NSDictionary` that performs these duties. An `NSDictionary` stores a value (which can be any kind of Objective-C object) under a given key (usually an `NSString`). You can then use that key to look up the corresponding value. So, for example, if you have an `NSDictionary` that stores all the contact information for a person, you can ask that dictionary "Give me the value for the key home-address." Or say, "Give me the value for the key email-address."

> **Note**   Why not just have an array and look at the values inside it? A dictionary (which is also known as a hash table or an associative array) uses a storage mechanism that's optimized for key lookups. Rather than scanning an entire array looking for an item, the dictionary can immediately put its electronic hands on the data it's after. For frequent lookups and for large data sets, a dictionary can be hundreds of times faster than an array. That's, like, really fast.

As you can probably guess, NSDictionary, like NSString and NSArray, is an immutable object. However, the NSMutableDictionary class lets you add and remove stuff at will. To make a new NSDictionary, you supply all the objects and keys that live in the dictionary at creation time.

The easiest way to get started with a dictionary is to use the dictionary literal syntax, which is similar to the class method dictionaryWithObjectsAndKeys:.

The literal syntax is defined as @{key:value,…};. Notice that it uses curly braces instead of square brackets. Also note that dictionaryWithObjectsAndKeys: uses objects followed by the key, but the literal syntax is reversed: key first, value second. Each key value is separated by a colon and each pair is separated by a comma.

```
+ (id) dictionaryWithObjectsAndKeys: (id) firstObject, …;
```

This method takes an alternating sequence of objects and keys, terminated by a nil value (as you're probably thinking, you can't store a nil value in an NSDictionary, and you likely guessed that nil is not required when using the literal syntax). Let's say we want to make a dictionary to hold the tires of our car using human-readable labels rather than arbitrary indexes in an array. You can create such a dictionary like this:

```
Tire *t1 = [Tire new];
Tire *t2 = [Tire new];
Tire *t3 = [Tire new];
Tire *t4 = [Tire new];
NSDictionary *tires = [NSDictionary dictionaryWithObjectsAndKeys: t1,
    @"front-left", t2, @"front-right", t3, @"back-left", t4, @"back-right", nil];
```

or

```
NSDictionary *tires = @{@"front-left" : ti, @"front-right" : t2, @"back-left" : t3,
    @"back-right" : t4};
```

To access a value in the dictionary, use the objectForKey: method, giving it the key you previously stored the value under:

```
- (id) objectForKey: (id) aKey;
```

or

```
tires[key];
```

So, to find the back-right tire, you can do this:

```
Tire *tire = [tires objectForKey:@"back-right"];
```

or

```
Tire *tire = tires[@"back-right"];
```

If there's no back-right tire in the dictionary (if it's a funky three-wheeler), the dictionary returns nil.

To make a new NSMutableDictionary, send the dictionary message to the NSMutableDictionary class. You can also create a new mutable dictionary and give Cocoa a hint of its eventual size by using dictionaryWithCapacity: (have you started to notice that Cocoa has a very regular naming system?).

```
+ (id) dictionaryWithCapacity: (NSUInteger) numItems;
```

As we mentioned earlier with NSMutableString and NSMutableArray, the capacity is just a hint, not a limit to the size of the dictionary. You can add things to the dictionary using setObject:forKey:.

```
- (void)setObject:(id)anObject forKey:(id)aKey;
```

Here's another way to make the dictionary that holds the tires:

```
NSMutableDictionary *tires = [NSMutableDictionary dictionary];
[tires setObject:t1 forKey:@"front-left"];
[tires setObject:t2 forKey:@"front-right"];
[tires setObject:t3 forKey:@"back-left"];
[tires setObject:t4 forKey:@"back-right"];
```

If you use setObject:forKey: on a key that's already there, it replaces the old value with the new one. If you want to take a key out of a mutable dictionary, use the removeObjectForKey: method:

```
- (void) removeObjectForKey: (id) aKey;
```

So, if we want to model one of our tires falling off, we can just remove it:

```
[tires removeObjectForKey:@"back-left"];
```

Just as with NSArrays, there is no literal syntax for NSMutableDictionary.

Use but Don't Extend

Because you're inventive, you might be tempted to create subclasses of NSString, NSArray, or NSDictionary. Resist the urge. In some languages, you do end up subclassing string and array classes to get work done. But in Cocoa, many classes are actually implemented as **class clusters**, which are a bunch of implementation-specific classes hidden behind a common interface. When you make an NSString object, you might actually end up getting an NSLiteralString, NSCFString, NSSimpleCString, NSBallOfString, or any number of undocumented implementation-detail objects.

As a user of NSString or NSArray, you don't have to care which class is being used under the hood. But trying to subclass a class cluster is an exercise in pain and frustration. Instead of subclassing, you can usually solve such programming problems by composing an NSString or NSArray into one of your classes or by using categories (described in Chapter 12).

Family Values

NSArrays and NSDictionarys hold only objects. They can't directly contain any primitive types, like int, float, or struct. But you can use objects that embed a primitive value. For example, stick an int into an object, and you can then put that object into an NSArray or NSDictionary.

If you want to use objects for basic types, you can use NSInteger and NSUInteger. These types also unify values for 32-bit and 64-bit processors.

NSNumber

Cocoa provides a class called NSNumber that **wraps** (that is, implements as objects) the primitive numeric types. You can create a new NSNumber using these class methods:

```
+ (NSNumber *) numberWithChar: (char) value;
+ (NSNumber *) numberWithInt: (int) value;
+ (NSNumber *) numberWithFloat: (float) value;
+ (NSNumber *) numberWithBool: (BOOL) value;
```

There are many more of these creation methods, including unsigned versions and varieties for long and long long integers, but these are the most common ones.

You can also use the literal syntax to create these objects:

```
NSNumber *number;
number = @'X'; // char
number = @12345; // integer
number = @12345ul; // unsigned long
number = @12345ll; // long long
number = @123.45f; // float
number = @123.45; // double
number = @YES; // BOOL
```

After you create an NSNumber, you can put it into a dictionary or an array:

```
NSNumber *number = @42;
[array addObject number];
[dictionary setObject: number forKey: @"Bork"];
```

Once you have a primitive type wrapped in an NSNumber, you can get it back out using one of these instance methods:

```
- (char) charValue;
- (int) intValue;
- (float) floatValue;
- (BOOL) boolValue;
- (NSString *)stringValue;
```

It's perfectly OK to mix and match the creation and extraction methods. For example, it's all right to create an NSNumber with numberWithFloat: and get the value back with intValue. NSNumber will do the proper conversions for you.

> **Note**   The wrapping of a primitive type in an object is often called **boxing**, and taking the primitive type out is **unboxing**. Some languages have an autoboxing feature that automatically converts a primitive to its corresponding wrapped type and back. Objective-C does not support autoboxing.

NSValue

NSNumber is actually a subclass of NSValue, which wraps arbitrary values. You can use NSValue to put structures into NSArrays and NSDictionary objects. Create a new NSValue using this class method:

```
+ (NSValue *) valueWithBytes: (const void *) value objCType: (const char *) type;
```

You pass the address of the value you want to wrap (such as an NSSize or your own struct). Usually, you take the address (using the & operator in C) of the variable you want to save. You also supply a string describing the type, usually by reporting the types and sizes of the entries in the struct. You don't actually have to write code to build this string yourself. There's a compiler directive called @encode that takes a type name and generates the proper magic for you. So, to put an NSRect into an NSArray, you do something like this:

```
NSRect rect = NSMakeRect (1, 2, 30, 40);
NSValue *value = [NSValue valueWithBytes:&rect objCType:@encode(NSRect)];
[array addObject:value];
```

You can extract the value using getValue:

```
- (void)getValue:(void *)buffer;
```

When you call getValue:, you pass the address of a variable that you want to hold the value:

```
value = [array objectAtIndex: 0]; [value getValue: &rect];
```

> **Note**   In the getValue: example, you can see the use of get in the name of the method to indicate that we're providing a pointer as the place to store the value the method generates.

Convenience methods are provided for putting common Cocoa structs into NSValues, and we have conveniently listed them here:

```
+ (NSValue *)valueWithPoint:(NSPoint)aPoint;
+ (NSValue *)valueWithSize:(NSSize)size;
+ (NSValue *)valueWithRect:(NSRect)rect;
- (NSPoint)pointValue;
- (NSSize)sizeValue;
- (NSRect)rectValue;
```

To store and retrieve an NSRect in an NSArray, you do this:

```
value = [NSValue valueWithRect:rect];
[array addObject: value];
…
NSRect anotherRect = [value rectValue];
```

NSNull

We've told you that you can't put `nil` into a collection, because `nil` has special meaning to NSArray and NSDictionary. But sometimes, you really need to store a value that means "there's nothing here at all." For example, let's say you have a dictionary that holds a person's contact information, and under the key @"home fax machine", you store the user's home fax number. If that key holds a phone number value, you know that person has a fax machine. But if there's no value in the dictionary, does it mean that person has no home fax machine or that you don't know if they have one?

By using NSNull, you can eliminate the ambiguity. You can decide that a value of NSNull for the key @"home fax machine" means the person definitely does not have a fax machine, and no value for the key means that you don't know if the person has one or not.

NSNull is probably the simplest of all Cocoa classes. It has but a single method:

```
+ (NSNull *) null;
```

And you add it to a collection like this:

```
[contact setObject: [NSNull null]
forKey: @"home fax machine"];
```

You access it as follows:

```
id homefax = [contact objectForKey: @"home fax machine"];
if (homefax == [NSNull null])
{
// … no fax machine. rats.
}
```

[NSNull null] always returns the same value, so you can use == to compare it with other values.

Example: Looking for Files

OK, enough with the theoretical blah blah. Here's an actual working program that uses some of the classes found in this chapter. FileWalker (found in the *08-01 FileWalker project* folder) will paw through your Mac's home directory looking for *.jpg* files and print a list of what it finds. It's not terribly exciting, we admit, but it actually does something.

FileWalker uses NSString, NSArray, NSEnumerator, and two other Foundation classes to interact with the file system.

Our example also uses NSFileManager. The NSFileManager class lets you do stuff with the file system, like create directories, remove files, move files around, and get information about files. In this example, we're going to ask NSFileManager to make an NSDirectoryEnumerator for us, which we'll use to chug through a hierarchy of files.

This entire program resides in the main() function, because we're not making any of our own classes. Here is main() in its entirety:

```
int main (int argc, const char * argv[])
{
  @autoreleasepool
```

```
{
    NSFileManager *manager;
    manager = [NSFileManager defaultManager];

    NSString *home;
    home = [@"~" stringByExpandingTildeInPath];

    NSDirectoryEnumerator *direnum;
    direnum = [manager enumeratorAtPath:home];

    NSMutableArray *files;
    files = [NSMutableArray arrayWithCapacity:42];

    NSString *filename;
    while (filename = [direnum nextObject])
    {
        if ([[filename pathExtension] isEqualTo: @"jpg"]) {
            [files addObject: filename];
        }
    }

    NSEnumerator *fileenum;
    fileenum = [files objectEnumerator];

    while (filename = [fileenum nextObject])
    {
        NSLog (@"%@", filename);
    }
}
    return 0;

} // main
```

Now, let's deconstruct this program bit by bit. At the top is the @autoreleasepool boilerplate
code (Chapter 9 covers this in detail, as you'll see).

Our next step is to get hold of an NSFileManager to play with. NSFileManager has a class method
named defaultManager that gives us an NSFileManager object of our very own:

```
NSFileManager *manager = [NSFileManager defaultManager];
```

This is a common idiom in Cocoa. There are a number of classes that have a **singleton
architecture**: only one of them is needed. You really need only one file manager, or one font
manager, or one graphics context. These classes provide a class method to give you access to a
single, shared object, which you then use to get your work done.

In this case, we need a directory iterator. But before we can ask the file manager for a directory
iterator, we must figure out where in the file system to start looking at files. Starting from the top
level of your hard drive could take a long time, so let's just look in your home directory.

How do we specify this directory? We could start with an absolute path, like /Users/wmalik/,
but that has the limitation that it only works if your home directory is named *wmalik*. Luckily,
Unix (and OS X) has a shorthand character for the home directory, which is ~ (also known as
the *tilde*). Yes, there really is a use for that character even when you're not typing in *Español*).
~/Documents is the *Documents* directory, and *~/junk/oopack.txt* would be found at */Users/*

wmalik/junk/oopack.txt on Waqar's machine. NSString has a method that takes the tilde and expands it. That method is used in the next two lines of code:

```
NSString *home = [@"~" stringByExpandingTildeInPath];
```

stringByExpandingTildeInPath replaces ~ with the current user's home directory. On Waqar's machine, home is */Users/wmalik*. Next, we feed this path string to the file manager:

```
NSDirectoryEnumerator *direnum = [manager enumeratorAtPath: home];
```

enumeratorAtPath: returns an NSDirectoryEnumerator, which is a subclass of NSEnumerator. Each time you call nextObject on this enumerator object, it returns another path to a file in that directory. This method goes down into subdirectories too. By the time the iteration loop ends, you have the path for every single file in your home directory. Some extra features are provided by NSDirectoryEnumerator, such as getting a dictionary of attributes for every file, but we won't use those here.

Because we're looking for *.jpg* files (that is, path names that end in ".jpg"), and we're going to print their names, we need a place to store those names. We could just log them with NSLog() as we come across them in the enumeration, but in the future, we might want to do some operation on all the files at a different spot in the program. An NSMutableArray is a dandy choice here. We'll make a mutable array and add matching paths to it:

```
NSMutableArray *files = [NSMutableArray arrayWithCapacity:42];
```

We have no idea how many *.jpg* files will actually be found, so we just picked 42 because — well, you know why. And because the capacity isn't a permanent limitation on the size of the array, we'll be fine in any case.

Finally, we get to the real meat of the program. Everything else has been set up, and now, it's time for the loop:

```
NSString *filename;
while (filename = [direnum nextObject]) {
```

The directory enumerator returns an NSString with the path to the file it's pointing to. And, just like NSEnumerator, it will return nil when it's done, which will stop the loop when there's nothing else to do.

NSString provides a number of convenience utilities for dealing with pathnames and filenames. For example, the pathExtension method gives you the extension for the file (minus the dot that precedes it). So, calling pathExtension on a file named *oopack.txt* would return @"txt" and the pathExtension for *VikkiCat.jpg* would be @"jpg".

We use nested method calls to grab the path extension and send that string the message isEqualTo:. If that call returns YES, the filename is added to the array of files, like so:

```
if ([[filename pathExtension] isEqualTo: @"jpg"])
{
 [files addObject: filename];
}
```

After the directory loop ends, the files array is enumerated and its contents are printed using NSLog():

```
NSEnumerator *fileenum = [files objectEnumerator];
while (filename = [fileenum nextObject])
{
 NSLog (@"%@", filename);
}
```

Next, we tell main() to return 0 to indicate a successful exit:

```
return (0);
} // main
```

Here's the start of a sample run on Waqar's machine:

```
cocoaheads/DSCN0798.jpg
cocoaheads/DSCN0804.jpg
cow.jpg
Development/Borkware/BorkSort/cant-open-file.jpg
Development/Borkware/BSL/BWLog/accident.jpg
```

It works! It might take a while to show results though, because it may have to dig through many thousands of images to do its thing.

Behind the Sign That Says "Beware of the Leopard"

FileWalker uses the classic style of iteration. The project *08.02 FileWalkerPro* shows how to do this stuff with fast enumeration. One nifty feature of the fast enumeration syntax is that you can feed it an already existing NSEnumerator or subclass. And it just so happens that NSDirectoryEnumerator is a subclass of NSEnumerator, so we can happily send the results of -enumeratorAtPath: to fast enumeration:

```
int main (int argc, const char * argv[])
{
  @autoreleasepool
  {
    NSFileManager *manager;
    manager = [NSFileManager defaultManager];

    NSString *home;
    home = [@"~" stringByExpandingTildeInPath];

    NSMutableArray *files;
    files = [NSMutableArray arrayWithCapacity: 42];

    for(NSString *filename in [manager enumeratorAtPath:home])
    {
      if([[filename pathExtension] isEqualTo:@"jpg"])
      {
        [files addObject:filename];
      }
    }
```

```
   for(NSString *filename in files)
   {
     NSLog (@"%@", filename);
   }
 }
 return 0;

} // main
```

As you can see, this version is simpler than the previous one: we've jettisoned two enumerator variables and the supporting code for them.

Summary

We've covered a lot of stuff in this chapter! We introduced three new language features: class methods (which are methods that are handled by the class itself instead of a particular instance), the @encode() directive used for methods that need a description of a C type to do their work, and fast enumeration.

We looked at a number of useful Cocoa classes, including NSString, NSArray, and NSDictionary. NSString holds human-readable text, while NSArray and NSDictionary hold collections of objects. These objects are immutable: they can't change after you create them. Cocoa provides mutable versions of these classes, which let you change their contents at will.

Despite all our efforts (and despite the length of this chapter), we've just barely scratched the surface of the hundreds of different classes in Cocoa. You can have fun and get smarter by digging around and learning about more of these classes.

Finally, we used the classes we learned about to spin through our home directory looking for groovy pictures.

In the next chapter, we dive into the mysteries of memory management, and you'll learn how you can clean up after yourself if you make any messes.

Chapter 9

Memory Management

Next on our plate is memory management using Objective-C and Cocoa (yum!). Memory management is part of a more general problem in programming called **resource management**. Every computer system has finite resources for your program to use. These include memory, open files, and network connections. If you use a resource, such as by opening a file, you need to clean up after yourself (in this case, by closing the file). If you keep on opening files but never close them, you'll eventually run out of file capacity. Think about your public library. If everyone borrowed books but never returned them, eventually the library would close because it would have no more books, and everybody would be sad. Nobody wants that.

Of course, when your program ends, the operating system reclaims the resources it used. But as long as your program is running, it uses resources, and if you don't practice cleanliness, some resource will eventually be used up, and your program will probably crash. And as operating systems evolve, the notion of when a program actually ends is becoming more fuzzy.

Not every program uses files or network connections, but every program uses memory. Memory-related errors are the bane of every programmer who uses a C-style language. Our friends in the Java and scripting worlds have it easy: memory management happens automatically for them, like having their parents clean up their rooms. We, on the other hand, have to make sure to allocate memory when we need it and free that memory when we're finished with it. If we allocate without freeing, we'll **leak memory**: our program's memory consumption will grow and grow until we run out of memory, and then, the program will crash. We need to be equally careful not to use any memory after we free it. We might be using stale data, which can cause all sorts of errors, or something else might have moved into that memory, and then we end up corrupting the new stuff.

> **Note** Memory management is a hard problem. Cocoa's solutions are rather elegant but do take some time to wrap your mind around. Even programmers with decades of experience have problems when first encountering this material, so don't worry if it leaves your head spinning for a while.

Object Life Cycle

Just like the birds and the bees out here in the real world, objects inside a program have a life cycle. They're born (via `alloc` or `new`); they live (receive messages and do stuff), make friends (via composition and arguments to methods), and eventually die (get freed) when their lives are over. When that happens, their raw materials (memory) are recycled and used for the next generation.

Reference Counting

Now, it's pretty obvious when an object is born, and we've talked a lot about how to use an object, but how do we know when an object's useful life is over? Cocoa uses a technique known as **reference counting**, also sometimes called **retain counting**. Every object has an integer associated with it, known as its **reference count** or **retain count**. When some chunk of code is interested in an object, the code increases the object's retain count, saying, "I am interested in this object." When that code is done with the object, it decreases the retain count, indicating that it has lost interest in that object. When the retain count goes to 0, nobody cares about the object anymore (poor object!), so it is destroyed and its memory is returned to the system for reuse.

When an object is created via `alloc` or `new`, or via a `copy` message (which makes a copy of the receiving object), the object's retain count is set to 1. To increase its retain count, you send the object a `retain` message. To decrease its retain count, you send the object a `release` message.

When an object is about to be destroyed because its retain count has reached 0, Objective-C automatically sends the object a `dealloc` message. You can override `dealloc` in your objects. Do this to release any related resources you might have allocated. Don't ever call `dealloc` directly. You can rely on Objective-C to invoke your `dealloc` method when it's time to kill your object.

To find out the current retain count, send the `retainCount` message. Here are the signatures for retain, release and retainCount:

```
- (id) retain;
- (oneway void) release;
- (NSUInteger) retainCount;
```

A `retain` call returns an id. This enables you to chain a `retain` call with other message sends, incrementing the object's retain count and then asking it to do some work. For instance, `[[car retain] setTire: tire atIndex: 2];` asks `car` to bump up its retain count and perform the `setTire` action.

The first project in this chapter is RetainCount1, located in the *09.01 RetainCount-1* project folder. This program creates an object (`RetainTracker`) that calls `NSLog()` when it's initialized and when it gets deallocated:

```
@interface RetainTracker : NSObject
@end // RetainTracker

@implementation RetainTracker
 - (id) init
 {
  if (self = [super init]) {   NSLog (@"init: Retain count of %d.",
      [self retainCount]);
 }
```

```
  return (self);
} // init

- (void) dealloc
{
  NSLog (@"dealloc called. Bye Bye.");
  [super dealloc];

} // dealloc
@end // RetainTracker
```

The init method follows the standard Cocoa idiom for object initialization, which we'll explore in the next chapter. As we mentioned earlier, the dealloc message is sent (and, as a result, the dealloc method called) automatically when an object's retain count reaches 0. Our versions of init and dealloc use NSLog() to write out a message saying that they were called.

main() is where a new RetainTracker object is created, and the two methods defined by that class get called indirectly. When a new RetainTracker is created, retain and release messages are sent to increase and decrease the retain count, while we watch the fun, courtesy of NSLog():

```
int main (int argc, const char *argv[])
{
 RetainTracker *tracker = [RetainTracker new];
 // count: 1

[tracker retain]; // count: 2
NSLog (@"%d", [tracker retainCount]);

[tracker retain]; // count: 3
NSLog (@"%d", [tracker retainCount]);

[tracker release]; // count: 2
NSLog (@"%d", [tracker retainCount]);

[tracker release]; // count: 1
NSLog (@"%d", [tracker retainCount]);

[tracker retain]; // count 2
NSLog (@"%d", [tracker retainCount]);

[tracker release]; // count 1
NSLog (@"%d", [tracker retainCount]);

[tracker release]; // count: 0, dealloc it
return (0);
} // main
```

In real life, of course, you wouldn't be doing multiple retains and releases in a single function like this. Over its lifetime, an object might see patterns of retains and releases like this from a bunch of different places in your program over time. Running the program lets us see the retain counts:

```
init: Retain count of 1.
2
3
2
```

```
1
2
1
dealloc called. Bye Bye.
```

So, if you call alloc, new, or copy on an object, you just need to release it to make it go away and let the memory get reclaimed.

Object Ownership

"Wait," you're thinking, "didn't you say this was hard? What's the big deal? You create an object, use it, release it, and memory management is happy. That doesn't sound terribly complicated." It gets more complex when you factor in the concept of **object ownership**. When something is said to "own an object," that something is responsible for making sure the object gets cleaned up.

An object with instance variables that point to other objects is said to **own** those other objects. For example, in CarParts, a car owns the engine and tires that it points to. Similarly, a function that creates an object is said to own that object. In CarParts, main() creates a new car object, so main() is said to own the car.

A complication arises when more than one entity owns a particular object, which is why the retain count can be larger than 1. In the case of the RetainCount1 program, main() owned the RetainTracker object, so main() is responsible for cleaning up the object.

Recall the engine setter method for Car:

```
- (void) setEngine: (Engine *) newEngine;
```

and how it was called from main():

```
Engine *engine = [Engine new];
[car setEngine: engine];
```

Who owns the engine now? Does main() own it or does Car? Who is responsible for making sure Engine gets a release message when it is no longer useful? It can't be main(), because Car is using the engine. It can't be Car, because main() might use the engine later.

The trick is to have Car retain the engine, increasing its retain count to 2. That makes sense, since two entities, Car and main(), are now using the engine. Car should retain the engine inside setEngine:, and main() should release the engine. Then Car releases the engine when it's finished (in its dealloc method), and the engine's resources are reclaimed.

Retaining and Releasing in Accessors

A first crack at writing a memory-management-savvy version of setEngine might look like this:

```
- (void) setEngine: (Engine *) newEngine
{
  engine = [newEngine retain];

  // BAD CODE: do not steal. See fixed version below.
} // setEngine
```

Unfortunately, that's not quite enough. Imagine this sequence of calls in `main()`:

```
Engine *engine1 = [Engine new]; // count: 1
[car setEngine: engine1]; // count: 2
[engine1 release]; // count: 1

Engine *engine2 = [Engine new]; // count: 1
[car setEngine: engine2]; // count: 2
```

Oops! We have a problem with engine1 now: its retain count is still 1. `main()` has already released its reference to engine1, but Car never did. We have now leaked engine1, and leaky engines are never good. That first engine object will sit around idling and consuming a chunk of memory.

Here's another attempt at writing `setEngine:`.

```
- (void) setEngine: (Engine *) newEngine
{
  [engine release];
  engine = [newEngine retain];

// More BAD CODE: do not steal. Fixed version below.
} // setEngine
```

That fixes the case of the leaked engine1 that you saw previously. But it breaks when newEngine and the old engine are the same object. Ponder this case:

```
Engine *engine = [Engine new]; // count: 1
Car *car1 = [Car new];
Car *car2 = [Car new];

[car1 setEngine: engine]; // count: 2
[engine release]; // count 1

[car2 setEngine: [car1 engine]]; // oops!
```

Why is this a problem? Here's what's happening. `[car1 engine]` returns a pointer to engine, which has a retain count of 1. The first line of setEngine is `[engine release]`, which makes the retain count 0, and the object gets deallocated. Now, both newEngine and the engine instance variable are pointing to freed memory, which is bad. Here's a better way to write setEngine:

```
- (void) setEngine: (Engine *) newEngine
{
  [newEngine retain];
  [engine release];
  engine = newEngine;

} // setEngine
```

If you retain the new engine first, and newEngine is the same object as engine, the retain count will be increased and immediately decreased. But the count won't go to 0, and the engine won't be destroyed unexpectedly, which would be bad. In your accessors, if you retain the new object before you release the old object, you'll be safe.

> **Note**   There are different schools of thought on how proper accessors should be written, and arguments and flame wars erupt on various mailing lists on a semiregular basis. The technique shown in the "Retaining and Releasing in Accessors" section works well and is (somewhat) easy to understand, but don't be surprised if you see different accessor management techniques when you look at other people's code.

Autorelease

Memory management can be a tough problem, as you've seen so far when we encountered some of the subtleties of writing setter methods. And now it's time to examine yet another wrinkle. You know that objects need to be released when you're finished with them. In some cases, knowing when you're done with an object is not so easy. Consider the case of a description method, which returns an NSString that describes an object:

```
- (NSString *) description
{
 NSString *description;
 description = [[NSString alloc]
   initWithFormat: @"I am %d years old", 4];

 return (description);
} // description
```

Here we're making a new string instance with alloc, which gives it a retain count of 1, and then we return it. Who is responsible for cleaning up this string object?

It can't be the description method. If you release the description string before returning it, the retain count goes to 0, and the object is obliterated immediately.

The code that uses the description could hang onto the string in a variable and then release it when finished, but that makes using the descriptions extremely inconvenient. What should be just one line of code turns into three:

```
NSString *desc = [someObject description];
NSLog (@"%@", desc);
[desc release];
```

There has got to be a better way. And luckily, there is!

Everyone into the Pool!

Cocoa has the concept of the **autorelease pool**. You've probably seen @autoreleasepool or NSAutoreleasePool in the boilerplate code generated by Xcode. Now it's time to see what that's all about.

The name provides a good clue. It's a pool (collection) of stuff, presumably objects, that *auto*matically gets *released*.

NSObject provides a method called `autorelease`:

```
- (id) autorelease;
```

This method schedules a release message to be sent at some time in the future. The return value is the object that receives the message; `retain` uses this same technique, which makes chaining together calls easy. When you send `autorelease` to an object, that object is actually added to an autorelease pool. When that pool is destroyed, all the objects in the pool are sent a `release` message.

> **Note**   There's no magic in the autorelease concept. You could write your own autorelease pool by using an `NSMutableArray` to hold the objects and sending all those objects a `release` message in the `dealloc` method. But there's no need for reinvention—Apple has done the hard work for you.

We can now write a description method that does a good job with memory management:

```
- (NSString *) description
{
 NSString *description;
 description = [[NSString alloc]
   initWithFormat: @"I am %d years old", 4];

 return ([description autorelease]);
} // description
```

So you can write code like this:

```
NSLog (@"%@", [someObject description]);
```

Now, memory management works just right, because the `description` method creates a new string, autoreleases it, and returns it for the `NSLog()` to use. Because that description string was autoreleased, it's been put into the currently active autorelease pool, and, sometime later, after the code doing the `NSLog()` has finished running, the pool will be destroyed.

The Eve of Our Destruction

When does the autorelease pool get destroyed so that it can send a release message to all the objects it contains? For that matter, when does a pool get created in the first place? There are two ways you can create an autorelease pool.

- Using the `@autoreleasepool` language keyword.
- Using the `NSAutoreleasePool` object.

In the Foundation tools we've been using, the creation and destruction of the pool has been done by using the language keyword. So when you use `@autoreleasepool{}`, all the code between the curly braces is put into this new pool. If your calculations are very memory intensive, you can nest autorelease pools.

One thing to keep in mind is that any variables that are defined within the curly braces are not visible outside of them; standard C scope applies, just like in loops.

The second, and more explicit, method is to use the NSAutoreleasePool object. When you do this, the code between new and release gets to use the new pool.

```
NSAutoreleasePool *pool;
pool = [NSAutoreleasePool new];
…
[pool release];
```

When you create an autorelease pool, it automatically becomes the active pool. When you release that pool, its retain count goes to 0, so it gets deallocated. During the deallocation, the pool releases all its objects.

So which method should you use? Use the keyword method. It's faster than the object method, because the language knows how to create and destroy memory better than we do.

When you're using the AppKit, Cocoa automatically creates and destroys an autorelease pool for you on a regular basis. It does so after the program handles the current event (such as a mouse click or key press). You're free to use as many autoreleased objects as you like, and the pool will clean them up for you automatically whenever the user does something.

> **Note**   You may have seen in Xcode's autogenerated code an alternate way of destroying an autorelease pool's objects: the -drain method. This method empties out the pool without destroying it. -drain is available in Mac OS X 10.4 (Tiger) and later. In our own code (not generated by Xcode), we'll be using -release, just to demonstrate how to support ancient versions of OS X.

Pools in Action

RetainCount2 shows the autorelease pool doing its thing. It's found in the *09-02 RetainCount-2* project folder. This program uses the same RetainTracker class we built in RetainCount1, which NSLog()s when a RetainTracker object is initialized and when it's released. For completeness, we'll demonstrate the use of both an NSAutoreleasePool object and the @autoreleasepool keyword.

RetainCount2's main() looks like this:

```
int main (int argc, const char *argv[])
{
 NSAutoreleasePool *pool;
 pool = [[NSAutoreleasePool alloc] init];

 RetainTracker *tracker;
 tracker = [RetainTracker new]; // count: 1

 [tracker retain]; // count: 2
 [tracker autorelease]; // count: still 2
 [tracker release]; // count: 1
```

```
NSLog (@"releasing pool");
[pool release];
// gets nuked, sends release to tracker

@autoreleasepool
  {
    RetainTracker *tracker2;
    tracker2 = [RetainTracker new]; // count: 1

    [tracker2 retain]; // count: 2
    [tracker2 autorelease]; // count: still 2
    [tracker2 release]; // count: 1

    NSLog (@"auto releasing pool");
  }
return (0);
} // main
```

To start, we create the autorelease pool:

```
NSAutoreleasePool *pool;
pool = [[NSAutoreleasePool alloc] init];
```

Now, any time we send the autorelease message to an object, it jumps into this pool:

```
RetainTracker *tracker;
tracker = [RetainTracker new]; // count: 1
```

Here, a new tracker is created. Because it's being made with a new message, it has a retain count of 1:

```
[tracker retain]; // count: 2
```

Next, it gets retained, just for fun and demonstration purposes. The object's retain count goes to 2:

```
[tracker autorelease]; // count: still 2
```

Then the object gets autoreleased. Its retain count is unchanged: it's still 2. The important thing to note is that the pool that was created earlier now has a reference to this object. When pool goes away, the tracker object will be sent a release message.

```
[tracker release]; // count: 1
```

Next, we release it to counteract the retain call that we used earlier. The object's retain count is still greater than 0, so it's still alive:

```
NSLog (@"releasing pool");
[pool release];
// gets nuked, sends release to tracker
```

Now, we release the pool. An NSAutoreleasePool is an ordinary object, subject to the same rules of memory management as any other. Because we made the pool with an alloc, it has a retain count of 1. The release decreases its retain count to 0, so the pool is destroyed and its dealloc method called.

Finally, `main` returns 0 to indicate that everything was successful:

```
return (0);
} // main
```

Can you guess what the output is going to look like? Which will come first, the `NSLog()` before we release the pool or the `NSLog` from `RetainTracker`'s `dealloc` method?

The `@autoreleasepool` method does the same thing but without the hassle of allocating an object and destroying.

Here's the output from a run of RetainCount2:

```
init: Retain count of 1.
releasing pool
dealloc called. Bye Bye.
init: Retain count of 1.
auto releasing pool
dealloc called. Bye Bye.
```

As you probably guessed, the `NSLog()` before releasing the pool happens prior to the `NSLog()` from `RetainTracker`.

The Rules of Cocoa Memory Management

Now you've seen it all: `retain`, `release`, and `autorelease`. Cocoa has a number of memory management conventions. They're pretty simple rules, and they're applied consistently throughout the toolkit.

> **Note** Forgetting Cocoa's memory management rules is a common mistake, as is trying to make them too complicated. If you find yourself scattering `retains` and `releases` around aimlessly, hoping to fix some bug, you're probably not clear on the rules. That means it's time to slow down, take a deep breath, maybe go get a snack, and read them again.

Here are the rules:

- When you create an object using `new`, `alloc`, or `copy`, the object has a retain count of 1. You are responsible for sending the object a `release` or `autorelease` message when you're finished with it. That way, it gets cleaned up when its useful life is over.

- When you get hold of an object via any other mechanism, assume it has a retain count of 1 and that it has already been autoreleased. You don't need to do any further work to make sure it gets cleaned up. If you're going to hang on to the object for any length of time, retain it and make sure to release it when you're finished.

- If you retain an object, you need to (eventually) release or autorelease it. Balance these `retains` and `releases`.

That's it—just three rules.

You'll be safe if you remember the mantra, "If I get it from new, alloc, or copy, I have to release or autorelease it."

Whenever you get hold of an object, you must be aware of two things: how you got it and how long you plan on hanging on to it (see Table 9-1).

In the next sections we'll discuss the particulars of transient use of objects versus longer-term use.

Table 9-1. Memory Management Rules

Obtained Via...	Transient Use	Hang On (Longer Use)
new, alloc, or copy	Release when finished	Release in dealloc
Any other way	Don't need to do anything	Retain when acquired, release in dealloc

Transient Objects

Let's take a look at some common memory-management life cycle scenarios. In the first, you're using an object, temporarily, in the course of some code, but you're not going to be keeping it around for very long. If you get the object from new, alloc, or copy, you need to arrange its demise, usually with a release:

```
NSMutableArray *array;
array = [[NSMutableArray alloc] init]; // count: 1
// use the array
[array release]; // count: 0
```

If you get the object from any other mechanism, such as arrayWithCapacity:, you don't have to worry about destroying it:

```
NSMutableArray *array;
array = [NSMutableArray arrayWithCapacity: 17];
// count: 1, autoreleased
// use the array
```

arrayWithCapacity: is not alloc, new, or copy, so you can assume that the object being returned has a retain count of 1 and has already been autoreleased. When the autorelease pool goes away, array is sent the release message; its retain count goes to 0, and its memory is recycled.

Here's some code that uses an NSColor:

```
NSColor *color;
color = [NSColor blueColor];
// use the color
```

blueColor is not alloc, new, or copy, so you can assume it has a retain count of 1 and is autoreleased. blueColor returns a global **singleton** object—a single object that's shared by every program that needs it—and won't actually ever get destroyed, but you don't need to worry about those implementation details. All you need to know is that you do *not* need to explicitly release color.

Hanging on to Objects

Frequently, you'll want to keep an object around for more than a couple of lines of code. Typically, you'll put these objects into instance variables of other objects, add them to a collection like NSArray or NSDictionary, or more rarely, keep them as global variables.

If you're getting an object from init, new, or copy, you don't need to do anything special. The object's retain count will be 1, so it will stick around. Just be sure to release the object in the dealloc method of the owner-object that's hanging on to it:

```
- (void) doStuff
{
  // flonkArray is an instance variable
  flonkArray = [NSMutableArray new]; // count: 1
} // doStuff

- (void) dealloc
{
  [flonkArray release]; // count: 0
  [super dealloc];
} // dealloc
```

If you get an object from something other than init, new, or copy, you need to remember to retain it. When you're writing a GUI application, think in event loops. You want to retain autoreleased objects that will survive for longer than the current event loop.

What's an event loop? A typical graphical user interface (GUI) application spends a lot of time waiting on the user to do something. The program sits twiddling its thumbs until the very slow human at the controls decides to click the mouse or tap the screen. When one of these events happens, the program wakes up and gets to work doing whatever is necessary to respond to the event. After the event is handled, the application goes back to sleep waiting for the next event. To keep your program's memory footprint low, Cocoa creates an autorelease pool before it starts handling the event and destroys the pool after the event is handled. This keeps the amount of accumulated temporary objects to a minimum.

The previous methods would be written as follows when using autoreleased objects:

```
- (void) doStuff
{
  // flonkArray is an instance variable
  flonkArray = [NSMutableArray arrayWithCapacity: 17];
  // count: 1, autoreleased
  [flonkArray retain]; // count: 2, 1 autorelease
} // doStuff
- (void) dealloc
{
  [flonkArray release]; // count: 0
  [super dealloc];
} // dealloc
```

At the end of the current event loop (if it's a GUI program) or when the autorelease pool gets destroyed, flonkArray is sent a release message, which lowers its retain count from 2 to 1. Because the count is greater than 0, the object lives on. We still need to release the object in our dealloc so that it gets cleaned up. If we didn't have retain in doStuff, flonkArray would get destroyed unexpectedly.

Remember that the autorelease pool is purged at well-defined times: when it's explicitly destroyed in your own code or at the end of the event loop when using the AppKit. You don't have to worry about a demon that goes around destroying autorelease pools at random. You also don't have to retain each and every object you use, because the pool won't go away in the middle of a function.

Keeping The Pool Clean   Sometimes autorelease pools don't get cleaned out as often as you would like. Here's a common question that comes up on Cocoa mailing lists: "I'm autoreleasing all the objects I use, but my program's memory is growing to absolutely huge levels." That problem is usually caused by something like this:

```
int i;
for (i = 0; i < 1000000; i++) {
 id object = [someArray objectAtIndex: i];
 NSString *desc = [object description];
 // and do something with the description
}
```

This program is running a loop that generates an autoreleased object (or two or ten) every time through a whole bunch of iterations. Remember that the autorelease pool is only purged at well-defined times, and the middle of this loop is not one of those times. Inside this loop, a million description strings are being created, and all of them are put into the current autorelease pool, so we have a million strings sitting around. Once the pool gets destroyed, the million strings will finally go away, but it won't happen before then.

The way to work around this is to create your own autorelease pool inside the loop. This way, every thousand times through the loop, you can nuke the pool and make a new one (as follows, with added code in bold):

```
NSAutoreleasePool *pool;
pool = [[NSAutoreleasePool alloc] init];
int i;
for (i = 0; i < 1000000; i++) {
 id object = [someArray objectAtIndex: i];
 NSString *desc = [object descrption];
 // and do something with the description
 if (i % 1000 == 0) {
 [pool release];
 pool = [[NSAutoreleasePool alloc] init];
 }
}
[pool release];
```

Every thousand times through the loop, the new pool is destroyed and a newer one is created. Now, no more than a thousand description strings will be in existence at one time, and the program can breathe easier. Autorelease pool allocation and destruction are pretty cheap operations, so you could even make a new pool in every iteration of the loop.

Autorelease pools are kept as a stack: if you make a new autorelease pool, it gets added to the top of the stack. An `autorelease` message puts the receiver into the topmost pool. If you put an object into a pool, and then make a new pool and destroy it, the autoreleased object will still be around, because the pool holding that object is still in existence.

The keyword method will not work here, because it has to be balanced using braces.

Take Out Those Papers and the Trash

Objective-C 2.0 introduced automatic memory management, also called garbage collection. Programmers used to languages like Java or Python are well acquainted with the concept of garbage collection. You just create and use objects and then, shockingly, forget about them. The system automatically figures out what's still being used and what can be recycled. Turning on garbage collection is very easy, but it's an opt-in feature. Just go to the Build Settings of the project information window, and choose *Required [-fobjc-gc-only]*, as shown in Figure 9-1.

Figure 9-1. *Enabling garbage collection*

Note   `-fobjc-gc` is for code that supports both garbage collection and `retain/release`, such as library code that can be used in both environments.

When you enable garbage collection, the usual memory management calls all turn into no-op instructions; that's a fancy way of saying they don't do anything.

The Objective-C garbage collector is a generational garbage collector. Newly created objects are much more likely to turn into garbage than objects that have been hanging around for a while. At regular times, the garbage collector starts looking at your variables and objects and follows the pointers between them. Any object it discovers without anything pointing to it is garbage, which is fit to be thrown away. The worst thing you can do is keep a pointer to an object that you're finished with. So if you point to an object in an instance variable (recall composition), be sure to assign `nil` to your instance variable, which removes your reference to this object and lets the garbage collector know it can be purged.

Like the autorelease pool, garbage collection is triggered at the end of an event loop. You can also trigger garbage collection yourself if you're not in a GUI program, but that's beyond the scope of what we want to talk about here.

With garbage collection, you don't need to worry too much about memory management. There are some subtle nuances when using memory received from the `malloc` function or with Core Foundation objects, but they're obscure enough that we won't be covering them. For now, you can just create objects and not worry about releasing them. We'll be discussing garbage collection as we go along.

Note that garbage collection is only for OS X programming; you can't use it for iOS apps. In fact, in iOS programming, Apple recommends you avoid using `autorelease` in your own code and that you also avoid convenience methods that give you autoreleased objects.

Typically, convenience methods are class methods that return a new object. For example, for `NSString`, all the methods that start with `stringWith` are convenience methods.

Automatic Reference Counting

What's the deal with no garbage collection in iOS? The main argument against garbage collection in iOS is that you don't know exactly when the garbage collector is going to show up. Just like in real life, you might know that your garbage will be picked up on Monday, but you're never sure of the exact time. What if you're trying to leave your house right when the garbage truck shows up? Garbage collection can have a big impact on the usability of a mobile device, which is more personal than a computer and typically has far more modest resources than a computer. Users don't want to have a game or phone call pause while the system cleans up memory.

Apple's solution is called **automatic reference counting (ARC)**. As the name suggests, ARC keeps track of your objects and decides which ones you meant to keep and which ones you didn't. It's a little like having a butler or personal assistant in your memory management. When you use ARC, you allocate and use objects as you would normally, and the compiler inserts the `retains` and `releases` for you – you don't put them in yourself.

ARC is *not* a garbage collector. As we've already discussed, garbage collection does its work at runtime, via code that runs and checks your objects periodically. In contrast, ARC does its thing at compile time. It inserts the proper retains and releases, so memory management happens as it would in well-written manually managed code. But instead of you having to do the memory management, the compiler does it for you. When the program runs, retains and releases happen as they should. The system doesn't know or care whether these commands were inserted by you or by the compiler.

ARC is an opt-in feature, which means you must explicitly enable or disable it.

Here are the pieces you need for writing ARC code:

- Xcode 4.2+
- Apple LLVM 3.0+ compiler (which comes with Xcode)
- OS X 10.7+

And here's what you need to run your code:

- iOS 4.0+ or OS X 10.6+ with 64-bit runtime
- Zeroing weak references (more on this later) requires iOS 5.0+ or OS X 10.7+

Note   ARC only works with retainable object pointers (ROPs). There are three kinds of retainable object pointers:

1) Block pointers

2) Objective-C object pointers

3) Typedefs marked with `__attribute__((NSObject))`

We'll talk a lot more about ROPs later in this chapter, especially while describing Xcode's ARC conversion tool.

All other pointer types, such as `char *` and CF objects such as `CFStringRef`, are not ARC compatible.

If you use pointers that aren't handled by ARC, you'll have to manage them yourself. That's OK, because ARC interoperates with manually managed memory.

If you want to use ARC in your code, you must meet three requirements:

- You must be able to reliably identify which objects are to be managed.
- You must be able to indicate how to manage an object.
- You must have a reliable way of passing ownership of an object.

Let's deal with these one at a time. The first requirement means that a root-level object of collections of objects must know how to manage its child objects. For example, let's say you have an array of strings created with `malloc`:

```
NSString **myString;
myString = malloc(10 * sizeof(NSString *));
```

This code creates a C array that points to ten strings. Because C arrays are not retainable, you can't use ARC on this structure.

This leads to the second requirement. This requirement usually means you must be able to increment and decrement the retain count on an object, which pretty much means anything that is derived from `NSObject` is cool. This category includes most of the objects you'll need to manage.

The third requirement states that when passing around an object, your program needs to be able to pass ownership of the object between the caller and the callee—more about that later.

With all of those restrictions, you might be asking yourself, do I really need to bother with using ARC? The answer is yes, absolutely! We guarantee it will save you aggravation and time in the long run.

Sometimes Weak Is Good

As we discussed earlier in this chapter, when you have a pointer to an object, you can either manage its memory (with `retain`/`release`) or just point to it without participating in its memory management. If you manage the memory of an object, you're said to have a **strong reference** to the object. If you are not managing its memory, you have (you guessed it) a weak reference. For example, when you use the `assign` attribute with a property, you're making a **weak reference**.

Why do we have weak references? Because they help us deal with retain cycles. We'll discuss that.

Let's say you have an object A that was created by some other object and has a retain count of 1 (Figure 9-2). Object A creates an object B as its child, and object B has a retain count of 1 (see Figure 9-3). Object B needs to have access to its parent; this turns out to be a very common pattern in Objective-C programs).

Figure 9-2. Object A has a retain count of 1

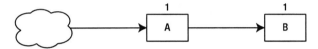

Figure 9-3. Object B, a child of object A, also has a retain count of 1

In this example, object A has a strong reference to Object B, because object A created object B. Now, if object B gets a strong reference to object A, the retain count on Object A increases to 2 (see Figure 9-4).

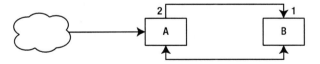

Figure 9-4. Object B has a strong reference to A, and Object A's retain count increases

All things must end, and eventually, the owner of object A no longer needs it. The owner calls `release` on Object A, which decrements its retain count to 1.

But object B, which was created by object A, owns that 1 retain count. Because both objects have nonzero retain counts, neither of them is released. This is a classic memory leak: the program has no access to the objects, but they're still using memory (see Figure 9-5).

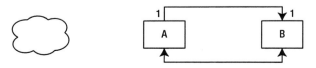

Figure 9-5. A classic memory leak

To solve this problem, we use a weak reference. We use `assign` to get object B's reference to object A. With the weak reference, the retain count doesn't increase. So when object A's owner releases it, its retain count goes to zero, it releases B, and both A and B relinquish their precious memory (see Figure 9-6). Perfect! Right?

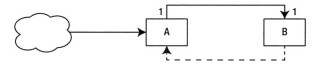

Figure 9-6. Object B has a weak reference to Object A

Better, but not quite perfect yet. When you have three objects involved (let's call them objects A, B, and C), you can end up with object A owning and having a strong reference to object B, while object C has a weak reference to object B (see Figure 9-7).

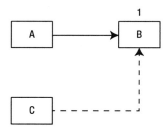

Figure 9-7. Two objects refer to B: one strongly, one weakly

If object A then releases object B, object C still has a weak reference to it, but that reference is no longer valid, and using it is likely to cause a crash, because there is no valid object at that location (see Figure 9-8).

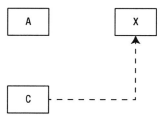

Figure 9-8. Object C still has a reference to a released object. This is bad

Here's the solution: objects that automagically clean up their weak references. These special weak references are called **zeroing weak references**, because when the object they point to is released, they are set to zero (`nil`) and can be handled like any other nil pointer (see Figure 9-9). Zeroing weak references are only available on iOS 5 or later and OS X 10.7 or later.

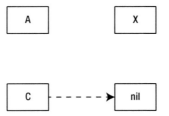

Figure 9-9. *Object C has a zeroing weak reference, which converts to nil when no longer valid*

To use zeroing weak references, you have to explicitly declare them. There are two ways to declare zeroing weak references: by using the __weak keyword when declaring a variable, or by using the weak attribute on properties:

```
__weak NSString *myString;
@property(weak) NSString *myString;
```

What do you do if you want to use ARC on older systems where zeroing weak references are not available? Apple provides the __unsafe_unretained keyword and unsafe_unretained attribute, both of which tell ARC that the specified reference is weak.

There are a couple of naming restrictions to watch out for when using ARC:

- You can't have a property whose name starts with "new." For example, @property NSString *newString is not allowed.

- You can't have a read-only only property without memory management attributes. Without ARC, you could use @property (readonly) NSString *title. But with ARC enabled, you must specify who manages memory, so a simple fix would be just to use unsafe_unretained, because of the default assign attribute.

Just to be orthogonal, there is also a __strong keyword and strong attribute. Keep in mind that memory management keywords and attributes are mutually exclusive.

OK! We're now ready to convert CarParts to use ARC. And when we're done, you'll notice that there is even less code than before. Our motto, and the motto of all programmers, is "less is more."

A New Convertible

Xcode provides a handy procedure to convert our existing projects to ARC. Before we start, we must make sure garbage collection is not turned on; garbage collection and ARC don't mix. If you try to convert a project without turning off garbage collection, you'll see a warning, as in Figure 9-10.

Let's walk through the process of turning off garbage collection for a target. The first step is selecting the target for which you want to disable garbage collection. Open your project (if it's not already open) and in the navigator, select the project. In the editor pane, you will see the project editor with your project at the top and targets below that (see Figure 9-11).

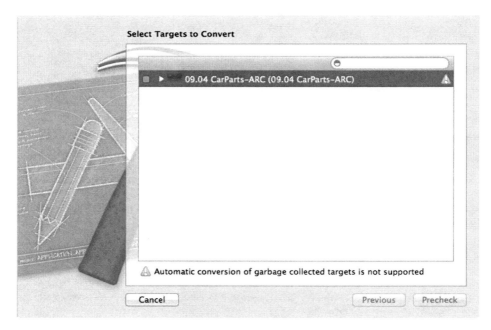

Figure 9-10. *You must turn off garbage collection before converting a project*

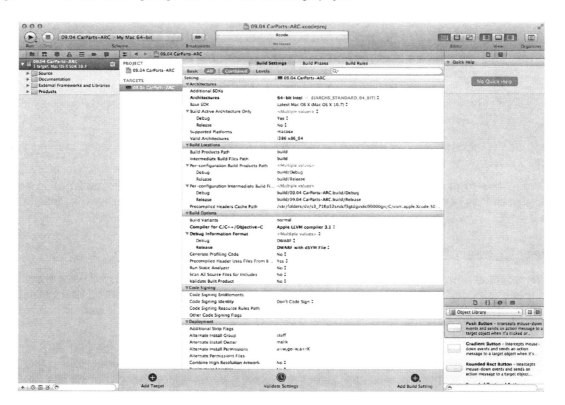

Figure 9-11. *Open your project in Xcode*

Now, select the target that should have garbage collection disabled. Then, click the Build Settings tab at the top in the editor pane. You will see that there are roughly one million settings for your target, which can be overwhelming. You can scan through the options to look for "Objective-C Garbage Collection," but there is a better way.

Apple knows it can be hard to find the setting your want, so if you look just below the build settings, you'll see a handy search field. Enter the text *garbage collection*. The search field narrows your choices to settings that relate to garbage collection. That's a lot better! Now, you have two items to look at.

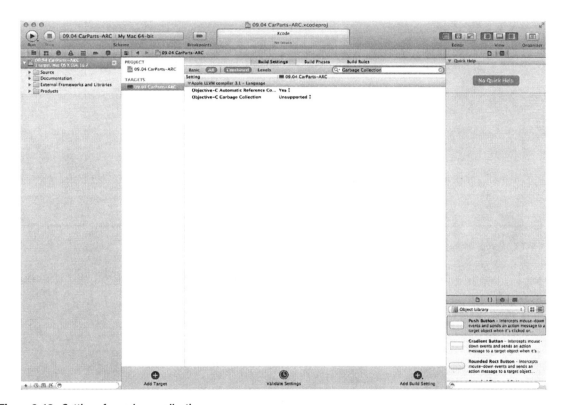

Figure 9-12. *Settings for garbage collection*

When you look at the "Objective-C Garbage Collection" item, a pop-up option menu gives you three choices:

- *Unsupported*: You must select this option when your project uses ARC, or you don't want to enable garbage collection for some reason.

- *Supported*: Your application can use garbage collection.

- *Required*: Your application *must* use garbage collection.

Our choice is the first one: unsupported (see Figure 9-13). This turns off garbage collection.

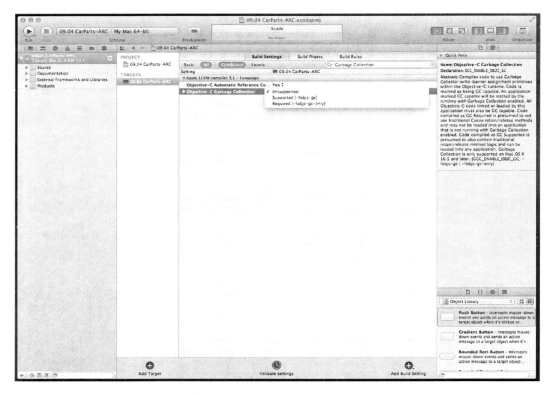

Figure 9-13. Select unsupported to turn off garbage collection

The conversion is a two-step process. First, you must make sure your code complies with the ARC requirements, and then, you perform the actual conversion.

> **Note** ARC conversion is a one-way trip. Once you go ARC, you can't go back.

To start the process, select the target you want to convert, then choose Edit ➤ Refactor ➤ Convert to Objective-C ARC (see Figure 9-14).

Because ARC works at the file level, you can mix ARC and non-ARC files in the same target.

Next, you'll see a list of targets to convert (see Figure 9-15). If your target depends on other targets, you can choose to do this process in baby steps. For instance, you can start with frameworks and libraries, and once you're finished with those, you can move on to targets that use them.

When you select a target to convert, by default, you select all the implementation files. If you have some files that are shared among different projects and you don't want to convert those, you can select just the ones you want. When you're finished selecting files, click Precheck. After the precheck process finishes, you can proceed to the next step: actual conversion (at last), as shown in Figure 9-16.

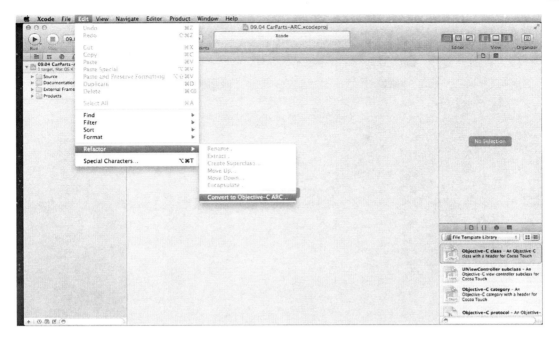

Figure 9-14. *Use the Edit menu to choose the ARC conversion item*

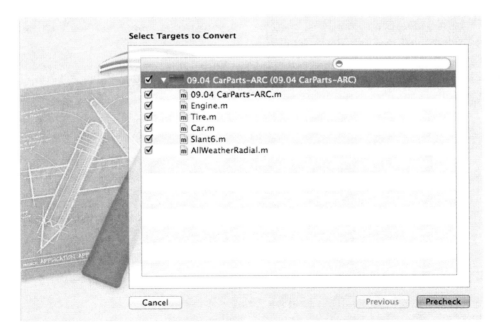

Figure 9-15. *Pick the files you want to convert*

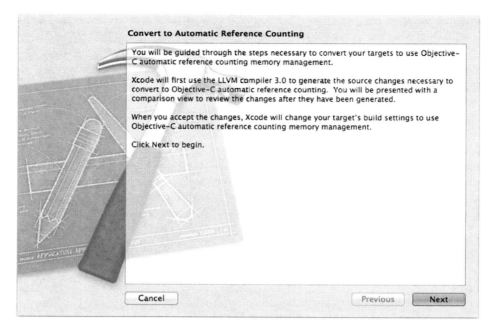

Figure 9-16. *ARC conversion introductory screen*

After you read the helpful introductory message and click *Next*, the conversion step processes your project and converts it to use ARC. In this step, Xcode finds each file that is to be compiled with ARC and modifies your source code as needed.

Once the process is finished, Xcode shows you a source compare view where you can see each file before and after conversion so you can decide if you like the changes.

We're getting closer, but the project is not fully converted yet. These changes have been made to copies of your files, to give you a chance to change your mind and back out of the process (did we mention it's not reversible?). To complete the conversion, you'll have a chance to save a copy of your "before" files, and then you're finished.

This was pretty easy, but we have to point out that this is the best-case scenario, where everything goes perfectly and automatically. But real life is not always that simple. The converter only works with source; it doesn't look at comments, and the current version is unable to read your mind to determine your intent. If the converter finds any ambiguity, it will be flagged, and you'll have to fix the issue before the conversion can proceed.

Ownership Has Its Privileges

One of the requirements we discussed earlier is that pointers in ARC code must be retainable object pointers (ROPs). This means, for example, that you can't simply assign an ROP to a non-ROP, because that transfers ownership of the pointer. Consider the following code:

```
NSString *theString = @"Learn Objective-C";
CFStringRef cfString = (CFStringRef)theString;
```

If you've looked at much Objective-C code, you've probably seen this pattern. What is it doing? One pointer, theString, is an ROP, while the other, CFStringRef, is not. For a happy ARC experience, we need to tell the compiler who owns the pointer. To do this, we can use a C technique called a **bridged cast**. This is a standard C type cast, but with extra keywords: __bridge, __bridge_retained, or __bridge_transfer. The term "bridge" refers to the ability to use different data types for the same purpose, and not to the thing you feel like jumping off of when you're stuck in a really tricky ARC conversion. Here's a description of each of the three types of bridged casts:

- (__bridge Type) *operand*: This type of cast transfers a pointer but does not transfer its ownership. In our example above, the operand is theString, and Type is CFStringRef. When using this keyword, one pointer is a ROP, and the other is not. With this cast, ownership of the pointer stays with the operand. Here's how our example would look with this case:

  ```
  cfString = (__bridge CFStringRef)theString;
  cfString gets the assignment, but ownership stays with theString.
  ```

- (__bridge_retained Type) *operand*: In this type, ownership is transferred to the non-ROP. One pointer is an ROP, and the other is not. Because ARC only takes care of ROP, you are responsible for releasing this object when you're done with it. This cast increments the object's retain count, so you have to decrement it, just as with standard old-fashioned memory management. Here's how our example would look:

  ```
  cfString = (__bridge_retained CFStringRef)theString
  ```

  In this case, cfString string owns the pointer and its retain count is incremented. You're responsible for managing it with retain/release.

- (__bridge_transfer Type) *operand*: This cast does the opposite of the previous kind; it transfers ownership to the ROP. In this case, ARC owns the object and will ensure it's released like any other ARC object.

Another restriction is that structs and unions can't have ROPs as members, so code like this is not allowed:

```
// Bad code. Do not steal or sell.
struct {
  int32_t foo;
  char *bar;
  NSString *baz;
} MyStruct;
```

You can get around this requirement by using a void * and a bridged cast. To assign and get the string back, our code would look like this:

```
struct {
  int32_t foo;
  char *bar;
  void *baz;
} MyStruct;
MyStruct.baz = (__bridge_retained void *)theString;
NSString *myString = (__bridge_transfer NSString *)MyStruct.baz;
```

As you can see, at the edges, ARC code is not always so automatic to write. It's a pretty deep topic that deserves plenty of study. To complete this conversation about ARC, we'll list memory management methods that you shouldn't call on ARC-managed objects:

- retain
- retainCount
- release
- autorelease
- dealloc

Because you sometimes need to free non-ARC objects or perform other cleanup, you can still write dealloc methods, but you can't call [super dealloc].

There are also methods you're not permitted to override on ARC objects:

- retain
- retainCount
- release
- autorelease

Being Exceptional

What is an exception? It's an unexpected event, such as an array out of bounds, that disrupts program flow because the program really doesn't know what to do about it.

When this happens, the program can create an exception object and hand it to the runtime system, which then figures out what to do next. Exceptions in Cocoa are represented by the NSException class. Cocoa requires that all exceptions must be of type NSException, so even though you can throw an exception from other objects, Cocoa isn't set up to deal with those. Instead, you should subclass NSException to create your own exceptions.

> **Note**   Exception handling is really intended for errors that are generated by your programs. Cocoa frameworks usually handle errors by exiting the program, which is not what you want. You should throw and catch exceptions in your code, instead of letting them escape to the framework level.

To enable support for exceptions, make sure the -fobj-exceptions flag is turned on. You can enable this with the *Enable Objective-C Exceptions* build option in Xcode (Figure 9-17).

The act of creating an exception and handing it to the runtime system is known as **throwing** an exception, or sometimes **raising** an exception. Notice that NSException has a few methods that start with raise. Some of these are class methods, and raise itself is an instance method.

Catching an exception is the act of handling an exception that has been thrown.

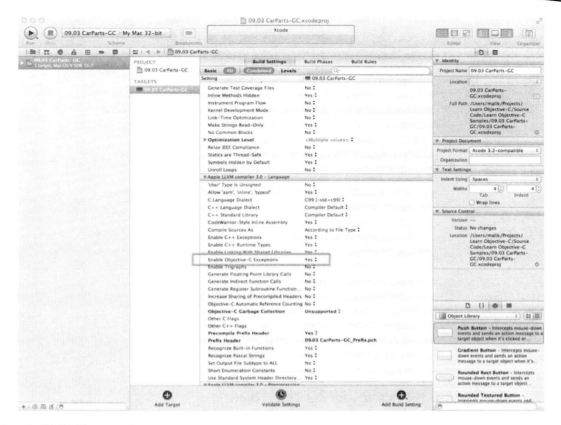

Figure 9-17. *Enabling exceptions*

> **Note**   When an exception is thrown and is not caught, the program stops at the exception point and propagates the exception.

Keywords for Exceptions

All the keywords for exceptions start with @. Here's what each one does:

- @try: Defines a block of code that will be tested to determine if an exception should be thrown.

- @catch(): Defines a block of code for handling a thrown exception. Takes an argument, typically of type NSException, but can be of other types.

- @finally: Defines a block of code that gets executed whether an exception is thrown or not. This code will always be executed.

- @throw: Throws an exception.

> **Note**   Earlier, we mentioned that you can throw exceptions from objects other than NSException instances, but that you should avoid doing so. The reason is that not every Cocoa framework catches exceptions thrown by objects other than NSException. To ensure that Cocoa works right with your exceptions, you should throw NSException objects only. Think of it like the old saying that you don't have to floss all your teeth, just the ones you want to keep.

You'll typically use @try, @catch, and @finally together in one structure. It goes a little something like this:

```
@try
{
    // code you want to execute that might throw an exception.
}
@catch (NSException *exception)
{
    // code to execute that handles exception
}
@finally
{
    // code that will always be executed. Typically for cleanup.
}
```

Catching Different Types of Exceptions

You can have multiple @catch blocks depending on which type of exception you want to handle. Your handlers should go in order from most to least specific, with a general handler after all the others. Here's an example:

```
@try{
} @catch (MyCustomException *custom) {
} @catch (NSException *exception) {
} @catch (id value) {
} @finally {
}
```

> **Note**   C programmers often use setjmp and longjmp in exception handling code. You can't use setjmp and longjmp within a @try block if the jump goes outside the @try braces. However, you can use goto and return to exit exception-handling code.

Throwing Exceptions

When the program detects an exception, it must propagate the exception to a block of code that handles it, cleverly called an exception handler. As we noted earlier, the process of propagating an exception is called throwing, or raising, an exception.

A program throws an exception by creating an instance of NSException and using one of two techniques:

- Using @throw exception;

- Sending a raise message to an NSException object

For example, we'll create an exception:

```
NSException *theException = [NSException exceptionWithName: …];
```

We can then throw with either

```
@throw theException;
```

or

```
[theException raise];
```

Use one technique or the other, but not both. The difference between the techniques is that raise can only be used with NSException objects, while @throw works with other objects as well.

You'll usually throw exceptions from inside the exception handling code. Your code can propagate the exception by sending another raise message or @throw keyword.

```
@try
{
  NSException *e = …;
  @throw e;
}
@catch (NSException *e) {
    @throw; // rethrows e.
}
```

> **Note**   In a @catch exception handling block, you can rethrow the exception without specifying the exception object.

The @finally block that is associated with a local @catch exception handler is executed before @throw causes the next higher exception handler to be called, because @finally is called before the @throw happens.

Objective-C exceptions are compatible with the C++ exception system.

> **Note**   Exceptions in Objective-C are resource intensive. You should not use exceptions for general flow control or simply to signify errors. Setting up an exception with @try has zero cost, but catching an exception has a substantial cost in program resources and speed.

Exceptions Need Memory Management Too

Memory management can be tricky when exceptions are involved. Let's take a look at this simple code:

```
- (void)mySimpleMethod
{
    NSDictionary *dictionary = [[NSDictionary alloc] initWith….];
    [self processDictionary:dictionary];
    [dictionary release];
}
```

Now let's imagine that processDictionary throws an exception. The program jumps out of this method and looks for an exception handler. But because the method exits at this point, the dictionary object is not released, and we have a memory leak.

One simple way to handle this is to use @try and @finally, doing some cleanup in @finally because it's always executed (as we said earlier).

```
- (void)mySimpleMethod
{
    NSDictionary *dictionary = [[NSDictionary alloc] initWith….];
    @try {
     [self processDictionary:dictionary];
    }
    @finally {
    [dictionary release];
    }
}
```

This pattern can be used with C-style memory management as well, such as malloc and free.

Exceptions and Autorelease Pools

Exception handling can sometimes suffer from a subtle problem of automatically releasing an exception object. Exceptions are almost always created as autoreleased objects because you don't know when they will need to be released. When the autorelease pool is destroyed, all objects in that pool are destroyed also, including the exception. Consider the following code, which sure looks innocent enough:

```
  - (void)myMethod
{
  NSAutoreleasePool *pool = [[NSAutoreleasePool alloc] init];
  NSDictionary *myDictionary =
    [[NSDictionary alloc] initWithObjectsAndKeys:@"asdfads", nil];
  @try {
    [self processDictionary:myDictionary];
  } @catch (NSException *e) {
    @throw;
  } @finally {
    [pool release];
  }
}
```

This looks like fine code: we create objects, and we release them, because we are good citizens. But wait! There's a problem when we think about exception handling. We discussed earlier that we can rethrow exceptions in the @catch block, which causes the @finally block to execute before the exception is rethrown. This will cause the local pool to be released before the exception can be delivered, thus turning it into a dreaded **zombie exception**. Luckily, we have a simple fix for this: we simply retain it outside our pool.

Our new method looks like this:

```
- (void)myMethod
{
  id savedException = nil;
  NSAutoreleasePool *pool = [[NSAutoreleasePool alloc] init];
  NSDictionary *myDictionary =
    [[NSDictionary alloc] initWithObjectsAndKeys:@"asdfads", nil];
  @try {
       [self processDictionary:myDictionary];
  } @catch (NSException *e) {
      savedException = [e retain];
      @throw;
  } @finally {
      [pool release];
      [savedException autorelease];
  }
}
```

By using retain, we saved the exception in the parent pool. When our pool is released, we already have a pointer saved, and when the parent pool is released, the exception will be released with it.

Summary

In this chapter, you learned about Cocoa's memory management methods: retain, release, and autorelease. We also discussed garbage collection and spent time delving into automatic reference counting (ARC), Apple's latest technique for memory management.

Each object maintains a retain count. Objects start their lives with a retain count of 1. When an object is retained, its retain count increases by 1, and when it's released, its retain count is decreased by 1. When the retain count reaches 0, the object is destroyed. The object's dealloc message is called first, and then its memory is recycled, ready for use by other objects.

When an object receives the autorelease message, its retain count doesn't change immediately; instead, the object is placed into an NSAutoreleasePool. When this pool is destroyed, all the objects in the pool are sent a release message. Any objects that have been autoreleased will then have their retain counts decremented by 1. If the count goes to 0, the object is destroyed. When you use the AppKit or UIKit, an autorelease pool is created and destroyed for you at well-defined times, such as when the current user event has been handled. Otherwise, you are responsible for creating your own autorelease pool. The template for Foundation tools includes code for this.

Cocoa has three rules about objects and their retain counts:

* If you get the object from a `new`, `alloc`, or `copy` operation, the object has a retain count of 1.

* If you get the object any other way, assume it has a retain count of 1 and that it has been autoreleased.

* If you retain an object, you must balance every `retain` with a `release`.

In general, ARC handles `retain` and `release` for you by inserting those calls at compile time.

Coming up next, we'll talk about `init` methods: how to make your objects hit the ground running.

Chapter 10

Object Initialization

So far, we've created new objects in two different ways. The first way is [SomeClass new], and the second is [[SomeClass alloc] init]. These two techniques are equivalent, but the common Cocoa convention is to use alloc and init rather than new. Typically, Cocoa programmers use new as training wheels until they have enough background to be comfortable with alloc and init. It's time for your training wheels to come off.

Allocating Objects

Allocation is the process by which a new object is born. It's the happy time when a chunk of memory is obtained from the operating system and designated as the location that will hold the object's instance variables. Sending the alloc message to a class causes that class to allocate a chunk of memory large enough to hold all its instance variables. alloc also conveniently initializes all the memory to 0. That way, you don't have the problem of uninitialized memory causing all sorts of random bugs that afflicts many languages. All your BOOLs start out as NO; all your ints are 0; all your floats become 0.0; all your pointers are nil; and all your base are belong to us (sorry, couldn't resist).

A newly allocated object isn't ready to be used right away: you need to initialize it before you can work with it. Some languages, including C++ and Java, perform object allocation and initialization in a single operation using a constructor. Objective-C splits the two operations into explicit allocation and initialization stages. A common beginner's error is to use only the alloc operation, like this:

```
Car *car = [Car alloc];
```

This might work, but without the initialization, you can get some strange behavior (also known as "bugs") later on. The rest of this chapter is all about the vital concept of initialization.

Initializing Objects

The counterpart to allocation is initialization. **Initialization** takes a chunk of memory and gets it ready to become a productive member of society. init methods—that is, methods that do initialization—almost always return the object they're initializing. You can (and should) chain your allocs and initializations like this:

```
Car *car = [[Car alloc] init];
```

and not like this:

```
Car *car = [Car alloc]; [car init];
```

This chaining technique is important because an initialization method might return an object that's not the same as the one that was allocated. If you think that's pretty odd, you're right. But it can happen.

Why might a programmer want an init method to return a different object? If you recall the discussion on class clusters at the end of Chapter 8, you saw that classes like NSString and NSArray are really just false fronts for a whole lot of specialized classes. An init method can take arguments, so the method code gets a chance to look at the arguments and decide that another class of object would be more appropriate. For example, let's say a new string is being made from a very long string, or maybe from a string of Arabic characters. Based on this knowledge, the string initializer might decide to create an object of a different class, one better suited to the needs of the desired string, and return that instead of the original object.

Writing Initialization Methods

Earlier, we asked you to endure some nod-and-smile moments when we presented initialization methods, mainly because they looked a little weird. Here's the init method from an earlier version of CarParts:

```
(id) init
{
 if (self = [super init])
 {
   engine = [Engine new];
   tires[0] = [Tire new];
   tires[1] = [Tire new];
   tires[2] = [Tire new];
   tires[3] = [Tire new];
 }
  return (self);
} // init
```

The main weirdness hits you on the very first line:

```
if (self = [super init]) {
```

This code implies that self might change. Change self in the middle of a method? Are we crazy? Well, maybe, but not this time. The first bit of code that runs in that statement is [super init]. That code lets the superclass do its initialization work. For classes that inherit from NSObject, calling on the superclass lets NSObject do any processing it needs to do so that objects can respond to messages and deal with retain counts. For classes that inherit from another class, this is their chance to do their own version of clean-slate initialization.

We just said that init methods like this one can return totally different objects. Remember that instance variables are found at a memory location that's a fixed distance from the hidden self parameter. If a new object is returned from an init method, we need to update self so that any subsequent instance variable references affect the right places in memory. That's why we need the self = [super init] assignment. Keep in mind that this assignment affects the value of self only for this method. It doesn't change anything outside the method's scope.

An init method can return nil if there's a problem initializing an object. For example, you might be using an init method that takes a URL and initializes an image object using an image file from a web site. If the network is down, or a redesign of the web site has moved the picture, you won't get a useful image object. The init method would then return nil, indicating the object couldn't be initialized. The test if (self = [super init]) won't run the body code if nil is returned from [super init]. Combining the assignment with a check for a nonzero value like this is a classic C idiom that lives on in Objective- C.

The code to get the object up and running is in the braces of the if statement's body. In the original Car init method, the body of the if statement creates an engine and four tires. From a memory management perspective, this code does the right thing, because objects returned via new start out with their reference counts set to 1.

Finally, the last line of the method is return (self);.

An init method returns the object that was just initialized. Since we assigned the return value of [super init] to self, that's what we should return.

Init to Win it   Some programmers don't like the combined assignment and test for a nonzero value. Instead, they write their init methods like this:

```
self = [super init];
if (nil != self)
{
}
return (self);
```

And that's fine. The key is that you assign back to self, especially if you're accessing any instance variables. No matter which way you do it, be aware that combining the assignment and test is a common technique, and you'll see it a lot in other people's code.

The self = [super init] style is the source of some controversy. One faction says you should always do this, just in case the superclass changes something in the initialization. The other camp says that this object changing is so rare and obscure that you need not bother—just use a plain [super init]. Those in this camp point out that if even if the init changes the object, that new object probably doesn't take any new instance variables you have added.

This problem is truly thorny in the abstract, but in the real world, it doesn't happen very often. We recommend always using the if (self = [super init]) technique just to be safe and to catch the "init returning nil" behavior of some init methods. But if you choose to use a plain [super init], that's fine too. Just be prepared to do a little debugging if you happen to catch one of the obscure corner cases.

What to Do When You're Initializing

What should you put in your init methods? This is the place to do your clean-slate initialization work. You assign values to instance variables and create the other objects that your object needs to do its work. When you write your init methods, you must decide how much work you want to do there. The CarParts programs showed two different approaches over the course of its evolution.

The first way used the init method to create the engine and all four tires. This made the Car immediately useful out of the box: call alloc and init, and take the car out for a test drive. We changed the next version to create nothing at all in the init method. We just left empty spaces for the engine and tires. The code that created the object would then have to create an engine and tires and set them using accessor methods.

Which way is right for you? The decision comes down to flexibility over performance, as do many tradeoffs in programming. The original Car init method is very convenient. If the intended use of the Car class is to create a basic car and then use it, that's the right design.

On the other hand, if the car will often be customized with different kinds of tires and engines, as in a racing game, we'll be creating the engine and tires just to have them thrown away. Such a waste! Objects would be created and then destroyed without ever being used.

Note Even if you don't provide calls to customize your object's attributes, you can still wait to create them until a caller asks for them. This is a technique known as **lazy evaluation**, and it can give you a performance boost if you're creating complex objects in your -init that might not actually be used.

Isn't That Convenient?

Some objects have more than one method that starts with the word init. In fact, it's important to remember that init methods are nothing special. They're just ordinary methods that follow a naming convention.

Many classes have **convenience initializers**. These are init methods that do some extra work, saving you the trouble of doing it yourself. To give you an idea of what we're talking about, here's a sampling of some of NSString's init methods:

```
- (id) init;
```

This basic method initializes a new, empty string. For immutable NSStrings, this method isn't terribly useful. But you can allocate and initialize a new NSMutableString and start throwing characters into it. You'd use it like this:

```
NSString *emptyString = [[NSString alloc] init];
```

That code gives you an empty string.

```
- (id) initWithFormat: (NSString *) format, …;
```

This version initializes a new string to the result of a formatting operation, just like we did with NSLog() and with the stringWithFormat: class method you saw in Chapter 7. Here's an example that gives the flavor of using this init method:

```
string = [[NSString alloc]
initWithFormat: @"%d or %d", 25, 624];
```

This gives you a string with the value of "25 or 624".

```
- (id) initWithContentsOfFile:(NSString *) path encoding:(NSStringEncoding) enc error:(NSError **) error
```

The initWithContentsOfFile:encoding:error: method opens the text file at the given path, reads everything there, and initializes a string with the contents. The following code reads the file /tmp/words.txt:

```
NSError *error = nil;
NSString *string =
[[NSString alloc] initWithContentsOfFile:@"/tmp/words.txt"
                encoding:NSUTF8StringEncoding
                    error:&error];
```

The encoding argument tells the API what type of contents are in the file. Typically, you'll want NSUTF8StringEncoding, indicating the file is encoded using the UTF8 format.

The third argument is returned nil if there is no error. If there is an error, you can find out what happened using the localizedDescription method. Putting everything together, we have

```
NSError *error = nil;
NSStringEncoding encoding = NSUTF8StringEncoding;
NSString *string = [[NSString alloc] initWithContentsOfFile:@"/tmp/words.txt"
                    usedEncoding:&encoding
                        error:&error];
if(nil != error)
{
  NSLog(@"Unable to read data from file, %@", [error localizedDescription]);
}
```

That's some pretty powerful stuff. This would take a whole bunch of code in C (you would have to open the file, read blocks of data, append to a string, make sure the trailing zero-byte is in the right place, and close the file). For us Objective-C devotees, it becomes a single line of code. Nice.

> **Note**   The general rule for different initializers is that if your object must have some information to initialize itself, you should provide that information as part of the init method. These are typically immutable objects.

More Parts Is Parts

Let's revisit CarParts, last seen in Chapter 6 when we broke out each class into its own source file. This time, we'll add some initialization goodness to the `Tire` class and clean up `Car`'s memory management along the way. For those of you following along at home, the project directory that has the finished program for this chapter is *10.01 CarPartsInit*.

> **Note**   As we discussed in detail in Chapter 9, Apple is moving from garbage collection in memory management to a newer technology called Automatic Reference Counting (ARC). For iOS development, you *must* use ARC; garbage collection isn't supported. We have an ARC version of this chapter's program in *10.01 CarPartsInit-ARC*. But because garbage collection is still around, we've also included a version that uses garbage collection as well. That one is named *10.01 CarPartsInit-GC*.

Init for Tires

Tires in the real world are more interesting creatures than the ones we've simulated in CarParts so far. In your real tires, you have to keep track of the tire pressure (don't want it to get too low) and the tread depth (once it goes below a couple of millimeters, the tires aren't safe anymore). Let's extend `Tire` to keep track of the pressure and tread depth. Here's the class declaration that adds two instance variables and the corresponding accessor methods:

```
#import <Cocoa/Cocoa.h>
@interface Tire : NSObject
 {
 float pressure;
 float treadDepth;
}
-(void) setPressure: (float) pressure;
-(float) pressure;
-(void) setTreadDepth: (float) treadDepth;
-(float) treadDepth;
@end // Tire
```

And here's the implementation of Tire, which is pretty straightforward:

```
#import "Tire.h"
@implementation Tire
- (id) init
{
 if (self = [super init])
 {
  pressure = 34.0; treadDepth = 20.0;
 }
 return (self);
} // init
- (void) setPressure: (float) p
{
  pressure = p;
```

```
} // setPressure
- (float) pressure
{
   return (pressure);
} // pressure
- (void) setTreadDepth: (float) td
{
   treadDepth = td;
} // setTreadDepth
- (float) treadDepth
{
 return (treadDepth);
} // treadDepth
- (NSString *) description
{
 NSString *desc;
   desc = [NSString stringWithFormat:
    @"Tire: Pressure: %.1f TreadDepth: %.1f", pressure, treadDepth];
   return (desc);
} // description
@end // Tire
```

The accessor methods provide a way for users of the tire to change the pressure and the tread depth. Let's take a quick look at the init method:

```
- (id) init
{
   if (self = [super init])
   {
    pressure = 34.0;
    treadDepth = 20.0;
   }
 return (self);
} // init
```

There should be no surprises here. The superclass (NSObject, in this case) is told to initialize itself, and the return value from that call is assigned to self. Then, the instance variables are assigned to useful default values. Let's make a brand new tire like this:

```
Tire *tire = [[Tire alloc] init];
```

The tire's pressure will be 34 psi, and its tread depth will be 20 mm. We should change the description method too:

```
- (NSString *) description
{
 NSString *desc;
 desc = [NSString stringWithFormat:
  @"Tire: Pressure: %.1f TreadDepth: %.1f", pressure, treadDepth];
 return (desc);
} // description
```

The description method now uses NSString's stringWithFormat: class method to make a string that includes the tire pressure and tread depth. Does this method follow our rules of good memory management behavior? Yes, it does. Because the object was not created by an alloc, copy, or new, it has a retain count of 1, and we can consider it to be autoreleased. So, this string will get cleaned up when the autorelease pool is destroyed.

Updating main()

Here is the main.m file, which is a hair more complicated than it was before:

```
#import "Engine.h"
#import "Car.h"
#import "Slant6.h"
#import "AllWeatherRadial.h"
int main (int argc, const char * argv[])
{
@autoreleasepool
{
 Car *car = [[Car alloc] init];
 for (int i = 0; i < 4; i++)
{
 Tire *tire;
 tire = [[Tire alloc] init];
 [tire setPressure: 23 + i]; [tire setTreadDepth: 33 - i];
 [car setTire: tire atIndex: i];
 [tire release];
}
 Engine *engine = [[Slant6 alloc] init];
 [car setEngine: engine];
 [car print];
 [car release];
}
 return (0);
} // main
```

Let's pull main() apart, piece by piece. We start by making an autorelease pool for autoreleased objects to swim around in while they await the pool's destruction:

```
@autoreleasepool {
```

Then, we create a new car using alloc and init:

```
Car *car = [[Car alloc] init];
```

After that, a loop spins around four times (from 0 to 3). This is where the new tires are made:

```
for (int i = 0; i < 4; i++) {
```

Each time through the loop, a new tire is created and initialized:

```
Tire *tire;
tire = [[Tire alloc] init];
```

Each tire starts out with its pressure and tread depth set in Tire's init method. But we're going to customize the values, just for fun. Because no two tires are identical in the real world, we're going to tweak the pressure and tread depths using the accessor methods:

```
[tire setPressure: 23 + i];
[tire setTreadDepth: 33 - i];
```

Next, we'll give the tire to the car:

```
[car setTire: tire atIndex: i];
```

Now that we're done with the tire, we release it:

```
[tire release];
```

This code assumes that Car is doing the right memory management thing, arranging to retain the object. Note that the Car as shown in Chapter 6 doesn't follow our memory management guidelines—we were so young and naive then—but we'll show you how to fix that in a little while.

After the tires are assembled, a new engine is created, just as before, and the engine is placed in the car:

```
Engine *engine = [[Slant6 alloc] init];
[car setEngine: engine];
[engine release];
```

As with the tires, the engine is released, because we're done using it. It's up to the Car to make sure the engine gets deallocated.

Finally, the Car is told to print itself out, and the Car is released because we're done with it:

```
[car print];
[car release];
```

Now the autorelease pool gets released, which causes its retain count to go to 0, deallocates the pool, and sends the release message to every object in the pool. When this happens, the NSStrings generated by the Tire description method get cleaned up, and then main ends, at last. But before we can run the program, we need to fix up the Car class so that it handles its memory management correctly. But first, here's what main would look like in a garbage-collected world:

```
int main (int argc, const char * argv[])
{
Car *car = [[Car alloc] init];
for (int i = 0; i < 4; i++)
{
 Tire *tire;
 tire = [[Tire alloc] init];
 [tire setPressure: 23 + i];
 [tire setTreadDepth: 33 - i];
 [car setTire: tire atIndex: i]; }
 Engine *engine = [[Slant6 alloc] init];
 [car setEngine: engine];
 [car print];
 return (0);
} // main
```

As you can see, it's a fair bit shorter and simpler without the extra memory management calls.

Cleaning Up the Car

Instead of using a regular C array in Car, let's use an NSMutableArray. Why? Because that will give us bounds checking for free. To do this, we'll change the @interface section of the Car class to use a mutable array (the changed line of code is in bold):

```
#import <Cocoa/Cocoa.h>
@class Tire;
@class Engine;

@interface Car : NSObject
{
NSMutableArray *tires;
Engine *engine;
}
- (void) setEngine: (Engine *) newEngine;
- (Engine *) engine;
- (void) setTire: (Tire *) tire
atIndex: (int) index;
- (Tire *) tireAtIndex: (int) index;
- (void) print;
@end // Car
```

We've upgraded pretty much every method of Car to follow the memory management rules. Let's start with init:

```
- (id) init
{
 if (self = [super init])
{
  tires = [[NSMutableArray alloc] init];
  for (int i = 0; i < 4; i++)
 {
   [tires addObject: [NSNull null]];
 }
}
 return (self);
} // init
```

You've seen self = [super init] a bajillion times already; you've practically memorized it. As you know by now, it just makes sure that the superclass gets the object up and running.

Next, we create an NSMutableArray. There's a handy NSMutableArray method called replaceOb jectAtIndex:withObject: that's perfect for implementing setTire:atIndex:. To use replaceOb jectAtIndex:withObject:, we need to have an object at the given index so it can be replaced. A fresh NSMutableArray doesn't have any contents, so we need some object as a placeholder. NSNull is great for that kind of thing. So, we put four NSNull objects (which you first saw in Chapter 8) into the array. In general, you don't have to prepack your NSMutableArrays with NSNulls, but in this case, doing so makes things a little easier later on.

At the end of init, we return self, because that's the object we just finished initializing.

Next come the accessor methods for the engine. These are setEngine: and engine. setEngine: uses the "retain the object passed in and release the current object" technique that we showed earlier:

```
- (void) setEngine: (Engine *) newEngine
{
 [newEngine retain];
 [engine release];
 engine = newEngine;
} // setEngine
```

And the engine accessor method simply returns the current engine:

```
- (Engine *) engine
{
 return (engine);
} // engine
```

Now let's do the tire accessors. First comes the setter:

```
- (void) setTire: (Tire *) tire
atIndex: (int) index
{
 [tires replaceObjectAtIndex: index withObject: tire];
} // setTire:atIndex:
```

This method uses replaceObjectAtIndex:withObject: to remove the existing object from the collection and replace it with the new object. We don't have to do any explicit memory management with the tire, because NSMutableArray will automatically retain the new tire and release the object that lives at the index, whether it's an NSNull placeholder or a previously stored tire object. NSMutableArray will release all of its objects when it gets destroyed, so the tire will get cleaned up.

The tireAtIndex: getter uses the objectAtIndex: method provided by NSArray to get the tire from the array:

```
- (Tire *) tireAtIndex: (int) index
{
 Tire *tire;
 tire = [tires objectAtIndex: index];
 return (tire);
} // tireAtIndex:
```

Rapid Return   It's perfectly legal to make the following method a one-liner by directly returning the result value of objectAtIndex:

```
(Tire *) tireAtIndex: (int) index
 {
 return ([tires objectAtIndex: index]);
 } // tireAtIndex:
```

The extra variable in the original makes the code a little easier to read (at least, to us) and setting a breakpoint easier, so we can see which object is being returned. This technique also makes it easier for the caveman debuggers to stick an NSLog() between the objectAtIndex: call and the end of the method when we return the tire object.

We still need to make sure the car cleans up after the objects it's hanging onto—specifically, the engine and the tires array. The dealloc method is the place to do this:

```
- (void) dealloc
{
  [tires release];
  [engine release];
  [super dealloc];
} // dealloc
```

That's enough to make sure all memory is reclaimed when this car gets sent to the junkyard. Be sure to call the superclass's dealloc method! Leaving that out is a common mistake. Also, make sure that [super dealloc] is the last statement in your dealloc method.

Finally, there's the print method for the car, which prints out the tires and the engine:

```
- (void) print
{
for (int i = 0; i < 4; i++)
{
  NSLog (@"%@", [self tireAtIndex: i]);
}
  NSLog (@"%@", engine);
} // print
```

The print method loops through the tires and logs each one. It's interesting that the loop uses the tireAtIndex: method rather than poking at the array itself. If you want to touch the array directly, you're welcome to do so. However, if you use the accessors, even in the implementation of a class, you'll insulate that code from any changes. For example, if the tire storage mechanism changes again in the future (say, back to a C-style array), you won't have to change the print method.

Now (finally!), we can run CarPartsInit. The results look like this:

```
Tire: Pressure: 23.0 TreadDepth: 33.0
Tire: Pressure: 24.0 TreadDepth: 32.0
Tire: Pressure: 25.0 TreadDepth: 31.0
Tire: Pressure: 26.0 TreadDepth: 30.0
I am a slant- 6. VROOOM!
```

Car Cleaning, GC and ARC Style

OK, so what about garbage collection? What does this class look like in that world? `setEngine` gets simpler.

```
- (void) setEngine: (Engine *) newEngine
{
 engine = newEngine;
} // setEngine
```

We change the `engine` instance variable. When Cocoa's garbage collection machinery runs, it realizes nobody else is pointing to the old engine, so the garbage collector makes that engine go away. On the other hand, because we have an instance variable pointing to the `newEngine`, it won't be collected; the garbage collector knows somebody is using it.

The `dealloc` method goes away completely: there is no use for `dealloc` in the garbage-collected world. If you need to do some work when an object goes away, you can override `-finalize`, which is called when the object is finally collected, but there are some subtleties associated with `finalize`. But for the kind of programming you'll be doing in Cocoa, you won't need to worry about `finalize`.

The ARC version is very similar to the GC version. The only thing we need to add is `@autoreleasepool` to tell the compiler we want it to handle the retain and release cycle.

Making a Convenience Initializer

No code is created perfect. You can always make improvements. Think back to the `main()` function and how we created the tires:

```
tire = [[Tire alloc] init];
[tire setPressure: 23 + i];
[tire setTreadDepth: 33 - i];
```

That's four message sends and three lines of code. Doing that in one operation would be nice. Let's make a convenience initializer that takes both the pressure and tread depth at the same time. Here's `Tire` with a convenience initializer added (in bold):

```
@interface Tire : NSObject
{
 float pressure;
 float treadDepth;
}
- (id) initWithPressure: (float) pressure
treadDepth: (float) treadDepth;
- (void) setPressure: (float) pressure;
- (float) pressure;
- (void) setTreadDepth: (float) treadDepth;
- (float) treadDepth;
@end // Tire
```

The implementation of that method is pretty plain, with no new surprises:

```
- (id) initWithPressure: (float) p treadDepth: (float) td
{
  if (self = [super init]) {
     pressure = p;
     treadDepth = td;
  }
  return (self);
} // initWithPressure:treadDepth:
```

Now, allocating and initializing a tire is a single-step operation:

```
Tire *tire;
tire = [[Tire alloc]
initWithPressure: 23 + i
treadDepth: 33 - i];
```

The Designated Initializer

Unfortunately, not all is well in initialization land. A couple of subtleties crop up when we start adding convenience initializers. Let's add two more convenience initializers to Tire:

```
@interface Tire : NSObject
{
 float pressure;
 float treadDepth;
}
- (id) initWithPressure: (float) pressure;
- (id) initWithTreadDepth: (float) treadDepth;
- (id) initWithPressure: (float) pressure treadDepth: (float) treadDepth;
- (void) setPressure: (float) pressure;
- (float) pressure;
- (void) setTreadDepth: (float) treadDepth;
- (float) treadDepth;
@end // Tire
```

The two new initializers, initWithPressure: and initWithTreadDepth:, are for folks who know they want a tire with either a particular pressure or a particular tread depth but don't care about the value of the other attribute and are happy to accept the default. Here's a first attempt at an initialization (which we'll be fixing later):

```
- (id) initWithPressure: (float) p
{
 if (self = [super init])
 {
  pressure = p;
  treadDepth = 20.0;
 }
 return (self);
} // initWithPressure
- (id) initWithTreadDepth: (float) td
{
 if (self = [super init])
```

```
{
  pressure = 34.0;
  treadDepth = td;
}
return (self);
} // initWithTreadDepth
```

We now have four init methods: init, initWithPressure:, initWithTreadDepth:, and initWithPressure:treadDepth:. Each of these knows the default pressure (34), the tread depth (20), or both. That works out OK, and the code is correct.

The problems come when we start subclassing Tire.

The Subclassing Problem

We already have a subclass of Tire named AllWeatherRadial. Now, suppose that AllWeatherRadial wants to add two new instance variables, rainHandling and snowHandling, which are floating point values that indicate how the tire handles on wet and on snowy roads. We need to make sure these get set to reasonable values when a new AllWeatherRadial is made.

So, here is the new interface for AllWeatherRadial, with the new instance variables and accessors:

```
@interface AllWeatherRadial : Tire
{
  float rainHandling;
  float snowHandling;
}
- (void) setRainHanding: (float) rainHanding;
- (float) rainHandling;
- (void) setSnowHandling: (float) snowHandling;
- (float) snowHandling;
@end // AllWeatherRadial
```

And the accessor methods are *trés* boring:

```
- (void) setRainHandling: (float) rh
{
  rainHandling = rh;
} // setRainHandling
- (float) rainHandling
{
  return (rainHandling);
} // rainHandling
- (void) setSnowHandling: (float) sh
{
  snowHandling = sh;
} // setSnowHandling
- (float) snowHandling
{
  return (snowHandling);
} // snowHandling
```

We updated the description method to show the various tire parameters:

```
- (NSString *) description
{
 NSString *desc;
 desc = [[NSString alloc] initWithFormat:
  @"AllWeatherRadial: %.1f / %.1f / %.1f / %.1f",
 [self pressure], [self treadDepth],
 [self rainHandling],
 [self snowHandling]];
 return (desc);
} // description
```

Here's the for loop in main(), which creates new AllWeatherRadials with their default values:

```
for (int i = 0; i < 4; i++)
{
AllWeatherRadial *tire;
 tire = [[AllWeatherRadial alloc] init];
 [car setTire: tire atIndex: i];
 [tire release];
}
```

When we run the program, though, there's a problem:

```
AllWeatherRadial: 34.0 / 20.0 / 0.0 / 0.0
AllWeatherRadial: 34.0 / 20.0 / 0.0 / 0.0
AllWeatherRadial: 34.0 / 20.0 / 0.0 / 0.0
AllWeatherRadial: 34.0 / 20.0 / 0.0 / 0.0
I am a slant- 6. VROOOM!
```

The AllWeatherRadial attributes didn't get set to reasonable default values. What happened? We need to set the values in an init method, so we'll have to override init. But Tire also has initWithPressure:, initWithTreadDepth:, and initWithPressure:treadDepth:. Do we have to override all of those? And even if we do, what happens if Tire adds a new initializer? It would be bad if a change in Tire breaks AllWeatherRadial.

Luckily, the folks who brewed up Cocoa anticipated this problem. They came up with the concept of the **designated initializer**. One init method in a class is the designated initializer. All the initializer methods of the class use the designated initializer to do the initialization work. Subclasses use their superclass's designated initializer for their superclass initialization. The init method that takes the most arguments usually ends up being the designated initializer. If you're using someone else's code, be sure to check the documentation to see which method is the designated initializer.

Fixing Tire's Initializers

First, we need to decide which of Tire's initializers should be dubbed the designated initializer. initWithPressure:treadDepth: is a good choice. It has the most arguments, and it's the most flexible of the initializers.

To fulfill the promise of the designated initializer, all other initializers should be implemented in terms of initWithPressure:treadDepth:. It looks something like this:

```
- (id) init
{
 if (self = [self initWithPressure: 34 treadDepth: 20])
 {
 }
 return (self);
} // init
- (id) initWithPressure: (float) p
{
 if (self = [self initWithPressure: p treadDepth: 20.0])
 {
 }
 return (self);
} // initWithPressure
- (id) initWithTreadDepth: (float) td
{
 if (self = [self initWithPressure: 34.0 treadDepth: td])
 {
 }
return (self);
} // initWithTreadDepth
```

> **Note**   You don't really need the empty bodies for the if statements, as in initWithPressure: treadDepth:. We like to do that so that all the init methods have a consistent look.

Adding the AllWeatherRadial Initializer

Now, it's time to add an initializer to AllWeatherRadial. The only method we need to add is an override of the designated initializer:

```
- (id) initWithPressure: (float) p
treadDepth: (float) td
{
 if (self = [super initWithPressure: p treadDepth: td])
 {
  rainHandling = 23.7;
  snowHandling = 42.5;
 }
 return (self);
} // initWithPressure:treadDepth
```

Now, when we run the program, the proper defaults are set:

```
AllWeatherRadial: 34.0 / 20.0 / 23.7 / 42.5
AllWeatherRadial: 34.0 / 20.0 / 23.7 / 42.5
AllWeatherRadial: 34.0 / 20.0 / 23.7 / 42.5
AllWeatherRadial: 34.0 / 20.0 / 23.7 / 42.5
I am a slant- 6. VROOOM!
```

VROOM, indeed!

Initializer Rules

You're not required to create an initializer method for your class. If you don't have any state you need to set up or the default behavior of alloc in clearing everything out to zero is good enough, you might choose not to bother with an init.

If you do write an initializer, be sure you call the superclass's designed initializer in your own designated initializer.

If you have more than one initializer, pick one to be the designated initializer. That method will be the one that calls the superclass's designated initializer. Implement all of your other initializers in terms of your designated initializer, as we did previously.

Summary

In this chapter, you learned all about object allocation and initialization. In Cocoa, these are two separate operations: alloc, a class method that comes from NSObject, allocates a chunk of memory and clears it to zero. init methods, which are instance methods, get an object up and running.

A class can have more than one init method. These init methods are usually convenience methods that make it easier to get the object configured the way you want. You'll choose one of these init methods to be the designated initializer. All other init methods are coded in terms of the designated initializer.

In your own init methods, you need to call either your own designated initializer or the superclass's designated initializer. Be sure to assign the value of the superclass's initializer to self and return that value from your init method. It's possible for a superclass to decide to return an entirely different object.

Coming next are properties, a quick and easy way to make your accessor methods.

Properties

Remember back in the mists at the dawn of time when we wrote accessor methods for our instance variables? We wrote a lot of boilerplate code, creating both a –setBlah method to set the object's blah attribute (obviously) and a –blah method to retrieve it. If the attribute is an object, we needed to retain the new one and release the old one. Utilities are out there that will turn your class definition into method declarations and definitions that you can paste into your files. But still, writing accessor methods is a lot of mind-numbing work that can better be applied to doing the cool stuff that's unique to your program.

In Objective-C 2.0, Apple introduced **properties**, a combination of new compiler directives and a new attribute accessor syntax. The new properties feature greatly reduces the amount of mindless code you have to write. Throughout this chapter, we'll be modifying *10.01 CarPartsInit* to use properties. The final code for this chapter can be found in the *11.01 CarProperties* project.

Remember that Objective-C 2.0 features can only be used on Mac OS X 10.5 (Leopard) or later, so if you must support ancient systems, you have to think twice. Properties are used heavily in newer parts of Cocoa (especially the snazzy Core Animation features) and are also used a lot in iOS development, so they're worth getting familiar with.

Shrinking Property Values

First off, we're going to convert one of the simpler classes, AllWeatherRadial, to use properties. To make the discussion a little more interesting, we'll add a couple of calls in main to change some values on the AllWeatherRadials we create. We're simulating someone buying four tires on sale from different stores, so all four have different handling characteristics.

Here is main again, with the new lines in bold:

```
int main(int argc, const char * argv[])
{
  @autoreleasepool
  {
    Car *car = [[Car alloc] init];
```

```
    for (int i = 0; i < 4; i++)
    {
      AllWeatherRadial *tire;

      tire = [[AllWeatherRadial alloc] init];
      [tire setRainHandling:20+i];
      [tire setSnowHandling:28+i];
      NSLog(@"tire %d's handling is %.f %.f", i,
        [tire rainHandling], [tire snowHandling]);

      [car setTire:tire atIndex:i];

      [tire release];
    }
    Engine *engine = [[Slant6 alloc] init];
    [car setEngine:engine];

    [car print];
    [car release];
  }
    return (0);
}
```

If you run the program now, you'll get this output, showing our newly changed tire handling values:

```
tire 0's handling is 20 28
tire 1's handling is 21 29
tire 2's handling is 22 30
tire 3's handling is 23 31
AllWeatherRadial: 34.0 / 20.0 / 20.0 / 28.0
AllWeatherRadial: 34.0 / 20.0 / 21.0 / 29.0
AllWeatherRadial: 34.0 / 20.0 / 22.0 / 30.0
AllWeatherRadial: 34.0 / 20.0 / 23.0 / 31.0
I am a slant-6. VROOOM!
```

Shrinking the Interface

Now let's look at AllWeatherRadial's class interface:

```
#import <Foundation/Foundation.h>
#import "Tire.h"
@interface AllWeatherRadial : Tire
{
 float rainHandling;
 float snowHandling;
}
- (void) setRainHandling: (float) rainHanding;
- (float) rainHandling;
- (void) setSnowHandling: (float) snowHandling;
- (float) snowHandling;
@end // AllWeatherRadial
```

This should be old hat for you by now. Let's clean it up, property-style:

```
#import <Foundation/Foundation.h>
#import "Tire.h"
@interface AllWeatherRadial : Tire
{
 float rainHandling;
 float snowHandling;
}
@property float rainHandling;
@property float snowHandling;
@end // AllWeatherRadial
```

A bit simpler, isn't it? No need for the four method definitions. Notice that we've grown two keywords preceded by at signs. Recall that the at sign is a signal for "Objective-C weirdness coming your way"! @property is a new compiler feature that says a new object attribute is being declared.

@property float rainHandling; says that objects of the class AllWeatherRadial have an attribute, of type float, called rainHandling. It also says that you can set the property by calling –setRainHanding: and that you can access the attribute by calling -rainHandling. You can run the program now, and it behaves just as it did before. All @property is doing is automatically declaring the setter and getter methods for the attribute. The attribute doesn't actually have to match the name of the instance variable, but it will in most cases. We'll talk about this a bit later. There are also some additional knobs you can turn on the properties; we'll talk about them later too, so please hang on.

Shrinking the Implementation

Now, let's look at the AllWeatherRadial implementation again:

```
#import "AllWeatherRadial.h"
@implementation AllWeatherRadial
- (id) initWithPressure: (float) p treadDepth: (float) td
{
 if (self = [super initWithPressure: p treadDepth: td])
 {
   rainHandling = 23.7;
   snowHandling = 42.5;
 }
return (self);
} // initWithPressure:treadDepth
- (void) setRainHandling: (float) rh
{
 rainHandling = rh;
} // setRainHandling

- (float) rainHandling
{
   return (rainHandling);
} // rainHandling
- (void) setSnowHandling: (float) sh
```

```
{
 snowHandling = sh;
} // setSnowHandling
- (float) snowHandling
{
  return (snowHandling);
} // snowHandling
- (NSString *) description
{
 NSString *desc;
 desc = [[NSString alloc] initWithFormat:
  @"AllWeatherRadial: %.1f / %.1f / %.1f / %.1f",
  [self pressure], [self treadDepth],
  [self rainHandling],
  [self snowHandling]];
 return (desc);
} // description
@end // AllWeatherRadial
```

In the previous chapter, we discussed the init method, the designated initializer, all the setter and getter methods, and the description. We're now going to ruthlessly eliminate all the setter and getter methods and replace them with two lines of code:

```
#import "AllWeatherRadial.h"
@implementation AllWeatherRadial
@synthesize rainHandling;
@synthesize snowHandling;
- (id) initWithPressure: (float) p
treadDepth: (float) td
{
 if (self = [super initWithPressure: p treadDepth: td])
 {
  rainHandling = 23.7;
  snowHandling = 42.5;
 }
 return (self);
} // initWithPressure:treadDepth
- (NSString *) description
{
 NSString *desc;
 desc = [[NSString alloc] initWithFormat:
  @"AllWeatherRadial: %.1f / %.1f / %.1f / %.1f", [self pressure], [self treadDepth],
  [self rainHandling], [self snowHandling]];
 return (desc);
} // description
@end // AllWeatherRadial
```

@synthesize is a compiler feature that says "create the accessors for this attribute." For the line of code @synthesize rainHandling;, the compiler emits the compiled code for –setRainHandling: and –rainHandling.

> **Note**   You may be familiar with code generation: Cocoa accessor-writing utilities and UI builders
> on other platforms generate source code, which is then compiled. But @synthesize is not code
> generation. You won't ever see the code that implements −setRainHandling: and −rainHandling,
> but these methods will exist and will be callable. This gives Apple the flexibility of changing the way
> accessors are generated in Objective-C, possibly leading to safer implementations or better performance.
>
> If you provide the methods in your class for the property, the compiler doesn't create them. The compiler
> only creates methods that are missing.

If you run the program now, you'll get the same results as before the changes.

Most properties are backed by a variable, so when you synthesize the getter and setter,
the compiler automatically creates an instance variable with the same name as the property.
Notice that the header file has two variables called rainHandling and snowHandling. The
setter and getter will use these variables. If you don't declare those variables, the compiler
creates them. There are two places where we can add the instance variables: the header file
or the implementation file. We can even mix the two, with some in the header and some in the
implementation.

Why would we want to put them in one place instead of another? Let's say you have a subclass,
and from the subclass, you want to access the variables directly instead of via properties. In this
case, the variables need to be in the header file. If the variables are only for your class, you can
move them into the .*m* file and clean up the public interface. The header file will look like this:

```
@interface AllWeatherRadial : Tire
@property float rainHandling;
@property float snowHandling;
@end // AllWeatherRadial
```

and the implementation file will look like this:

```
@implementation AllWeatherRadial
{
  float rainHandling;
  float snowHandling;
}

@synthesize rainHandling;
@synthesize snowHandling;

- (id) initWithPressure: (float)p treadDepth: (float)td
{
  if (self = [super initWithPressure: p treadDepth: td])
  {
    rainHandling = 23.7;
    snowHandling = 42.5;
  }
  return (self);
} // initWithPressure:treadDepth
```

```
- (NSString *) description
{
    NSString *desc;
    desc = [[NSString alloc] initWithFormat:
            @"AllWeatherRadial: %.1f / %.1f / %.1f / %.1f",
        [self pressure], [self treadDepth],
        [self rainHandling],
        [self snowHandling]];
    return (desc);
} // description
@end // AllWeatherRadial
```

As you can see, the header file looks much cleaner and has less code, which usually means it will cause you less trouble.

We can go a step further: remember that if we don't specify the instance variables, the compiler creates them for us. So we can eliminate this code without any negative consequences:

```
{
    float rainHandling;
    float snowHandling;
}
```

(We can remove the whole thing, including the braces.) Now we have deleted lots of code, which is likely to save us time typing and debugging.

Dots Incredible

Objective-C 2.0 properties introduce a new bit of syntactic sugar that makes accessing object attributes easier. These new features also make Objective-C a bit more approachable for folks who are used to languages like C++ and Java.

Recall the two new lines we added to main to change the tire's handling values:

```
[tire setRainHandling: 20 + i];
[tire setSnowHandling: 28 + i];
```

We can replace that code with this:

```
tire.rainHandling = 20 + i;
tire.snowHandling = 28 + i;
```

If you run the program again, you'll see the same results. We use NSLog to report the handling values of the tires:

```
NSLog(@"tire %d's handling is %.f %.f", i, [tire rainHandling], [tire snowHandling]);
```

We can now replace that code with this:

```
NSLog(@"tire %d's handling is %.f %.f", i, tire.rainHandling, tire.snowHandling);
```

The dot notation looks a lot like structure access in C and object access in Java—on purpose. When you see a dot on the left-hand side of an equal sign, the setter for that attribute name (–setRainHandling: and –setSnowHandling:) will be called. Otherwise, if you see a dot next to an object variable, the getter for that attribute name (–rainHandling and –snowHandling) is called.

If you're using properties, and you get strange error messages about accessing something that is not a `struct`, make sure you've included all the necessary header files for the classes you're using.

That's pretty much it for the stuff that properties introduce. Of course, we have some additional cases to discuss for the proper handling of object attributes and for avoiding the exposure of both setters and getters. Let's talk about those next.

Objecting to Properties

So far, we've looked at properties for scalar types—`float` in particular—but the same techniques apply for `int`, `char`, `BOOL`, and `struct`. For example, you can have an `NSRect` property if you want.

Objects bring some added complications. Recall that we retain and release objects as they flow through our accessors. For some object values, particularly string values, you want to always `-copy` them. Yet for other object values, like delegates (which we'll talk about in the next chapter), you don't want to retain them at all.

Let's add a new feature to Car so that we can play with some new property syntax. That's gonna be exciting! We'll give the car a name. We'll start out old school and use traditional accessor methods. First is *Car.h*, with the new goodies in bold:

```
@class Tire;
@class Engine;
@interface Car : NSObject
{
   NSString *name;
   NSMutableArray *tires;
   Engine *engine;
}
- (void)setName: (NSString *) newName;
- (NSString *) name;
- (void) setEngine: (Engine *) newEngine;
- (Engine *) engine;
-(void) setTire: (Tire *) tire atIndex: (int) index;
- (Tire *) tireAtIndex: (int) index;
- (void) print;
@end // Car
```

Now, we add the implementation of the accessors (notice that we're copying the name), along with choosing a default name for the car and displaying it in the description:

```
#import "Car.h"
@implementation Car
- (id) init
{
   if (self = [super init])
   {
   name = [[NSString alloc] initWithString:@"Car"];
   tires = [[NSMutableArray alloc] init];
   int i;
   for (i = 0; i < 4; i++) {
    [tires addObject: [NSNull null]];
   }
  }
 return (self);
} // init

- (void) dealloc
{
 [name release];
 [tires release];
 [engine release];
 [super dealloc];
} // dealloc

- (void)setName: (NSString *)newName
{
   [name release];
   name = [newName copy];
} // setName
```

```
- (NSString *)name
{
  return (name);
} // name

- (Engine *) engine
{
 return (engine);
} // engine

- (void) setEngine: (Engine *) newEngine
{
 [newEngine retain];
 [engine release];
 engine = newEngine;
} // setEngine

- (void) setTire: (Tire *) tire atIndex: (int) index
{
  [tires replaceObjectAtIndex: index withObject: tire];
} // setTire:atIndex:
- (Tire *) tireAtIndex: (int) index
{
 Tire *tire;
  tire = [tires objectAtIndex: index];
  return (tire);
} // tireAtlndex:
- (void) print
{
  NSLog (@"%@ has:", name);
 for (int i = 0; i < 4; i++)
  {
   NSLog (@"%@", [self tireAtIndex: i]);
  }
  NSLog (@"%@", engine);
} // print
@end // Car
```

And we'll set the name in `main`:

```
Car *car = [[Car alloc] init];
[car setName: @"Herbie"];
```

Run the program, and you'll see the car's name at the beginning of the output. OK, let's start adding properties to Car. Here is *Car.h* in all its glory:

```
@class Tire;
@class Engine;
@interface Car : NSObject
{
  NSString *name;
  NSMutableArray *tires;
  Engine *engine;
}
@property (copy) NSString *name;
```

```
@property (retain) Engine *engine;
- (void) setTire: (Tire *) tire atIndex: (int) index;
- (Tire *) tireAtIndex: (int) index;
- (void) print;
@end // Car
```

You'll notice the declarations of the simple accessors are gone, and they have been replaced by @property declarations. You can decorate @property with additional attributes to express your exact intentions on how the property is to behave. Because copy is added to name, the compiler and users of the class know that name is going to be copied. This can simplify the life of programmers using this class, because programmers know they won't need to make a copy of strings they get out of text fields. On the other hand, engine is managed just by retain/release. If you don't supply either one, the compiler will default to assign, which is generally not what you want with objects.

> **Note**   You can use some other decorations, like nonatomic, which makes accessors a bit faster if they won't be used in a multithreaded environment. Desktop machines are so fast that there is no real performance gain by making a property nonatomic, but iOS developers frequently use it to eke out more performance on resource-constrained mobile devices. You can also use assign if you don't want the attribute object to be retained, to help avoid retain cycles.
>
> By default, if you don't specify any attributes for properties, they are given the default attributes of nonatomic, and assign. You can only specify retain and copy attributes for retainable pointers (i.e. Objective-C objects). All other types, such as C and nonretainable pointers, must use assign and manage memory manually.
>
> If you provide either or both the setter and getter yourself, you cannot use atomic attribute; you must use nonatomic.

Car.m has two major changes. The name and engine accessors are deleted and two @synthesize directives are added:

```
@implementation Car
```

```
@synthesize name;
@synthesize engine;
```

And finally, main uses dot notation to set stuff:

```
Car *car = [[Car alloc] init];
car.name = @"Herbie";
...
car.engine = [[Slant6 alloc] init];
```

Appellation Spring

In all the code in this chapter, the name of the property has been the same as the name of an instance variable that backs that property. This pattern is very common and probably one you'll use most of the time. Sometimes, though, you may want one name for the instance variable and another for the public attribute name.

Let's say we want to call the name instance variable in Car something else, like appellation. We just change the name of the instance variable in *Car.h*:

```
@interface Car : NSObject
{
  NSString *appellation;
  NSMutableArray *tires;
  Engine *engine;
}
@property (copy) NSString *name;
@property (retain) Engine *engine;
```

and then change the synthesize directive:

```
 @synthesize name = appellation;
```

The compiler will still create –setName: and –name but will use the appellation instance variable inside of their implementations.

But when you compile, you see a couple of errors. You may recall that we directly accessed the name instance variable, which has been changed. We can choose to do a search and replace on the "name", or we can change direct ivar access to use accessors instead. In init, change

```
name = @"Car";
```

to

```
self.name = @"Car";
```

What's that self-dot-name business? It's a bit of disambiguation to let the compiler know that we want to vector through the accessors. If we just use a naked name, the compiler assumes that we're directly modifying an instance variable. To go through the accessors, we can write [self setName:@"Car"]. Remember that the dot is just shorthand for making this exact same call, so self.name = @"Car" is just another way of saying the same thing.

Finally, we have to fix the first NSLog call:

```
NSLog (@"%@ has:", self.name);
```

Now, we can rename appellation to something else, like nickname or moniker. We just need to change the instance variable name and the name used in @synthesize.

Because subclasses of the car do not need to access variables directly, let's kick them out of the header file. We can eliminate the name and the engine variable, as they will be created by the compiler. And we can move the tires array into the implementation file. This makes our header file even simpler (which makes it better).

Now that we have fixed this, let's go back to the *AllWeatherRadial.m* file. Notice, attentive reader, that in the description method, we're still using methods to get the attributes of the tire. Let's change all of those to use dot syntax. Our description method now looks like this:

```
- (NSString *) description
{
  NSString *desc;
  desc = [[NSString alloc] initWithFormat:
```

```
        @"AllWeatherRadial: %.1f / %.1f / %.1f / %.1f",
        self.pressure, self.treadDepth, self.rainHandling, self.snowHandling];
    return (desc);

} // description
```

Next we'll fix the `Tire` class and properties for `pressure` and `treadDepth`, and we'll get rid of the getters and setters. We have simplified the `Tire` interface (and code) without losing any functionality.

```
@interface Tire : NSObject

@property float pressure;
@property float treadDepth;

- (id) initWithPressure: (float) pressure;
- (id) initWithTreadDepth: (float) treadDepth;

- (id) initWithPressure: (float) pressure
    treadDepth: (float) treadDepth;
@end // Tire
```

We also got rid of the setters and getters from the implementation file. We're having a great time getting rid of unnecessary clutter and ripping out code where bugs could hide.

One more thing: you might remember that we added the `name` property to `Car`, which had the `copy` attribute. That means that when we assign the `name`, `Car` makes a copy of the string and stores it. If we weren't using ARC, we would need to add a `release` to the `dealloc` method of `Car`, like so:

```
[name release];
```

But because we are using ARC, we don't need to worry about that; the compiler will insert it there for us. It's ARC-tastic!

Read-Only About It

You might have an object with an attribute that is read-only. This attribute might be a value that's computed on the fly, like the surface area of a banana, or might be one that you want other objects to read but not change, like your driver's license number. You can code for these situations with more attributes on `@property`.

By default, properties are mutable: you can read and write them. Properties have a `readwrite` attribute you can use for specifying this. Since properties are mutable by default, you won't usually use it, but it's there if you need it and you want to make your intentions clear. We could have used `readwrite` in *Car.h*:

```
@property (readwrite, copy) NSString *name;
@property (readwrite, retain) Engine *engine;
```

But we didn't, because we generally want to stamp out and abolish and get rid of redundancy and repetition and saying the same thing over again.

Returning to our read-only property discussion, let's say we have a property, such as our license number or shoe size, that we don't want to be changed by anybody. We can use the readonly attribute on @property for this. An example class would be something like this:

```
@interface Me : NSObject
{
  float shoeSize;
  NSString *licenseNumber;
}
@property (readonly) float shoeSize;
@property (readonly) NSString *licenseNumber;
@end
```

When the compiler sees that @property is readonly, it generates a getter but not a setter for that attribute. Users of Me can call –shoeSize and –licenseNumber, but if you try to call -setShoeSize:, the compiler will complain. You'll get the same behavior when using dot notation.

I'd Rather Do It Myself

We mentioned that properties are backed by variables, and that the compiler creates getters and setters for you. But what if you don't want any of that? What if you'd rather not have a variable, getter, and setter for your property?

In that case, you're covered. You can use the keyword @dynamic to tell the compiler not to generate any code or create a variable for the property. Continuing from the previous examples, let's add the bodyMassIndex property to the Me class.

Because body mass index is calculated from a person's height and weight, we can't store the value for it. Instead, we want to create an accessor to compute the value at runtime. So we use @dynamic to specify a property and tell the compiler not to worry about creating a variable or a getter—we'll take care of it.

```
@property (readonly) float bodyMassIndex;

@dynamic bodyMassIndex;
- (float)bodyMassIndex
{
 ///compute and return bodyMassIndex
}
```

If you declare a dynamic property and you try to call a getter or setter without providing one, you'll get an error.

I Don't Like the Method Names

Sometimes, you might not like the names of the methods that are generated by default. They're in the form of blah and setBlah:. To overcome this, you can specify the names of the getter and setter that the compiler generates. Use the attributes getter= and setter= to define the preferred names of your methods. If you do this, note that you'll break the key-value coding convention (described in detail in Chapter 19), so you should have a good reason for using this feature.

Here's an example of a pattern that's useful for properties of Boolean types:

```
@property (getter=isHidden) BOOL hidden;
```

This tells the compiler to generate `isHidden` for the getter and `setHidden:` for the setter.

Alas, Properties Don't Do Everything

You'll notice we didn't convert `Car`'s tire methods to properties:

```
- (void) setTire: (Tire *) tire atIndex: (int) index;
- (Tire *) tireAtIndex: (int) index;
```

That's because these methods don't fit into the fairly narrow range of methods that properties cover. Properties will let you replace only –setBlah and –blah methods, but not methods that take extra arguments, like the tire's position on the car.

Summary

In this chapter, we discussed properties, which are a way to reduce the amount of code you have to write (and read later) when doing common operations with object attributes. Use the @property directive to tell the world, "Hey, this object has this attribute of this name of this type." Also use the directive to pass on some information about the property, like its mutability (readonly or readwrite). Behind the scenes, the compiler automatically generates the method declarations for the setter and getter for the object's attribute.

Use the @synthesize directive to tell the compiler to generate the implementation for the accessors. You can control which instance variable is affected by the generated implementation. If you don't want to use the default behavior, you're free to write your own code for the accessors. You can use @dynamic to tell the compiler not to generate a variable or code.

Dot notation, although usually presented in the context of properties, is just shorthand for calling the setter and getter for objects. Dot notation reduces the amount of typing you have to do and is a little more comfortable for folks coming from other languages.

Coming up next are categories, Objective-C's way of letting you extend existing classes, even if you don't have the code for them! Don't miss that.

Chapter 12

Categories

When you write object-oriented programs, you'll often want to add some new behavior to an existing class: you can always create new hoops for objects to jump through. For example, you might have designed a new kind of tire, so you'd subclass Tire and add the new cool stuff. When you want to add behavior to an existing class, you'll often create a subclass.

But sometimes, subclassing isn't convenient. For example, you might want to add some new behavior to NSString, but you remember that NSString is really the front end for a class cluster, which makes it difficult to subclass. In other cases, you might be able to make a subclass, but you're using a toolkit or library that won't be able to handle objects of the new class. For example, your new subclass of NSString won't be returned when you make a new string with the stringWithFormat: class method.

The dynamic runtime dispatch mechanism employed by Objective-C lets you add methods to existing classes. Hey, that sounds pretty cool! The Objective-C term for these new methods is **categories**.

Creating a Category

A category is a way to add new methods to existing classes. Want to add a new method to a class? Go right ahead! You can do this to any class, even classes you don't have the source code for.

For example, let's say you are writing a crossword puzzle program that takes a series of strings, determines the length of each string, and puts those lengths into an NSArray or NSDictionary. You'll need to wrap each length in an NSNumber object before adding it into the NSArray or NSDictionary.

You could write this code:

```
NSNumber *number;
number = [NSNumber numberWithUnsignedInt: [string length]];
// … do something with number
```

But that would soon get tedious. Instead, you could add a category to NSString that does this work for you. In fact, let's do that. The LengthAsNSNumber project is located in the *12.01 LengthAsNSNumber* project directory and contains the code that adds such a category to NSString.

Programmers often put categories in their own files, typically named *ClassName+CategoryName*. So, in our case, this would be *NSString+NumberConvenience*. This isn't a requirement, but it's a good practice.

Let's Create a Category

Xcode makes adding categories very easy. It even names the files correctly according to the convention we just described.

To create a category, open the project, go to the Navigator, and select the group where you want the files to show up. Next, select **File ➤ New ➤ New File** or type ⌘N. In the New File window, click Cocoa in the left pane and *Objective-C category* on the right (see Figure 12-1).

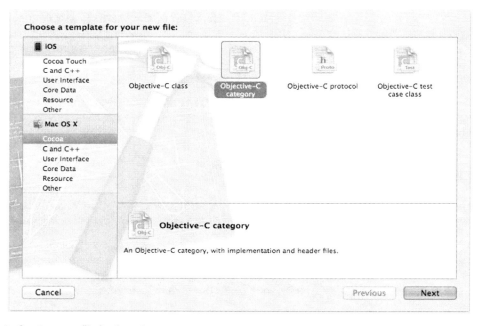

Figure 12-1. Create a new file for the category

Click Next, and on the next screen (see Figure 12-2), type *NumberConvenience* for the category and *NSString* in the Category on field; NSString is the class we want to add methods to. Click Next to go on.

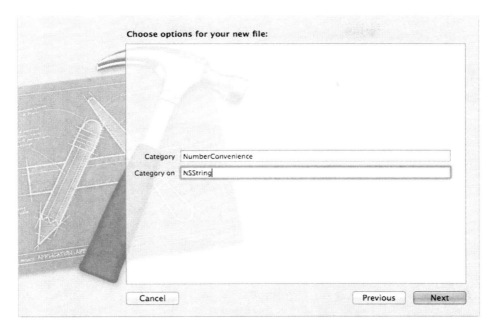

Figure 12-2. *Enter the category name and the associated class*

The next screen (shown in Figure 12-3) asks where to save the files and which target and group to add them to. Usually, you'll accept the selections Xcode has made. Click Create, and now, we have a header file with category interface and an implementation file ready for us to add methods.

@interface

The declaration of a category looks a lot like the declaration for a class:

```
@interface NSString (NumberConvenience)
- (NSNumber *) lengthAsNumber;
@end // NumberConvenience
```

You should notice a couple of interesting things about this declaration. First, an existing class is mentioned, followed by a new name in parentheses. This means that the category is called NumberConvenience, and it adds methods to NSString. Another way to say this is, "We're adding a category onto NSString called NumberConvenience." You can add as many categories to a class as you want, as long as the category names are unique.

You indicate the class you're putting the category onto (NSString) and the name of the category (NumberConvenience), and you list the methods you're adding, followed by @end. You can't add new instance variables, so there is no instance variable section as there is with a class declaration.

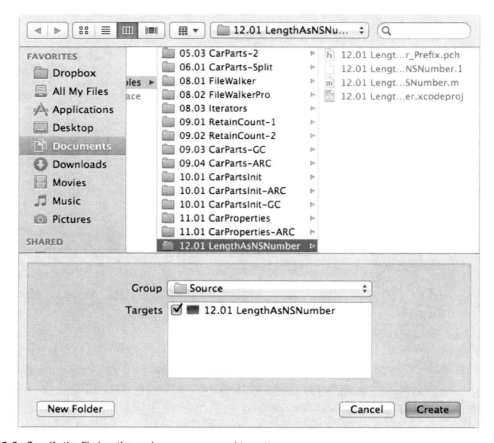

Figure 12-3. Specify the file location and source group and targets

You can also add properties to categories. Because you can't add instance variables, the properties must be of @dynamic type. The benefit of adding properties is that you can use dot notation to access the setters and getters.

@implementation

It comes as no surprise that the @interface section has an @implementation companion. You put the methods you're writing in @implementation:

```
@implementation NSString (NumberConvenience)
- (NSNumber *) lengthAsNumber
{
    NSUInteger length = [self length];
    return ([NSNumber numberWithUnsignedInt:length]);
} // lengthAsNumber
@end // NumberConvenience
```

Like @interface for the category, @implementation has the names of the class and the category, along with the bodies of the new methods.

The lengthAsNumber method gets the length of the string by calling [self length]. You will send the lengthAsNumber message to this string. Then, a new NSNumber is created with the length.

Let's take a quick time-out for one of our new favorite topics: memory management. Is this code correct? Yes! numberWithUnsignedInt is not an alloc, copy, or new method. Because it's not one of those three, it will return an object that we can assume has a retain count of 1 and has been autoreleased. The NSNumber object we create will get cleaned up when the currently active autorelease pool is destroyed.

And here is the new category in action. main() creates a new NSMutableDictionary, adds three strings as the keys and the length of the strings as the values:

```
int main(int argc, const char * argv[])
{
  @autoreleasepool
  {
    NSMutableDictionary *dict = [NSMutableDictionary dictionary];

    [dict setObject:[@"hello" lengthAsNumber]
         forKey:@"hello"];

    [dict setObject:[@"iLikeFish" lengthAsNumber]
         forKey:@"iLikeFish"];

    [dict setObject:[@"Once upon a time" lengthAsNumber]
         forKey:@"Once upon a time"];

    NSLog (@"%@", dict);
  }
  return 0;
}
```

Let's pull this apart, piece by piece, in our usual fashion.

The first thing we need to do is import the header file into main() so we know that we have this method defined for NSString. At the end of the other #import statements, we add the following:

```
#import "NSString+NumberConvenience.h"
```

Next, we create an autorelease pool, the ARC-tastic way:

```
@autoreleasepool {
```

Don't forget the closing brace at the end of your code. Just as a reminder, this pool is where all the autoreleased objects go. In particular, the mutable dictionary will end up in here, as will all of the NSNumbers our category creates.

After the pool is made, a new mutable dictionary is created. Recall that this handy Cocoa class lets us store pairs of keys and objects.

```
NSMutableDictionary *dict = [NSMutableDictionary dictionary];
```

We can't put primitive types like ints into a dictionary, so we have to use a wrapper class like NSNumber. Luckily, our shiny new category makes it easy to embed our string length into an NSNumber. Here is the code that adds the value 5 to the dictionary, using the key @"hello":

```
[dict setObject: [@"hello" lengthAsNumber] forKey: @"hello"];
```

That code looks weird, but it's actually doing the right thing. Remember that the @"string" kind of strings are actually full-blown NSString objects. They react to messages just like any other NSString object. Because we now have this category on NSString, any string will react to lengthAsNumber, even literal strings like these.

This bears repeating. This bears repeating! *Any* NSString will respond to lengthAsNumber—that includes literal strings, strings from description methods, mutable strings, strings from other parts of the toolkit, strings loaded from files, strings fetched from across the vast reaches of the Internet, and so on. This compatibility is what makes categories a hugely powerful idea. There is no need to subclass NSString to get this behavior—it *just works*.

When you run the program, you'll get output like this:

```
{
"Once upon a time" = 16;
hello = 5;
iLikeFish = 9;
}
```

Bad Categories

Now that you're all high on categories, let's bring you back to earth a bit. Categories have two limitations. The first is that you can't add new instance variables to a class. There's nowhere to put them.

The second limitation concerns name collisions, in which one of your category methods has the same name as an existing method. When names collide, the category wins. Your category method will completely replace the original method, with no way of getting the original back. Some programmers add a prefix to their category methods to make sure there won't be a conflict.

> **Note** There are techniques for getting around the inability to add new instance variables. For example, you can use a global dictionary to store a mapping between objects and any extra variables you want to associate with them. But if you find yourself relying on these tricks, you may want to consider if a category is really the best choice for what you're doing.

Good Categories

In Cocoa, categories are used mainly for three purposes: splitting a class's implementation across multiple files or multiple frameworks, creating forward references for private methods, and adding informal protocols to an object. Don't worry if you have no idea what "informal protocol" means. We'll cover that in a little bit.

Clint Eastwood Would Love This

Now that we've talked about bad and good categories, let's introduce one special category, with a special description: **class extension**. One of this category's special qualities is that it has no name. What does that mean? Well, we just went through the process of naming a category and using that name when defining the @interface. This special class extension category is not named. Here's a complete rundown on the class extension category:

- As we've pointed out, it doesn't have a name.

- You can use it for classes you have the source for (that is, your own classes).

- You can add instance variables.

- You can change the mutability of variables from readonly to readwrite.

- You can have any number of them.

Take a look at the project *12.02 Class Extension*. We have created a simple class called Things, and it looks like this:

```
@interface Things : NSObject
@property (assign) NSInteger thing1;
@property (readonly, assign) NSInteger thing2;

- (void)resetAllValues;
@end
```

The class has two properties and a method. We have marked the thing2 property as readonly, and that's all that's vsisible in the class's public interface. But there's more to it than that, as we'll see when we take a peek at the implementation. First, notice this code:

```
@interface Things ()
{
  NSInteger thing4;
}
@property (readwrite, assign) NSInteger thing2;
@property (assign) NSInteger thing3;
@end
```

This looks almost like we're defining a class, except that there's no parent class. What we're doing is basically taking the class Things and *extending* it by adding private properties and methods. That's why it's called *class extension*.

Looking at the thing2 property, you might notice that we already defined this property in the header file. What are we doing with it here? We're changing its mutability, marking it readwrite so that the compiler will generate a setter but keep access private to this class. The public interface has only a getter.

We have also added a private things3 property that can be only used by this class internally. And we added an instance variable named thing4, which is also private.

What's that siren? Yep, here come the memory police to find out what we're doing about our new objects. Because we're using ARC, we don't have to release the objects, as they will released for us at the end of the autorelease pool. The memory police are satisfied.

So why would you want to do something like this? One of the characteristics of object-oriented programming is information hiding. You want to expose only things that users need to see, and nothing else, such as implementation details. These techniques help you accomplish that.

We put this category in the *.m* file, but we could put it in the private header (*ThingsPrivate.h*) and allow Things subclasses or friend classes to have access to these items.

You can have multiple class extension categories, which can lead to bugs that are hard to find, so please use this feature wisely.

Running the program now gives us

```
1      0      0
200    300    400
```

Splitting an Implementation with Categories

As you saw in Chapter 6, you can put a class's interface into a header file and the implementation into a *.m* file. But you can't split an @implementation across multiple *.m* files. If you have a single large class you want to split across multiple *.m* files, you can use categories to do the job.

Take, for instance, the NSWindow class provided by the AppKit. If you look at the documentation for NSWindow, you'll find hundreds of methods; the NSWindow documentation is over 60 pages long when printed (don't try this at home).

Putting all the code for NSWindow into one file would make it huge and unwieldy for the Cocoa development team, not to mention us poor developers. If you look at the header file and search for "@interface," you'll see the official class interface:

```
@interface NSWindow : NSResponder
```

Then, there are a whole bunch of categories, including these:

```
@interface NSWindow(NSKeyboardUI)
@interface NSWindow(NSToolbarSupport)
@interface NSWindow(NSDrag)
@interface NSWindow(NSCarbonExtensions)
```

This use of categories allows all the keyboard user interface stuff to live in one source file, the toolbar code in another file, drag-and-drop features in yet another, and so on. These categories also break the methods into logical groups, making life easier for folks who are reading the header file. That's what we're going to try but on a smaller scale.

Using Categories in our Project

The CategoryThing project, found in the *12.03 CategoryThing* folder, has a simple class that's spread across a couple of implementation files.

First is *CategoryThing.h*, which has the class declaration and some categories. This file starts with the #import of the Foundation framework and the class declaration with three integer instance variables:

```
#import <Foundation/Foundation.h>
@interface CategoryThing : NSObject
{
  NSInteger thing1;
  NSInteger thing2;
  NSInteger thing3;
}
@end // CategoryThing
```

After the class declaration come three categories, and each category has accessor methods for one instance variable. We'll put the implementation of these into separate files.

```
@interface CategoryThing (Thing1)
- (void)setThing1:(NSInteger)thing1;
- (NSInteger)thing1;
@end // CategoryThing (Thing1)

@interface CategoryThing(Thing2)
- (void)setThing2:(NSInteger)thing2;
- (NSInteger)thing2;
@end // CategoryThing (Thing2)

@interface CategoryThing (Thing3)
- (void)setThing3:(NSInteger)thing3;
- (NSInteger)thing3;
@end // CategoryThing (Thing3)
```

And that's it for *CategoryThing.h*.

CategoryThing.m is pretty simple, containing a description method we can use with the %d format specifier in NSLog():

```
#import "CategoryThing.h"
@implementation CategoryThing
- (NSString *) description
{
NSString *desc;
desc = [NSString stringWithFormat: @"%d %d %d", thing1, thing2, thing3];
return (desc);
} // description
@end // CategoryThing
```

Time for a memory management check. Is description doing the right thing? Yes, it is. Because stringWithFormat is not an alloc, copy, or new, it returns an object we can assume has a retain count of 1 and has been autoreleased, so it will be cleaned up when the current autorelease pool goes away.

Now for the categories. *Thing1.m* has the implementation for the Thing1 category:

```
#import "CategoryThing.h"

@implementation CategoryThing (Thing1)
- (void)setThing1:(NSInteger)t1
```

```
{
  thing1 = t1;
} // setThing1

- (NSInteger) thing1
{
  return (thing1);
} // thing1

@end // CategoryThing
```

The interesting point to note is that a category can access the instance variables of the class it has been put onto. Category methods are first-class citizens.

The contents of *Thing2.m* are very similar to those of *Thing1.m*:

```
#import "CategoryThing.h"

@implementation CategoryThing (Thing2)

- (void)setThing2:(NSInteger) t2
{
  thing2 = t2;
} // setThing2

- (NSInteger)thing2
{
  return (thing2);
} // thing2

@end // CategoryThing
```

After reading this far, you can probably figure out what *Thing3.m* looks like (hint: cut; paste; search; replace).

The *main.m* file contains main(), which actually uses these categories we've been constructing. First comes the #import statement:

```
#import "CategoryThing.h"
```

We need to import the header for CategoryThing so that the compiler can see the class definition and the categories. After that comes main():

```
int main (int argc, const char *argv[])
{
@autoreleasepool {
 CategoryThing *thing = [[CategoryThing alloc] init];
 [thing setThing1: 5];
 [thing setThing2: 23];
 [thing setThing3: 42];
 NSLog (@"Things are %@", thing);
 }
return (0);
} // main
```

The first line of main() contains the standard autorelease pool code we've come to know and, uh, love. This pool will end up holding the autoreleased description string that's used by NSLog().

Next, a `CategoryThing` object is allocated and initialized:

```
CategoryThing *thing = [[CategoryThing alloc] init];
```

Here's our obligatory report to the memory management patrol: Because this is an `alloc`, its retain count is 1, and it's not in the autorelease pool. And because this project uses ARC, we don't need to worry about adding a `release`; our friend the compiler will do the correct thing and add one for us.

Next, some messages are sent to the object to set the values of `thing1`, `thing2`, and `thing3`:

```
[thing setThing1: 5];
[thing setThing2: 23];
[thing setThing3: 42];
```

When you're using an object, whether the methods are declared in the interface, in a superclass, or in a category doesn't matter.

After the `thing` values have been set, `NSLog()` prints out the object. As you saw in the description method for `CategoryThing`, this displays the values of the three thing instance variables:

```
NSLog (@"Things are %@", thing);
```

Finally, the autorelease pool is released, and `main()` returns 0:

```
}
return (0);
} // main
```

That's it for our little program. Running the program gives these results:

```
Things are 5 23 42
```

Not only can you split a class's implementation across multiple source files, you can divide it among multiple frameworks as well. `NSString` is a class that lives in the Foundation framework, which has a lot of data-oriented classes, such as strings, numbers, and collections. All the eye candy (windows, colors, drawing, and the like) lives in the AppKit and UIKit. Even though `NSString` is declared in Foundation, the AppKit has a category on `NSString` called `NSStringDrawing`, which lets you send draw messages to string objects. When you draw a string, the method renders the string's text on the screen. Because this is fancy graphics stuff, it's an AppKit feature. But `NSStrings` are Foundation objects. The Cocoa designers used categories to put the data functionality into Foundation and the drawing functionality into AppKit. We, as programmers, just deal with `NSStrings`, and we generally won't care where a particular method comes from.

Making Forward References with Categories

As we've mentioned before, Cocoa doesn't have any truly private methods. If you know the name of a method an object supports, you can call it, even if there is no declaration for that method in a class's `@interface`.

The compiler, though, tries to be helpful. If it sees you calling a method on an object, and it hasn't seen a declaration or definition for that method yet, it complains like this: `warning: 'CategoryThing' may not respond to '-setThing4:'`. Generally, this kind of complaint is good, because it will help you catch a lot of your typos.

But the compiler's vigilance can cause problems if your implementation uses methods that aren't listed in the `@interface` section of your class. There are a lot of good reasons why you don't want to list all your methods there. The methods might be pure implementation details, or you might be playing around with method names to decide which ones you want to use. But if you don't declare your methods before using them, you'll get warnings from the compiler. Fixing all compiler warnings is a good thing, so what can you do?

If you can arrange to define a method before you use it, the compiler will see your definition, and it won't produce a warning. But if that's not convenient to do, or if you're using a unpublished method in another class, you'll need to do something else.

Categories to the Rescue!

Declaring a method in a category is enough for the compiler to say, "OK, this method exists. I'm not going to complain if I see the programmer using it." You don't actually have to implement it if you don't want to.

One common technique is to place a category at the top of the implementation file. Say that `Car` has a method called `rotateTires`. We could implement `rotateTires` in terms of another method called `moveTireFromPosition:toPosition:` to swap the tires at two locations. This second method is an implementation detail and not something we want to put into the public interface of the car. By declaring it in a category, `rotateTires` can use `moveTireFromPosition:toPosition:` without generating any warnings from the compiler. The category would look like this:

```
@interface Car (Private)
- (void) moveTireFromPosition: (int) pos1 toPosition: (int) pos2;
@end // Private
```

When you implement this method, it doesn't have to exist in an `@implementation Car (Private)` block, but if it doesn't, the compiler will give you a warning, so it's good practice to put these in `@Implementations`. Plus, later on, if you need to look for those methods, they'll be all in one place and easy to find. You can leave this method in the `@implementation Car` section. This lets you separate your methods into categories as an organizational and documentation convenience, while still allowing you to keep all your methods in one big pile in the implementation file.

When you're accessing private methods of other classes, you don't even have to supply an implementation of the method. Just having it declared in a category is enough to keep the compiler happy. By the way, you really shouldn't access private methods of other classes, but sometimes, you must do so to work around bugs in Cocoa or other people's code, or to write test code.

Be careful, though. Apple has guidelines for accepting applications into the Mac and iOS App Stores. One guideline is that your app can't access private variables and methods of classes. If your app does so, Apple may reject it.

Informal Protocols and Delegation Categories

Now, it's time for more of those Big Words and Big Ideas that you often find in object-oriented programming—you know, the ones that sound more complicated than they actually are.

Cocoa classes often use a technique that involves a **delegate**, which is an object asked by another object to do some of its work. For example, the AppKit class NSApplication asks its delegate if it should open an Untitled window when the application launches. NSWindow objects ask their delegates if they should allow a window to be closed.

Most often, you will be the one writing the delegate object and giving it to some other object, typically something provided by Cocoa. By implementing specific methods, you can exert control over how the Cocoa object behaves.

Scrolling lists in Cocoa are handled by the AppKit class NSTableView. When the tableView is ready to do some work, such as selecting the row the user just clicked, the object asks its delegate if it can select the row. The tableView sends a message to its delegate:

```
- (BOOL) tableView: (NSTableView *) tableView shouldSelectRow: (NSInteger) rowIndex;
```

The delegate method can look at the tableView and the row to decide whether the row should be selected. If the table includes rows that shouldn't be selected, the delegate might implement the concept of disabled rows that are not selectable.

The ITunesFinder Project

The Cocoa class that lets you find network services published by Bonjour (the technology formerly called Rendezvous) is named NSNetServiceBrowser. You tell the net service browser what service you're looking for and give it a delegate object. The browser object then sends messages to the delegate object telling it when it sees new services.

ITunesFinder, which lives in the *12.04 ITunesFinder* project folder, uses NSNetServiceBrowser to list all the shared iTunes music libraries that it can find.

For this project, we'll start out with main(), which lives in *main.m*. The delegate object is an instance of the class ITunesFinder, so we need to import its header file:

```
#import <Foundation/Foundation.h>
#import "ITunesFinder.h"
```

And then main() starts. We set up the autorelease pool:

```
int main (int argc, const char *argv[]) {
@autoreleasepool {
```

Next, a new NSNetServiceBrowser is born:

```
NSNetServiceBrowser *browser = [[NSNetServiceBrowser alloc] init];
```

And then a new ITunesFinder is created:

```
ITunesFinder *finder = [[ITunesFinder alloc] init];
```

Because we're using alloc to create these, we must take responsibility for making sure they'll be released when we're finished with them. We're using ARC, so we don't have to add a release, but if you're not using ARC, you have to do this manually.

Next, we tell the net service browser to use the `ITunesFinder` object as a delegate:

```
[browser setDelegate: finder];
```

Then, we tell the browser to go look for iTunes shares:

```
[browser searchForServicesOfType: @"_daap._tcp" inDomain: @"local."];
```

The "`_daap._tcp`" string tells the net service browser to look for services of type daap ("daap" is short for "Digital Audio Access Protocol") using the TCP networking protocol. This incantation finds libraries published by iTunes. The domain `local.` means to look for the services on the local network. The Internet Assigned Numbers Authority (IANA) maintains a list of Internet protocol families, which usually map to the Bonjour service name.

Next, `main()` logs the fact that it has begun browsing and starts a `run` loop:

```
NSLog (@"begun browsing");
[[NSRunLoop currentRunLoop] run];
```

A `run` loop is a Cocoa construct that blocks (that is, doesn't do any processing) until something interesting happens. In this case, "interesting" means that the net service browser discovers a new iTunes share.

In addition to listening for network traffic, run loops handle other things like waiting for user events, such as key presses or mouse clicks. The `run` method actually will not return; it will keep running forever, so the code that follows it won't ever execute. However, we've left it in to let readers of the code know that we're aware of proper memory management (we could construct a `run` loop that runs only for a specific amount of time, but that code is more complicated and doesn't really contribute to our discussion of delegates). So here's the clean-up code that won't actually get run:

```
}
return (0);
} // main
```

Now, we have the net service browser and a run loop. The browser sends out network packets looking for particular services, and packets come back saying, "Here I am." When these packets come back, the run loop tells the net service browser, "Here are some packets for you." The browser then looks at the packets, and if they're from a service it hasn't seen before, it sends messages to the delegate object telling it what happened.

Now it's time to look at the code for our delegate, `ITunesFinder`. The interface for the `ITunesFinder` class is minimal:

```
#import <Foundation/Foundation.h>
@interface ITunesFinder : NSObject <NSNetServiceBrowserDelegate>
@end // ITunesFinder
```

Remember that we don't *have* to declare methods in the `@interface`. A delegate object only has to implement the methods it's interested in having called.

Notice that we have `<NSNetServiceBrowserDelegate>` after `NSObject`. That tells the compiler and other objects that the `iTunesFinder` class implements methods or conforms to the protocol with that name (more on that in the next chapter). For now, we simply add this so the compiler won't complain.

The implementation has two methods. First come the preliminaries:

```
#import "ITunesFinder.h"
@implementation ITunesFinder
```

and then the first delegate method:

```
- (void) netServiceBrowser: (NSNetServiceBrowser *) b
      didFindService: (NSNetService *) service
        moreComing: (BOOL) moreComing {
 [service resolveWithTimeout: 10];

 NSLog (@"found one! Name is %@",
   [service name]);
} // didFindService
```

When an NSNetServiceBrowser finds a new service, it sends the netServiceBrowser:didFindSer
vice:moreComing: message to the delegate object. The browser is passed as the first argument
(which would be the same as the value of the browser variable in main). If you have multiple
service browsers doing searches at the same time, examining this parameter lets you figure out
which one has found something.

The NSNetService object passed in the second argument is an object that describes the service
that was found, such as an iTunes share. The last argument, moreComing, is used to signal
when a batch of notifications is done. Why did the Cocoa designers include this moreComing
parameter? If you ran this program on a big college network with a hundred iTunes shares, this
method would get called 99 times with moreComing having the value YES and then once with a
value of NO. This information is handy to have when constructing the user interface, so you know
when to update your window. As new iTunes shares come and go, this method is called again
and again.

[service resolveWithTimeout: 10] tells the Bonjour system to go fetch all the interesting
properties about the service. In particular, we want the name of the share, like Scott's Groovy
Tunes, so we can print it out. [service name] gets us the name of the share.

iTunes shares can come and go, as people put their laptops to sleep or move off the network.
The ITunesFinder class implements a second delegate method that gets called when a network
service vanishes:

```
- (void) netServiceBrowser: (NSNetServiceBrowser *) b
      didRemoveService: (NSNetService *) service
        moreComing: (BOOL) moreComing
{
 [service resolveWithTimeout: 10];

 NSLog (@"lost one! Name is %@",
   [service name]);

} // didRemoveService
```

This is exactly like the didFindService method, except that it logs when a service is no longer
available.

Now, run the program, and see what happens. Waqar's network has an ancient Mac mini called *Waqar Malik's Home Library* that shares iTunes music around the house. That produces this output:

```
begun browsing
found one! Name is Waqar Malik's Home Library
```

We start up iTunes on a laptop and share the music under the library name indigo:

```
found one! Name is indigo
```

After quitting iTunes on the laptop, ITunesFinder tells us

```
lost one! Name is indigo
```

Delegates and Categories

OK, so what does all this delegate stuff have to do with categories? Delegates highlight another use of categories: the methods that can be sent to a delegate are declared as a category on NSObject. Here is part of the declaration of the NSNetService delegate methods:

```
@interface NSObject (NSNetServiceBrowserDelegateMethods)
- (void) netServiceBrowserWillSearch:(NSNetServiceBrowser *) browser;
- (void) netServiceBrowser:(NSNetServiceBrowser *) aNetServiceBrowser↵
 didFindService:(NSNetService *) service moreComing: (BOOL) moreComing;
- (void) netServiceBrowserDidStopSearch:(NSNetServiceBrowser *) browser;
- (void) netServiceBrowser:(NSNetServiceBrowser *) browser didRemoveService:↵
 (NSNetService *) service moreComing: (BOOL) moreComing;
@end
```

By declaring these methods as a category on NSObject, the implementation of NSNetServiceBrowser can send one of these messages to *any* object, no matter what class it actually is. This also means that any kind of object can be a delegate, as long as it implements the method.

> **Note**   By putting a category on NSObject like this, any kind of object can be used as a delegate object. There is no need to inherit from a specialized serviceBrowserDelegate class (like you do in C++) or to conform to a specific interface (as in Java).

Putting a category on NSObject is called creating an **informal protocol**. As you know, a "protocol" in computer-speak is a set of rules that govern communication. An informal protocol is simply a way to say, "Here are some methods you might want to implement so you can do cool stuff with them." There are methods declared in the NSNetServiceBrowserDelegateMethods informal protocol that we haven't implemented in ITunesFinder. That's OK. With informal protocols, you implement only what you want.

As you might guess, there's also the concept of a formal protocol. We'll cover that in the next chapter.

Responds to Selectors

You might be asking yourself, "How does NSNetServiceBrowser know if its delegate can handle those messages that are being sent to it?" You've probably encountered the Objective-C runtime error that appears when you try sending a message that an object doesn't understand:

```
-[ITunesFinder addSnack:]: selector not recognized
```

So how does NSNetServiceBrowser get away with it? It doesn't. NSNetServiceBrowser first checks with the object by asking it, "Can you respond to this selector?" If it can, NSNetServiceBrowser sends the message.

What is a **selector**? It's just the name of a method, but it's encoded in a special way that's used by the Objective-C runtime for quick lookups. You indicate a selector by using the @selector() compiler directive, with the name of the method nestled in the parentheses. So, the selector for the Car method setEngine: would be

```
@selector(setEngine:)
```

And this would be the selector for the setTire:atIndex: Car method:

```
@selector(setTire:atIndex:)
```

NSObject provides a method called respondsToSelector: that queries an object to see if it will respond to a given message. The following chunk of code uses respondsToSelector:

```
Car *car = [[Car alloc] init];
if ([car respondsToSelector: @selector(setEngine:)])
{
 NSLog (@"yowza!");
}
```

This code prints "yowza!", because a Car object does indeed respond to the setEngine: message.

Now, check out this block of code:

```
ITunesFinder *finder = [[ITunesFinder alloc] init];
if ([finder respondsToSelector:@selector(setEngine:)])
{
 NSLog (@"yowza!");
}
```

There will be no "yowza!" this time. ITunesFinder does not have a setEngine: method.

To find out what it needs to know, NSNetServiceBrowser would call respondsToSelector:@selector(netServiceBrowser:didFindService:moreComing:). If the delegate can respond to that message, the browser will send the message. Otherwise, the browser ignores that delegate for now and just goes on its merry way.

Other Uses for Selectors

Selectors can be passed around and used as arguments to methods and even stored as instance variables. This can lead to some very powerful and flexible constructs.

One of the classes in the Foundation framework is called `NSTimer`; it can send a message to an object repeatedly, which is very handy in games when you want to move a monster toward the player on a regular basis. When you make a new `NSTimer` object, you give it the object you want it to send a message to and a selector saying which method you want it to call. For example, you could have a timer call the `moveMonsterTowardPlayer:` method of your game engine. Or, you could have another timer call an `animateOneFrame:` method.

Summary

We introduced you to categories in this chapter. Categories provide a way to add new methods to existing classes, even if you don't have the source code for those classes.

In addition to adding functionality to existing classes, categories provide a way to split an object's implementation across multiple source files or even across multiple frameworks. For example, think back to `NSString`'s data-handling methods, which are implemented in the Foundation framework, separate from its drawing methods in UIKit and AppKit.

Categories let you declare informal protocols. An informal protocol is a category on `NSObject` that lists methods that objects might be able to respond to. Informal protocols are used to implement delegation, a technique that allows you to easily customize the behavior of an object. Along the way, you also learned about selectors, which are a way to indicate a particular Objective-C message in your code.

Coming up next are Objective-C protocols, the formal protocols that are the dressed-up cousins of informal protocols.

Chapter **13**

Protocols

In the previous chapter, we talked about the magic of categories and informal protocols. When you use an informal protocol, as you saw in Chapter 12, you implement only the methods you want to respond to. For the `NSNetServiceBrowser` delegate in Chapter 12, we implemented only the two methods that are called when a new service is added to or removed from the network: we didn't have to implement the six other methods in the `NSNetServiceBrowserDelegate` informal protocol. We also didn't have to declare anything in our object saying that we're usable as an `NSNetServiceBrowser` delegate. It all just worked with a minimum of fuss.

As you might guess, Objective-C and Cocoa also include the concept of a formal protocol, and in this chapter, we'll take a look at how those work.

Formal Protocols

A **formal protocol** (like an informal protocol) is a named list of methods and properties. However, a formal protocol requires that you explicitly adopt it. You **adopt** a protocol by listing the protocol's name in your class's `@interface` declaration. When you do this, your class is said to **conform** to the protocol (and you thought you were a nonconformist). Adopting a protocol means that you promise to implement all the methods of that protocol. If you don't, the compiler yells at you by generating a warning.

> **Note** Formal protocols are just like Java interfaces. In fact, Objective-C protocols were the inspiration for Java's interfaces.

Why would you want to create or adopt a formal protocol? It sounds like a lot of work is required to implement every method. Depending on the protocol, some busywork may even be involved. But, more often than not, a protocol has only a small number of methods to implement, and you have to implement them all to gain a useful set of functionality anyway, so the formal protocol requirements are generally not a burden. Objective-C 2.0 has added some nice features that make using protocols much less onerous, which we'll talk about at the end of this chapter.

Declaring Protocols

Let's take a look at a protocol declared by Cocoa, NSCopying. If you adopt NSCopying, your object knows how to make copies of itself:

```
@protocol NSCopying
- (id) copyWithZone: (NSZone *) zone;
@end
```

The syntax looks kind of the same as the syntax for declaring a class or a category. Rather than using @interface, you use @protocol to tell the compiler, "I'm about to show you what a new formal protocol will look like." That statement is followed by the protocol name. Protocol names must be unique.

You can also can have parent protocols, similar to parent classes. To specify the parent protocol, declare it in angle brackets after the name of the protocol.

```
@protocol MySuperDuberProtocol <MyParentProtocol>
@end
```

The preceding lines mean that MySuperDuperProtocol extends MyParentProtocol, so you have to satisfy the method implementation of all the required methods in both protocols. You can always use NSObject as the root protocol. Don't confuse that with the NSObject class. The NSObject class conforms to NSObject protocol, which means that all objects conform to the NSObject protocol. It's a good idea to have the NSObject protocol as the parent of the protocol you're defining.

Next is a list of method declarations, which every protocol adopter must implement. The protocol declaration finishes with @end. No instance variables are introduced with a protocol.

Let's look at another example. Here's the NSCoding protocol from Cocoa:

```
@protocol NSCoding
- (void) encodeWithCoder: (NSCoder *) encoder;
- (id) initWithCoder: (NSCoder *) decoder;
@end
```

When a class adopts NSCoding, that class promises to implement both of these messages. encodeWithCoder: is used to take an object's instance variables and freeze-dry them into an NSCoder object. initWithCoder: extracts freeze-dried instance variables from an NSCoder and uses them to initialize a new object. These are always implemented as a pair; there's no point in encoding an object if you'll never revive it into a new one, and if you never encode an object, you won't have anything to use to create a new one.

Adopting a Protocol

To adopt a protocol, you list the protocol in the class declaration, surrounded by angle brackets. For example, if Car adopts NSCopying, the declaration looks like this:

```
@interface Car : NSObject <NSCopying>
{
// instance variables
}
// methods
@end // Car
```

And if Car adopts both NSCopying and NSCoding, the declaration goes like this:

```
@interface Car : NSObject <NSCopying, NSCoding>
{
// instance variables
}
// methods
@end // Car
```

You can list the protocols in any order; it makes no difference.

When you adopt a protocol, you're sending a message to programmers reading the class declaration, saying that objects of this class can do two very important things: they can encode/decode themselves and copy themselves.

Implementing a Protocol

That's about all there is to know regarding protocols (save a little syntactic detail when declaring variables that we'll discuss later). We'll spend the bulk of this chapter going through the exercise of adopting the NSCopying protocol for CarParts.

Car-bon Copies

Let's all chant together the rule of memory management, "If you get an object from an alloc, copy, or new, it has a retain count of 1, and you're responsible for releasing it." We've covered alloc and new already, but we really haven't discussed copy yet. The copy method, of course, makes a copy of an object. The copy message tells an object to create a brand new object and to make the new object the same as the receiver.

Now, we'll be extending CarParts so that you can make a copy of a car (wait until Detroit hears about this). The code for this lives in the *13.01 CarParts-Copy* project folder. Along the way, we'll touch on some interesting subtleties involved in implementing the copy-making code.

Makin' Copies   Actually, you can make copies in a bunch of different ways. Most objects refer to—that is, point at—other objects. When you create a **shallow** copy, you don't duplicate the referred objects; your new copy simply points at the referred objects that already exist. NSArray's copy method makes shallow copies. When you make a copy of an NSArray, your copy only duplicates the pointers to the referred objects, not the objects themselves. If you copy an NSArray that holds five NSStrings, you still end up with five strings running around your program, not ten. In that case, each object ends up with a pointer to each string.

A **deep** copy, on the other hand, makes duplicates of all the referred objects. If NSArray's copy was a deep copy, you'd have ten strings floating around after the copy was made. For CarParts, we're going to use a deep copy. This way, when you make a copy of a car, you can change a value it refers to, such as a tire's pressure, without changing the pressure for both cars.

You are free to mix and match deep and shallow copies of your composed objects, depending on the needs of your particular class.

To copy a car, we'll need to be able to make copies of engines and tires too. Programmers, start (with) your engines!

Copying Engines

The first class we'll mess with is Engine. To be able to make a copy of an engine, the class needs to adopt the NSCopying protocol. Here is the new interface for Engine:

```
@interface Engine : NSObject <NSCopying>
@end // Engine
```

Because we've adopted the NSCopying protocol, we have to implement the copyWithZone: method. A **zone** is an NSZone, which is a region of memory from which you can allocate memory. When you send a copy message to an object, it gets turned into copyWithZone: before reaching your code. Back in days of yore, NSZones were more important than they are now, but we're still stuck with them like a small piece of baggage.

Here's Engine's copyWithZone:

```
implementation:
- (id) copyWithZone: (NSZone *) zone
{
    Engine *engineCopy;
    engineCopy = [[[self class]
    allocWithZone: zone] init];
    return (engineCopy);
} // copyWithZone
```

Engine has no instance variables, so all we have to do is make a new engine object. However, that's not quite as easy as it sounds. Look at that complex statement on the right side of engineCopy. The message sends are nested three levels deep!

The first thing this method does is get the class for self. Then, it sends that class an allocWithZone: message to allocate some memory and create a new object of that class. Finally, the init message is sent to this new object to get it initialized. Let's discuss why we need that complicated nest of messages, especially the [self class] business.

Recall that alloc is a class method. allocWithZone: is a class method too, which you can tell by the leading plus sign in its method declaration:

```
+ (id) allocWithZone: (NSZone *) zone;
```

We'll need to send this message to a class, rather than an instance. What class do we send it to? Our first instinct is to send allocWithZone: to Engine, like this:

```
[Engine allocWithZone: zone];
```

That will work for Engine, but not for an Engine subclass. Why not? Ponder Slant6, which is a subclass of Engine. If you send a Slant6 object the copy message, eventually the code will end up in Engine's copyWithZone:, because we ultimately use the copying logic from Engine. And if you send allocWithZone: directly to the Engine class, a new Engine object will be created, not a Slant6 object. Things can really get confusing if Slant6 adds instance variables. In that case, an Engine object won't be big enough to hold the additional variables, so you may end up with memory overrun errors.

Now you probably see why we used [self class]. By using [self class], the allocWithZone: will be sent to the class of the object that is receiving the copy message. If self is a Slant6 object, a new Slant6 instance is created here. If some brand new kind of engine is added to our program in the future (like a MatterAntiMatterReactor), that new kind of engine will be properly copied too.

The last line of the method returns the newly created object.

Let's double-check memory management. A copy operation should return an object with a retain count of one (and not be autoreleased). We get hold of the new object via an alloc, which always returns an object with a retain count of one, and we're not releasing it, so we're A-OK in the memory management department.

That's it for making Engine copy-capable. We don't have to touch Slant6. Because Slant6 doesn't add any instance variables, it doesn't have to do any extra work when making a copy. Thanks to inheritance, and the technique of using [self class] when creating the object, Slant6 objects can be copied too.

Copying Tires

Tires are trickier to copy than engines. Tire has two instance variables (pressure and treadDepth) that need to be copied into new Tires, and the AllWeatherRadial subclass introduces two additional instance variables (rainHandling and snowHandling) that also must be copied into a new object.

First up is Tire.

```
@interface Tire : NSObject <NSCopying>
@property float pressure;
@property float treadDepth;

// … methods

@end // Tire
```

and now the implementation of copyWithZone::

```
- (id) copyWithZone: (NSZone *) zone
{
 Tire *tireCopy;
 tireCopy = [[[self class] allocWithZone: zone] initWithPressure:
      pressure treadDepth: treadDepth];
 return (tireCopy);
} // copyWithZone
```

You can see the [[self class] allocWithZone: zone] pattern here, like in Engine. Since we have to call init when we create the object, we can easily use Tire's initWithPressure:treadDepth: to set the pressure and treadDepth of the new tire to be the values of the tire we're copying. This method happens to be Tire's designated initializer, but you don't have to use the designated initializer for copying. If you want, you can use a plain init along with accessor methods to change attributes.

> **A Handy Pointer for You**   You can access public instance variables directly via the C pointer operator, like this:
>
> ```
> tireCopy->pressure = pressure;
> tireCopy->treadDepth = treadDepth;
> ```
>
> Generally, we try to use `init` methods and accessor methods in the unlikely event that setting an attribute involves extra work.

Now, it's time for `AllWeatherRadial`. The `@interface` for `AllWeatherRadial` is unchanged:

```
@interface AllWeatherRadial : Tire
// … properties
// … methods
@end // AllWeatherRadial
```

Wait—where's the `<NSCopying>`? You don't need it, and you can probably guess why. When `AllWeatherRadial` inherits from `Tire`, it pulls along all of `Tire`'s baggage, including the conformance to the `NSCopying` protocol.

We'll need to implement `copyWithZone:` though, because we have to make sure `AllWeatherRadial`'s rain- and snow-handling instance variables are copied:

```
- (id) copyWithZone: (NSZone *) zone
{
 AllWeatherRadial *tireCopy;
 tireCopy = [super copyWithZone: zone];
 tireCopy.rainHandling = rainHandling;
 tireCopy.snowHandling = snowHandling;
 return (tireCopy);
} // copyWithZone
```

Because `AllWeatherRadial` is a subclass of a class that can be copied, it doesn't need to do the `allocWithZone:` and `[self class]` jazz we used earlier. This class just asks its superclass for a copy and hopes that the superclass does the right thing and uses `[self class]` when allocating the object. Because `Tire`'s `copyWithZone:` uses `[self class]` to determine the kind of object to make, it will create a new `AllWeatherRadial` instance, which is just what we want. That code also handles copying the `pressure` and `treadDepth` values for us. Now, isn't that convenient?

The rest of the work is to set the rain- and snow-handling values. The properties are good for doing that.

Copying the Car

Now that we can make copies of engines and tires and their subclasses, it's time to make the Car itself copyable.

As you'd expect, Car needs to adopt the NSCopying protocol:

```
@interface Car : NSObject <NSCopying>
// properties
// … methods
@end // Car
```

And to fulfill its promise to NSCopying, Car must implement our old friend copyWithZone:. Here is Car's copyWithZone: method:

```
- (id) copyWithZone: (NSZone *) zone
{
  Car *carCopy;
  carCopy = [[[self class] allocWithZone: zone] init];
  carCopy.name = self.name;
  Engine *engineCopy;
  engineCopy = [[engine copy] autorelease];
  carCopy.engine = engineCopy;
  for (int i = 0; i < 4; i++)
  {
    Tire *tireCopy;
    tireCopy = [[self tireAtIndex: i] copy];
    [tireCopy autorelease];
    [carCopy setTire: tireCopy atIndex: i];
  }
  return (carCopy);
} // copyWithZone
```

That's a little more code than we've been writing, but all of it is similar to what you've seen already.

First, a new car is allocated by sending allocWithZone: to the class of the object that's receiving this message:

```
Car *carCopy;
carCopy = [[[self class] allocWithZone: zone] init];
```

CarParts-copy contains no subclasses of Car, but it might someday. You never know when someone will make one of those time-traveling DeLoreans. We can future-proof ourselves by allocating the new object using self's class, as we've done so far.

We need to copy over the car's appellation:

```
carCopy.name = self.name;
```

Remember that the name property will copy its string, so the new car will have the proper name.

Next, a copy of the engine is made, and the car copy is told to use that for its engine:

```
Engine *engineCopy;
engineCopy = [[engine copy] autorelease];
carCopy.engine = engineCopy;
```

See that autorelease? Is it necessary? Let's think through our memory management for a second. [engine copy] will return an object with a retain count of 1. setEngine: will retain the engine that's given to it, making the retain count 2. When the car copy is (eventually) destroyed, the engine will be released by Car's dealloc, so its retain count goes back to 1. By the time that happens, this code will be long gone, so nobody will be around to give it that last release to cause it to be deallocated. In that case, the engine object would leak. By autoreleasing it, the reference count will be decremented sometime in the future when the autorelease pool gets drained.

Could we have done a simple [engineCopy release] instead of autoreleasing? Yes. You'd have to do the release after the setEngine: call; otherwise, the engine copy would be destroyed before being used. Which way you choose to manage the memory is up to your own tastes. Some programmers like to keep their memory cleanup in one place in their functions, and others like to autorelease the objects at the point of creation so they don't forget to release them later on. Either approach is valid, but note that for iOS apps, Apple recommends you release right away and not use autorelease, because you don't know when the autorelease will decrement the retain count.

After carCopy is outfitted with a new engine, a for loop spins around four times, copying each tire and installing the copies on the new car:

```
for (int i = 0; i < 4; i++)
{
 Tire *tireCopy;
 tireCopy = [[self tireAtIndex: i] copy];
 [tireCopy autorelease];
 [carCopy setTire: tireCopy atIndex: i];
}
```

The code in the loop uses an accessor method to get the tire at position 0, then position 1, and so on each time through the loop. That tire is then copied and autoreleased so that its memory is handled properly. Next, the car copy is told to use this new tire at the same position. Because we constructed the copyWithZone: methods in Tire and AllWeatherRadial carefully, this code will work correctly with either kind of tire. You will notice that we did not use the NSArray's copy method, because it makes a shallow copy and we want a deep copy.

Finally, here's main() in its entirety. Most of it is old code you've seen in previous chapters; the groovy new code appears in bold:

```
int main (int argc, const char * argv[]) {
@autoreleasepool
{
 Car *car = [[Car alloc] init];
 car.name = @"Herbie";
 for (int i = 0; i < 4; i++)
 {
  AllWeatherRadial *tire;
  tire = [[AllWeatherRadial alloc] init];
  [car setTire: tire atIndex: i];
  [tire release];
 }
 Slant6 *engine = [[Slant6 alloc] init];
 car.engine = engine; [engine release];
 [car print];
 Car *carCopy = [car copy];
 [carCopy print];
 [car release];
 [carCopy release];
}
return (0);
} // main
```

After the original car is printed out, a copy is made, and that one is printed out. We should, therefore, get two sets of identical output. Run the program,, and you'll see something like this:

```
Herbie has:
AllWeatherRadial: 34.0 / 20.0 / 23.7 / 42.5
AllWeatherRadial: 34.0 / 20.0 / 23.7 / 42.5
AllWeatherRadial: 34.0 / 20.0 / 23.7 / 42.5
AllWeatherRadial: 34.0 / 20.0 / 23.7 / 42.5
I am a slant-6. VROOOM!
Herbie has:
AllWeatherRadial: 34.0 / 20.0 / 23.7 / 42.5
AllWeatherRadial: 34.0 / 20.0 / 23.7 / 42.5
AllWeatherRadial: 34.0 / 20.0 / 23.7 / 42.5
AllWeatherRadial: 34.0 / 20.0 / 23.7 / 42.5
I am a slant-6. VROOOM!
```

Protocols and Data Types

You can specify protocol names in the data types you use for instance variables and method arguments. By doing this, you give the Objective-C compiler a little more information so it can help error-check your code.

Recall that the id type represents a pointer to any kind of object; it's the generic object type. You can assign any object to an id variable, and you can assign an id variable to any kind of object pointer. If you follow id with a protocol name, complete with angle brackets, you're telling the compiler (and any humans reading the code) that you are expecting any kind of object, as long as it conforms to that protocol.

For example, NSControl has a method called setObjectValue:, which requires an object that conforms to NSCopying:

```
- (void) setObjectValue: (id<NSCopying>) object;
```

When you compile this, the compiler checks the type of the argument and gives you a warning, like "class 'Triangle' does not implement the 'NSCopying' protocol." Handy!

Objective-C 2.0 Goodies

Apple never leaves well enough alone. Objective-C 2.0 added two new modifiers for protocols: @optional and @required. Wait a minute. Did we just say that if you conform to a protocol, you're required to implement all of the protocol's methods? Yes, that's true, unless you specify the @optional keyword. So you can do groovy stuff like this:

```
@protocol BaseballPlayer
- (void)drawHugeSalary;
@optional
- (void)slideHome;
- (void)catchBall;
- (void)throwBall;
@required
- (void)swingBat;
@end // BaseballPlayer
```

This code says a class that adopts the `BaseballPlayer` protocol is required to implement `-drawHugeSalary` and `-swingBat` but has the option of sliding home, catching the ball, or throwing the ball.

Why would Apple add this feature, when informal protocols seem to work OK? It's one more tool in our arsenal to explicitly express our intent in class declarations and our method declarations. Say you saw this in a header file:

```
@interface CalRipken : Person <BaseballPlayer>
```

You know immediately that we're dealing with someone who gets paid a lot and can swing a bat and who might slide home or catch or throw the ball. With an informal protocol, there's no way to say this. Likewise, you can decorate arguments to methods with a protocol:

```
-(void)draft:(Person<BaseballPlayer>);
```

This code makes it obvious what kind of person can get drafted to play baseball. And if you do any iOS development, you'll notice the things that are informal protocols in Cocoa become formal protocols with a lot of `@optional` methods.

The Delegation Will Come to Order

Now that we've covered protocols in Objective-C, let's discuss **delegation**, a feature that's often used with protocols. Delegation is a design pattern that allows an object to designate another object to handle a particular task.

If you've looked at much Objective-C code, you've probably seen examples of delegation. For example, `UITableView` and `NSTableView` have a `dataSource` property that is handled by a delegate. An object knows that a delegate can handle a task because the delegate conforms to a protocol for the task.

We'll use a real-world example to illustrate this. Let's say that at your programming job you have a boss whose task is to create an iOS or OS X application. Does your boss do all the work? Not likely. Instead, your boss breaks up the project into small chunks, does some of the work, and assigns (delegates) the rest to other programmers depending on their expertise. Some employees are better at doing some tasks than others. Because the boss is smart, the right programmers are chosen for the right tasks.

You have actually already seen an example of delegation in the previous chapter. In the *12.04 iTunesFinder* sample, the `ITunesFinder` class is a delegate for the `NSNetServiceBrowser`.

How can `NSNetServiceBrowser` trust that the object will perform the task it needs? Let's take a look at the delegate methods for `NSNetServiceBrowser`.

```
- (id <NSNetServiceBrowserDelegate>)delegate;
- (void)setDelegate:(id <NSNetServiceBrowserDelegate>)delegate;
```

The first method returns the current delegate if it is set, or `nil` otherwise. The second one sets the delegate. The type of the argument delegate tells us that we can set any object as a delegate as long as it conforms to the expected protocol.

If you look at `NSNetServices.h`, you'll see that the protocol has quite a few methods, and all of them are optional. We can implement all, some, or none of these optional methods.

We defined the ITunesFinder class to say that we can handle the tasks that are required by the protocol.

```
@interface ITunesFinder : NSObject <NSNetServiceBrowserDelegate>
@end // ITunesFinder
```

What if we took out the `<NSNetServiceBrowserDelegate>` part and then assigned the object as a delegate? The compiler will complain "You can't handle the method!" and will produce an error (OK, maybe it uses slightly different language):

```
Sending 'ITunesFinder *__strong' to parameter of incompatible type 'id<NSNetServiceBrowser
Delegate>'
```

Let's look at the example in *13.02 Delegation*. We have three objects: Worker1, Worker2, and Manager. Workers have some work that they're required to do, and they have the option to do extra work to impress the boss. Also, keep in mind that this project uses ARC, so we don't send the release methods to objects once we're done as we would if we were ARCless.

```
int main(int argc, const char * argv[])
{
  @autoreleasepool
  {
    Manager *manager = [[Manager alloc] init];
    Worker1 *worker1 = [[Worker1 alloc] init];
    manager.delegate = worker1;
    [manager doWork];

    Worker2 *worker2 = [[Worker2 alloc] init];
    manager.delegate = worker2;
    [manager doWork];
  }
  return 0;
}
```

When we run this program, we see the following output:

```
Worker1 doing required work.
I am a manager and I am working
Worker2 doing required work.
Worker doing optional work.
I am a manager and I am working
```

The Manager does its own work and also asks the Workers to perform required work. If the Workers can perform optional work, they do that too.

```
- (void)doWork
{
  [delegate doSomeRequiredWork];
  if(YES == [delegate
       respondsToSelector:@selector(doSomeOptionalWork)])
  {
    [delegate doSomeOptionalWork];
  }
  [self myWork];
}
```

The Manager uses a delegate to get the Workers to do their required and optional work. The code asks the delegate if it has implemented the method, and if so, it asks the delegate to handle the method. Finally, the Manager does its own work.

This code might give you an idea: why not ask every object whether it has a method before calling that method? That way, the program would never crash by calling a nonexistent method. This would work, but you'd pay a huge price in slowing down your program extremely. So it's a good idea to only do this for delegates.

Summary

In this chapter, we introduced the concept of a formal protocol. You define a formal protocol by listing a set of methods inside a @protocol block. Objects adopt this formal protocol by listing the protocol name in angle brackets after the class name in an @interface statement. When an object adopts a formal protocol, it promises to implement every required method that's listed in the protocol. The compiler helps you keep your promise by giving you a warning if you don't implement all the protocol's methods.

Along the way, we explored some of the nuances that occur with object-oriented programming, particularly the issues that crop up when making copies of objects that live in a hierarchy of classes.

And now, congratulations! You've covered a great majority of the Objective-C language and have delved deeply into a number of topics that come up often in OOP. You have a good foundation for moving on to Cocoa programming or jumping into your own projects. In the next chapter, we'll study blocks, a relatively new Objective-C feature that enables you to do more powerful things with functions. We'll also discuss concurrency, which is how you can keep your computers and mobile devices busy doing several things at once.

14

Blocks and Concurrency

In this chapter, we'll discuss **blocks**, an Objective-C feature that enhances what you can do with functions. You can use blocks in applications that run on iOS (version 4.0 and later) and OS X (10.6 and later). We'll also talk about concurrency, or how to take advantage of modern devices that can do more than one thing at a time.

You're Never Too Old to Play with Blocks

Block objects (usually called simply "blocks") are extensions to C functions. In addition to the code that's normally part of a function, blocks include variable bindings as well. Blocks are also known as **closures**.

Blocks have two types of bindings: automatic and managed. **Automatic bindings** use memory on the stack, and **managed bindings** are created on the heap.

Because blocks are actually implemented at the C language level, they're available in various C-based languages, including Objective-C, C++, and Objective-C++

Blocks are available in Xcode's GCC and Clang tools, but are not part of the ANSI C standard. A proposal for blocks has been submitted to the C programming language standards group.

Blocks and Function Pointers

Before we get into blocks, let's first spend a moment talking about good old-fashioned function pointers. Why, pray tell? Because the syntax for blocks is borrowed from the syntax of function pointers. So if you know how to declare a function pointer, you know how to declare a block. Like function pointers, blocks have the following characteristics:

- Return type can be inferred or declared
- Type argument list
- Name

Let's declare a function pointer:

```
void (*my_func)(void);
```

This very basic function pointer takes no arguments and returns no results. To convert this to a block definition we just replace * (the asterisk) with ^ (a caret), like so:

```
void (^my_block)(void);
```

You use the caret operator to declare a block variable and to mark the start of the block's implementation. Just as in functions, the body of the block is contained in {} (brackets)

"Show me the code," you say? Here you go (you'll find this code in *14.01 Square*):

```
int (^square_block)(int number) =
 ^(int number) {return (number * number);};
int result = square_block(5);
printf("Result = %d\n", result);
```

This particular block takes an integer and returns the square of that number. The part before the equals sign is the block definition, and the part after the equals sign is the implementation. We can state this in general terms:

```
<returntype> (^blockname)(list of arguments) = ^(arguments){ body; };
```

The compiler infers the return type of the block literal, so you can omit it. If the block has no arguments, you can omit those too. So blocks can often be very compact and concise, like this one from *14.02 Hello Blocks*:

```
void (^theBlock)() = ^{ printf("Hello Blocks!\n"); };
```

Using a Block

Because you declared the block as a variable, you can use it just as you would a function, as you can see in *14.01 Square*:

```
int result = square_block(5);
```

No doubt, you noticed there's no caret symbol in this line of code. That's because you only use a caret when you *define* a block, not when you *invoke* it.

Blocks have another cool property that might make you want to use them instead of functions: they have access to variables that are declared in the same (local) scope as the block. This means that any variables that are available at the time of the block's creation can be accessed:

```
int value = 6;
int (^multiply_block)(int number) = ^(int number)
 {return (value * number);};
int result = multiply_block(7);
printf("Result = %d\n", result);
```

Using a Block Directly

When you want to use a block, most of the time you won't need to create a block variable. Instead, you typically just create a block instance inline with your code. Usually, you'll need a method or function that takes a block as an argument (see the following code from *14.04 Sorting Array*).

```
    NSArray *array = [NSArray arrayWithObjects:
        @"Amir", @"Mishal", @"Irrum", @"Adam", nil];
NSLog(@"Unsorted Array %@", array);
NSArray *sortedArray = [array sortedArrayUsingComparator:^(NSString
    *object1, NSString *object2) {
        return [object1 compare:object2];
}];
NSLog(@"Sorted Array %@", sortedArray);
```

You simply create a block, then set it and forget it.

Use the typedef

As you can see, that long defining variable statement can be a bit daunting. It's easy to make a mistake when typing one of those. Luckily, typedef comes to the rescue (see *14.05 Typedefed Blocks*).

```
typedef double (^MKSampleMultiply2BlockRef)(double c, double d);
```

This statement defines a block variable named MKSampleMultiply2BlockRef that takes two double numbers as arguments and returns a double number. With this typedef in place, you can use this variable like so:

```
MKSampleMultiply2BlockRef multiply2 = ^(double c, double d)
  { return c * d; };
printf("%f, %f", multiply2(4, 5), multiply2(5, 2));
```

If you look at *14.06 More Typedefs*, you'll notice we have defined quite a few different type of block variables.

```
typedef void (^MKSampleVoidBlockRef)(void);
typedef void (^MKSampleStringBlockRef)(NSString *);
typedef double (^MKSampleMultiplyBlockRef)(void);
```

Blocks and Variables

When a block is declared, it captures its state at the point of creation. Blocks can access the standard kinds of variables that functions use:

- Global variables, including local static variables within the enclosing scope.
- Global functions (not really variables, of course).
- Parameters from an enclosing scope.
- __block variables at the function level (that is, the same level as the block is declared.) These are mutable variables.
- Nonstatic variables at the enclosing scope are captured as constants.
- Objective-C instance variables.
- Local variables within the block.

We'll delve into each of these variable types in greater detail.

Local Variables

Local variables are declared in the same scope as the block. Let's take a look at this example, which is part of *14.06 More Typedefs*:

```
typedef double (^MKSampleMultiplyBlockRef)(void);
double a = 10, b = 20;

MKSampleMultiplyBlockRef multiply = ^(void){ return a * b; };
NSLog(@"%f", multiply());
a = 20;
b = 50;

// what do you think it will print?
NSLog(@"%f", multiply());
```

What do you think the second NSLog statement will print? Anyone guess 1000? As Alex Trebek would say, "Sorry, no." Why? Because the variables are local, the block will copy them and save their states at the time of the block's definition. So in this case, the NSLog will print 200.

Global Variables

In our local variables example in the preceding section, we said that the variables had the same scope as the block. You can mark the variables as static (global) to get them to behave the way you probably expected them to.

```
static double a = 10, b = 20;

MKSampleMultiplyBlockRef multiply = ^(void){ return a * b; };
NSLog(@"%f", multiply());
a = 20;
b = 50;
NSLog(@"%f", multiply());
```

Parameter Variables

Parameter variables in a block act just like parameter variables passed to a function.

```
typedef double (^MKSampleMultiply2BlockRef)(double c, double d);
MKSampleMultiply2BlockRef multiply2 = ^(double c, double d) { return c * d; };
NSLog(@"%f, %f", multiply2(4, 5), multiply2(5, 2));
```

__*block* Variables

Local variables are captured as constants within blocks. If you want to be able to modify their values, you must declare them as mutable. So, for example, the following code will fail to compile:

```
double c = 3;
MKSampleMultiplyBlockRef multiply = ^(double a, double b) { c = a * b; };
```

The compiler will yell at you with this error:

```
Variable is not assignable (missing __block type specifier)
```

To fix the compilation error, you need to mark variable c as __block, as suggested by that friendly compiler message above (see *14.07 Mutable Variables*):

```
__block double c = 3;
MKSampleMultiplyBlockRef multiply = ^(double a, double b)
  { c = a * b; };
```

Some variables can't be declared as __block. These restrictions apply:

- No variable-length arrays
- No structures that contain variable-length arrays

Block Local Variables

These variables act the same as local variables within functions.

```
 void (^MKSampleBlockRef)(void) = ^(void){
    double a = 4;
    double c = 2;
    NSLog(@"%f", a * c);
};

MKSampleBlockRef();
```

Objective-C Objects

Blocks are first-class citizens in Objective-C, which means you can treat them like you would any other objects. The biggest issue you will run into when using blocks is likely to be memory management. As we just discussed, you have to be careful when accessing Objective-C objects from within blocks. As always, there are rules to help you with memory management:

- If you reference an Objective-C object, it is retained.
- If you access an instance variable by reference, self (the object performing the method) is retained.
- If you access an instance variable by value, the variable is retained.

The first one is pretty simple, but there's a subtle difference between the other two. Let's take a look at an example from *14.08 Objective Blocks*. In that project, look at *ProcessStrings.m*.

```
    NSString *string1 = ^{
     return [_theString stringByAppendingString:_theString];
   };
 ;
```

In this example, __theString is an instance variable for a class where this block is declared. Because the instance variable is accessed directly in the block, the containing object (self) is retained. Now, here's another example:

```
NSString *localObject = _theString;
NSString *string2 = ^{
  return [localObject stringByAppendingString:localObject];
};
```

In this one, we have indirection: we make a local reference to the instance variable and use that in the body of the block. This time, the localObject, and not self, is retained.

Because blocks are objects, you can send all the memory management messages to them. At the C level, you have to use the Block_copy() and Block_release() functions to properly manage memory. *14.09 Block Copy* shows you how to copy blocks.

```
MKSampleVoidBlockRef block1 = ^{
  NSLog(@"Block1");
};
block1();

MKSampleVoidBlockRef block2 = ^{
  NSLog(@"Block2");
};
block2();
Block_release(block2);

block2 = Block_copy(block1);
block2();
```

Concurrency, or Keeping Up with Yourself

Up to this point, most of the code we've discussed makes things happen one after the other, in sequential order. Now, we'll talk about moving past that limitation.

Your Mac that runs Xcode has at least two processor cores, and maybe a lot more. Even the latest iOS devices have multiple cores. This means you can have more than one thing happening at the same time. Apple provides various APIs to take advantage of multiple cores. Programs that have more than one thing executing at the same time are said to be **concurrent**.

The most basic technique for taking advantage of concurrency is using POSIX threads to handle different parts of your program that can execute independently. POSIX threads have both a C and an Objective-C API. To write concurrent applications requires creating multiple threads, and writing threaded code is challenging. Because threads are a low-level API, you have to manage them manually. Depending on the hardware and other software running, the conditions for the number of threads required can change. Handling all this is tricky, and once you've scoped out the problem, you might decide you're actually better off without threaded code.

Apple to the rescue! To reduce the burden of programming for multiple cores, Apple introduced Grand Central Dispatch, affectionately known as GCD. This technology takes much of the burden of thread management from you so you can concentrate on just writing code for your task. To use GCD, you submit blocks or functions to be run as threads. GCD is a system-level technology, so you can use it at any level of your code. GCD decides how many threads are needed and when to schedule them to run. Because it runs at the system level, it can balance your application's load along with everything else running, making the computer or device perform more efficiently.

Synchronize

OK, kids, it's analogy time. You're driving along a multilane highway, and other cars are going by you, while you're passing some slower cars. Imagine multiple paths of execution happening the same way on your computer. Just like in traffic, some execution paths take a long time, and some are quick. During rush hour, when you want to get on the freeway, you have to wait for cars in front of you as one car at a time joins the road. Lanes and traffic signals control the flow to keep the traffic moving as smoothly as possible. Stepping out of our cars and inside our computers, how do we manage traffic when it consists of processes? We use a synchronization device such as a flag or a **mutex** to gate access.

> **Note**   "Mutex" is short for "**mut**ual **ex**clusion," which refers to the problem of ensuring that no two threads can be in their critical section at the same time.

Objective-C provides a language-level keyword called @synchronized. This keyword takes an argument, typically the object that is being modified.

```
@synchronized(theObject)
{
// Critical section.
}
```

This ensures that the critical code section is accessed serially from different threads.

When you define a property and you don't specify the keyword nonatomic as an attribute of the property, the compiler generates getters and setters that enforce mutual exclusion. If you don't care, or you know that the values for the property will not be accessed from multiple threads, you can add the nonatomic attribute. Why would you want to do that? The reason is to squeeze out a bit more performance. How does that work? The compiler generates @synchronize (mutex, atomic) to ensure mutual exclusion. There's overhead involved in setting up code and variables to work that way, which can make access to them much slower than direct access.

Select Performance

If you simply want to have some code execute in the background, NSObject provides methods that allow you to do just that. These methods all have performSelector: in their names. The simplest of these is performSelectorInBackground:withObject:, which executes one of your methods in the background. It works by creating a thread to run your method. There are some restrictions (surprise!) on how those methods must be defined:

- ▓   Because these methods are running on their own threads, you must create an autorelease pool for Cocoa objects. The main autorelease pool is associated with the main thread.

- ▓   The methods must not return any values and must either take no arguments or have one object as an argument. In other words, the methods must have one of the following signatures:

```
- (void)myMethod;
- (void)myMethod:(id)myObject;
```

With those restrictions in mind, our method implementation looks like this (*14.10 Selectors*):

```
- (void)myBackgroundMethod
{
 @autoreleasepool
 {
   NSLog(@"My Background Method");
 }
}
```

or

```
- (void)myOtherBackgroundMethod:(id)myObject
{
 @autoreleasepool
 {
   NSLog(@"My Background Method %@", myObject);
 }
}
```

To execute your method in the background, just call performSelectorInBackground:withObject:, like so:

```
[self performSelectorInBackground:@selector(myBackgroundMethod)
 withObject:nil];
[self performSelectorInBackground:@selector(myOtherBackgroundMethod:)
 withObject:arugmentObject];
```

That's it. You're done. Once the method is finished executing, the Objective-C runtime takes care of cleaning up and getting rid of the thread. Note that you won't be notified when the method finishes executing: this is the bare bones, low-rent version. If you want to do anything more complicated, you need to read on to discover the exciting world of dispatch queues.

Every Day I Get in the Queue

GCD uses **dispatch queues**, which are similar to threads but much simpler to use. You just write your code, assign it a queue, and then have the system execute it. You can execute arbitrary code asynchronously or synchronously. There are three types of queues:

- *Serial*: Each serial queue executes tasks one at time in the order they were assigned. You can create as many of these queues you want, and they will operate in parallel, with one task executing per queue.

- *Concurrent*: Each concurrent queue executes one or more tasks concurrently. Tasks are started in the order they were assigned to the queue. You can't create concurrent queues. Instead, you use one of three queues provided by the system.

- *Main*: This is the main queue that is available for your application. This queue executes tasks on the main thread of your program.

Next, we'll discuss these various kinds of queues and how you might use them.

A Bowl of Serial

Sometimes, you have a series of tasks that need to happen in a given order. You can use a serial queue for that. Task execution order is first in, first out (FIFO): the queue ensures that the tasks are executed in predictable order, as long as the tasks are submitted asynchronously. These queues can never deadlock.

> **Not the hairstyle**   **Deadlock** is an unhappy condition in which two or more competing tasks are each waiting on the other to finish. You can observe this in real life when cars arrive simultaneously at a four-way stop.

Let's whip up a serial queue:

```
dispatch_queue_t my_serial_queue;
my_serial_queue = dispatch_queue_create
 ("com.apress.MySerialQueue1", NULL);
```

The first argument is the name of the queue, and the second provides attributes for the queue (although it's not used now and must be NULL). Once the queue is created, we can assign tasks to it. Queues are reference-counted objects, so we'll have the inevitable memory management discussion later in this section.

Concurrent Dispatch Queues

Concurrent dispatch queues are good for tasks that can run in parallel. Concurrent queues are first in, first out (FIFO), and a task can start before the previous one is finished. The number of tasks that can run at once is not predictable: it varies over time depending on what else is running. So every time you run the program, the number of concurrent tasks might be different.

> **Note**   If you need to be sure that you run same number of tasks every time, you can manage threads manually with the Threads API.

Each application gets three concurrent queues to use: high, default, and low priority. To get a reference to any of these, you call dispatch_get_global_queue (see *14.11 Hello Queue*).

```
dispatch_queue_t myQueue;
myQueue = dispatch_get_global_queue
 (DISPATCH_QUEUE_PRIORITY_DEFAULT, 0);
```

The other options for priority are DISPATCH_QUEUE_PRIORITY_HIGH and DISPATCH_QUEUE_PRIORITY_LOW. The second argument is always 0 for now. Because these are global, you don't have to manage memory for them. You don't need to keep a reference to these queues—just use the function to get access when you need it.

Right Down Main Street

Use `dispatch_get_main_queue` to access the serial queue associated with the application's main thread.

```
dispatch_queue_t main_queue = dispatch_get_current_queue(void);
```

Because this queue is associated with the main thread, you must be very careful about scheduling tasks on this queue, as they will block your main application. You typically use this queue for synchronization, submitting multiple tasks and performing some action when they are all complete.

I Am Jack's Dispatch Queue

You can find out which queue a block is running on by calling `dispatch_get_current_queue()`. If you call this function outside of a block object, it returns the main queue.

```
dispatch_queue_t myQueue = dispatch_get_current_queue();
```

Memory Management Is for Queues Too

Dispatch queues are reference-counted objects. You use `dispatch_retain()` and `dispatch_release()` to modify the retain count for queues. As you might guess, these are similar to `retain` and `release` for conventional objects. You can use these functions only with queues you create, and not the global dispatch queues. In fact, if you send these messages to global queues, they'll simply be ignored, so no harm done. If you're writing an OS X application that uses garbage collection, you must manage these queues manually.

Context for Queues

You can assign a global data context to your dispatch objects, including dispatch queues. You can assign just about any kind of data, such as Objective-C objects or pointers, to this context. The system only knows that the context contains data associated with your queue. You must manage the memory for the context data. You have to allocate memory when you need it and clean up the data before the queue is deallocated. Once you have allocated your context data, you can use the `dispatch_set_context()` and `dispatch_get_context()` functions.

```
NSMutableDictionary *myContext =
 [[NSMutableDictionary alloc] initWithCapacity:5];
[myContext setObject:@"My Context" forKey:@"title"];
[myContext setObject:[NSNumber numberWithInt:0] forKey:@"value"];
dispatch_set_context(_serial_queue,
 (__bridge_retained void *)myContext);
```

In this example, we created the context as a dictionary, but we can use any pointer type. We could even allocate raw memory and use that.

In the last line, we need to say that the queue must keep track of this object. We use `__bridge_retained` to increment the retain count on `myContext`.

Cleanup Function

Once you have set up the data for the context object, when do you get rid of it? The easy answer is that you don't really know when and where the context object will go away. To handle this situation, you can tell the object to call a function when it's going away, similar to the dealloc method for classes. The signature of the function must be as follows:

```
void function_name(void *context);
```

We'll create an example function to be called when the context object is going away, typically called a **finalizer** function:

```
void myFinalizerFunction(void *context)
{
  NSLog(@"myFinalizerFunction");
  NSMutableDictionary *theData = (__bridge_transfer
   NSMutableDictionary*)context;
  [theData removeAllObjects];
}
```

Let's talk a little about the __bridge_transfer keyword. This keyword transfers the management of the object's memory from the global pool to our function. When our function terminates, ARC will decrement its retain count, and when the retain count reaches zero, the object will be released. But if the object is not released, myContext will hang around until the heat death of the universe (approximately).

How do we access the context from inside of our block?

```
NSMutableDictionary *myContext = (__bridge NSMutableDictionary *)
    dispatch_get_context(dispatch_get_current_queue());
```

Why did we add the __bridge keyword here? We're telling ARC that we're not interested in managing the memory for the context. We want the system to keep managing it.

Adding Tasks

There are two ways to add tasks to the queue:

- *Synchronously*: The queue waits until the task is finished.

- *Asynchronously*: The task is added, and the function returns immediately, without waiting for the task to finish. This technique is preferred because it doesn't block other code from running.

You can submit either a block or a function to execute on the queue. There are four dispatch functions: each of sync and async, for a block or for a function. We'll take a look at each type of dispatch function.

> **Note**   To avoid deadlock, you should never call dispatch_sync or dispatch_sync_f from a task that is running on the same queue.

Programming with Dispatch

The easiest way to add a task to a queue is via a block. The block must be of type `dispatch_block_t`, which is defined as taking no arguments and returning no results:

```
typedef void (^dispatch_block_t)(void)
```

Let's add our async block. It's a function that takes two arguments, the queue and the block, respectively.

```
dispatch_async(_serial_queue, ^{ NSLog(@"Serial Task 1"); });
```

If you prefer, you can define a block ahead of time, instead of inline.

```
dispatch_block_t myBlock = ^{ NSLog(@"My Predfined block"); };
dispatch_async(_serial_queue, myBlock);
```

To add the function synchronously instead, use `dispatch_sync`.

As we said earlier, we can also add a function to the queue. The prototype for the function must be as follows:

```
void function_name(void *argument)
```

Here's an example function:

```
void myDispatchFuction(void *argument)
{
  NSLog(@"Serial Task %@", (__bridge NSNumber *)argument);
  NSMutableDictionary *context = (__bridge NSMutableDictionary *)
    dispatch_get_context(dispatch_get_current_queue());
  NSNumber *value = [context objectForKey:@"value"];
  NSLog(@"value = %@", value);
}
```

Next, we need to add this function to the queue. The dispatch function takes three arguments: the queue, any context you need to pass, and the function. If you don't need to send extra information to the function, you can just pass NULL.

```
dispatch_async_f(_serial_queue, (__bridge void *)[NSNumber numberWithInt:3],
    (dispatch_function_t)myDispatchFuction);
```

As soon as the queue is created, it's ready and waiting for tasks. When we add a task, the queue schedules it. To add to the queue synchronously instead, call `dispatch_sync_f`.

If you want to stop the queue for any reason, call `dispatch_suspend()` and pass the queue.

```
dispatch_suspend(_serial_queue);
```

Once you have suspended the queue, you can resume it by calling `dispatch_resume()`. You are the master of time and space.

```
dispatch_resume(_serial_queue);
```

Operation Queues

You probably noticed that this stuff is pretty low level. Whatever happened to Objective-C, you might ask? Weren't you recently reading a book about that language? In fact, there are APIs, called **operations**, at the Objective-C level that make working with queues somewhat easier.

To use operations, you first create an operation object; then, you assign it to the operation queue, and let the queue execute it. There are three ways to create operations:

- NSInvocationOperation: Use this when you already have a class that does your work, and you want to perform it on a queue.

- NSBlockOperation: This is just like calling dispatch_async with a block of code to execute.

- *Your custom operation*: If you need more flexibility in operation types, you can get fancy and create your own custom type. You must define your operation by subclassing NSOperation.

We'll spend some time and ink (or electrons, for you eBook readers) discussing each of these techniques.

Creating an Invocation Operation

NSInvocationOperation invokes a selector for your class that performs your work. That's why this is handy if you already have a class built with selectors (see *14.12 Objective Queue*).

```
@implementation MyCustomClass
- (NSOperation *)operationWithData:(id)data
{
  return [[NSInvocationOperation alloc] initWithTarget:self
    selector:@selector(myWorkerMethod:) object:data];
}
// This is the method that does the actual work
- (void)myWorkerMethod:(id)data
{
    NSLog(@"My Worker Method %@", data);
}
@end
```

Once you add the operation to the queue and the task is ready to be executed, the myWorkerMethod: method of the class will be called.

Creating a Block Operation

If you have block of code that you want to execute on the queue, you can create this operation and have the queue run it.

```
NSBlockOperation *blockOperation =
 [NSBlockOperation blockOperationWithBlock:^{
  // Do my work
}];
```

The blocks for these operations are of the same type that we used in dispatch queues. Once you have created a block operation with your first block, you can add more blocks using the `addExecutionBlock:` method. Depending on the queue type (serial or concurrent) the blocks will run in serial or parallel, respectively.

```
[blockOperation addExecutionBlock:^{
    // do some more work
}];
```

Adding Operations to the Queue

Once you have created an operation, you need to add blocks to the queue. Instead of using `dispatch_queue_t` as in the previous section, this time, we'll use `NSOperationQueue`. `NSOperationQueue` always executes operations concurrently. It also takes dependencies into account, so if one operation depends on the another, they will execute accordingly.

If you want to make sure you always execute your operation serially, you can set the maximum concurrent operations to 1 and tasks will execute in FIFO order. Before you can add an operation to a queue, you need a way to refer to that queue. You can create a queue or use one of the predefined queues, such as the current queue:

```
NSOperationQueue *currentQueue = [NSOperationQueue currentQueue];
```

or the main queue:

```
NSOperationQueue *mainQueue = [NSOperationQueue mainQueue];
```

Here's how we create a queue of our very own:

```
NSOperationQueue *_operationQueue = [[NSOperationQueue alloc] init];
```

Now that we have a queue, we can use `addOperation:` to add an operation:

```
[theQueue addOperation:blockOperation];
```

Or we can add a block to execute instead of creating an operation object:

```
[theQueue addOperationWithBlock:^{
  NSLog(@"My Block");
}];
```

Once you add the operation to the queue, it will be scheduled and executed.

Summary

In this chapter, we presented blocks, a relatively recent addition to Objective-C that enhances what you can do with functions. Blocks let you bind variables to functions to create objects you can use in your programs. Blocks are especially useful for implementing concurrency.

The topic of concurrency is vast and complicated. In this chapter, we described some of the concurrency features available to your programs in OS X and iOS.

Apple's Grand Central Dispatch (GCD) feature provides a way for your apps to use concurrency without having to spend all your time programming at the low levels of the system. You should experiment with GCD and other concurrent programming features to find out what's possible for your apps and what you're comfortable doing.

As your skills evolve and as Apple adds more tools, your apps will be able to do more tasks in parallel, which will make them more responsive. However, there's always a point of diminishing returns at which the cost (in extra time spent coding and debugging) of adding parallel processing to your apps outweighs the benefits.

As you work more with concurrent tasks, heed warnings about creating deadlocks (tasks that depend on each other and so can never finish) and other bad bugs. These are things that you probably don't want to happen.

Chapter 15

Introduction to UIKit

So far, we have had a lot of fun learning about writing apps for OS X, the Mac operating system. But enough of that Mac stuff for a while. It's time to switch gears and take a look at how to write an app for iOS. Just as Mac apps use AppKit, iOS apps use UIKit. It has all the UI components and goodness that make iOS apps what they are.

iOS doesn't have command-line access, so we can't create a command-line tool as we did for OS X. Instead, we'll start by duplicating the CaseTool program we wrote for OS X in Chapter 14. You don't even need an iOS device to do this exercise. All you need is Xcode with the iOS SDK, which installs by default when you get Xcode from the Mac App Store.

Keep in mind a few ways that iOS differs from OS X:

- There is no shell or console.

- Applications run in a simulator on your Mac.

- Some non-UI APIs are not available.

- Most programmers think it's much easier to develop iOS apps.

Our finished product will look like Figure 15-1 on an iPhone. Like CaseTool back in Chapter 14, this app changes your strings into all uppercase or all lowercase.

Let's start our adventure by launching Xcode (if it's not already running). The first thing we need to do is make a project using the iOS SDK. Select **File ➤ New ➤ New Project** or ⌘+shift+N, as shown in Figure 15-2.

This will bring up a sheet to select the project type. We'll choose iOS Application from the list at the left, which then displays the application types (see Figure 15-3).

We select Single View Application. As the name implies, this application just displays a view. Apps of this type are typically very simple and don't require much of a user interface.

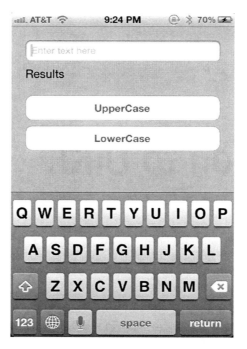

Figure 15-1. *A preview of CaseTool on an iPhone*

Figure 15-2. *Create a new project*

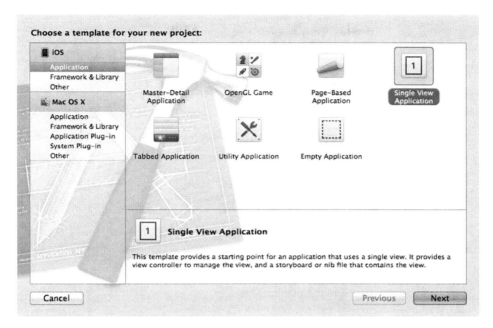

Figure 15-3. Choose the application type

Here are what the other templates are for:

- *Master-Detail* uses a navigation controller and a table view for a list of items and details of those items when selected.

- *OpenGL Game* is for making super awesome time-wasting games.

- *Page-Based* lets you build book-like apps that have page flip animations (for iPad only).

- *Tabbed* makes multiview applications, which you commonly see on iPhone apps that have a tab bar at the bottom and a view associated with each tab.

- The *Utility Application* template has a main view, which is similar to what you get in Single View applications, but adds a flip view.

- *Empty Application* is an advanced option you can use if none of the templates fit or you know exactly how you want to build your app.

Once you have selected *Single View Application*, click *Next*. You'll see the dialog that asks you to name your app. We're going to use the same name we used for our OS X application: CaseTool.

On this screen, make sure *Use Storyboard* and *Include Unit Tests* are not selected, but be sure *Use Automatic Reference Counting* is selected. For Device Family, we'll choose *Universal*, which means our application will run on the iPhone, iPod touch, and iPad. Once you've made all your selections, click *Next* to move to the next screen, where you'll select which directory to use for saving your project (see Figure 15-5).

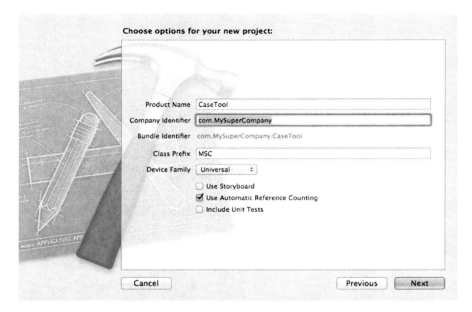

Figure 15-4. It's time to play "name that app"

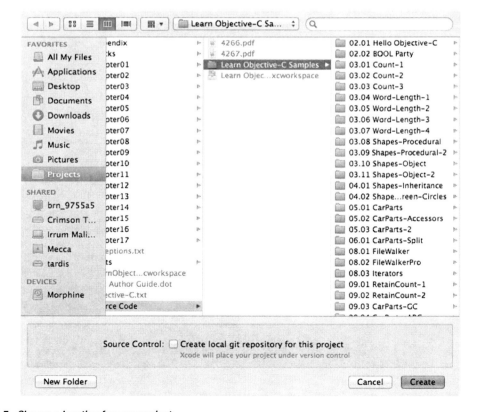

Figure 15-5. Choose a location for your project

When you have created your project, Xcode opens it and shows it to you (see Figure 15-6).

Figure 15-6. *Our new project*

Take a look in the file list. We have files for the application delegate, plus another class and two nib files, one for iPhone and one for iPad. (If you don't choose *Universal* when you create the project, you only get one of those files.)

Let's delve into our application delegate header file. First is our trusty #import, which you probably remember from all the way back in Chapter 14. Interface elements for iOS start with the prefix UI, because we're using UIKit instead of AppKit. We also have the Foundation framework, which works on iOS just as for OS X. So classes like NSString are available, and they work like they do in OS X.

```
#import <UIKit/UIKit.h>
@class MSCViewController;
@interface MSCAppDelegate : UIResponder <UIApplicationDelegate>
@property (strong, nonatomic) UIWindow *window;
@property (strong, nonatomic) MSCViewController *viewController;
@end
```

In the code, you'll see that we have a window object and a view controller object. Here's the implementation:

```
- (BOOL)application:(UIApplication *)application
    didFinishLaunchingWithOptions:(NSDictionary *)launchOptions
```

```
{
  self.window = [[UIWindow alloc] initWithFrame:[[UIScreen mainScreen] bounds]];
  // Override point for customization after application launch.
  if ([[UIDevice currentDevice] userInterfaceIdiom] == UIUserInterfaceIdiomPhone) {
    self.viewController = [[MSCViewController alloc] initWithNibName:
@"MSCViewController_iPhone" bundle:nil];
  } else {
    self.viewController = [[MSCViewController alloc] initWithNibName:
@"MSCViewController_iPad" bundle:nil];
  }
  self.window.rootViewController = self.viewController;
  [self.window makeKeyAndVisible];
  return YES;
}
```

This code kicks off by creating a window object. All applications run in this main window. Next, we create our view controller, which varies depending on the device that's running the code. Then, we ask the view controller for the view to add to your hierarchy. This is boilerplate code that pretty much every app uses. In fact, even if you create your application based on other templates, it will look very similar to this.

View Controllers

The main pattern Cocoa uses is Model-View-Controller, as we discussed in Chapter 14. Sure enough, in our application we have a view, a controller, and a kind of model.

Our view comes from a nib file. This is handy because it's faster to design and load a view from a nib file than to create one by hand.

Our class MCSViewController is a subclass of UIViewController. UIViewController knows how to do the typical tasks of managing a view, such as putting it on the screen, resizing, rotating, and so on. Since we are managing a view, it makes sense to subclass our class from it.

Why can't we just use UIViewController? We need to add few items to the view, and the UIViewController doesn't know about those. So we subclass it and teach the subclass to deal with the things we add.

Adding Items to the Nib File

Select the iPhone-specific nib file MSCViewControler_iPhone.xib. You'll see the app's view at the size of an iPhone screen. You'll also notice that the object pane displays items that are specific to iOS (see Figure 15-7).

Let's work on the nib file. Select a Text Field object from the Objects pane at the lower right and drag it to the view. Adjust the size to fit inside the width of the screen, paying attention to the guides when you adjust the size (see Figure 15-8).

Next, we're going to drag a label object and add it to the view, then adjust its size. The result is in Figure 15-9.

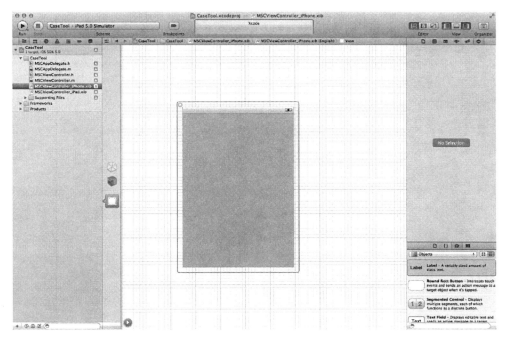

Figure 15-7. The iPhone nib file

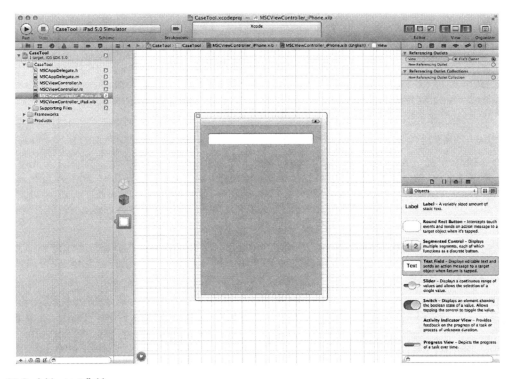

Figure 15-8. Add a text field

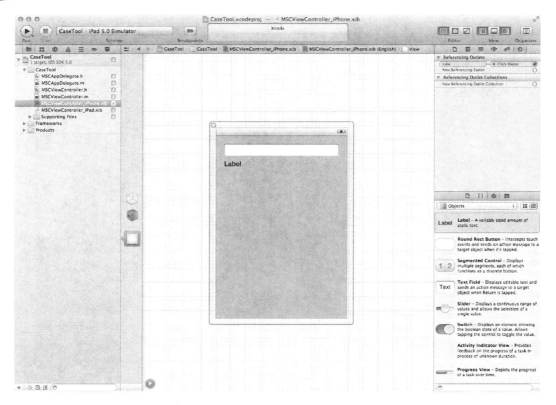

Figure 15-9. *Put a label under the text field*

The next step is to add a button. In the Objects pane, select Round Rect Button, and drag one to the view under the text field and label. Once the button is there, adjust its size and layout to match the text field's width, as in Figure 15-10.

Now double-click the round rect button to give it a title. We shall call it UpperCase (see Figure 15-11).

We have a button for changing text to uppercase. We also need one for the opposite function. Drag another round rectangular button to the view, and put it under the first one. Adjust its size so it looks like its fellow button, and name it LowerCase, as shown in Figure 15-12. (Here's a shortcut tip: you can also create the second button by selecting the first one and then choosing **Edit ➤ Duplicate**, or just pressing ⌘+D.)

Of course, you don't have to lay out your view the way we have. You can adjust the size and position of the objects however you want, so feel free to go crazy. Our complete view layout looks like Figure 15-13.

Now that we have the view just as we want it, it's time for the fun of connecting outlets and actions. On the right side of the toolbar, click the middle button of the Editor group to open the assistant, or press ⌘+option+return on the keyboard if you prefer shortcuts. Arrange the nib file and the header file `MCSViewController.h` so it's easy to drag and connect between them. Remember the control-drag fun we had back in Chapter 14? Let's do that again. Control-drag from the text field in the view and toward the header file (see Figure 15-14).

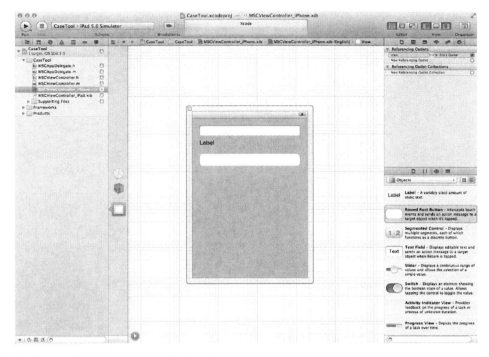

Figure 15-10. *We've added a wide round rect button. Round rects are everywhere!*

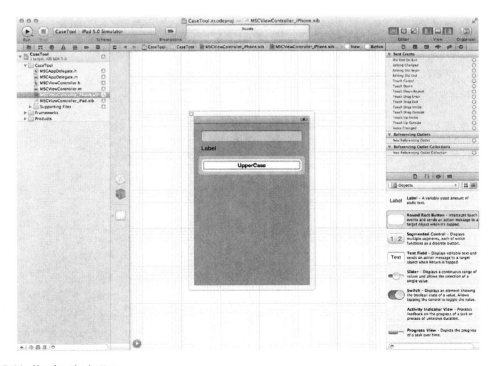

Figure 15-11. *Naming the button*

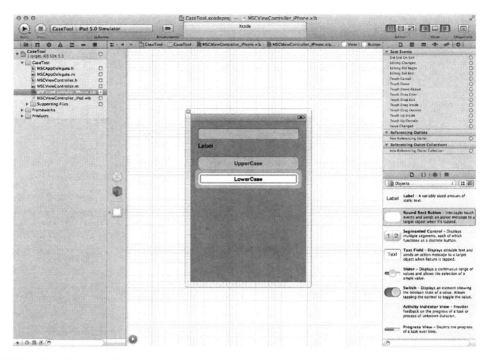

Figure 15-12. *Putting the second button into place*

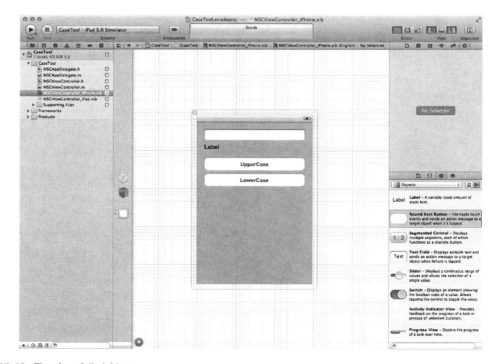

Figure 15-13. *The view, fully laid out*

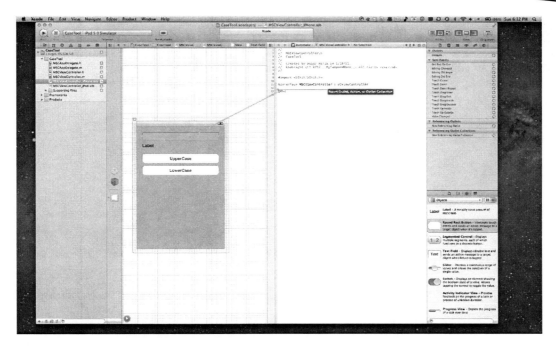

Figure 15-14. *Control-drag to make the first connection*

Drop the line you're dragging between the @interface and @end in the header file (also in Figure 15-14). Xcode pops up a groovy little window (see Figure 15-15).

Figure 15-15. *This appears when you create a new connection*

The window in Figure 15-15 asks you to enter the name of the outlet. But before we do that, notice that next to Object are the words "File's Owner." What is that? Well, when you load a nib file, it's owned by a controller. When the template created the nib file and the controller file, it made our controller the nib file's owner. If you need to, you can change the nib file's owner by selecting File's Owner from the nib file and changing its class. But for now, we'll leave it as it is.

Now we're ready to name the outlet. Type **textField**, and click Connect.

By performing this procedure, we just added an outlet (see Figure 15-16). If you look at the header file, you'll see that code has been added to specify the outlet. Note that the name of the class is UITextField. If you remember back in Chapter 14 with our Mac example, we used NSTextField, which is similar to UITextField but not exactly the same.

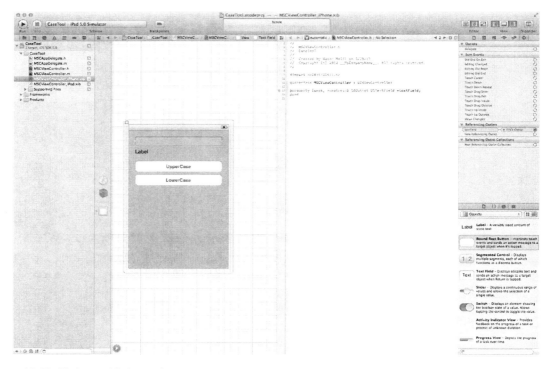

Figure 15-16. We have added an outlet

Now, let's connect the label to hold the result. Control-drag from the label to just below the code for the textField outlet.

Figure 15-17. Name the outlet for the label

Enter resultsField for the name, and click Connect. Now, we have two outlets, as shown in the header file (see Figure 15-18).

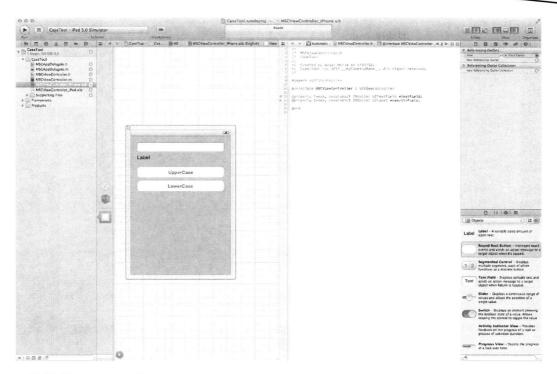

Figure 15-18. *We have two outlets*

Now it's time to make our buttons work. We do this by adding actions for the buttons. We don't need outlets for them, because outlets would be used to change their values, which we don't need to do.

To create the first button action, control-drag from the UpperCase button, and drop it below `resultsField` in the header, as shown in Figure 15-19.

This time we want to create an action, so click Outlet, and change it to Action. This changes the options available in the box (see Figure 15-20).

Here's some information about each item in the Connection dialog:

- *Name*: This item contains the name of the action we're creating.

- *Type*: This is the class name for the action's argument. By default, this value is `id` (the generic class), but you can change that to whichever class is sending the action. In our case, the class sending the action is `UIButton`.

- *Event*: This differs greatly between OS X and iOS. In iOS, there are many more event types, due to the touch interface. In this case, we're going to use the Touch Up Inside event. This means that the button action will be called when the user's finger stops touching the screen while still inside the button. Figure 15-21 shows all the different kinds of events available for iOS actions.

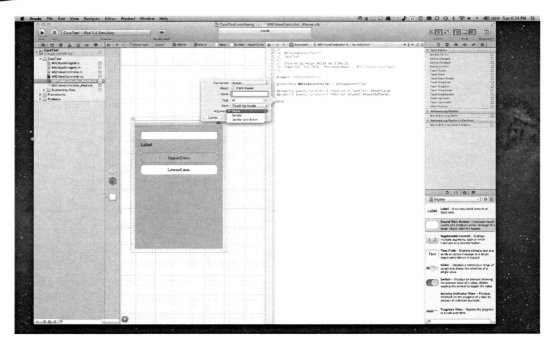

Figure 15-19. *Control-drag to create the first button action*

Figure 15-20. *Dialog box for setting up the UpperCase button*

■ *Arguments*: In OS X applications, we don't get an option for arguments, because all actions have one argument. In the happy world of iOS, we have three options: *None*, *Sender* (which is what happens in OS X), and *Sender and Event* (which includes a `UIEvent` argument that you can query to decide what to do). We're going to choose *None* for our action (see Figure 15-22).

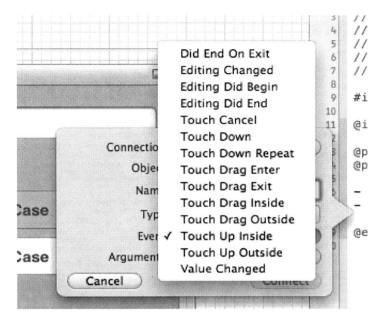

Figure 15-21. Choose the event kind for the action

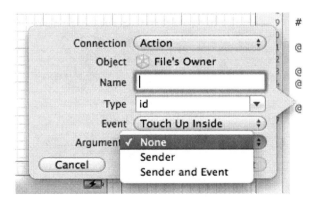

Figure 15-22. Choose None for the arguments

Completing this step creates the code for the action, and the code is added to the header file.

Next, we create an action for the LowerCase button.

Now that we're done with the interface connections, let's add some code. (Sadly, programming still requires this.) Some of the boilerplate code is already there, such as synthesizing properties and empty implementations of actions.

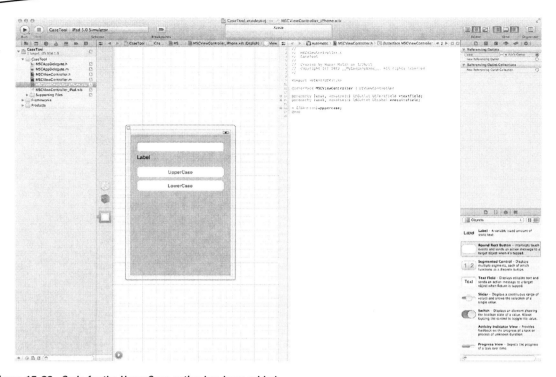

Figure 15-23. *Code for the UpperCase action has been added*

Figure 15-24. *Create the action for the second button*

Recall from Chapter 14 that from our application delegate we call

```
- (id)initWithNibName:(NSString *)nibNameOrNil bundle:(NSBundle *)nibBundleOrNil
```

This method is in our parent class, so we don't need to implement it. We call this method to load the nib file, which we'll need if we want access to outlets. So we'll call the method:

```
- (id)initWithNibName:(NSString *)nibNameOrNil bundle:(NSBundle *)nibBundleOrNil
{
  self = [super initWithNibName:nibNameOrNil bundle:nibBundleOrNil];
  if(nil != self)
```

```
  {
    NSLog (@"init: text %@ / results %@", textField, resultsField);
  }
  return self;
}
```

Also in Chapter 14, we talked about awakeFromNib. The view controller calls viewDidLoad after the nib has been loaded and objects have been initialized. Some previous versions of iOS also called awakeFromNib, but in iOS 5, it does not get called.

Let's add awakeFromNib:

```
- (void)awakeFromNib
{
    NSLog(@"awake: text %@ / results %@", textField, resultsField);
}
```

We'll add a minimal implementation of viewDidLoad. This is typically where you'll modify your outlets or set up other UI items, as you're guaranteed to have your nib file loaded when viewDidLoad is called. We'll use it to set some of the defaults for our text fields.

```
- (void)viewDidLoad
{
  [super viewDidLoad];
  // Do any additional setup after loading the view, typically from a nib.
  NSLog (@"viewDidLoad: text %@ / results %@", textField, resultsField);

  [textField setPlaceholder:@"Enter text here"];
  resultsField.text = @"Results";
}
```

This code sets the placeholder for textField, which is the gray text displayed before the user enters anything in the field. We also set the defaults for the label to let the user know where to expect to see the results.

Next in the code, you'll see viewDidUnload. This method is called after the view is removed from the view hierarchy. Why do we care about that? The answer is memory conservation.

iOS does not use virtual memory. Apps are constrained by available memory in the device. Plus, if we use too much memory, iOS will strike down **upon us** with great vengeance and furious anger, killing our app. We can use viewDidUnload to help clean up after ourselves.

In iOS (particularly iPhone) apps, most of the time when a view goes away, it's replaced on the screen by another one. When this happens, the previous view is no longer visible, so we don't need to keep it around. iOS unloads the view to save memory, so viewDidUnload gives us a chance to remove items from the view so we can save some memory. In this case, we remove textField and resultsField. These two methods are called once for the lifetime of the view.

There are four other methods (viewWillAppear:, viewDidAppear:, viewWillDisappear:, and viewDidDisappear:) that get called when a view is going away or appearing. These get called every time it's appropriate, even if the view does not get unloaded.

Now, let's add the code that actually does the uppercasing and lowercasing.

```
- (IBAction)uppercase
{
  NSString *original = textField.text;
  NSString *uppercase = [original uppercaseString];
  resultsField.text = uppercase;
}
- (IBAction)lowercase
{
  NSString *original = textField.text;
  NSString *lowercase = [original lowercaseString];
  resultsField.text = lowercase;
}
```

For iOS text fields, we ask the field to use an NSString method to convert its text (just as we did in OS X code in Chapter 14) and then set the label's text property to the modified string. Just like the OS X version, we'll use stringValue and setStringValue: for this.

We claimed we're building a universal app, one that runs on both iPhone and iPad, but we haven't worked on the iPad nib file yet. Let's fix that.

Select the iPad version of the nib file, ViewController_iPad.xib. Add the required UI elements to make it look like the iPhone version we created earlier. We can create the elements one at a time as we did for the iPhone version, or for faster service we can shift-select multiple items in the iPhone view, copy them, and paste them into the iPad view. The result looks something like Figure 15-25.

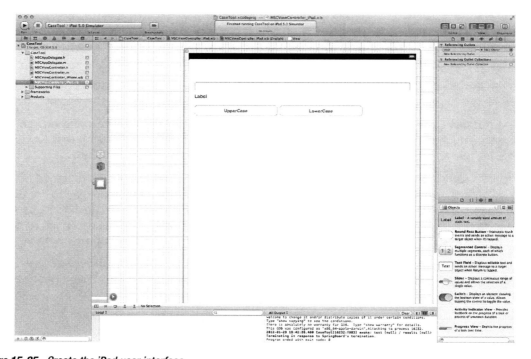

Figure 15-25. Create the iPad user interface

We're getting closer, but we're not quite there yet. If we build and run the app now, we can actually type in the text field and click the buttons, but they don't do anything. To make it work, we have to connect our outlets and actions.

In the iPad nib, control-drag from File's Owner, and drop on the text field (see Figure 15-26).

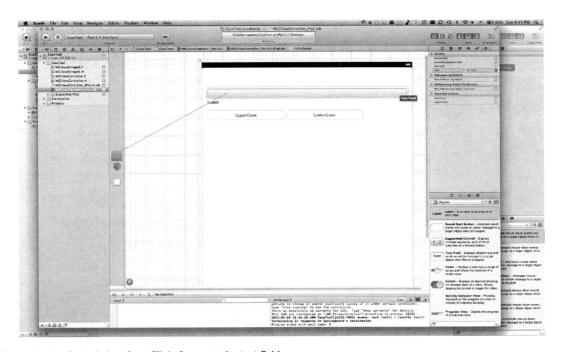

Figure 15-26. Control-drag from File's Owner to the text field

When the little pop-up menu appears, select textField (see Figure 15-27).

Repeat the process for the label: control-drag from File's Owner to the label (see Figure 15-28), and choose resultsField from the pop-up menu (see Figure 15-29).

OK, let's make it do something! We're ready to connect the actions. Control-drag from the UpperCase button to File's Owner (see Figure 15-30). And obviously, choose UpperCase from the pop-up menu.

Do the same for the LowerCase button (see Figure 15-31).

You might notice that there's a minus sign next to the upperCase method in the pop-up menu. That means there's already a connection to this method. You can assign a method to multiple actions.

Finally, click the Scheme pop-up menu, and choose iPad. Then, click Run on the left side of the toolbar. This starts the iPad Simulator and runs our app. Woohoo! We can also see our app in its iPhone version. In the Simulator, choose **Hardware ➤ Device ➤ iPhone**.

Figure 15-27. Choose textField from the pop-up window

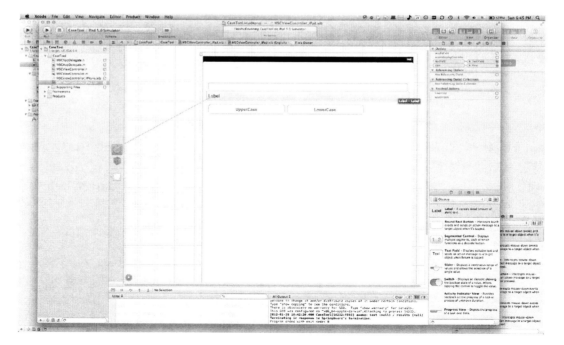

Figure 15-28. Connect the label to File's Owner

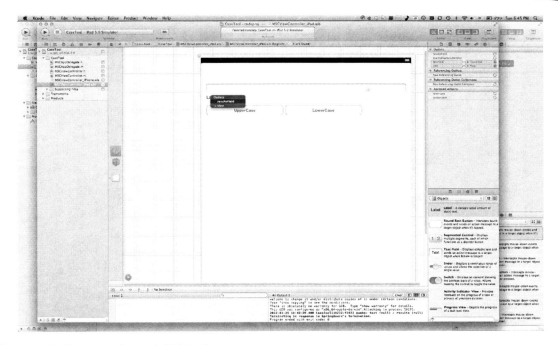

Figure 15-29. Connect to the resultsField outlet

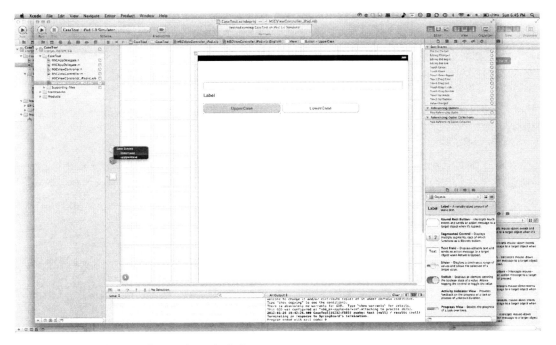

Figure 15-30. Connect the upperCase action to its button

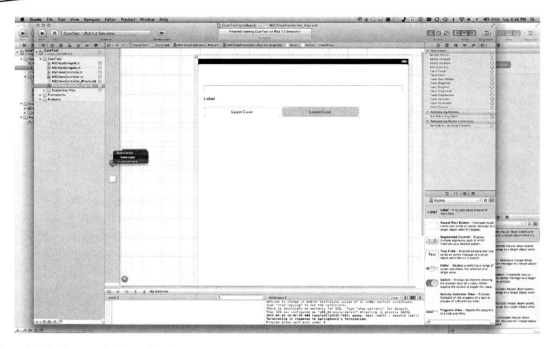

Figure 15-31. Connect the LowerCase button

Summary

Whew! That was a lot of information just to get a simple app to run in the simulator, although Xcode did help us a lot. Obviously, we have only scratched the surface of the vast set of APIs you can use to develop iOS apps.

In this chapter, we showed you how to use a view controller in your iOS app and how iOS manages memory for views. We discussed classes that are specific to iOS. We spent time on the ways in which iOS is both similar to and different from OS X.

If you plan on developing application for iOS and you want to know more, check out the book *Beginning iOS 5 Development* by David Mark, Jack Nutting, and Jeff LaMarche (Apress, 2011).

Chapter 16

Introduction to the Application Kit

So far in this book, all our programs have used the Foundation Kit and have communicated with us through the time-honored method of sending text output to the console. That's fine for getting your feet wet, but the real fun begins when you see a Mac-like interface that includes things you can click and play with. We'll take a detour in this chapter to show you some highlights of the Application Kit (or AppKit), Cocoa's user-interface treasure trove for OS X.

The program we'll construct in this chapter is called CaseTool, and you can find it in the *16.01 CaseTool* project folder. CaseTool puts up a window that looks like the screenshot shown in Figure 16-1. The window has a text field, a label, and a couple of buttons. When you type some text into the field and click a button, the text you entered is converted to uppercase or lowercase. Although that's very cool indeed, you'll no doubt want to add additional useful features before you post your application on the Mac App Store with a $4.99 price tag.

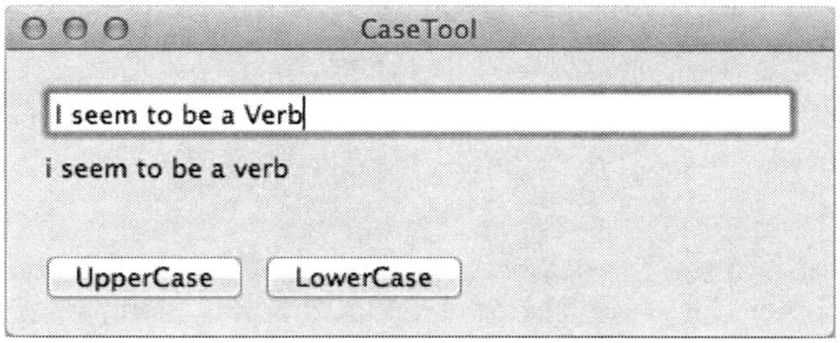

Figure 16-1. The finished product

Making the Project

You'll be using Xcode to build this project, and we'll lead you step-by-step through the process of doing so. The first thing is to create the project files. Then, we'll lay out the user interface, and finally, we'll make the connections between the UI and the code.

Let's get started by going to Xcode and making a new Cocoa Application project. Run Xcode. On the startup screen, click Create a New Xcode Project. (If Xcode is already running, choose **File ➤ New ➤ New Project**.) Select Application from the table on the left under Mac OS X, if it is not already selected. Select Cocoa Application (as shown in Figure 16-2), and then click Next to set some options for our app.

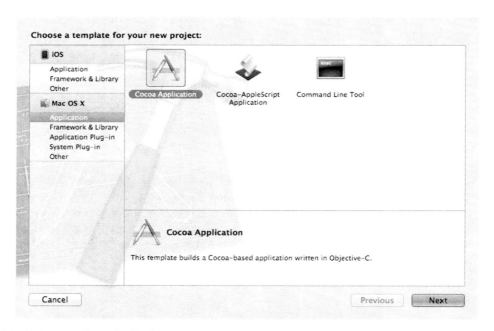

Figure 16-2. *Make a new Cocoa Application*

Take a look at Figure 16-3 to see the screen where we set options. The first item is Product Name; we're going to enter *CaseTool*. The next field, Company Identifier, is used by the App Store to differentiate your app from others. Company Identifiers usually are in **reverse-domain-name** format; that is, they start with *com*, then a period and the company name. In our example, we use com.MySuperCompany. This field is case-sensitive, so keep that in mind when you choose yours.

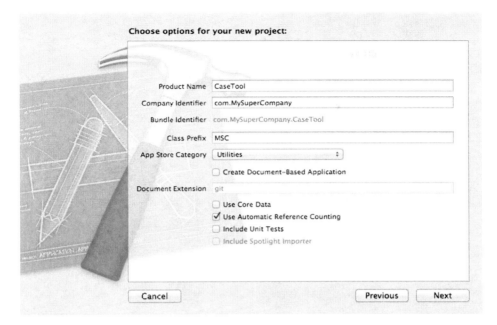

Figure 16-3. Name the new project

The next field is Class Prefix. It's customary to enter three or more characters here. This string is prepended to the names of classes you create. We'll use MSC, which of course stands for "My Super Company." For example, if you create a class named `Circle`, Xcode will actually name the class `MSCCircle`. Why do this? Because Objective-C doesn't have namespaces, this is a kind of pseudo-namespace, a way to reserve some names for your application. This way, if you're using a third-party framework, and it has a class named `Circle`, that name won't collide with yours.

For App Store category, we select Utilities, because that correctly describes our app.

For other options, make sure to deselect Create Document-Based Application, Use Core Data, and Include Unit Tests. The only checkbox that should be selected is Use Automatic Reference Counting.

Finally, a sheet drops down (see Figure 16-4) to let you select the directory for saving the project. We won't be discussing source code control in this book, but if you want, you can create a Git repository by selecting the Source Control option on this sheet. Xcode has built-in support for source control with Subversion (SVN) and Git.

That's it—your new project has been created. If you open the CaseTool group on the left side of the Xcode window, you'll see that there are already some files in the project: *MSCAppDelegate.h*, *MSCAppDelegate.m*, and *MainMenu.xib*.

`MSCAppDelegate` is the controlling object for our application.

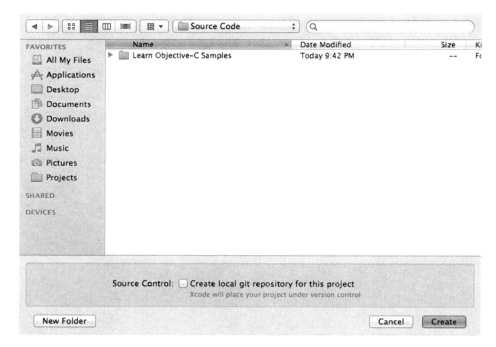

Figure 16-4. *Specify where you want to save your project*

Making the Delegate @interface

We'll use the Interface Builder editor in Xcode to lay out the window's contents and hook up various connections between MSCAppDelegate and the user interface controls. Interface Builder is also used to lay out iOS applications, so time in Interface Builder is well spent no matter which platform you'll end up programming for. We'll add stuff to the MSCAppDelegate class, and then Interface Builder will notice our additions and let us build the user interface.

First, let's take a look at the header file for the delegate:

```
#import <Cocoa/Cocoa.h>
@interface MSCAppDelegate : NSObject <NSApplicationDelegate>
@property (assign) IBOutlet NSWindow *window;
@end
```

You will see a quasi-keyword in there called IBOutlet. This isn't really an Objective-C keyword, but it's reserved by Apple for use by Interface Builder. You will also notice that there is a little dot in the gutter to the left of the IBOutlet line. You can click that dot to jump directly to the associated object in Interface Builder.

Another quasi-keyword we'll encounter is IBAction. IBAction is defined to be void, which means the return type of the methods declared will be void (that is, returning nothing).

If IBOutlet and IBAction don't do anything, why are they even there? The answer is that they're not there for the compiler: IBOutlet and IBAction are actually flags to Interface Builder, as well as the humans who read the code. By looking for IBOutlet and IBAction, Interface Builder learns that MSCDelegate objects have two instance variables that can be connected to stuff, and MSCDelegate provides methods that can be the target of button clicks (and other user interface actions). We'll talk about how this works in a little bit.

Interface Builder

Now, it's time to crank up Xcode's Interface Builder editor, affectionately known as IB to its friends. We want to edit the *MainMenu.xib* file that comes along with the project. This file is outfitted with a menu bar, along with a window we can put user controls into.

In the Xcode project window, find and click *MainMenu.xib* (see Figure 16-5).

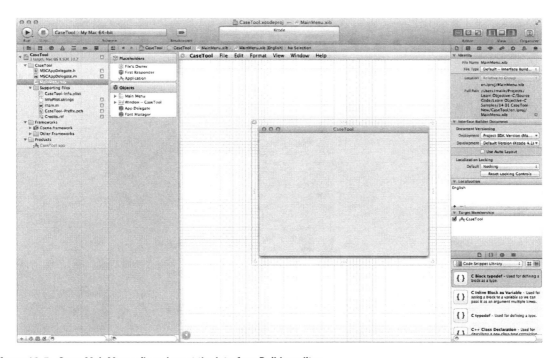

Figure 16-5. Open MainMenu.xib and meet the Interface Builder editor

This opens the Interface Builder editor in Xcode and displays the contents of the file. Even though the file extension is *.xib*, we call these **nib files**. "Nib" is an acronym for "NeXT Interface Builder," an artifact of Cocoa's heritage as part of a company called NeXT. Nib files are binary files that contain freeze-dried objects, and *.xib* files are nib files in XML format. They get compiled into nib format at compile time.

Look at the left side of the editor area. The Interface Builder dock holds icons that represent the contents of the nib file. You might not be able to tell at a glance what these are and what they do, but don't worry, you'll get there before long. For now, we can expand the dock to show the names of the objects. See the arrow in a circle (looks like a Play button) at the bottom of the dock, just to its right? Click it, and the dock items will reveal their names.

At the top of the editor window is the menu bar for the application we're building. You can add and edit menus and menu items there. We won't be messing with menus in this project.

Below the menu bar is an empty window where we'll put some text fields and buttons. This real, live window corresponds to the miniature window-shaped icon over in the dock. Now, we're going to use the library pane, the area in the lower-right corner that we talked about back in Chapter 7. In the library pane, click the third icon from the left, the one that looks like a box. The pane switches to show the Object Library (see Figure 16-6), which contains a whole bunch of different kinds of objects you can drag out into your window—there's a lot of stuff in there. You can type some text in the search box at the bottom to narrow down what you see. For your convenience, a description is provided for each kind of object you can play with.

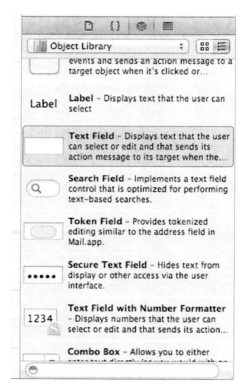

Figure 16-6. *Object Library in the library pane*

Laying Out the User Interface

Now, it's time to lay out the user interface. Find Text Field in the library, and drag it into the window, as shown in Figure 16-7. As you drag things around in the window, you'll see blue guidelines appear. These help you lay out your objects according to Apple user interface specifications.

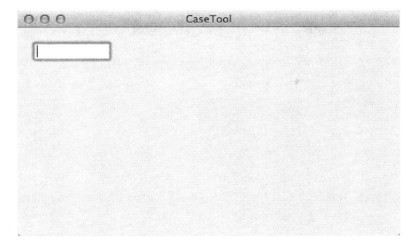

Figure 16-7. Drag out a text field

Now, we'll drag out a label. Click Label from the library, and drag it into the window, as shown in Figure 16-8. This is where the uppercase and lowercase results will go.

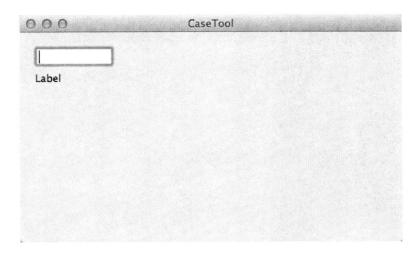

Figure 16-8. Drag out a label

Next, find a push button in the library, and drag that over. Position it under the label as shown in Figure 16-9. This is fun, isn't it?

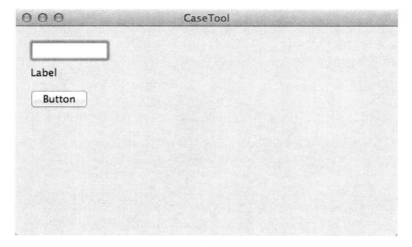

Figure 16-9. *Drag a button into the window*

Now, double-click the newly deposited button. The label becomes editable. Type *UpperCase,* and press return to accept the edit. Figure 16-10 shows the button being edited.

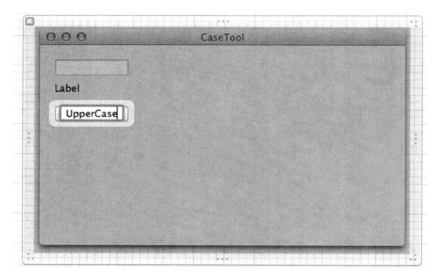

Figure 16-10. *Edit the button's label*

Now, drag another button from the palette and change its label to *LowerCase.* Figure 16-11 shows the window after the second button has been added.

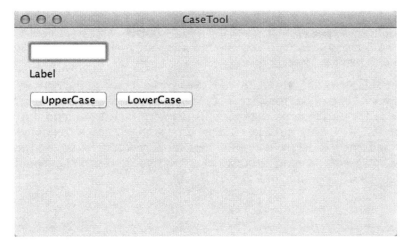

Figure 16-11. *All the items have been added*

Next, we did a little interior decorating, resizing the text fields and the window itself to make it a little nicer, as shown in Figure 16-12. We also resized the label to span the width of the window (although you can't see that in the figure). The label must be wide enough to display whatever text you type into the field. Now, the window looks just the way we want it.

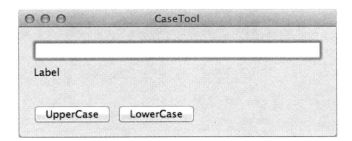

Figure 16-12. *The window is cleaned up*

Making Connections

In this section, we'll show you how to wire up your code to the lovely user interface elements we just finished creating.

Hooking Up the Outlets

Now, it's time to hook up some connections. First, we need to tell the object which NSTextField its textField and resultsField instance variables should point to. We're going to use the

Assistant Editor, which we discussed briefly in Chapter 7. At the top right of the Xcode window is a set of three buttons labeled Editor. Click the middle button, and you'll split the editor in two vertically; that's the Assistant Editor. If you need more room, make sure you have the dock in its minimal version, with just the icons showing.

Next, hold down the Control key, and drag from the text field over to the header file—yes, you're crossing the streams!—and under the @property line, until the message "Insert Outlet or Action" appears (see Figure 16-13). Once you let go of the pointer, you will get a pop-up dialog like the one shown in Figure 16-14. Enter textField in the name area, and click Connect. This creates the textField property in the header file and other required keywords. So far, we haven't typed in any code, but we've already "written" a bunch of it. That's very cool. Let's repeat the connection process for the label and name that one resultsField.

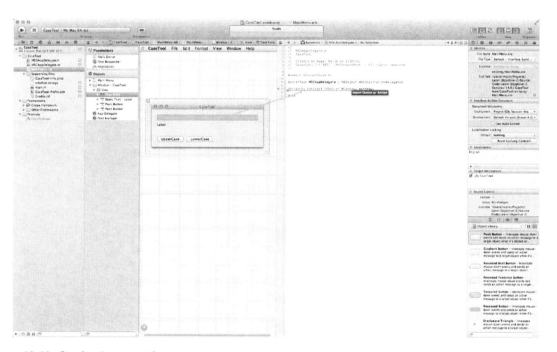

Figure 16-13. Starting the connection

Figure 16-14. Editing the connection

Double-check your work in the Connections panel of the Inspector. To see that panel, choose **View ➤ Utilities ➤ Show Connection Inspector**, or click the Connections button (the one that looks like a right-facing arrow) on the Inspector. You'll see the connections at the top of the Inspector, as shown in Figure 16-15.

Figure 16-15. Double-checking the connections

Hooking Up the Actions

Now, we're ready to wire the buttons to actions so they'll trigger our code. We'll control-drag again to make our love connections, this time from the button to the MSCAppDelegate.

Note   Knowing which way to drag a connection is a common source of confusion when using Interface Builder. The direction of the drag is *from* the object that needs to know something *to* the object it needs to know about.

MSCAppDelegate needs to know which NSTextField to use for the user's input, so the drag is from MSCAppDelegate to the text field.

The button needs to know which object to tell, "Hey! Someone pushed me!" So you drag from the button to AppController.

Control-click the UpperCase button, and drag a wire below the last @property in the header file, as shown in Figure 16-16. The connection box pops up again. This time, change the connection type to Action. Enter **uppercase** in the name field, and click Connect. This creates the method prototype in the header file and a dummy (empty) implementation in the .m file.

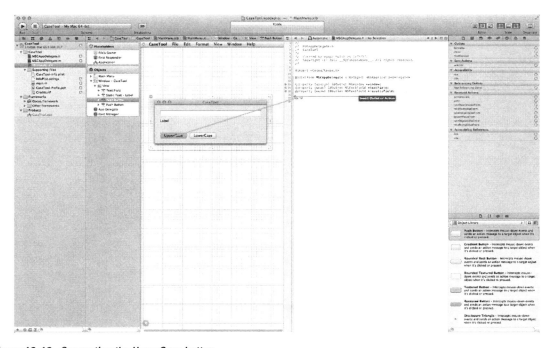

Figure 16-16. *Connecting the UpperCase button*

Now, whenever the button is clicked, the uppercase: message will be sent to the MSCAppDelegate instance, just like we always wanted. We can then take whatever action we want in our uppercase: method.

Finally, we make the last connection by hooking up the LowerCase button. Control-drag from the LowerCase button to the header file, and change the type to Action and name to lowercase (see Figure 16-17) And now we're done in Interface Builder.

Figure 16-17. *Make the connection (again)*

Chances are you moved along fairly slowly laying out the objects and making the connections. That's OK. With practice, you'll get a lot faster. An experienced IB jockey can zip through all these steps in less than a minute.

AppDelegate Implementation

Now, let's get back to coding. It's time to implement MSCAppDelegate—but first, a little bit on how an IBOutlet works.

When a nib file is loaded (*MainMenu.xib* is loaded automatically when the application starts, and you can create your own nib files and load them yourself), any objects that were stored in the nib file are re-created. This means that alloc and init both take place under the hood. When the application starts, an MSCAppDelegate instance is allocated and initialized. During the init method, all the IBOutlet instance variables are nil. Only after *all* the objects in the nib file are created (including the window and text fields and buttons) will all the connections be set up.

Once all the connections are made (which simply involves putting the address of the NSTextField objects into the MSCAppDelegate's instance variables), the message awakeFromNib is sent to every object that was created. Note that there is no predefined order in which the objects are created, and no predefined order in which awakeFromNib messages are sent.

A very, very common error is to try to do some work with IBOutlets in the init method. Because all the instance variables are nil, all messages to them are no-ops, so any work you try to do in init will silently fail (this is one of the places where Cocoa can let you down and cost you some debugging time). If you think this is happening and you're wondering why your code isn't working, use NSLog to print the values of your instance variables and see if they're all nil.

Let's get on with MSCAppDelegate's implementation. Here are the necessary preliminaries:

```
#import "MSCAppDelegate.h"
@implementation MSCAppDelegate
```

Next are the properties that we defined. But where did that code come from? We didn't add it. Well, we sort of did: when we dragged items from the nib file to the header, Interface Builder added this code for us.

Next we'll add an init method. We don't really need this, but we want to show that outlets have no values at init time.

```
- (id) init
{
  if (nil != (self = [super init]))
  {
  NSLog (@"init: text %@ / results %@", _textField, _resultsField);
  }
  return self;
}
```

To have a nicer user interface, we should set the text fields to some reasonable default value, rather than Label. True, it's an accurate default value, but it's not terribly interesting. We'll put Enter text here into the text field, and the results field will be preset to Results. awakeFromNib is the ideal place for this (although we could have also set this up in Interface Builder).

```
- (void)awakeFromNib
{
 NSLog (@"awake: text %@ / results %@", _textField, _resultsField);
 [_textField setStringValue:@"Enter text here"];
 [_resultsField setStringValue:@"Results"];
}
```

NSTextField has a method called setStringValue:, which takes an NSString as its parameter and changes the contents of the text field to reflect that string value. That's the method we're using to change the text fields to something more interesting for users to look at.

Now, for the action methods—first is uppercase:

```
- (IBAction) uppercase: (id) sender
{
    NSString *original = [_textField stringValue];
    NSString *uppercase = [original uppercaseString];
    [_resultsField setStringValue:uppercase];
} // uppercase
```

We get the original string from the _textField using the stringValue message, and we make an uppercase version. NSString provides us with the handy uppercaseString method, which creates a new string built from the contents of the receiving string, but with every letter kicked to uppercase. That string is then set as the contents of the _resultsField.

Time for our obligatory memory management check: is everything groovy? You betcha. Both of the new objects that are created (the original and uppercase strings) come from methods that are not alloc, copy, or new, so they're in the autorelease pool and will get cleaned up. It's the responsibility of setStringValue: to either copy or retain the incoming string. What setStringValue: does is its own business. But we know our memory management is correct.

lowercase: is just like uppercase:, but on the down-low.

```
- (IBAction) lowercase: (id) sender {
    NSString *original = [_textField stringValue];
    NSString *lowercase = [original lowercaseString];
    [_resultsField setStringValue:lowercase];
} // lowercase
```

And that's it! When you run the program, you'll see the window appear. Type a string, and change its case, just like in Figure 16-18.

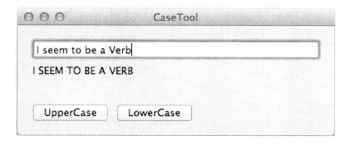

Figure 16-18. The finished CaseTool program does what it does

Summary

This chapter has been a whirlwind tour that just touched the surface of Interface Builder and the Application Kit. We used only one AppKit class directly (NSTextField) and a couple of classes indirectly (NSButton, which powers the buttons, and NSWindow, which is the object controlling the window). There are over 100 different classes in the AppKit for you to play with, many of which appear in Interface Builder.

At this point, you're fully qualified to dive into a Cocoa book or project. We'll continue in the next chapter with an exploration of some of Cocoa's features for saving and loading files.

Chapter 17

File Loading and Saving

Many computer programs (applications) end up creating some kind of semi-permanent artifact of the user's work. Maybe it's an edited photo. Maybe it's a chapter of a novel. Maybe it's your band's cover of "Free Bird." In each of these cases, the user ends up with a saved file.

The standard C library provides function calls to create, read, and write files, such as open(), read(), write(), fopen(), and fread(). These functions are well documented elsewhere, so we won't talk about them. Cocoa provides Core Data, which handles all this file stuff behind the scenes for you. We won't be talking about this either.

So what does that leave us to discuss? Cocoa provides two general classes of file handling: property lists and object encoding, which we'll talk about here.

Property Lists

In Cocoa, there is a class of objects known as **property list** objects, frequently abbreviated as **plist**. These lists contain a small set of objects that Cocoa knows how to do stuff with, in particular, how to save them to files and load them back. The property list classes are NSArray, NSDictionary, NSString, NSNumber, NSDate, and NSData, along with their mutable counterparts if they have any.

You've seen the first four before but not the last two. We'll chat about those before we start filing things away. You can find all the code for this part of the chapter in the project *15.01 PropertyListing*.

NSDate

Time and date handling are pretty common in programs. iPhoto knows the date when you took that picture of your dog, and your personal accounting application knows the closing date when reconciling your bank statement. NSDate is the fundamental class in Cocoa's date and time handling.

To get the current date and time, use [NSDate date], which gives you an autoreleased object. So this code

```
NSDate *date = [NSDate date];
NSLog (@"today is %@", date);
```

would print something like this:

```
today is 2012-01-23 11:32:02 -0400
```

There are methods you can use to compare two dates, so you can sort lists. There are also methods to get a date as a delta from the current time. For instance, you might want the date for exactly 24 hours ago:

```
NSDate *yesterday = [NSDate dateWithTimeIntervalSinceNow: -(24 * 60 * 60)];
NSLog (@"yesterday is %@", yesterday);
```

The preceding code prints out:

```
yesterday is 2012-01-23 11:32:02 -0400
```

+dateWithTimeIntervalSinceNow: takes an argument of an NSTimeInterval, which is a typedef of a double representing some interval of seconds. This lets you specify a time displacement in the future with a positive time interval or in the past with a negative time interval, as we're doing here.

> **Note**   If you would like to format how the date is printed, Apple provides a class called NSDateFormatter, it conforms to Unicode Technical Standard #35. This gives you various ways to format the date for the user.

NSData

A common idiom in C is passing buffers of data around to functions. To do this, you usually pass to a function the pointer to the buffer and the length of the buffer. Plus, memory management issues may arise in C. For example, if the buffer has been dynamically allocated, who is responsible for cleaning it up when it's no longer useful?

Cocoa provides us the NSData class that wraps a hunk of bytes. You can get the length of the data and a pointer to the start of the bytes. Because NSData is an object, the usual memory management behaviors apply. So, if you're passing a hunk of data to a function or method, you can pass an autoreleased NSData instead without worrying about cleaning it up. Here is an NSData object that will hold an ordinary C string, which is just a sequence of bytes, and print out the data:

```
const char *string = "Hi there, this is a C string!";
NSData *data = [NSData dataWithBytes: length: strlen(string) + 1];
NSLog (@"data is %@", data);
```

Here are the results:

```
data is <48692074 68657265 2c207468 69732069 73206120 43207374 72696e67 2100>
```

That's, uh, special. But, if you have an ASCII chart handy (you can find one by firing up the terminal and typing the command man ascii), you can see that this chunk of hexadecimal is actually our string. 0x48 is "H", 0x69 is "i", and so on. The -length method gives us the number of bytes, and the -bytes method gives us a pointer to the beginning of the string. Notice the + 1 in the +dataWithBytes: call? That's to include the trailing zero-byte that C strings need. Also notice the 00 at the end of the results of the NSLog. By including the zero-byte, we can use the %s format specifier to print the string:

```
NSLog (@"%d byte string is '%s'", [data length], [data bytes]);
```

which results in the following output:

```
30 byte string is 'Hi there, this is a C string!'
```

NSData objects are immutable. Once you create them, that's it. You can use them, but you can't change them. NSMutableData, though, lets you add and remove bytes from the data's contents.

Writing and Reading Property Lists

Now that you have seen all of the property list classes, what can we do with them? The collection property list classes (NSArray and NSDictionary) have a method called -writeToFile: atomically:, which writes the property lists to files. NSString and NSData also have a writeToFile:atomically: method, but it just writes out strings or blobs of data.

So, we could load up an array with strings and then save it:

```
NSArray *phrase;
phrase = [NSArray arrayWithObjects: @"I", @"seem", @"to", @"be", @"a", @"verb", nil];
[phrase writeToFile: @"/tmp/verbiage.txt" atomically: YES];
```

Now, look at the file */tmp/verbiage.txt*, and you should see something like this:

```
<?xml version="1.0" encoding="UTF-8"?>
<!DOCTYPE plist PUBLIC "-//Apple//DTD PLIST 1.0//EN"
"http://www.apple.com/DTDs/PropertyList-1.0.dtd"> <plist version="1.0"> <array>
<string>I</string>
<string>seem</string>
<string>to</string>
<string>be</string>
<string>a</string>
<string>verb</string> </array> </plist>
```

This code, while a bit verbose, is exactly what we tried to save: an array of strings. These property list files can be arbitrarily complex, with arrays of dictionaries containing arrays of strings and numbers and dates. Xcode also includes a property list editor, so you can poke around plist files and modify them. If you look around the operating system, you'll find lots of property list files, like all of your preference files in *Library/Preferences* in your home directory and system configuration files like those in */System/Library/LaunchDaemons*.

> **Note**   Some property list files, especially the preferences files, are stored in a compressed binary format. You can convert these files to something human-readable using the `plutil` command: `plutil -convert xml1 `*`filename.plist`*.

Now that we have our *verbiage.txt* file sitting on disk, we can read it in with `+arrayWithContentsOfFile:` method, like this:

```
NSArray *phrase2 = [NSArray arrayWithContentsOfFile: @"/tmp/verbiage.txt"];
NSLog (@"%@", phrase2);
```

And our output happily matches what we saved earlier:

```
(
I,
seem,
to,
be,
a,
verb
)
```

> **Note**   Did you notice the word "atomically" in our `writeToFile:` method? Are these calls radioactive? Nope. The `atomically:` argument, which takes a BOOL, tells Cocoa whether it should save the contents of the file in a temporary file first and, later, swap this temporary file with the original file when the file save is successful. This argument is a safety mechanism—if something bad happens during the save, you won't clobber the original file. But that safety does come at a price: you're consuming double the disk space while the save happens because the original file is still there. Unless you're saving huge files that might fill the users' hard drives, you should save your files atomically.

If you can boil your data down to property list types, you can use these very convenient calls to save stuff to disk and read it back later. When you're playing around with new ideas or bootstrapping a new project, you can use these conveniences to get your programs up and running quickly. Even if you just want to save a blob of data to disk and you're not using objects at all, you can use `NSData` to ease the work. Just wrap your data in an `NSData` object and call `writeToFile:atomically:` on the `NSData` object.

One downside to these functions is that they don't return any error information. If you can't load a file, you'll just get a nil pointer back from the method, without any idea of what went wrong.

Modifying Objects

Notice that when you read data from a file using the collection types, you can't modify the data. One way to modify things would be to use brute force, traversing the plist and creating a parallel structure that is mutable. But you don't have to go to that extreme: there is another way. In fact, if you're doing something in Cocoa and it seems convoluted, Apple has probably generously provided a simpler solution.

There is a class called NSPropertyListSerialization (and that's a mouthful to say). As the name implies, it will save and load your property lists with pretty much the options you want.

In particular we will be looking at the method propertyListFromData:mutabilityOption:format: errorDescription:. This will give you your plist data; plus, you'll get an error when things don't go so well.

Here is the code to write the plist data in binary format.

```
NSString *error = nil;
NSData *encodedArray = [NSPropertyListSerialization dataFromPropertyList:capitols
        format:NSPropertyListBinaryFormat_v1_0 errorDescription:&error];
[encodedArray writeToFile:@"/tmp/capitols.txt" atomically:YES];
```

As you can see, we convert the array data to NSData to file.

To read that data back into memory takes one extra step when we specify the file format. We create a pointer, so if the format is different than what we specified, we can use the pointer with the original format or convert it to a new format.

```
NSPropertyListFormat propertyListFormat = NSPropertyListXMLFormat_v1_0;
NSString *error = nil;
NSMutableArray *capitols = [NSPropertyListSerialization propertyListFromData:data
        mutabilityOption:NSPropertyListMutableContainersAndLeaves
                format:&propertyListFormat
        errorDescription:&error];
```

One of the options is how we want to read the data: do we want to be able to modify the plist or not? Also do we want to modify the structure of the list or just data?

Encoding Objects

Unfortunately, you can't always express your objects' information as property list classes. If we could express everything as dictionaries of arrays, we wouldn't need our own classes. Luckily, Cocoa has machinery for letting objects convert themselves into a format that can be saved to disk. Objects can encode their instance variables and other data into a chunk of data, which can be saved to disk. That chunk of data can be read back into memory later, and new objects can be created based on the saved data. This process is called **encoding and decoding**, or **serialization and deserialization**.

If you remember our foray into Interface Builder in the last chapter, we dragged objects out of the library and into the window, and things were saved to the nib file. In other words, the NSWindow and NSTextField objects were serialized and saved to disk. When the nib file was loaded into memory when the program ran, the objects were deserialized, and new NSWindow and NSTextField objects were created and hooked together.

As you can probably guess, you can do the same thing with your own objects by adopting the NSCoding protocol. The protocol looks like this:

```
@protocol NSCoding
- (void) encodeWithCoder: (NSCoder *) encoder;
- (id) initWithCoder: (NSCoder *) decoder;
@end
```

By adopting this protocol, you promise to implement both of these methods. When your object is asked to save itself, -encodeWithCoder: will be called. When your object is asked to load itself, -initWithCoder: will be called.

So what's this coder thing? NSCoder is an abstract class that defines a bunch of useful methods for converting your objects into NSData and back. You never create a new NSCoder instance because it doesn't actually do much. But there are a couple of concrete subclasses of NSCoder that you actually use to encode and decode your objects. We'll be using two of them, NSKeyedArchiver and NSKeyedUnarchiver.

Probably the easiest way to understand these guys is with an example. You can look in the project *15.02 SimpleEncoding* for all of the code.

Let's start off with a simple class with some instance variables:

```
@interface Thingie : NSObject <NSCoding>
{
 NSString *name;
 int magicNumber;
 float shoeSize;
 NSMutableArray *subThingies;
}
@property (copy) NSString *name;
@property int magicNumber;
@property float shoeSize;
@property (retain) NSMutableArray *subThingies;
- (id)initWithName: (NSString *) n magicNumber: (int) mn shoeSize: (float) ss;
@end // Thingie
```

This should be pretty familiar. We have four instance variables of object and scalar types, including one collection. Properties default to readwrite, so we did not mention that in the property definitions. There are public properties for each of them and a handy one-stop-shopping init method to create a new Thingie from scratch.

Notice that Thingie adopts NSCoding. That means we're going to provide an implementation for the encodeWithCoder and initWithCoder methods. For now, we'll make those two empty.

```
@implementation Thingie
@synthesize name;
@synthesize magicNumber;
@synthesize shoeSize;
@synthesize subThingies;
- (id)initWithName: (NSString *) n magicNumber: (int) mn shoeSize: (float) ss
{
 if (self = [super init])
```

```
    {
        self.name = n;
        self.magicNumber = mn;
        self.shoeSize = ss;
        self.subThingies = [NSMutableArray array];
    }
    return (self);
}
- (void) dealloc
{
    [name release];
    [subThingies release];
    [super dealloc];
} // dealloc
- (void) encodeWithCoder: (NSCoder *) coder
{
    // nobody home
} // encodeWithCoder
- (id) initWithCoder: (NSCoder *) decoder
{
    return (nil);
} // initWithCoder
- (NSString *) description
{
    NSString *description =
        [NSString stringWithFormat: @"%@: %d/%.1f %@", name,
            magicNumber, shoeSize, subThingies];
    return (description);
} // description
@end // Thingie
```

This chunk of code will initialize a new object, clean up any messes we have made, create the stub methods to make the compiler happy over us adopting NSCoding, and return a description.

Notice that in the init method we're using self.attribute on the left-hand side of the assignments. Remember that this actually means that we're calling the accessor methods for those attributes, and these methods were created by @synthesize. We're not doing a direct instance variable assignment. This object creation technique will get us proper memory management for the passed in NSString and for the NSMutableArray we create, so we don't have to provide it explicitly.

So, inside of main(), make a Thingie, and print it:

```
Thingie *thing1;
thing1 = [[Thingie alloc] initWithName: @"thing1" magicNumber: 42 shoeSize: 10.5];
NSLog (@"some thing: %@", thing1);
```

The preceding code will print out this:

```
some thing: thing1: 42/10.5 ( )
```

That was fun. Now, let's archive this object. Implement Thingie's encodeWithCoder: like this:

```
- (void) encodeWithCoder: (NSCoder *) coder
{
  [coder encodeObject: name forKey: @"name"];
  [coder encodeInt: magicNumber forKey: @"magicNumber"];
  [coder encodeFloat: shoeSize forKey: @"shoeSize"];
  [coder encodeObject: subThingies forKey: @"subThingies"];
} // encodeWithCoder
```

We'll be using NSKeyedArchiver to do all of the work of archiving our objects into an NSData. The keyed archiver, as its name implies, uses key/value pairs to hold an object's information. Thingie's -encodeWithCoder encodes each instance variable under a key that matches the instance variable name. You don't have to do this. You could encode the name under the key flarblewhazzit, and nobody would care. Keeping the key names similar to the instance variable names makes it easy to know what maps to what.

You're welcome to use naked strings like this for your encoding keys, or you can define a constant to prevent typos. You can do something like #define kSubthingiesKey @"subThingies", or you can have a variable local to the file, like static NSString *kSubthingiesKey = @"subThingies";.

Notice that there's a different encodeSomething:forKey: method for each type. You need to make sure you use the proper method to encode your types. For any Objective-C object type, you use encodeObject:forKey:

When you're restoring an object, you'll use decodeSomethingForKey: methods:

```
- (id) initWithCoder: (NSCoder *) decoder
{
  if (self = [super init]) {
    self.name = [decoder decodeObjectForKey: @"name"];
    self.magicNumber = [decoder decodeIntForKey: @"magicNumber"];
    self.shoeSize = [decoder decodeFloatForKey: @"shoeSize"];
    self.subThingies = [decoder decodeObjectForKey: @"subThingies"];
  }
  return (self);
} // initWithCoder
```

initWithCoder: is like any other init method. You need to have your superclass initialize things before you can do your stuff. You have two ways to do this, depending on what your parent class is. If your parent class adopts NSCoding, you should call [super initWithCoder: decoder]. If your parent class does not adopt NSCoding, you just call [super init]. NSObject does not adopt NSCoding, so we do the simple init.

When you use decodeIntForKey:, you pull an int value out of the decoder. When you use decodeObjectForKey:, you pull an object out of the decoder, recursively using initWithCoder: on any embedded objects. Memory management works the way you would expect: you're getting objects back from a method that's not called alloc, copy, or new, so you can assume the objects are autoreleased. Our property declarations make sure that all memory management is handled correctly.

You'll notice that we have the encoding and decoding in the same order as the instance variables. You don't have to do that; it's just a handy habit to make sure that you're encoding and decoding everything and haven't skipped something. That's one of the reasons for using keys with the call—you can put them in and pull them out in any order.

Now, let's actually use this stuff. We have thing1 we created earlier. Let's archive it:

```
NSData *freezeDried;
freezeDried = [NSKeyedArchiver archivedDataWithRootObject: thing1];
```

The +archivedDataWithRootObject: class method encodes that object. First, it creates an NSKeyedArchiver instance under the hood; it then passes it to the -encodeWithCoder method of the object thing1. As thing1 encodes its attributes, it can cause other objects to be encoded, like the string, the array, and any contents we might put in that array. Once the entire pile of objects has finished encoding keys and values, the keyed archiver flattens everything into an NSData and returns it.

We can save this NSData to disk if we want by using the -writeToFile:atomically: method. Here, we're just going to dispose of thing1, re-create it from the freeze-dried representation, and print it out:

```
[thing1 release];
thing1 = [NSKeyedUnarchiver unarchiveObjectWithData: freezeDried];
NSLog (@"reconstituted thing: %@", thing1);
```

It prints out the exact same thing we saw earlier:

```
reconstituted thing: thing1: 42/10.5 ( )
```

Seeing a gun on the wall in the first act of a Chekhov play makes you wonder, and, similarly, you're probably wondering about that mutable array called subThingies. We can put objects into the array, and they will get encoded automatically when the array gets encoded. NSArray's implementation of encodeWithCoder: invokes encodeWithCoder on all of the objects, eventually leading to everything being encoded. Let's add some subThingies to thing1:

```
Thingie *anotherThing;
anotherThing = [[[Thingie alloc]
    initWithName: @"thing2"
    magicNumber: 23
    shoeSize: 13.0] autorelease];
[thing1.subThingies addObject: anotherThing];
anotherThing = [[[Thingie alloc]
    initWithName: @"thing3"
    magicNumber: 17
    shoeSize: 9.0] autorelease];
[thing1.subThingies addObject: anotherThing];

NSLog (@"thing with things: %@", thing1);
```

And this prints out thing1 and the subthings:

```
thing with things: thing1: 42/10.5 (
 thing2: 23/13.0 (
 ),
 thing3: 17/9.0 (
 )
)
```

Encoding and decoding works exactly the same:

```
freezeDried = [NSKeyedArchiver archivedDataWithRootObject: thing1];
```

```
thing1 = [NSKeyedUnarchiver unarchiveObjectWithData: freezeDried];
NSLog (@"reconstituted multithing: %@", thing1);
```

and prints out the same logging seen previously.

What happens if there are cycles in the data being encoded? For example, what if thing1 is in its own subThingies array? Would thing1 encode the array, which encodes thing1, which encodes the array, which encodes thing1 again, over and over again? Luckily, Cocoa is clever in its implementation of the archivers and unarchivers so that object cycles can be saved and restored.

To test this out, put thing1 into its own subThingies array: [thing1.subThingies addObject: thing1];

Don't try using NSLog on thing1, though. NSLog isn't smart enough to detect object cycles, so it's going to go off into an infinite recursion trying to construct the log string, eventually dropping you into the debugger with thousands upon thousands of -description calls.

But, if we try encoding and decoding thing1 now, it works perfectly fine, without running off into the weeds:

```
freezeDried = [NSKeyedArchiver archivedDataWithRootObject: thing1];
thing1 = [NSKeyedUnarchiver unarchiveObjectWithData: freezeDried];
```

Summary

As you saw in this chapter, Cocoa provides two techniques for loading and saving files: property lists (plists) and object encoding. Property list data types are a collection of classes that know how to load and save themselves. If you have a collection of objects that are all property list types, you can use handy convenience functions for saving them to disk and reading them back in.

If, like most Cocoa programmers, you have your own objects that aren't property list types, you can adopt the NSCoding protocol and implement methods to encode and decode the objects: You can turn your own pile of objects into an NSData, which you can then save to disk and read back in later. From this NSData, you can reconstruct the objects.

Coming next is key-value coding, which lets you interact with your objects on a higher plane of abstraction.

18

Key-Value Coding

One idea we keep coming back to is indirection. Many programming techniques are based on indirection, including this whole object-oriented programming business. In this chapter, we'll look at another indirection mechanism. This is not an Objective-C language feature, but one provided by Cocoa.

So far, we've been changing an object's state directly by calling methods directly or via a property's dot-notation or by setting instance variables. Key-value coding, affectionately known as KVC to its friends, is a way of changing an object's state indirectly, by using strings to describe what piece of object state to change. This chapter is all about key-value coding.

Some of the more advanced Cocoa features, like Core Data and Cocoa Bindings (which we'll not talk about in this book), use KVC as cogs in their fundamental machinery.

A Starter Project

We'll be working with our old friend CarParts again. Check out the project called *18.01 Car-Value-Coding* for the goodies. To get things rolling, we've added some attributes to the Car class, like the make and model, to play around with. We renamed appellation back to name to make things more uniform:

```
@interface Car : NSObject <NSCopying>
{
 NSString *name;
 NSMutableArray *tires;
 Engine *engine;
 NSString *make;
 NSString *model;
 int modelYear;
 int numberOfDoors;
 float mileage;
}
@property (readwrite, copy) NSString *name;
@property (readwrite, retain) Engine *engine;
```

```
@property (readwrite, copy) NSString *make;
@property (readwrite, copy) NSString *model;
@property (readwrite) int modelYear;
@property (readwrite) int numberOfDoors;
@property (readwrite) float mileage;
...
@end // Car
```

And we've added the @synthesize directives so that the compiler will automatically generate the setter and getter methods:

```
@implementation Car
@synthesize name;
@synthesize engine;
@synthesize make;
@synthesize model;
@synthesize modelYear;
@synthesize numberOfDoors;
@synthesize mileage;
```

We've also updated the -copyWithZone method to move the new attributes over:

```
- (id) copyWithZone: (NSZone *) zone
{
 Car *carCopy;
 carCopy = [[[self class]allocWithZone: zone] init];
 carCopy.name = name;
 carCopy.make = make;
 carCopy.model = model;
 carCopy.numberOfDoors = numberOfDoors;
 carCopy.mileage = mileage;
// plus copying tires and engine, code in chapter 13.
```

And we changed the -description to print out these new attributes and to leave out the Engine and Tire printing:

```
- (NSString *) description
{
  NSString *desc;
  desc = [NSString stringWithFormat:
  @"%@, a %d %@ %@, has %d doors, %.1f miles, and %d tires.", name, modelYear, make, model,
numberOfDoors, mileage, [tires count]];
  return desc;
} // description
```

Finally, in main, we'll set these properties for the car and print them out. We've also used autorelease along with the alloc and init so that all memory management is kept in one place.

```
int main (int argc, const char * argv[])
{
  @autoreleasepool
{
  Car *car = [[[Car alloc] init] autorelease];
  car.name = @"Herbie";
  car.make = @"Honda";
```

```
car.model = @"CRX";
car.numberOfDoors = 2;
car.modelYear = 1984;
car.mileage = 110000;
int i;
for (i = 0; i < 4; i++)
{
  AllWeatherRadial *tire;
  tire = [[AllWeatherRadial alloc] init];
  [car setTire: tire atIndex: i];
  [tire release];
}
Slant6 *engine = [[[Slant6 alloc] init] autorelease];
car.engine = engine;
NSLog (@"Car is %@", car);
}
return (0);
} // main
```

After running the program, you get a line like this:

```
Car is Herbie, a 1984 Honda CRX, has 2 doors, 110000.0 miles, and 4 tires.
```

Introducing KVC

The fundamental calls in key-value coding are -valueForKey: and -setValue:forKey:. You send the message to an object and pass in a string, which is the key for the attribute of interest.

So, we can ask for the name of the car:

```
NSString *name = [car valueForKey:@"name"];
NSLog (@"%@", name);
```

This gives us Herbie. Likewise, we can get the make:

```
NSLog (@"make is %@", [car valueForKey:@"make"]);
```

valueForKey: performs a little bit of magic and figures out what the value of the make is and returns it.

valueForKey: works by first looking for a getter named after the key: -key or -isKey. So for these two calls, valueForKey: looks for -name and -make. If there is no getter method, it looks inside the object for an instance variable named _key or key. If we had not supplied accessor methods via @synthesize, valueForKey would look for the instance variables _name and name or _make and make.

That last bit is huge: -valueForKey uses the metadata in the Objective-C runtime to crack open objects and poke inside them looking for interesting information. You can't really do this kind of stuff in C or C++. By using KVC, you can get values where there are no getter methods and without having to access an instance variable directly via an object pointer.

The same technique works for the model year:

`NSLog (@"model year is %@", [car valueForKey: @"modelYear"]);`

which would print out `model year is 1984`.

Hey, wait a minute! `%@` in NSLog prints out an object, but `modelYear` is an `int`, not an object. What's the deal? For KVC, Cocoa automatically boxes and unboxes scalar values. That is, it automatically puts scalar values (`int`s, `float`s, and some `struct`s) into `NSNumber`s or `NSValue`s when you use `valueForKey`, and it automatically takes scalar values out of these objects when you use `-setValueForKey`. Only KVC does this autoboxing. Regular method calls and property syntax don't do this.

In addition to retrieving values, you can set values by name by using `-setValue:forKey`.

`[car setValue: @"Harold" forKey: @"name"];`

This method works the same way as `-valueForKey:`. It first looks for a setter for name, like `-setName` and calls it with the argument `@"Harold"`. If there is no setter, it looks in the class for an instance variable called `name` or `_name` and then assigns it.

> **We Must Underscore this Rule**   Both the compiler and Apple reserve instance variable names that begin with an underscore, promising dire consequences to you and your dog if you try to use one. There's no actual enforcement of this rule, but there might be someday, so disobey at your own risk.

If you're setting a scalar value, before calling `-setValue:forKey:`, you need to wrap it up (box it):

`[car setValue: [NSNumber numberWithFloat: 25062.4] forKey: @"mileage"];`

And `-setValue:forKey:` will unbox the value before it calls `-setMileage:` or changes the mileage instance variable.

A Path! A Path!

In addition to setting values by key, key-value coding allows you to specify a key path, which, like a file system path, lets you follow a chain of relationships.

To give us something to dig into, how about we add some horsepower to our engines? We'll add a new instance variable to `Engine`:

```
@interface Engine : NSObject <NSCopying>
{
  int horsepower;
}
@end // Engine
```

Notice that we're not adding any accessors or properties. Usually, you'll want to have accessors or properties for interesting object attributes, but we'll avoid them here to really show you that KVC digs into objects directly.

We're adding an init method so that the engine starts off with a nonzero horsepower:

```
- (id) init
{
  if (self = [super init])
  {
    horsepower = 145;
  }
  return (self);
} // init
```

We also added copying of the horsepower instance variable in -copyWithZone so that copies will get the value, and we added it to the -description, which is pretty old hat by now, so we'll leave out further explanation.

Just to prove we can get and set the value, you can add the following code to *18.01 Car-Value-Coding.m*:

```
NSLog (@"horsepower is %@", [engine valueForKey: @"horsepower"]);
[engine setValue: [NSNumber numberWithInt: 150]forKey: @"horsepower"];
NSLog (@"horsepower is %@", [engine valueForKey: @"horsepower"]);
```

This prints out:

```
horsepower is 145
horsepower is 150
```

What about those key paths? You specify different attribute names separated by dots. By asking a car for its "engine.horsepower", you get the horsepower value. In fact, let's try accessing key paths using the -valueForKeyPath and -setValueForKeyPath methods. We'll send these messages to the car instead of the engine:

```
[car setValue: [NSNumber numberWithInt: 155]forKeyPath: @"engine.horsepower"];
NSLog (@"horsepower is %@", [car valueForKeyPath: @"engine.horsepower"]);
```

These key paths can be arbitrarily deep, depending on the complexity of your object graph (which is just a fancy way of saying your collection of related objects); you can have key paths like "car.interior.airconditioner.fan.velocity". In some ways, digging into your objects can be easier with a key path than doing a series of nested method calls.

Aggregated Assault

One cool thing about KVC is that if you ask an NSArray for a value for a key, it will actually ask every object in the array for the value for that key and then pack things up in another array, which it gives back to you. The same works for arrays that are inside of an object (recall composition?) that you access by key path.

NSArrays that are embedded in other objects are known in the KVC vernacular as having a to-many relationship. For instance, a car has a relationship with many (well, four) tires. So we can say that Car has a to-many relationship with Tire. If a key path includes an array attribute, the remaining part of the key path is sent to every object in the array.

> **Out of Many, One**   Since you now know about to-many relationships, you're probably wondering what a to-one relationship is. Ordinary object composition is a to-one relationship. A car has a to-one relationship with its engine, for instance.

Remember that Car has an array of tires, and each tire has its air pressure. We can get all of the tire pressures in one call:

```
NSArray *pressures = [car valueForKeyPath: @"tires.pressure"];
```

After making the following call

```
NSLog (@"pressures %@", pressures);
```

we can print out these results:

```
pressures (
34,
34,
34,
34 )
```

What's happening here exactly, aside from us being vigilant about our tire maintenance? valueForKeyPath: breaks apart your path and processes it from left to right. First, it asks the car for its tires. Once it has the tires in hand, it asks the tires object for its valueForKeyPath: with the rest of the key path, "pressure" in this case. NSArray implements valueForKeyPath: by looping over its contents and sending each object the message. So the NSArray sends each tire it has inside itself a valueForKeyPath: using "pressure" for the key path, which results in the tire pressure being returned, boxed up in an NSNumber. Pretty handy!

Unfortunately, you can't index these arrays in the key path, such as by using "tires[0]. pressure" to get to the first tire.

Pit Stop

Before we head to the next bit of key-value goodness, we'll be adding a new class, called Garage, which will hold a bunch of classic cars. You can find all this stuff in the project named *16.02 Car-Value-Garaging*. Here's Garage's interface:

```
#import <Cocoa/Cocoa.h>
@class Car;
@interface Garage : NSObject
{
 NSString *name;
 NSMutableArray *cars;
}
@property (readwrite, copy) NSString *name;
- (void) addCar: (Car *) car;
- (void) print;
@end // Garage
```

Nothing's new here. We're forward-declaring Car, because all we need to know is that it's an object type to use as an argument to the -addCar: method. The name is a property, and the @ property statement says that users of Garage can access and change the name. And there's a method to print out the contents. To implement a collection of cars, we've got a mutable array behind the scenes.

The implementation is similarly straightforward:

```
#import "Garage.h"
@implementation Garage
@synthesize name;
- (void) addCar: (Car *) car
{
  if (cars == nil)
  {
    cars = [[NSMutableArray alloc] init];
  }
  [cars addObject: car];
} // addCar
- (void) dealloc
{
  [name release];
  [cars release];
  [super dealloc];
} // dealloc
- (void) print
{
  NSLog (@"%@:", name);
  for (Car *car in cars)
  {
    NSLog (@" %@", car);
  }
} // print
@end // Car
```

We include the *Garage.h* header file as usual and @synthesize the name accessor methods.

-addCar: is an example of lazy initialization of the cars array; we only create it when necessary. -dealloc cleans up the name and the array, and -print walks through the array and prints out the cars.

We've also totally overhauled the main *Car-Value-Garaging.m* source file compared to previous versions of the program. This time, the program makes a collection of cars and puts them into the garage.

First off are the necessary #imports for the objects we're going to be using:

```
#import <Foundation/Foundation.h>
#import "Car.h"
#import "Garage.h"
#import "Slant6.h"
#import "Tire.h"
```

Next, we have a function to make a car from a pile of attributes. We could have made a class method on Car, or made some kind of factory class, but Objective-C is still C, so we can use functions. Here, we're using a function, because it keeps the code for assembling a car close to where it is actually being used.

```
Car *makeCar (NSString *name, NSString *make, NSString *model, int modelYear, int numberOfDoors,
float mileage, int horsepower)
{
  Car *car = [[[Car alloc] init] autorelease];
  car.name = name;
  car.make = make;
  car.model = model;
  car.modelYear = modelYear;
  car.numberOfDoors = numberOfDoors;
  car.mileage = mileage;
  Slant6 *engine = [[[Slant6 alloc] init] autorelease];
  [engine setValue: [NSNumber numberWithInt: horsepower]
    forKey: @"horsepower"];
  car.engine = engine;
// Make some tires.

for (int i = 0; i < 4; i++)
{
  Tire * tire= [[[Tire alloc] init] autorelease];
  [car setTire: tire atIndex: i];
 }
  return (car);
} // makeCar
```

Most of this should be familiar by now. A new car is made and autoreleased per Cocoa convention, because the folks who will be getting the car from this function won't themselves be calling new, copy, or alloc. Then, we set some properties—remember that this technique is different from KVC, since we're not using setValue:forKey. Next, we make an engine and use KVC to set the horsepower, since we didn't make an accessor for it. Finally, we make some tires and put those on the car. At last, the new car is returned.

And here's the new version of main():

```
int main (int argc, const char * argv[])
 {
@autoreleasepool
{
 Garage *garage = [[Garage alloc] init];
 garage.name = @"Joe's Garage";
 Car *car; car = makeCar (@"Herbie", @"Honda", @"CRX", 1984, 2, 110000, 58);
 [garage addCar: car];
 car = makeCar (@"Badger", @"Acura", @"Integra", 1987, 5, 217036.7, 130);
 [garage addCar: car];
 car = makeCar (@"Elvis", @"Acura", @"Legend", 1989, 4, 28123.4, 151);
 [garage addCar: car];
 car = makeCar (@"Phoenix", @"Pontiac", @"Firebird", 1969, 2, 85128.3, 345);
 [garage addCar: car];
```

```
car = makeCar (@"Streaker", @"Pontiac", @"Silver Streak", 1950, 2, 39100.0, 36);
[garage addCar: car];
 car = makeCar (@"Judge", @"Pontiac", @"GTO", 1969, 2, 45132.2, 370);
 [garage addCar: car];
car = makeCar (@"Paper Car", @"Plymouth", @"Valiant", 1965, 2, 76800, 105);
[garage addCar: car];
[garage print];
[garage release];
};
return (0);
} // main
```

`main()` does some bookkeeping, makes a garage, and builds a small stable of cars to be kept there. Finally, it prints out the garage and then releases it.

Running the program gives this terribly exciting output:

```
Joe's Garage:
    Herbie, a 1984 Honda CRX, has 2 doors, 110000.0 miles, 58 hp and 4 tires
    Badger, a 1987 Acura Integra, has 5 doors, 217036.7 miles, 130 hp and 4 tires
    Elvis, a 1989 Acura Legend, has 4 doors, 28123.4 miles, 151 hp and 4 tires
    Phoenix, a 1969 Pontiac Firebird, has 2 doors, 85128.3 miles, 345 hp and 4 tires
    Streaker, a 1950 Pontiac Silver Streak, has 2 doors, 39100.0 miles, 36 hp and 4 tires
    Judge, a 1969 Pontiac GTO, has 2 doors, 45132.2 miles, 370 hp and 4 tires
    Paper Car, a 1965 Plymouth Valiant, has 2 doors, 76800.0 miles, 105 hp and 4 tires
```

Now, we have the foundation for the next bit of key-value goodness we promised.

Smooth Operator

Key paths can refer to more than object values. A handful of operators can be stuck into the key paths to do things like getting the average of an array of values or returning the minimum and maximum of those values.

For example, here's how we count the number of cars:

```
NSNumber *count;
count = [garage valueForKeyPath: @"cars.@count"];
NSLog (@"We have %@ cars", count);
```

When we run this, it prints out

```
We have 7 cars
```

Let's pull apart this key path, "cars.@count". cars says to get the cars property, which we know is an NSArray, from garage. Well, OK, we know it's an NSMutableArray, but we can consider it just to be an NSArray if we're not planning on changing anything. The next thing is @count. The at sign, as you know, is a signal that there's some magic coming up. For the compiler, @"blah" is a string, and @interface is the introduction for a class. Here, @count tells the KVC machinery to take the count of the result of the left-hand part of the key path.

We can also get the sum of a particular value, like the total number of miles our fleet has covered. The following snippet

```
NSNumber *sum;
sum = [garage valueForKeyPath: @"cars.@sum.mileage"];
NSLog (@"We have a grand total of %@ miles", sum);
```

prints out

```
We have a grand total of 601320.6 miles
```

which gets us from the Earth to the moon and back, with some spare change.

So how does this work? The @sum operator breaks the key path into two parts. The first part is treated as a key path to some to-many relationship, the cars array in this case. The other part is treated like any key path that has a to-many relationship in the middle. It is treated as a key path used against each object in the relationship. So mileage is sent to every object in the relationship described by cars, and the resulting values are added up. Of course, each of these key paths can be of arbitrary length.

If we wanted to find out the average mileage per car, we can divide this sum by the count. But there's an easier way—the following lines

```
NSNumber *avgMileage;
avgMileage = [garage valueForKeyPath: @"cars.@avg.mileage"];
NSLog (@"average is %.2f", [avgMileage floatValue]);
```

print out

```
average is 85902.95
```

Pretty simple, huh? Without all this key-value goodness, we'd have to write a loop over the cars (assuming we could even get hold of the cars array from the garage), ask each car for its mileage, accumulate that into a sum, and then divide by the count of cars—not hard stuff but still a small pile of code.

Let's pull apart the key path we used this time: "cars.@avg.mileage". Like @sum, the @avg operator splits the key path into two parts, the part that comes before it, cars in this case, is a key path to the to-many relation for cars. The part after @sum is another key path, which is just the mileage. Under the hood, KVC happily spins a loop, adds up the values, keeps a count, and does the division.

There are also @min and @max operators, which do the obvious things:

```
NSNumber *min, *max;
min = [garage valueForKeyPath: @"cars.@min.mileage"];
max = [garage valueForKeyPath: @"cars.@max.mileage"];
NSLog (@"minimax: %@ / %@", min, max);
```

with the result of minimax: 28123.4 / 217036.7.

> **KVC Is Not for Free**   KVC makes digging around in collections pretty easy. So why not use KVC for everything, then, and forget about accessor methods and writing code? There's never a free lunch, unless you work at some of the wilder Silicon Valley technology companies. KVC is necessarily slower, because it needs to parse strings to figure out what it is you want. There is also no error checking by the compiler. You might ask for `karz.@avg.millage`: the compiler has no idea that's a bad key path, and you'll get a runtime error when you try to use it.

Sometimes, you have an attribute that can take on only a small set of values, like the make of all of the cars. Even if we had a million cars, we would have a small number of unique makes. You can get just the makes from your collection with the key path "cars.@distinctUnionOfObjects. make":

```
NSArray *manufacturers; manufacturers =
[garage valueForKeyPath: @"cars.@distinctUnionOfObjects.make"];
NSLog (@"makers: %@", manufacturers);
```

When the preceding code is run, you get this:

```
makers: (
    Honda,
    Plymouth,
    Pontiac,
    Acura
)
```

The operator there in the middle of this key path, with the distinctly scary name of "@distinctUnionOfObjects", does just what it says. It applies the same logic as the other operators: it takes the collection specified on the left and uses the key path on the right against each object of that collection, then turns the resulting values into a collection. The "union" part of the name refers to taking the union of a bunch of objects. The "distinct" part of the name weeds out all of the duplicates. There are a couple other operators along the lines of this one, but we'll leave them for you to discover. Also, you can't add your own operators. Bummer.

Life's a Batch

KVC has a pair of calls that let you make batch changes to objects. The first is `dictionaryWithValuesForKeys:`. You give it an array of strings. The call takes the keys, uses `valueForKey:` with each of the keys, and builds a dictionary with the key strings and the values it just got.

Let's pick a car from the garage and get a dictionary of some of its attributes:

```
car = [[garage valueForKeyPath: @"cars"] lastObject];
NSArray *keys = [NSArray arrayWithObjects: @"make", @"model",
@"modelYear", nil];
NSDictionary *carValues = [car dictionaryWithValuesForKeys: keys];
NSLog (@"Car values : %@", carValues);
```

Running this gives us some information from Paper Car:

```
Car values : {
make = Plymouth;
model = Valiant;
modelYear = 1965;
}
```

And we can change these values turning our Valiant into something new and (arguably) improved—a Chevy Nova:

```
NSDictionary *newValues =
[NSDictionary dictionaryWithObjectsAndKeys:
@"Chevy", @"make",
@"Nova", @"model",
[NSNumber numberWithInt:1964], @"modelYear",
nil];
[car setValuesForKeysWithDictionary: newValues];
NSLog (@"car with new values is %@", car);
```

And after we run these lines of code, we see it's actually a new car:

```
car with new values is Paper Car, a 1964 Chevy Nova, has 2 doors, 76800.0 miles, and 4 tires.
```

Notice that some values have changed (make, model, and year), but others haven't, like the name and mileage.

This tool isn't terribly useful for this program, but it allows you to do some nifty tricks in user interface code. For example, you could have something like Apple's Aperture Lift and Stamp tool, which lets you move some, but not all, alterations you made to a picture onto other pictures. You could lift all of the attributes using dictionaryWithValuesForKeys and let the contents of the dictionary drive all the stuff displayed in the user interface. The user can take stuff out of the dictionary and then use this modified dictionary to change the other pictures using setValuesForKeysWithDictionary. If you design your user interface classes the right way, you can use the same lift and stamp panel with disparate things like photos, cars, and recipes.

You might wonder what happens with nil values, such as a car with no name, because dictionaries can't contain nil values. Think back to Chapter 7, where [NSNull null] is used to represent nil values. The same thing happens here. For a no-name car, [NSNull null] will be returned under the @"name" when you call dictionaryWithValuesForKeys, and you can supply [NSNull null] for a setValuesForKeysWithDictionary to do the same, but in reverse.

The Nils Are Alive

This discussion of nil values brings up an interesting question. What does "nil" mean for a scalar value, like for mileage. Is it zero? Is it –1? Is it pi? There's no way for Cocoa to know. You can try like this:

```
[car setValue: nil forKey: @"mileage"];
```

But Cocoa gives you the smack-down:

```
'[<Car 0x105740> setNilValueForKey]: could not set nil as the value for the key mileage.'
```

To fix this problem, you override -setNilValueForKey in *18.01 Car-Value-Garaging.m* and provide whatever logic makes sense. We'll make an executive decision and say that nil mileage means to zero out the car's mileage, rather than using some other value like –1:

```
- (void) setNilValueForKey: (NSString *) key
{
  if ([key isEqualToString: @"mileage"])
  {
  mileage = 0;
  } else {
  [super setNilValueForKey: key];
  }
} // setNilValueForKey
```

Notice that we call the superclass method if we get an unexpected key. That way, if someone tries to use key-value coding for a key we don't understand, the caller will get the proper complaint. Generally, unless there's a rare, good reason not to (like a specific action you're intentionally trying to avoid), always invoke the superclass method when you're overriding.

Handling the Unhandled

The last stop on our key-value tour (three-hour tour?) is handling undefined keys. If you've tried your hand at any KVC and mistyped a key, you've probably seen this:

```
'[<Car 0x105740> valueForUndefinedKey:]: this class is not key value coding-compliant for the key garbanzo.'
```

This basically says that Cocoa can't figure out what you mean by using that key, so it gives up.

If you look closely at the error message, you notice it mentions the method valueForUndefinedKey:. As you can probably guess, we can handle undefined keys by overriding this method. You also can probably guess that there's a corresponding setValue:forUndefinedKey:, if you try to change a value with an unknown key.

If the KVC machinery can't find a way to do its magic, it falls back and asks the class what to do. The default implementation just throws up its hands, as you saw previously. We can change that behavior, though. Let's turn Garage into a very flexible object that lets us set and get any key. We start by adding a mutable dictionary:

```
@interface Garage : NSObject
{
  NSString *name;
  NSMutableArray *cars;
  NSMutableDictionary *stuff;
}
… @end // Garage
```

Next, we add the valueForUndefinedKey methods:

```objc
- (void) setValue: (id) value forUndefinedKey: (NSString *) key
{
  if (stuff == nil)
  {
    stuff = [[NSMutableDictionary alloc] init];
  }
  [stuff setValue: value forKey: key];
} // setValueForUndefinedKey
- (id) valueForUndefinedKey:(NSString *)key
{
  id value = [stuff valueForKey: key];
  return (value);
} // valueForUndefinedKey
```

and release the dictionary in -dealloc.

Now, you can set any arbitrary values on the garage by adding code to *18.01 Car-Value-Garaging.m*:

```objc
[garage setValue: @"bunny" forKey: @"fluffy"];
[garage setValue: @"greeble" forKey: @"bork"];
[garage setValue: [NSNull null] forKey: @"snorgle"];
[garage setValue: nil forKey: @"gronk"];
```

and get them back out:

```objc
NSLog (@"values are %@ %@ %@ and %@", [garage valueForKey: @"fluffy"], [garage valueForKey: @"bork"], [garage valueForKey: @"snorgle"], [garage valueForKey: @"gronk"]);
```

This NSLog prints out

```
values are bunny greeble <null> and (null)
```

Notice the difference between <null> and (null). <null> is an [NSNull null] object, and (null) is a real live nil value that we got back because "gronk" was not in the dictionary. Also notice we used the KVC method setValue:forKey: when using the stuff dictionary. Using this method allows callers to pass in a nil value without requiring us to check for it in the code. The NSDictionary setObject:forKey: will complain if you give it nil, while setValue:forKey: with a nil value on a dictionary will remove that key from the dictionary.

Summary

Key-value coding includes a lot more than we can cover in this chapter, but you should now have a solid foundation for exploring other aspects of KVC. You've seen examples of setting and getting of values with a single key, where KVC looks for setter and getter methods to accomplish what you ask. If it can't find any methods, KVC digs directly into an object and changes values.

You've also seen key paths, which are dot-separated keys that specify a path through a network of objects. These key paths may look a lot like they're accessing properties, but they are actually very different mechanisms. You can stick various operators in a key path to have KVC do extra work on your behalf. Last, we looked at several methods you can override to customize corner-case behavior.

Next up, we'll have a look at Xcode's static analyzer.

Chapter 19

Using the Static Analyzer

When you build applications, most compilers can detect code that looks fishy and issue a warning, indicating code that might turn into a bug at runtime. In an effort to move beyond this kind of warning, a few years ago, Apple added a **static analyzer** to Xcode version 3.2. The static analyzer is a tool that logically examines your code without actually running it, looking for errors that can turn into bugs. In this chapter, we'll take a look at how you can use the static analyzer to find problems in your code.

Getting Some Static

What does the static analyzer do? How does it work? The static analyzer knows a lot about how Objective-C programs are supposed to work, then checks your program against that knowledge. It doesn't simply look at your source; it actually moves through code paths in your application looking for logical errors and then reports those errors to you. You can fix them before you even build and run.

The static analyzer can spot various kinds of errors:

- Security problems, such as memory leaks and buffer overflows
- Concurrency issues, such as race conditions (when two or more tasks can fail depending on timing)
- Logic problems, including dead code and various poor coding practices

This is great! But along with the goodness, there are some negatives to using the analyzer.

- It slows down your build process, because it takes time to perform the analysis.
- The analyzer sometimes generates false positives, telling you about problems that aren't really problems.

> ▨   It changes your familiar workflow, because you have to figure out how it fits in.

Going Into Analysis

OK, even with the negatives, that really doesn't sound so bad. Let's give it a try. How do we get started using this fancy tool?

It really couldn't be easier. Start by opening a project; we'll use *19-01 CarParts Error*. Click the *Product* menu and choose *Analyze* (see Figure 19-1), or press ⌘+shift+B. That's it! You've been analyzed. But you're not finished—that's just the beginning of how you interact with this tool.

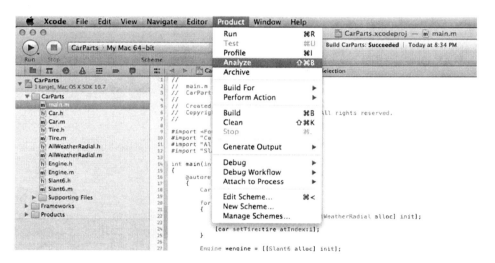

Figure 19-1. *Choose* Analyze *from the* Product *menu*

When we build *19.01 CarParts Error*, we see that it compiles without any errors and seems to run fine. With the static analysis step, you might notice that our program takes a bit longer to compile.

No doubt you also noticed that the analyzer had a few things to report, indicated by the branching arrows icon. The static analyzer found four issues for us that we didn't know we had. Cool—let's take a look.

The Issue Navigator (see Figure 19-2) lists the issues the analyzer found. We'll examine the errors one by one.

Dead Store Is Not Where Vampires Buy Milk

The first one says "Dead store." The description "Dead store" means we created an object (in this case, it's named pool), but we never actually accessed it in our code directly—we never sent it method calls or tried to modify it (see Figure 19-3).

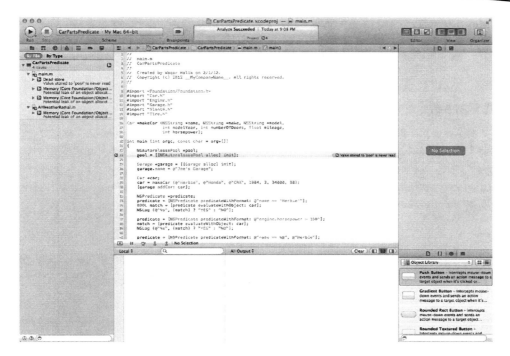

Figure 19-2. The analyzer found four issues

Figure 19-3. The code that caused the analyzer to report an issue

Even though our program is technically correct, the process of allocating and releasing memory takes time and (obviously) uses storage, both of which are especially important in iOS. Thanks to the analyzer, we can remove this variable from our application, making our program a little more efficient.

Airtight Garage

Now, we'll move on to the second issue. This one claims we have a "potential leak of an object," specifically the garage object. But how can that be? We release garage at the end of main, just before we release pool. The plot thickens.

To find out more, we click the analyzer bubble that appears inline with the code. When we do, we get the amazing squiggly drawing shown in Figure 19-4.

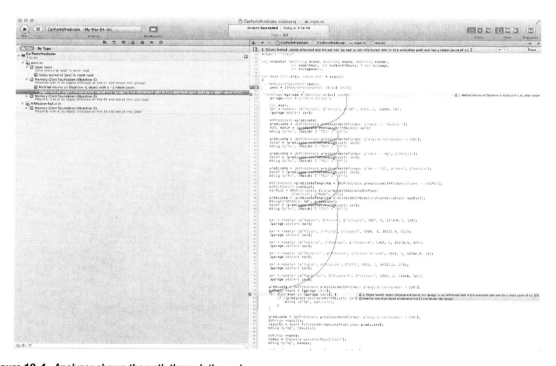

Figure 19-4. Analyzer shows the path through the code

Figure 19-4 shows you the path through the code, which, tellingly, never reaches the line where garage is released. Looking more closely, we see there's a stray return statement at line 177 that ends the function before we can clean up memory.

Surprisingly, this mistake is very common. It typically happens when you return too early from a method or function without releasing allocated objects.

Remember Where You Park

Two issues down, two to go. The next analyzer issue says that we're leaking an object stored into carsCopy. A closer look shows that we made carsCopy a mutableCopy of cars, but we never released the copy (see Figure 19-5). We can fix this by releasing carsCopy at the end of main.

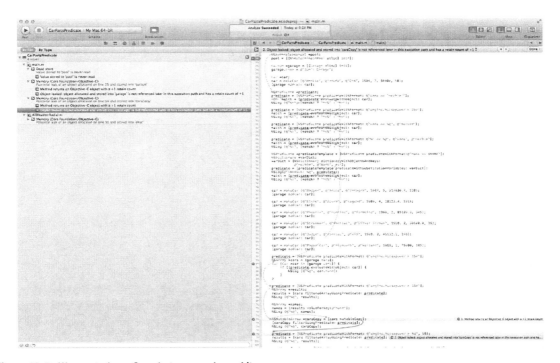

Figure 19-5. We created carsCopy but never released it

You Can't Take It with You

We have one analyzer issue left, a leak in AllWeatherRadial. When we look at this one, we see that description allocated a string desc but never released it before returning (see Figure 19-6). In this case, we can tell the pool to get rid of it when ready, by editing the return statement to say return [desc autorelease].

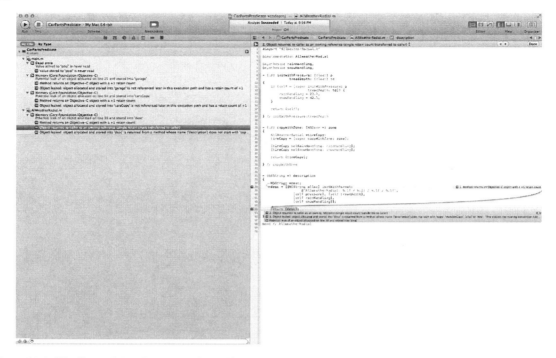

Figure 19-6. *We allocated desc but never released it*

Assisting the Analyzer

The static analyzer is a great tool, but it's not perfect. To help give the analyzer some hints to do its job better, you can use keywords in your methods to avoid getting false positives. These keywords let you tell the analyzer, "I know this doesn't look good, but I promise I know what I'm doing here, so please don't yell at me."

Returning a Retained Object

You can use NS_RETURNS_RETAINED to mark a method that returns an object with a retain count greater than zero. Assume you have the following method:

```
- (NSMutableArray *)superDuperArrayCreator
{
  NSMutableArray *myArray = [[NSMutableArray alloc] init];
  // … process the myArray
  return myArray;
}
```

You know that you want this method to return myArray, and you plan to release the array after you get it back. But the analyzer doesn't know that; it only knows that, by convention, you must clean up the memory in the place where it was allocated.

To placate the analyzer, you can mark the method NS_RETURNS_RETAINED. It looks like this:

```
- (NSMutableArray *)superDuperArrayCreator NS_RETURNS_RETAINED;
```

Similarly, you can use the Core Foundation version for C objects. To return one of those, you can use the keyword CF_RETURNS_RETAINED. So for the following code:

```
- (CFMutableArrayRef)superDuperArrayCreator
{
  CFMutableArrayRef myArrayRef = CFArrayCreateMutable(kCFAllocatorNull, 10, NULL);
  // … process the myArray
  return myArrayRef;
}
```

Your method will look like this:

```
- (CFMutableArrayRef)superDuperArrayCreator CF_RETURNS_RETAINED;
```

Returning a Nonretained Object

You can also point the analyzer in the opposite direction, telling it to complain when you try to return a *nonretained* object. The keywords for this are NS_RETURNS_NOT_RETAINED and CF_RETURNS_NOT_RETAINED.

Given this definition

```
- (NSMutableArray *)superDuperArrayCreator NS_RETURNS_NOT_RETAINED;
```

the analyzer will raise an issue if we return an object that is retained.

Returning Nothing

To make sure a method returns void (nothing), you can use the keyword CLANG_ANALYZER_ NORETURN when you define the method. In this case, an analyzer issue will appear if you try to return a value.

What's That Sound?   Where did the "CLANG" prefix come from on that last keyword? Clang is an open-source project that enhances C compilers and provides the foundation of the static analyzer in Xcode. For more information on Clang, you can check out http://clang.llvm.org.

On Further Analysis

The static analyzer found four problems of various kinds in our little program. In this section, we'll describe just a few of the other kinds of issues the static analyzer can reveal.

Compare Error

A common pattern in Objective-C programs is getting a value and testing it at the same time in conditional statements such as if and while.

```
if(myValue = [self getValue])
  {
    // do something
  }
```

There are two ways you can interpret the if statement:

- myValue is assigned a value and then tested for nil.

- myValue is equal to the value that is returned by the method.

Because there's some ambiguity here and the analyzer can't read our minds (yet), the analyzer flags this as an issue. If we really intended the first meaning, we can rewrite it as if((myValue = [self getValue])) or if(nil != (myValue = [self getValue])).

If we intended the second meaning, this really is an error, and we need to fix it by correctly comparing the two values:

```
if(myValue == [self getValue])
```

Leaking Memory

Let's take a look at this code:

```
- (void)myMethod
{
  NSString *string = [[NSString alloc] initWithFormat:@"%d, %d", 1, 2];
  if(nil == string)
  {
    return;
  }
  NSArray *array = [[NSArray alloc] initWithObjects:string, nil];

  if(nil == array)
  {
    return;
  }
  // do some stuff
  // Much later
  [array release];
  [string release];
}
```

At first glance, this code looks very nice. We're being good citizens by allocating memory and then releasing it when the method finishes. All is well and good, right? Not really! The analyzer reveals the sordid truth.

One path in the code will result in a memory leak. If the memory allocation for array fails, the method can't proceed, and the method returns immediately. But at this point, we have already allocated string, and it's not getting released, because we never get to the end of the method where the sweet `release` happens. This points out a general good practice: whenever you exit a method, you should think about what's been allocated and not released.

To fix this, we modify the second `if` statement as follows:

```
if(nil == array)
{
  [string release];
  return;
}
```

Over-Releasing

Often you'll create an object, use it, and eventually send an `autorelease` so when the method finishes, the object goes away.

```
NSString *myString = [[[NSString alloc] initWithFormat:…] autorelease];

// later that same app

[myString autorelease];
```

In this case, `myString` originally had 0 as its retain count, but then we told the compiler to release it anyway, and the static analyzer points the finger. To fix this, we remove one of the autorelases.

Synchronizing on nil

In this pattern, we need to modify an object, but we want to make sure no one else can access it while it is being modified. We know we can use `@synchronized(object)` so that when we're finished modifying the value, it's valid and generally accessible.

But wait! If the object is `nil`, the static analyzer will notice, and `@synchronized` won't have any effect. To fix this, we have to make sure the object isn't `nil`.

The Static Analyzer Is Not a Concern Troll

The static analyzer will report these and many other kinds of potential problems in your code, and it's getting smarter with each release. You don't have to heed everything it says, and sometimes, its messages will mystify you, but spending some time figuring out just what it's telling you is a good idea. Think of the static analyzer as your well-meaning, slightly annoying friend who is very often right.

On the other hand, don't get too dependent on the static analyzer to catch every memory leak and poor coding practice. You're still in charge of your code!

Summary

The static analyzer found four issues in a small program like this one. Wow! Imagine what the analyzer will find when you turn it loose on a big, complicated project. You don't have to run the analyzer every time you build, but including it in your workflow as you develop is definitely good practice.

A word of caution: as you've seen in this chapter, the analyzer helps point you at problems, but you still need to do a bit of your own sleuthing to figure out exactly what's wrong. No doubt, one day the analyzer will pinpoint exactly what you've done wrong and will then fix the problem for you. But today is not that day.

Chapter 20

NSPredicate

A fairly common operation when writing software is to take a collection of objects and evaluate them against some kind of known truth. You hang on to objects that conform to the truth and throw out objects that don't, leaving you with a pile of interesting objects to play with.

You see this all the time with software you use, like iPhoto. If you tell iPhoto to show you only pictures with a rating of three stars or better, the truth you've specified is "photo must have a rating of three stars or better." All of your photos are run through this filter. Those that have a rating of three or more stars pass through it, and the rest don't. iPhoto then shows you all your good pictures.

Similarly, iTunes has its search box. The truth you're seeking might be that the artist is Marilyn Manson or Barry Manilow. So all of your non-head-banging and noncrooning music will be hidden, allowing you to create one of the strangest dance mixes around.

Cocoa provides a class called NSPredicate that lets you specify these truth filters. You can create NSPredicate objects that describe exactly what you think is the truth and run each of your objects through the predicate to see if they match.

"Predicate" in this sense is different than the "predicate" you might have learned about in an English grammar class. "Predicate" here is used in the mathematical and computer science sense: a function that evaluates to a true or false value.

NSPredicate is Cocoa's means of describing queries, like you might use with a database. You can use NSPredicates with database-style APIs like Core Data and Spotlight, although we won't be covering either of those here (but you can apply much of what's in this chapter to those two technologies as well as to your own objects). You can think of NSPredicate as yet another means of indirection. You can use a predicate object that does your checking, rather than asking explicitly in code, "Are these the droids I'm looking for?" By swapping predicate objects around, you can have common code sift through your data without hard-coding the conditions you're looking for. This is another application of the Open/Closed Principle that you encountered back in Chapter 3.

Creating a Predicate

Before you can use an NSPredicate object against one of your objects, you need to create it, which you can do in two fundamental ways. One involves creating a lot of objects and assembling them. This requires a lot of code and is handy if you're building a general user interface for specifying searches. The other way involves query strings you put into your code. These are much easier to deal with when just getting started, so we'll concentrate on query strings in this book. The usual caveats with string-oriented APIs apply here, especially lack of error checking by the compiler and, sometimes, curious runtime errors.

There is no escape from CarParts—we'll be basing this chapter's examples on the garage of cars built in Chapter 18. You can find everything in the *20.01 Car-Part-Predicate* project.

To start, we'll look at just one car:

```
Car *car;
car = makeCar (@"Herbie", @"Honda", @"CRX", 1984, 2, 34000, 58);
[garage addCar: car];
```

Recall that we wrote the makeCar function to build up a car and give it an engine and some tires. In this case, we have Herbie, a two-door 1984 Honda CRX with a 58-horsepower engine with 34,000 miles on it.

Now, let's make a predicate:

```
NSPredicate *predicate;
predicate = [NSPredicate predicateWithFormat: @"name == 'Herbie'"];
```

Let's pull this apart. predicate is one of our usual Objective-C object pointers, which will point to an NSPredicate object. We use the NSPredicate class method +predicateWithFormat: to actually create the predicate. We give it a string, and +predicateWithFormat: takes that string and builds a tree of objects behind the scenes that will be used to evaluate the predicate.

predicateWithFormat sounds a lot like stringWithFormat, provided by NSString, which lets you plug in stuff using printf-style format specifiers. As you'll see later, you will be able to do the same thing with predicateWithFormat. Cocoa has consistent naming schemes — it's nice like that.

This predicate string looks like a standard C expression. On the left-hand side is a key path, name. Next come an operator for equality (==) and a quoted string on the right-hand side. If a chunk of text in the predicate string is not quoted, it is treated as a key path. If it's quoted, it's treated as a literal string. You can use single quotes or double quotes (as long as they're balanced). Usually, you'll use single quotes; otherwise, you'll have to escape each double quote in the string.

Evaluate the Predicate

OK, so we've got a predicate. What now? We evaluate it against an object!

```
BOOL match = [predicate evaluateWithObject: car];
NSLog (@"%s", (match) ? "YES" : "NO");
```

-evaluateWithObject: tells the receiving object (the predicate) to evaluate itself with the given object. In this case, it takes the car, applies valueForKeyPath: using name as the key path to get the name. Then, it compares it for equality to "Herbie." If the name and "Herbie" are the same, -evaluateWithObject: returns YES; otherwise, NO. The NSLog uses the ternary operator to convert the numerical BOOL to a human-readable string.

Here's another predicate:

```
predicate = [NSPredicate predicateWithFormat:
  @"engine.horsepower > 150"];
match = [predicate evaluateWithObject: car];
```

The predicate string has a key path on the left-hand side. This key path digs into the car, finds the engine, and then finds the horsepower of the engine. Next, it compares that value with 150 to see if it's larger.

After we evaluate this against Herbie, match has the value of NO, because little Herbie's horsepower (58) is not greater than 150.

Checking an object against a particular predicate's truth is all well and good, but things get more interesting when you have collections of objects. Say we wanted to see which cars in our garage are the most powerful. We can loop through the cars and test each one with this predicate:

```
NSArray *cars = [garage cars];
for (Car *car in [garage cars])
{
  if ([predicate evaluateWithObject: car])
  {
    NSLog (@"%@", car.name);
  }
}
```

We get the cars from the garage, loop over them all, and evaluate each one against the predicate. This chunk of code prints the cars with highest horsepower:

```
Elvis
Phoenix
Judge
```

Makes sense, no? Before we go on, let's make sure you're clear about all the pieces of syntax involved. Take a good look at the car's name call in NSLog. That's using the Objective-C 2.0 dot syntax and is the equivalent of call [car name];. There's no magic involved. The predicate string here is "engine.horsepower > 150". engine.horsepower is a key path, which might involve all sorts of magic under the hood.

Fuel Filters

One famous virtue/vice of programmers is laziness. Wouldn't it be nice if we didn't have to write that for loop and if statement? It's only a couple of lines of code, but zero lines of code would be even better. Luckily, a couple of categories add predicate filtering methods to Cocoa's collection classes.

-filteredArrayUsingPredicate: is a category method on NSArray that will spin through the contents of the array, evaluate each object against a predicate, and accumulate objects that evaluate to YES into a new array that is returned:

```
NSArray *results;
results = [cars filteredArrayUsingPredicate: predicate];
NSLog (@"%@", results);
```

This produces the following results:

```
(
Elvis, a 1989 Acura Legend, has 4 doors, 28123.4 miles, 151 hp and 4 tires,
Phoenix, a 1969 Pontiac Firebird, has 2 doors, 85128.3 miles, 345 hp and 4 tires,
Judge, a 1969 Pontiac GTO, has 2 doors, 45132.2 miles, 370 hp and 4 tires
)
```

OK, so these results are not identical to the previous ones. This is an array of cars; in the previous example, we had names. We can use key-value coding (KVC) to extract the names, remembering that when valueForKey: is sent to an array, the key is applied to all elements of the array:

```
NSArray *names;
names = [results valueForKey:@"name"];
NSLog (@"%@", names);
```

If we print out names, we'll see this:

```
(
    Elvis,
    Phoenix,
    Judge
)
```

Let's say you have a mutable array, and you want to yank out all the items that don't belong. NSMutableArray has a method -filterUsingPredicate, which, handily enough, will do just the yanking we're looking for:

```
NSMutableArray *carsCopy = [cars mutableCopy];
[carsCopy filterUsingPredicate: predicate];
```

If you print out carsCopy, it will be the set of three cars we saw earlier.

You can still use -filteredArrayUsingPredicate: with an NSMutableArray to make a new (nonmutable) array, because NSMutableArray is a subclass of NSArray. NSSets have similar calls, too.

As we mentioned with KVC, using predicates is really convenient, but it runs no faster than writing all the code yourself. That's because there's no way to avoid looping over all the cars and doing some work with each of them. For the most part, this looping is no big deal if you're writing for OS X, because computers are very fast these days. Go ahead and write the most convenient code possible and then measure your performance using one of Apple's tools like Instruments if you run into speed problems. iOS programmers, though, should pay very close attention to program performance at all times.

Format Specifiers

Experienced programmers know that hard-coding isn't necessarily a good idea. What if we wanted to know which cars have over 200 horsepower and then later which cars have over 50 horsepower? We could have predicate strings like "engine.horsepower > 200" and "engine.horsepower > 50", but we'd have to recompile the program and get back to the bad world we escaped in Chapter 3.

We can put varying stuff into our predicate format strings in two ways: format specifiers and variable names. First, we'll take a look at format specifiers. You can put in numerical values with %d and %f like you're familiar with:

```
predicate = [NSPredicate predicateWithFormat: @"engine.horsepower > %d", 50];
```

Of course, rather than using 50 right there in your code, you could have that value driven by the user interface or some external mechanism.

In addition to the usual printf specifiers, you can also use %@ to insert a string value. %@ is treated just like a quoted string:

```
predicate = [NSPredicate predicateWithFormat: @"name == %@", @"Herbie"];
```

Notice that the %@ is not quoted in the format string here. If you quoted %@, like with "name == '%@'", the characters % and @ would be in the predicate string.

NSPredicate strings also let you use %K to specify a key path. This predicate is the same as the others, using name == 'Herbie' as the truth:

```
predicate =
  [NSPredicate predicateWithFormat: @"%K == %@", @"name", @"Herbie"];
```

Using format specifiers is one way to have flexible predicates. The other involves putting variable names into the string, similar to environment variables:

```
NSPredicate *predicateTemplate =
  [NSPredicate predicateWithFormat:@"name == $NAME"];
```

Now that we have a predicate with a variable in it, we can make new specialized predicates using the predicateWithSubstitutionVariables call. You create a dictionary of key-value pairs, in which the key is the variable name (without the dollar sign), and the value is what should be plugged into the predicate:

```
NSDictionary *varDict;
varDict = [NSDictionary dictionaryWithObjectsAndKeys:
      @"Herbie", @"NAME", nil];
```

This uses the string "Herbie" for the value under the key "NAME". So make this the new predicate:

```
predicate =
  [predicateTemplate predicateWithSubstitutionVariables: varDict];
```

This predicate works exactly like the other ones you've seen.

You can use different kinds of objects for the variable values, like NSNumbers, with this predicate that filters for engine power:

```
predicateTemplate =
  [NSPredicate predicateWithFormat: @"engine.horsepower > $POWER"];
varDict = [NSDictionary dictionaryWithObjectsAndKeys:
  [NSNumber numberWithInt: 150], @"POWER", nil];
predicate =
  [predicateTemplate predicateWithSubstitutionVariables: varDict];
```

This creates a predicate whose truth is an engine horsepower that's more than 150.

In addition to NSNumbers and NSStrings, you can use [NSNull null] for nil values, and you can even use arrays, as you'll see a little later in this chapter. Note that you can't use $VARIABLE for key paths, only values. If you want to vary key paths programmatically when using predicate format strings, you'll need to use the %K format specifier.

No type checking is done by the predicate machinery. You can accidentally plug in a string where a number was expected, which might end up as an error message complaint at runtime or just a baffling behavior.

Hello Operator, Give Me Number 9

NSPredicate's format string includes a lot of different operators you can use. We'll touch on most of the operators and give a quick example of each one. The rest can be found in Apple's online documentation, available from Xcode.

Comparison and Logical Operators

The predicate string syntax supports some of your favorite operators from C, such as the equality operators == and =.

The inequality operators come in various flavors, as shown in Table 20-1.

Table 20-1. Inequality operators

Operator	Meaning
>	Greater than
>= and =>	Greater than or equal to
<	Less than
<= and =<	Less than or equal to
!= and <>	Not equal to

The syntax also supports parenthetical expressions (really!) and the AND, OR, and NOT logical operators, or their C-looking equivalents &&, ||, and !.

Here's an example. You can filter out the most and least powerful cars, leaving the midrange ones:

```
predicate = [NSPredicate predicateWithFormat:
        @"(engine.horsepower > 50) AND
          (engine.horsepower < 200)"];
results = [cars filteredArrayUsingPredicate: predicate];
NSLog (@"oop %@", results);
```

And if we actually apply this to our fleet, we get the following results:

```
Herbie, a 1984 Honda CRX, has 2 doors, 34000.0 miles, 58 hp and 4 tires,
Badger, a 1987 Acura Integra, has 5 doors, 217036.7 miles, 130 hp and 4 tires,
Elvis, a 1989 Acura Legend, has 4 doors, 28123.4 miles, 151 hp and 4 tires,
Paper Car, a 1965 Plymouth Valiant, has 2 doors, 76800.0 miles, 105 hp and 4 tires
```

Operators in predicate strings are case insensitive. You can use AnD, ANd, AND, or and at your whim. We'll be using all capitals here, but you don't have to in real code.

The inequalities work with numeric values and string values as well. To see all the cars from the beginning of the alphabet, use this predicate:

```
predicate = [NSPredicate predicateWithFormat: @"name < 'Newton'"];
results = [cars filteredArrayUsingPredicate: predicate];
NSLog (@"%@", [results valueForKey: @"name"]);
```

```
(
    Herbie,
    Badger,
    Elvis,
    Judge
)
```

Array Operators

The predicate string "(engine.horsepower > 50) OR (engine.horsepower < 200)" is a pretty common pattern. We're looking for horsepower values between these two numbers. Wouldn't it be cool if we could use an operator to see what's BETWEEN two values? Turns out we can:

```
predicate = [NSPredicate predicateWithFormat:
      @"engine.horsepower BETWEEN { 50, 200 }"];
```

The curly braces denote an array, and BETWEEN treats the first element of the array is the lower bound and the second element as the upper bound.

You can plug in your own NSArrays by using the %@ format specifier:

```
NSArray *betweens = [NSArray arrayWithObjects:
  [NSNumber numberWithInt: 50],
  [NSNumber numberWithInt: 200], nil];
predicate = [NSPredicate predicateWithFormat:
  @"engine.horsepower BETWEEN %@", betweens];
```

You can use variables too:

```
predicateTemplate =
  [NSPredicate predicateWithFormat: @"engine.horsepower BETWEEN $POWERS"];
varDict =
  [NSDictionary dictionaryWithObjectsAndKeys: betweens, @"POWERS", nil];
predicate = [predicateTemplate predicateWithSubstitutionVariables: varDict];
```

Arrays have more uses than just specifying the endpoints of an interval. You can use the IN operator to see if a particular value is contained in an array. This should be familiar to programmers with SQL experience:

```
predicate = [NSPredicate predicateWithFormat:
 @"name IN { 'Herbie', 'Snugs', 'Badger', 'Flap' }"];
```

We have cars named Herbie and Badger, so those will survive a filtering:

```
results = [cars filteredArrayUsingPredicate: predicate];
NSLog (@"%@", [results valueForKey: @"name"]);
```

Sure enough, this only returns two:

```
(
  Herbie,
  Badger
)
```

SELF Sufficient

Sometimes, you'll be applying predicates to simple values, like plain old string strings, rather than fancy objects that can be manipulated with key paths. Say we have an array of the car names, and we want to apply the same filter we used previously. What would we use in place of name, since NSString does not react well when you ask it for a name?

SELF to the rescue! SELF refers to the object being evaluated by the predicate. In fact, we can express all of our key paths in the predicates as being relative to SELF. This predicate is exactly the same as the previous one:

```
predicate = [NSPredicate predicateWithFormat:
 @"SELF.name IN { 'Herbie', 'Snugs', 'Badger', 'Flap' }"];
```

Now, back to that array of strings. How do we tell if a string is also in that array of names? Let's take a look.

First, you'll need that array of just the names from somewhere. Since we're already hip-deep in CarParts, we'll deal with those, using the KVC trick of getting the valueForKey: against an array:

```
names = [cars valueForKey: @"name"];
```

This is an array of strings containing all the names of the cars we own. Next, make a predicate:

```
predicate = [NSPredicate predicateWithFormat:
 @"SELF IN { 'Herbie', 'Snugs', 'Badger', 'Flap' }"];
```

And then, evaluate it:

```
results = [names filteredArrayUsingPredicate: predicate];
```

If you look at `results` now, it's the same two names we've seen before: Herbie and Badger. Here's a quiz. What output is produced by the following?

```
NSArray *names1 = [NSArray arrayWithObjects:
 @"Herbie", @"Badger", @"Judge", @"Elvis", nil];
NSArray *names2 = [NSArray arrayWithObjects:
 @"Judge", @"Paper Car", @"Badger", @"Phoenix", nil];

predicate = [NSPredicate predicateWithFormat: @"SELF IN %@", names1];
results = [names2 filteredArrayUsingPredicate: predicate];
NSLog (@"%@", results);
```

Here's the answer:

```
(
    Judge,
    Badger
)
```

This is a clever way of taking the intersection of two arrays. OK, so how does it work? The predicate includes the contents of the first array, so it looks something like

```
SELF IN {"Herbie", "Badger", "Judge", "Elvis"}
```

Now, the second name array is filtered with this predicate. Strings that are in both arrays will be in `names2` and will cause the `SELF IN` clause to say it's true, so the string will be in the results array. Objects only in the second array will get dropped on the floor, since they won't match any of the strings in the predicate. Strings only in the first array will just sit there, waiting to be compared against and will never make it into the results.

String Operations

The relational operators you saw before work with strings. There are also some that are string-specific, as shown in Table 20-2.

Table 20-2. String-Specific Operators

Operator	Meaning
BEGINSWITH	Check whether a string begins with another string.
ENDSWITH	Check whether a string ends with another string.
CONTAINS	Check whether a string lives somewhere inside another string.

Using relational operators lets you do tricks like using `"name BEGINSWITH 'Bad'"` to match "Badger", `"name ENDSWITH 'vis'"` to match "Elvis", and `"name CONTAINS udg"` to match "Judge".

What happens if you write a predicate string like "name BEGINSWITH 'HERB'"? This won't match "Herbie" or anything else, because these matches are case sensitive. Likewise, "name BEGINSWITH 'Hérb'" won't match, because the "e" has an accent mark. To relax the rules for name matching here, we can decorate these operators with [c], [d], or [cd]. The c stands for "case insensitive," the d for "diacritic insensitive" (that is, ignoring accent marks), and [cd] for both. Usually, you'll use [cd] unless there's a good reason to be case and accent sensitive. You never know when a user will have a sticky caps lock key and end up talking to your application IN ALL CAPS.

This predicate string will match Herbie: "name BEGINSWITH[cd] 'HERB'"

Like, Fer Sure

Sometimes, doing string matches at the beginning or end (or middle) of a string isn't powerful enough. For these situations, the predicate format string includes the LIKE operator. With this operator, a question mark matches one character, and an asterisk matches any number of characters. SQL and Unix shell programmers will recognize this behavior (sometimes called "globbing").

The predicate string "name LIKE '*er*'" will match any name that has "er" in the middle of it. This is equivalent to CONTAINS.

The predicate string "name LIKE '???er*'" will match "Paper Car", because it has three characters, an "er", and any number of characters after the "er". It does not match "Badger" because that has four characters before the "er".

LIKE also accepts the [cd] decoration for case and diacritic insensitivity.

If you're into regular expressions, you can use the MATCHES operator. Give it a regular expression, and the predicate will evaluate it.

Express Yourself   Regular expressions are a very powerful, very compact way of specifying string-matching logic. Sometimes, regular expressions can become dense and obscure, and entire books have been written on the subject. The NSPredicate regular expressions use the International Components for Unicode (ICU) syntax, which you can learn about with the help of your favorite Internet search engine.

While regular expressions are powerful, they also can be computationally expensive. If you have simpler operations in your predicate, such as the basic string operators and comparison operators, perform those first before using MATCHES. That should give you a speed boost.

That's All, Folks

This discussion of predicates wraps up *Learn Objective-C*. We've covered a lot of ground, from indirection and the basics of object-oriented programming, all the way through sophisticated tools like key-value coding and filtering objects with NSPredicate. Congratulations on surviving this entire book! You are now officially ready to tackle the next stage of your iOS and OS X programming career. Thank you for joining us.

Coming to Objective-C from Other Languages

Many programmers come to Objective-C and Cocoa from other languages and have a hard time learning Objective-C because it behaves differently from most other popular languages. New Objective-C programmers often assert that Objective-C is a bad language because it does not have behaviors X, Y, Z, which TheirFavoriteLanguage has. And feature checklists aside, let's face it: in some respects, Objective-C is just plain weird.

The advice we can offer new Objective-C and Cocoa programmers—even those with years of experience in other languages and other platforms—is to set aside any preconceived notions of how things are *supposed to* work and accept Objective-C, Cocoa, and Xcode on their own terms for a while. Work through a few books and tutorials. Once you have some Objective-C experience under your belt, you can see which techniques and approaches from other languages apply to Cocoa and Objective-C and which ones don't. No language is ideal for all circumstances, and no toolkit is perfect for every job. The best things to do are to learn enough to decide if a particular language and toolkit will do what you need and be aware of the tradeoffs involved.

In this appendix, we'll present some information that should help smooth your transition from other popular languages to Objective-C.

Coming from C

Objective-C is just plain old C with a few additional features for handling object orientation. The bulk of this book describes these extra features, so we won't repeat everything here. But a couple of interesting topics are worth covering.

Remember that Objective-C programmers get access to all the goodies that come with C, such as the standard C library. For example, you are welcome to use `malloc()` and `free()` to deal with dynamic memory or `fopen()` and `fgets()` for handling files.

Occasionally, someone on the Internet asks, "I'm calling an ANSI C library that uses callbacks to do its work. How can I have it call a method instead?" This question also comes up when you're using low-level Apple frameworks like Core Foundation and Core Graphics.

The short answer is, "You can't." The callbacks work only for C functions that have the signature required by the library. The functions that implement Objective-C methods need to have the `self` and `selector` arguments first, so they'll never match the required signatures.

Most callback-oriented libraries let you supply some user data or a pointer. You can think of this as a rock under which you can hide. You give the library some meaningful pointer when you register your callback, and the library gives you back your pointer when it calls your callback.

All Objective-C objects are dynamically allocated, so it's safe to use the address of an object as this context pointer. You don't need to worry about some stack-allocated object disappearing underneath you. Inside the callback, you cast the context pointer into your object type and then start sending it messages.

For example, let's say you're using an imaginary C API XML parsing library, and you feed data to a class called TreeWalker as the XML file is parsed. Make a new TreeWalker:

```
TreeWalker *walker = [[TreeWalker alloc] init];
```

Then, make the XML parser:

```
XMLParser parser;
parser = XMLParserLoadFile ("/tmp/badgers.xml");
```

Set the callback function (a C function) for the parser, and use the TreeWalker object as the context:

```
XMLSetParserCallback (parser, elementCallback, walker);
```

Then, as the XML file is parsed, the callback is called:

```
void elementCallback (XMLParser *parser, XMLElement *element, userData *context)
{
   TreeWalker *walker = (TreeWalker *) context;
   [walker handleNewElement: element inParser: parser];
} // someElementCallback
```

You can see that the context pointer is cast to an object pointer, and messages are sent to that object.

Coming from C++

C++ has a lot of features that Objective-C lacks: multiple inheritance, namespaces, operator overloading, templates, class variables, abstract classes, the Standard Template Library (STL), and so on. If you miss these, Objective-C has features and techniques that can replace them, or at least simulate them.

For example, you can use categories and protocols as a form of multiple inheritance or for implementing abstract base classes. One common use for multiple inheritance is to provide an interface so that other code can invoke particular methods on your object. Categories and protocols are perfect for this pattern. You can use protocols to provide pure abstract base classes.

Categories and protocols won't help you if you're using multiple inheritance to bring in extra instance variables (called **member variables** in C++). To do this, you can use composition to include an object in another object and then use stub methods to redirect messages to the second object (which is a common technique in Java). You can also simulate multiple inheritance by overriding the forwardInvocation: method. This method gets called if a message is received that the object doesn't know how to handle. By examining the NSInvocation object, you can see if it should be forwarded on to your "multiply inherited" object and then send it if necessary. This technique saves you from having to write a lot of little stub methods. However, it's much slower than real multiple inheritance and can be a pain to set up.

Other conventions can replace still more C++ features, such as stub methods that call abort for abstract classes that shouldn't be instantiated, though some features have weak replacements, such as name prefixes instead of namespaces.

C++ vtable vs. Objective-C Dynamic Dispatch

One of the biggest differences between C++ and Objective-C is the mechanism of dispatching methods (or **member functions**, as they're known in C++). C++ uses a vtable-based mechanism for determining what code to invoke for virtual functions.

You can think of each C++ object as having a pointer to an array of function pointers. When the compiler sees that the code wants to invoke a virtual function, it calculates an offset from the start of the vtable, emits machine code to take the function pointer at that offset from the start of the vtable, and uses that as the chunk of code to execute. This process requires the compiler to know, at compile time, the type of the object that is calling the member function so that it can calculate the correct offset into the vtable. This kind of dispatch is very fast, requiring just a couple of pointer operations and one read to get the function pointer.

The Objective-C way, described in detail in Chapter 3, uses a runtime function to poke around in the various class structures searching for the code to invoke. This technique can be several times slower than the C++ route.

Objective-C adds flexibility and convenience at the expense of speed and safety, which is a classic trade-off. With the C++ model, the member function dispatch is fast. It is also very safe, because the compiler and linker make sure that the object being used can handle that method. But the C++ method can also be inflexible, because you can't change the kind of object you're dealing with. You have to use inheritance to allow different classes of objects to react to the same message.

A lot of information about a class is not retained by the C++ compiler, such as its inheritance chain and the members that compose it. At runtime, the ability to treat objects generically is limited. The most you can do at runtime is a dynamic cast, which tells you if an object is a specific kind of subclass of another object.

The C++ inheritance hierarchy can't be changed at runtime. Once the program has been compiled and linked, it's pretty much set in stone. Dynamic loading of C++ libraries is frequently problematic, due in part to the complexities of C++ name mangling—the way it performs type-safe linking using the primitive Unix linkers it has to work with.

In Objective-C, an object needs only a method implementation for it to be callable, which allows arbitrary objects to become data sources and/or delegates for other objects. The lack of multiple inheritance can be an inconvenience, but one that is greatly eased by the ability to send any message to any object without having to worry about its inheritance pedigree.

Of course, this ability to send any message to any object makes Objective-C less type safe than C++. You can get runtime errors if the object being sent a message can't handle it. There are no type-safe containers in Cocoa. Any object can be put into a container.

Objective-C carries around a lot of metadata about a class, so you can use reflection to see if an object responds to a particular message. This practice is very common for objects that have data sources or delegates. By first checking to see if the delegate responds to a message, you can avoid some of the runtime errors you might get. You can also use categories to add methods to other classes.

Because of this metadata, it's easier to reverse engineer the classes used in a program. You can determine the instance variables, their layout in the object structure, and the methods defined by the class. Even stripping the executable of its debugging information doesn't remove the Objective-C metadata. If you have highly confidential algorithms, you may want to implement them in C++ or at least obfuscate their names—don't use class or method names like `SerialNumberVerifier`, for example.

In Objective-C, you can send messages to the `nil` (zero) object. There is no need to check your message sends against `NULL`. Messages to `nil` are no-ops. The return values from messages sent to `nil` depend on the return type of the method. If the method returns a pointer type (such as an object pointer), the return value will be `nil`, meaning you can safely chain messages to a `nil` object—the `nil` will just propagate. If the method returns an `int` the same size of a pointer or smaller, it will return zero. If it returns a float or a structure, you will have an undefined result. Because of this, you can use a `nil` object pattern to keep you from having to test object pointers against `NULL`. On the other hand, this technique can mask errors and cause bugs that are difficult to track down.

All objects in Objective-C are dynamically allocated. There are no stack-based objects, automatic creation and destruction of temporary objects, or automatic type conversion between class types, so Objective-C objects are more heavyweight than C++ stack-based objects. That's one of the reasons why small lightweight entities (like `NSPoint` and `NSRange`) are structures instead of first-class objects.

Finally, Objective-C is a very loose language. Where C++ has public, protected, and private member functions, Objective-C has full support for public, protected, and private instance variables, but no protection at all for member functions. Anyone who knows the name of a method can send that message to the object. Using the Objective-C reflection features, you can see all the methods supported by a given object. Methods are callable even if they never appear in a header file, and you have no reliable way to figure out which object is calling the method, because message sends can come from C functions (as discussed earlier in this appendix).

As you've seen, you don't have to redeclare methods you override in subclasses or mark them as virtual. Any method can be overridden in a subclass or category. There are two schools of thought on whether this is a good idea. One camp says that redeclaring provides information to the reader about which changes the class makes to its superclasses, while the other faction says that these are just implementation details that class users don't have to be bothered with and are not worth causing recompilations of all dependent classes when a new method is overridden.

Objective-C has no class variables. You can simulate them by using file-scoped global variables and providing accessors for them. An example class declaration might look like this (other stuff, like declarations for instance variables and method declarations, is included):

```
@interface Blarg : NSObject
{
}
+ (int) classVar;
+ (void) setClassVar: (int) cv;
@end // Blarg
```

And then the implementation would look like this:

```
#import "Blarg.h"
static int g_cvar;
@implementation Blarg
+ (int) classVar
{
  return (g_cvar);
} // classVar
+ (void) setClassVar: (int) cv
{
  g_cvar = cv;
} // setClassVar
@end // Blarg
```

The Cocoa object hierarchy has a common ancestor class: NSObject. When you create a new class, you'll almost always subclass NSObject or an existing Cocoa class. C++ object hierarchies tend to be several trees with distinct roots.

Objective-C++

There is a way to have the best of both worlds. The Clang compiler that comes with Xcode supports a hybrid language called Objective-C++. This compiler lets you freely mix C++ and Objective-C code, with a couple of small restrictions. You can get type safety and low-level performance when you need them, and you can use Objective-C's dynamic nature and the Cocoa toolkit where it makes sense.

A common development scenario is to put all of the application's core logic into a portable C++ library (if you're building a cross-platform application) and write the user interface in the platform's native toolkit. Objective-C++ is a great boon to this style of development. You get the performance and type safety of C++, and the users get applications created with the native toolkit that fits in seamlessly with their platform.

To have the compiler treat your code as Objective-C++, use the .*mm* file extension on your source. The .*M* extension also works, but the Mac's HFS+ file system is case insensitive but case preserving, so it's best to avoid any kind of case dependency.

Like matter and antimatter, the Objective-C and C++ object hierarchies cannot mix. So you can't have a C++ class that inherits from NSView, and you can't have an Objective-C class inheriting from std::string.

You can put pointers to Objective-C objects into C++ objects. Since all Objective-C objects are dynamically allocated, you can't have complete objects embedded in a class or declared on a stack. You'll need to `alloc` and `init` any Objective-C objects in your C++ constructors (or wherever it's convenient) and release them in your destructors (or somewhere else). So this would be a valid class declaration:

```
class ChessPiece
{
  ChessPiece::PieceType type;
  int row, column;
  NSImage *pieceImage;
};
```

You can put C++ objects into Objective-C objects:

```
@interface SWChessBoard : NSView
{
  ChessPiece *piece[32];
}
@end // SWChessBoard
```

C++ objects embedded in Objective-C objects, rather than having a pointer relationship, have their constructors called when the Objective-C object is allocated and have their destructors called when the Objective-C object is deallocated.

Exceptions

`NSExceptions` and C++ exceptions are interoperable: you can freely throw and catch blocks. C++ destructors and `@finally` blocks are honored when the exception unwinds. Also, `catch( . . . )` and `@catch( . . . )` can catch and rethrow any exceptions.

Coming from Java

Like C++, Java has numerous features that Objective-C does not have or implements in different ways. For instance, classic Objective-C has no garbage collector but has retain/release and the autorelease pool with ARC. You can turn on garbage collection in your OS X Objective-C programs if you want.

Java interfaces are like Objective-C formal protocols; both require the implementation of a set of methods. Java has abstract classes, but Objective-C does not. Java has class variables, and in Objective-C, you use static file-scoped global variables and provide accessors to them, as shown in the "Coming from C++" section. Objective-C is pretty loose with public and private methods. As we've noted, any method that an object supports can be invoked, even if it doesn't appear in any external form, such as a header file. Java lets you declare classes final, preventing any subclasses from being made. Objective-C goes to the other extreme by letting you add methods to any class at runtime.

Class implementations in Objective-C are usually split into two files: the header file and the implementation itself. This separation isn't required, though, for small private classes, as you've seen with some of the code in this book. The header file (with a *.h* extension) holds the public information related to the class, such as any new enums, types, structures, and objects that will be used by the code that uses this class. Other bodies of code import this file with the preprocessor (using #import). Java lacks the C preprocessor, which is a textual substitution tool that automatically processes C, Objective-C, and C++ source code before it is given to the compiler. When you see directives that start with #, you know that line is a command to the preprocessor. The C preprocessor actually knows nothing about the C family of languages; it just does blind text substitutions. The preprocessor can be a very powerful—and dangerous—tool. Many programmers consider the lack of the preprocessor in Java to be a feature.

In Java, almost every error is handled with exceptions. In Objective-C, error handling depends on the API you're using. The Unix API typically returns a –1 value, and a global error number (errno) is set to a specific error. The Cocoa APIs typically throw exceptions only on programmer errors or situations where cleanup is not possible. The Objective-C language provides exception handling features similar to Java and C++: @try, @catch, and @finally.

In Objective-C, the null (zero) object is termed *nil*. You can send messages to nil and not have to worry about a NullPointerException. Messages to nil are no-ops, so there is no need to check your message sends against NULL. Messages to nil are discussed earlier in the "Coming from C++" section.

In Objective-C, you can change a class's behavior at runtime by adding methods to existing classes using categories. There are no such things as final classes in Objective-C; you can subclass anything, as long as you have a header file for it, because the compiler needs to know how big an object the superclass defines.

In practice, you end up doing a lot less subclassing in Objective-C than in Java. Through mechanisms like categories and the dynamic runtime, which allows sending any message to any object, you can put functionality into fewer classes, and you can also put the functionality into the class that makes the most sense. For instance, you can put a category on NSString to add a feature, such as reversing a string or removing all white space. Then, you can invoke that method on any NSString, no matter where it comes from. You're not restricted to your own string subclass to provide those features.

Generally, the only times you need to subclass in Cocoa are when you are creating a brand new object (at the top of an object hierarchy), fundamentally changing the behavior of an object, or working with a class that requires a subclass because it doesn't do anything useful out of the box. For instance, the NSView class used by Cocoa for making user interface components has no implementation for its drawRect: method. You need to subclass NSView and override that method to draw in the view. But for many other objects, delegation and data sources are used. Because Objective-C can send any message to any object, an object does not need to be of a particular subclass or to conform to a particular interface, so a single class can be a delegate and data source to any number of different objects.

Because data source and delegate methods are declared in categories, you don't have to implement all of them. Cocoa programming in Objective-C has few empty stub methods, or methods that turn around and invoke the same method on an embedded object just to keep the compiler quiet when adopting a formal protocol.

With power comes responsibility, of course. With Objective-C's manual retain, release, and autorelease memory management system, you can easily create tricky memory errors inadvertently. Placing categories on other classes can be a very powerful mechanism, but if abused, doing so can make your code difficult to untangle and impossible to give to someone else. Plus, Objective-C is based on C, so you get all of C's baggage, along with its dangers when using the preprocessor, including the possibility of pointer-related memory errors.

Coming from BASIC

Many programmers learned how to program using Visual Basic or REALbasic, and their transition to Cocoa and Objective-C can be a confusing one.

BASIC (Visual and REAL) environments provide an integrated development environment that makes up the complete workspace. Cocoa splits your development into two environments: the Interface Builder editor and the text editor, both in Xcode. You use Interface Builder to create the user interface and to tell the user interface the name of the methods to invoke on a particular object, and then you put your control logic into source code edited in Xcode's text editor (or TextMate, BBEdit, emacs, or whichever text editor is your favorite).

In BASIC, the user interface items and the code they work with are tightly integrated. You put chunks of code into the buttons and text fields to make them behave the way you want. You can factor this code into a common class and have the code in the buttons talk to that class, but for the most part, BASIC programming involves putting code on user interface items. If you're not careful, this style can lead to messy programs with the logic scattered across a lot of different items. BASIC programming typically involves changing properties of objects to get them to behave the way you want.

In Cocoa, you find a clear separation between the interface and the logic that goes on behind that interface. You have a collection of objects that talk to each other. Rather than setting a property on an object, you ask the object to change its property. This distinction is subtle but important. The bulk of the think-time you spend in Cocoa is figuring out what message you need to send rather than what property you need to set.

BASIC has a very rich market in third-party controls and support code. Frequently, you can buy something off the shelf and integrate it into your codebase rather than build it yourself.

Coming from Scripting Languages

Programmers coming from scripting languages, such as Perl, PHP, Python, and Tcl, probably have the hardest transition to the Objective-C and Cocoa world.

Scripting languages excel in programmer conveniences, such as very robust string handling and processing, automatic memory management (whether by reference counting or garbage collection under the hood), very quick turnaround in development, flexible typing (being able to move between numbers, strings, and lists with ease), and a plethora of packages you can download and use. The runtime environment is often very flexible in scripting languages too, letting you design your own object types and control structures at will.

If you're coming from a scripting language, in many ways Objective-C will seem like a big step backward in time. It is a language of the '80s, compared to scripting languages that evolved in the '90s. String handling can be painful, since there is no built-in regular expression capability. Making strings with `printf()` style formats is about as fancy as Cocoa gets. Even though Objective-C has added ARC and garbage collection, a lot of existing code you'll see on the Internet uses the manual memory management techniques with retain and release. Development includes a compile and link phase, causing a delay between making a code change and seeing the result. You have to manually deal with distinct types, such as integers, character arrays, and string objects. Plus, you have all the baggage C brings along, such as pointers, bitwise operations, and easy-to-make memory errors.

Why go through this pain to use Objective-C? Performance is one reason: depending on the kind of application, Objective-C can perform better than a scripting language. Access to the native user interface toolkit (Cocoa) is another important advantage. Most scripting languages support the Tk toolkit originally developed for the Tcl language. This package is workable, but it doesn't have the depth and breadth of user interface features that you get with Cocoa. And, most importantly, applications built with Tk typically don't look and feel like iOS or Mac programs.

You can have the best of both worlds, though, by using scripting bridges. There are bridges between Objective-C and Python (called PyObjC) and Ruby (RubyObjC), so both of those scripting languages can be first-class citizens. When you use these bridges, you can subclass Cocoa objects in Python or Ruby and have access to all of Cocoa's features.

Summary

Objective-C and Cocoa aren't like any other programming languages and toolkits. Objective-C has some neat features and behaviors that derive from its dynamic runtime dispatch qualities. You can do things in Objective-C that you can't do in other languages.

Objective-C lacks some niceties that have been added to other languages over the years. In particular, robust string handling, name spaces, and metaprogramming are features in these other languages that you don't have in Objective-C.

Everything in programming comes down to trade-offs. You have to decide whether what you would gain in Objective-C compared to your current language of choice is worth what you would lose. For us, being able to use Cocoa for building applications more than pays for the time and effort it took to get familiar with Objective-C.

Index

P

Q

R

S, T

U, W

X, Y, Z

CPSIA information can be obtained at www.ICGtesting.com
Printed in the USA
LVOW112001050712

288907LV00001B/5/P